Conte

This *Handbook*, along with the National Trust's website at **www.nationaltrust.org.uk**, provides the complete guide for members and visitors to 469 places to visit in England, Wales and Northern Ireland in 2014.

Pictured: **Marsden Moor Estate, West Yorkshire**

Using your Handbook

Your 2014 *Handbook* covers the period from 1 January to 31 December inclusive.

Entries for individual places to visit are grouped geographically into areas and then ordered alphabetically. Each area opens with a general look at its coast and countryside, followed by a selection of coast and countryside places (listed alphabetically), then the remainder of entries.

Maps
Maps are grouped together at the back of this *Handbook* (see pages 381 to 394) and show the places mentioned in the text, including the London Partner Museums and Historic House Hotels.

Measurements
Where mentioned, areas are shown in hectares (1 hectare = 2.47 acres) with acres in brackets. Short distances are in yards (1 yard = 0.91 metre); longer distances are in miles. Heights are shown in metres.

Getting there
We recommend consulting the Trust's website for up-to-date details of how to reach each place.

Corfe Castle in Dorset

Opening arrangements
These are shown in tables in date order, with special notes underneath. Please see the example below.

Occasionally opening arrangements may be changed at short notice and/or facilities withdrawn (reasons include special events or dangerous weather conditions).

Coast and countryside places which are open every day all year do not have an opening arrangements table.

Please be aware that, unless otherwise indicated, last admission is 30 minutes before the time shown in the table. This is to allow enough time for you to enjoy your visit fully.

Black type indicates that the place or facility is **open** on these days.	A grey dot indicates that the place or facility is **closed** on these days.

Hinton Ampner		M	T	W	T	F	S	S
House								
11 Feb–4 Nov	11–5	M	T	W	T	F	S	S
5 Nov–28 Nov	11–5	M	T	W	·	·	S	S
1 Dec–9 Dec	10:30–4:30	M	T	W	T	F	S	S
Garden, shop and tea-room								
11 Feb–30 Mar	10–5	M	T	W	T	F	S	S
31 Mar–30 Sep	10–6	M	T	W	T	F	S	S
1 Oct–4 Nov	10–5	M	T	W	T	F	S	S
5 Nov–28 Nov	10–5	M	T	W	·	·	S	S
1 Dec–9 Dec	10–4:30	M	T	W	T	F	S	S

Last entry to house and tea-room 20 minutes before closing. 7 December: open to 7.

Special notes or important information relating to opening arrangements.

Extra copies of the National Trust *Handbook* are available to buy, while stocks last.

Before you visit

Here are the 'need to know' essentials before your visit – see also page 377 for Q and As.

What you pay
National Trust members enjoy free entry virtually everywhere for an unlimited number of visits. However, there may be a charge for everyone, including members, on special event days.

At the few places where there is a charge for members, this is indicated in the entry as a special note, which appears at the end of the description.

For accurate up-to-date admission prices visit **www.nationaltrust.org.uk** or call Supporter Services on 0844 800 1895.

Prices may vary during off-peak and busy periods – check the website, which is definitive. Admission prices include VAT and may change if VAT rates change. Most prices include a voluntary 10 per cent donation under the Gift Aid on Entry scheme.

Children
Under-fives are free, and five to 16 year olds enjoy a reduced admission price (typically 50 per cent). Seventeens and over pay the adult price. Children not accompanied by an adult are admitted at the Trust's discretion. Discounted prices apply to families in most cases and we offer a range of family-friendly facilities (see 'Making the most of your day' in each entry).

Concessions
Free entry is offered on Heritage Open Days and occasionally at other times.

Group visits
All group visits should be booked in advance with your destination. Discounts are usually available for groups of 15 plus. Travel trade information is at **www.nationaltrust.org.uk/groups**, telephone 0844 800 2329 or email traveltrade@nationaltrust.org.uk

Guided tours
Many tours are available at a range of Trust places; check website for details.

Facilities
You can assume that all the places mentioned have car parking on site or nearby; in the rare situations where this isn't the case, this is indicated. The same is true for toilets, which are only mentioned when there aren't any or they're more than about 300 yards away.

Eating and shopping
We offer the best of local and seasonal food and fine gift shops at most places, and in some tourist centres, such as York.

Dogs
Assistance dogs always welcome. See 'Dogs' at the end of the 'Making the most of your day' section for more information and page 376.

Events
Our website has full details of a great range of events. Sometimes places have to close for bigger events and many are chargeable, including members.

Booking in advance
At some smaller places such as Mr Straw's House, advance booking is essential. Timed tickets are sometimes issued to all visitors – including members – on busy days.

Safety
We take your safety very seriously and aim to provide a safe and healthy environment for your visit. However, it is important that you are prepared for every landscape you may encounter – especially when exploring our coast and countryside places.

For practical advice on planning, clothing and equipment, please visit our website.

Extra copies of the National Trust *Handbook* are available to buy, while stocks last.

Access

Symbols (see inside front cover) indicate access provisions at each place.

The usual membership fee or admission price applies to the disabled person. Carers or essential companions of a disabled visitor enjoy free entry on request.

An Admit One card can be issued to make this easier, call 01793 817634 or email enquiries@nationaltrust.org.uk

Getting there

Each entry gives its address, a grid reference to help locate the place on the maps at the back of the book and Sat Nav details where necessary. Up-to-date details of how to get there without a car are given on our website and other helpful resources are below.

Further information to help plan your journey

Transport Direct: plan how to get there by public transport or car from any UK location or postcode using **www.transportdirect.info**

Sustrans: for NCN routes and cycling maps visit **www.sustrans.org.uk** or telephone 0117 929 0888.

National Rail Enquiries: for train times visit **www.nationalrail.co.uk** or telephone 08457 48 49 50.

Traveline: for bus routes and times for England, Wales and Scotland visit **www.traveline.info** or telephone 0871 200 2233.

Taxis from railway stations: **www.traintaxi.co.uk**

Public transport in Northern Ireland (train and bus): **www.translink.co.uk** or telephone 028 9066 6630.

Transport for London: for all travel information visit **www.tfl.gov.uk** or telephone 0843 222 1234.

National Trust online

See **www.nationaltrust.org.uk** for a vast range of information, news and events. You can sign up for regular e-newsletters at **www.nationaltrust.org.uk/email**

All the information relating to places featured in the *Handbook* can be downloaded for free as an app for your iPhone, iPad, Nokia or Android device.

 Find us on Facebook at facebook.com/nationaltrust

 Follow us on Twitter at twitter.com/nationaltrust

South West

The stout harbour walls at Mullion Cove, Cornwall, are much needed in winter, when gentle waves become towering breakers

Outdoors in the South West

Many of the natural features in the South West would be a highlight on their own; when you take into account the sheer number and scale of these places, it's easy to see why this region is such a popular destination for lovers of the great outdoors.

Where else could you spend the morning on the beach, explore deep wooded valleys at lunchtime and step out on the high moors or soaring chalk downland in the afternoon?

Above: **the South West Coast Path above the expanse of Sandymouth Beach, near Bude, Cornwall**

So much to do, so much to see

Getting a breath of fresh air can mean different things to each person, but whatever your favourite outdoor pursuit, you can do it all with us. If you want to run the South West Coast Path – you can; if you'd rather find a quiet car park with a great view – we've got loads. No matter what your idea of a great day out might be, we've probably got the key ingredients, be they butterflies on Brean Down, 'barrel waves' at Godrevy or blossoms at Branscombe.

If you prefer the active life, we've got brilliant biking, coasteering, kiting and walking. In fact pretty much any outdoor activity you can think of, you can do on Trust land.

We also care for some of the most beautiful and sensitive sites in the South West. Our rangers have a huge depth of conservation knowledge, and all you need to do is pick their brains if you want to know more about the amazing wildlife here.

Where to start

The Trust protects more than 50,000 hectares (123,500 acres) of countryside in the counties of Cornwall, Devon, Dorset, Somerset, Wiltshire and Gloucestershire; that's around 190 square miles of farmland, moors, woods, downs and some 380 miles of the coast. Around the South West peninsula from Minehead in Somerset to Poole in Dorset runs the 630-mile South West Coast Path – the longest national trail in the country. We look after nearly 300 miles of it.

Many of the South West's most iconic and wildlife-rich landscapes are in the Trust's care: swathes of Exmoor and Dartmoor; long stretches of the Jurassic Coast of Dorset and East Devon and the historic mining areas of Cornwall and West Devon (both World Heritage Sites); the islands of Brownsea and Lundy; the famous cliffs of Cheddar Gorge in Somerset; some of the best beaches in Dorset, Devon and Cornwall; the chalk downs of Wiltshire and Dorset; and the woods, meadows and commons of the Cotswolds; along with nature reserves, heathlands and ancient woods throughout the six counties.

Below: **cycling on the Saltram Estate, near Plymouth, Devon; canoeing on the Fowey Estuary, Cornwall**

Above: **Dancing Ledge on the Purbeck coast, near Swanage, Dorset**

It's your membership that helps us protect and manage these precious landscapes for everyone to enjoy in their own way, and with all the accompanying health benefits – mental, spiritual and physical – that can come from something as simple as going for a walk in a beautiful place.

How can you find out about all of this open country, and the many things you can do once you get there? Some of the best-known places have their own entries in the following pages, but there are hundreds more. To discover them, and to find the many small coastal and countryside car parks that are the threshold to wonderful outdoor experiences, visit **www.nationaltrust.org.uk/southwest**

Immerse yourself in the South West: stay in one of hundreds of the Trust's holiday cottages or bunkhouses (ideal for groups) in some extraordinary places, or get that bit closer to nature in one of our campsites. Visit **www.nationaltrust.org.uk/holidays**

Outdoors in the South West

The ultimate holiday peninsula, for locals and visitors, blessed with a spectacular variety of landscapes, seascapes and natural wonders for you to explore and enjoy.

Baggy Point

Moor Lane, Croyde, Devon EX33 1PA

Map ① E5  1939

Baggy Point is the impressive headland at Croyde, once owned by the Hyde family and overlooking one of the best surfing beaches in the South West. Huge coastal views, great walks and opportunities to climb, surf and coasteer make it a must-do destination for anyone visiting North Devon. **Note**: toilets (not National Trust) on main beach slipway, 500 yards from Trust car park.

Eating and shopping: Sandleigh tea-room, garden and shop (tenant-run) serving drinks and food grown on site in the walled garden. There's a new outdoor covered seating area overlooking the garden. Tea-room is next to car park, close to beach slipway.

The impressive headland at Baggy Point, North Devon

Making the most of your day: free children's activity pack (to borrow), cold drinks and snacks and walks leaflets available from car park kiosk. Nearby Arlingon Court is well worth a visit. **Dogs**: welcome on leads (except for seasonal ban on Croyde Beach from May to September).

Access for all: ♿🏢➡

Getting here: see website for details.
Parking: free.

Finding out more: 01271 870555 or baggypoint@nationaltrust.org.uk

Baggy Point
Car park is usually manned March to November and at busy periods and locked at dusk.

Bolberry Down

near Salcombe, Devon

Map ① F9  1938

Dramatic clifftop with far-reaching views. Bolberry Down has levelled circular trails through a breathtaking coastal landscape. **Note**: sorry no toilet.

Finding out more: 01752 346585 or bolberrydown@nationaltrust.org.uk

---

Brean Down

Brean, North Somerset

Map ① H4  1954

One of Somerset's most striking coastal landmarks: a miniature downland rich in wildlife and history and offering magnificent views. Relax on the beach at the foot of the downs or take a walk along this spectacular 'natural pier' to the Palmerston fort, which provides a unique insight into Brean's past. **Note**: steep climbs and cliffs; please stay on main paths. Dangerous beach, tide comes in quickly.

Cheddar Gorge

The Cliffs, Cheddar, Somerset

Map ① I4  1910

At almost 400 feet deep and three miles long, Cheddar is England's largest gorge. It was formed during successive Ice Ages, when glacial meltwater carved into the limestone, creating steep cliffs. The gorge is a haven for wildlife and contains many rare plants, including the Cheddar pink. **Note**: terrain is steep away from the road. Caves and car parks privately owned (charge including members).

Eating and shopping: gift shop and information centre.

Making the most of your day: 5-mile circular gorge walk (details from shop and information centre) and Strawberry Line (NCN26) cycle route to Cheddar. **Dogs**: welcome on leads in shop and gorge.

Beach at the foot of Brean Down, North Somerset, above, and craggy Cheddar Gorge, Somerset, right

Eating and shopping: Cove Café serving cooked breakfast, lunch or tea and cakes. Shop selling ice-cream, buckets and spades and beach games.

Making the most of your day: fort with gun magazines (open most weekends). Welcome beach hut. Wild Wednesdays during school holidays for children. Downloadable circular walk. **Dogs**: welcome on leads.

Access for all: 🚻 **Building** ♿

Getting here: see website for details. **Sat Nav**: use TA8 2RS. **Parking**: pay and display (charges for non-members).

Finding out more: 01643 862452 or breandown@nationaltrust.org.uk

Getting here: see website for details. **Sat Nav**: use BS27 3QE. **Parking**: pay and display car parks on both sides of gorge, not National Trust (charge including members).

Finding out more: 01643 862452 or cheddargorge@nationaltrust.org.uk

Brean Down		M	T	W	T	F	S	S
Café and shop								
15 Mar–2 Nov	10–5	M	T	W	T	F	S	S

Café and shop opening hours vary according to weather. Close at dusk if earlier.

Cheddar Gorge		M	T	W	T	F	S	S
Information centre and shop								
15 Mar–20 Jul	11–5	M	T	W	.	F	S	S
21 Jul–7 Sep	11–5	M	T	W	T	F	S	S
8 Sep–2 Nov	11–5	M	T	W	.	F	S	S

Information centre and shop open Bank Holidays. Opening times vary according to weather.

Glastonbury Tor

near Glastonbury, Somerset

Map (1) I5  1933

Iconic tor, topped by a 15th-century tower offering spectacular views of the Somerset Levels, Dorset and Wiltshire.
Note: sorry no toilet.

Finding out more: 01643 862452 or glastonburytor@nationaltrust.org.uk

Fyne Court

Broomfield, Bridgwater, Somerset TA5 2EQ

Map (1) H5  1967

A hidden Somerset gem (above). While the house (the former home of amateur scientist Andrew Crosse) no longer stands, the site, within woods and meadows, is simply beautiful. Families will enjoy discovering the walled garden, boathouse and lake and following the trails. Information room in courtyard.

Eating and shopping: Courtyard tea-room serving light lunches, cream teas and cakes. Bags of charcoal for sale in tea-room.

Making the most of your day: events including bushcraft skills, open-air theatre, three walking trails and a children's play trail. Wild Wednesdays for children in school holidays and free Thursday tours of the grounds.
Dogs: welcome on leads.

Access for all: **Grounds**

Getting here: see website for details.
Parking: free, 150 yards.

Finding out more: 01643 862452 or fynecourt@nationaltrust.org.uk

Fyne Court		M	T	W	T	F	S	S
Tea-room								
22 Mar–2 Nov	10:30–4	M	·	·	T	F	S	S
Estate								
Open all year		M	T	W	T	F	S	S

Tea-room has extended opening hours in the summer.
Opening times can vary according to weather conditions.

Leigh Woods

near Bristol, Avon

Map (1) I4  1909

Beautiful haven on Bristol's doorstep (below), with diverse woodland and wonderful views of Avon Gorge and the suspension bridge. Excellent network of paths, including a 1¾-mile easy-access trail, links to the National Cycle Network and new 'Yer Tiz' off-road cycle trail.
Note: sorry no toilets.

Eating and shopping: picnics welcome.

Making the most of your day: natural play area. Permanent orienteering course (map available from office).
Dogs: welcome (but be aware of cattle).

Getting here: see website for details.
Parking: roadside parking on North Road, off A369, or Forestry Commission car park.

Finding out more: 0117 973 1645 or leighwoods@nationaltrust.org.uk

---

Minchinhampton and Rodborough Commons

near Stroud, Gloucestershire

Map ① J2/3 🏛️📶 1913

These historic Cotswolds commons, traditionally grazed, are famed for rare flowers and butterflies, prehistoric remains and far-reaching views.

Stroud, as seen from Rodborough Common, Gloucestershire

Minchinhampton Common contains a nationally important complex of Neolithic and Bronze Age burial mounds, while the limestone grasslands of Rodborough Common have abundant wild flowers, including the rare pasqueflower and many different varieties of orchids.

Eating and shopping: many great picnic spots, although there are no picnic tables. The historic Winstones ice-cream factory is on Rodborough Common and ice-cream vans are usually found in the reservoir car park in summer. Several pubs around the edge of both commons.

Making the most of your day: the commons are great places to walk, picnic, spot butterflies or fly a kite, and there are regular events throughout the year. Downloadable Rodborough Common butterfly walk available.
Dogs: welcome everywhere, but keep under close control near livestock.

Access for all: ♿

Getting here: see website for details.
Parking: Reservoir car park on Minchinhampton Common: SO 855 013; Rodborough Fort car park on Rodborough Common: SO 852 035.

Finding out more: 01452 814213 or minchinhampton@nationaltrust.org.uk

Parke

near Bovey Tracey, Devon TQ13 9JQ

Map (1) G7 1974

Set on the south-eastern edge of Dartmoor, this tranquil country park contains numerous delights. Riverside paths follow the course of the Bovey, as it meanders through woodlands and meadows rich in plant and wildlife. There is also a medieval weir, walled garden and orchard with historic apple trees.

Eating and shopping: Home Farm Café (not National Trust). Seasonal produce from the walled garden for sale.

Making the most of your day: orienteering trails and geocaching. Events and apple days. Self-guided garden, woodland trails and quizzes. Outdoor Tracker Packs.
Dogs: on leads where stock grazing.

Access for all: 🚻♿🅿 Countryside 👣

Getting here: see website for details.
Parking: free.

Finding out more: 01626 834748 or parke@nationaltrust.org.uk

Parke		M	T	W	T	F	S	S
Parkland, woodland and walks								
Open all year	Dawn–dusk	M	T	W	T	F	S	S
Home Farm Café								
Open all year	10–5*		M	T	W	T	F	S	S

*Café opening and closing times in winter are dependent on weather. Closed 25 and 26 December.

Parke, Devon, on the edge of wild Dartmoor

Off-road biking at Plymbridge Woods, Devon

Plymbridge Woods and Plym Valley

near Plymouth, Devon

Map (1) F8  1968

The wooded valley of the River Plym creates a 'green bridge' from Plymouth to the heights of Dartmoor. At its lower end, Plymbridge is the starting point for cycle trails and walks, discovering birdlife and industrial ruins. The upper valley climbs through rocky crags to open onto the high moors.

Eating and shopping: mobile refreshment van in Plymbridge car park (weekends). Perfect picnic spots beside the river.

Making the most of your day: old railway line cycle path and wooded mountain-bike trail. Watch peregrine falcons from viaduct (spring). Paddle or swim in the river. Geocaching, den-building, downloadable Tracker Packs, orienteering and events.
Dogs: welcome under control.

Access for all: 👣

Getting here: see website for details. **Parking**: at Plymbridge (SX 524 585), Shaugh Prior (SX 533 636) and Cadover Bridge (SX 554 645).

Finding out more: 01752 341377 or plymvalley@nationaltrust.org.uk

Purbeck Countryside

near Corfe Castle, Dorset

Map ① K7 🖼️🎣🍴🏛️🚻♿🏊‍♂️🚴🧺🪑 ⛺ 1976

A world in miniature – heaths, hills, cliffs and coast ready to be explored on foot or by bike.

Finding out more: 01929 450002 or purbeck@nationaltrust.org.uk

---

South Milton Sands

Thurlestone, near Kingsbridge, Devon TQ7 3JY

Map ① F9 🏊‍♂️🚴 1980

Thurlestone Rock off South Milton Sands, Devon

This popular long, golden, sandy beach, with rock pools and dunes, edges a sheltered bay of crystal-clear water and looks out to the iconic Thurlestone Rock offshore. The nearby wetland is home to many bird species and is an ideal place to spot rare migratory visitors.

Eating and shopping: Beach House café (Trust-approved concession) serving refreshments and lunch (locally caught fish).

Making the most of your day: numerous activities available, from rock-pooling and beachcombing to swimming, windsurfing and kayaking. For divers, the wreck of the *Louis Sheid* lies just offshore.

Access for all: 🅿️♿🚻♿🚶 Café 🪑♿

Getting here: see website for details.
Parking: free (charge for non-members).

Finding out more: 01548 561144 or southmiltonsands@nationaltrust.org.uk

South Milton Sands
Beach café seasonal opening.

A line of old trees beside Bronze Age burial mounds on King Barrow Ridge, Stonehenge World Heritage Site, Wiltshire

Stonehenge Landscape

near Amesbury, Wiltshire

Map (1) K5  1927

Within the Stonehenge World Heritage Site, 827 hectares (2,100 acres) of Trust downland surrounds the stone circle, with a huge complex of Neolithic and Bronze Age monuments to explore, including the Stonehenge Cursus (older than Stonehenge itself), ancient burial mounds and Durrington Walls – once a mid-winter feasting site. **Note**: stone circle, visitor centre and shuttle managed by English Heritage (admission free to Trust members).

Eating and shopping: indoor café at visitor centre (not National Trust).

Making the most of your day: guided walks and family activities throughout the year.
Dogs: welcome under close control (assistance dogs only at stone circle).

Access for all: P & WC

Getting here: see website for details.
Parking: 50 yards to visitor shuttle service (not National Trust) to landscape and stone circle (Trust members free). Access on foot to some areas may be temporarily restricted due to construction works.

Finding out more: 01980 664780 or stonehenge@nationaltrust.org.uk

Studland Beach

Studland, near Swanage, Dorset

Map (1) K7 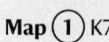    1982

Glorious slice of Purbeck coastline with a four-mile stretch of golden, sandy beach, gently shelving bathing waters and views of Old Harry Rocks and the Isle of Wight. Includes the most popular naturist beach in Britain. The heathland behind the beach is a haven for native wildlife and features all six British reptiles. Designated trails through the sand dunes and woodlands allow for exploration and spotting of deer, insects and bird life as well as numerous wild flowers. Studland was the inspiration for Toytown in Enid Blyton's *Noddy*. **Note**: Shell Bay toilets are low-water flush, only other toilets at Knoll Beach and Middle Beach.

Eating and shopping: seaside café with spectacular views of Old Harry Rocks serving fresh, locally sourced food (inside and outside seating). Log burner in winter. Knoll Beach shop sells seaside-themed goods, including buckets and spades, swimwear and local gifts.

Dunes on the glorious Studland Beach in Dorset, below, and fun in the water, right

Making the most of your day: year-round events, including children's trails, wildlife-themed guided walks, slacklining, beach volleyball, food events and Discovery Centre for private hire. Watersports. Coastal change interpretation hut open all year.
Dogs: restrictions apply 1 May to 30 September.

Access for all: ♿🚻♿🛗 **Grounds** ♿♿

Getting here: see website for details.
Parking: mainly pay and display. Shell Bay and South Beach, 9 to 11; Knoll Beach and Middle Beach, 9 to 8 (or dusk if earlier).

Finding out more: 01929 450500 or studlandbeach@nationaltrust.org.uk

Studland Beach		M	T	W	T	F	S	S
Shop and café								
1 Jan–29 Mar	10–4	M	T	W	T	F	S	S
30 Mar–29 Jun	9:30–5*	M	T	W	T	F	S	S
30 Jun–7 Sep	9–6	M	T	W	T	F	S	S
8 Sep–25 Oct	9:30–5*	M	T	W	T	F	S	S
26 Oct–31 Dec	10–4	M	T	W	T	F	S	S

*Shop and café open one hour later at weekends. Shop and café opening hours may be longer in fine weather and shorter in poor. Shop and café closed 6 March and 25 December.

Wembury

Wembury Beach, Wembury, Devon PL9 0HP

Map (1) F9  1939

A great beach, and more: some of the best rock pools in the country, good surfing, masses of wildlife and views of a distinctive island – the Great Mewstone. Starting point for lovely inland and coastal walks to Wembury Woods and the Yealm Estuary, and around Wembury Point.

Eating and shopping: historic Old Mill Café serving coffees, homemade cakes, soups, pasties and ice-cream. Beach shop selling everything from spades and wetsuits to windbreaks.

Making the most of your day: rock-pooling with Wembury Marine Centre (01752 862538, not National Trust), birdwatching, sailing, surfing, kayaking, diving, snorkelling, walking, horse-riding and fishing at nearby Cellars Beach. **Dogs**: welcome on coast path and on beach (except for 1 May to 30 September).

Access for all: [P][WC][access icons] Café [access icon]
Marine Centre [icon] Beach [icon]

Getting here: see website for details.
Parking: free (charge for non-members).

Finding out more: 01752 346585 or wembury@nationaltrust.org.uk

Wembury
For details of the Old Mill Café seasonal opening, telephone 01752 863280.

The sun sets over Cornwall, seen from Wembury Point in Devon

Old boat house in Woodchester Park, Gloucestershire

Woodchester Park

Nympsfield, near Stonehouse, Gloucestershire GL10 3TS

Map (1) J3  1994

The tranquil wooded valley contains a 'lost landscape': remains of an 18th- and 19th-century landscape park with a chain of five lakes. The restoration of this landscape is an ongoing project. Waymarked trails (steep in places) lead through picturesque scenery, passing an unfinished Victorian mansion (not National Trust).
Note: toilet not always available.

Making the most of your day: waymarked trails through valley. **Dogs**: under close control, on leads where requested.

Access for all: Grounds [icon]

Getting here: see website for details.
Parking: £3 (pay and display), no change given from ticket machine. Accessible from Nympsfield road, 300 yards from junction with B4066.

Finding out more: 01452 814213 or woodchesterpark@nationaltrust.org.uk

Cornish coast

Cornwall is all about the coast, laden with memories of childhood holidays: sandy beaches, harbours and secret coves, cafés on the water's edge, breathtaking clifftop paths.

Boscastle

Cornwall PL35 0HD

Map (1) D7 ![icons] 1955

Much of the land in and around Boscastle is owned by the National Trust. This includes the cliffs of Penally Point and Willapark, which guard the sinuous harbour entrance, Forrabury Stitches, high above the village and divided into ancient 'stitchmeal' cultivation plots, as well as the lovely Valency Valley. **Note**: toilet by main car park (not National Trust).

Eating and shopping: café with courtyard seating (wi-fi available), shop and visitor centre.

Making the most of your day: children's quiz/trail. Holiday cottages. Combine with a visit to Tintagel Old Post Office, just a few miles along the coast. **Dogs**: welcome on walks and in café courtyard.

Access for all: ![icons] Grounds ![icon]

Getting here: see website for details.
Parking: pay and display, 100 yards (not National Trust).

Finding out more: 01840 250010 or boscastle@nationaltrust.org.uk

Boscastle		M	T	W	T	F	S	S
Shop, café and visitor centre								
1 Jan–28 Feb	10:30–4	M	T	W	T	F	S	S
1 Mar–3 Aug	10–5	M	T	W	T	F	S	S
4 Aug–30 Aug	10–5:30	M	T	W	T	F	S	S
31 Aug–2 Nov	10–5	M	T	W	T	F	S	S
3 Nov–31 Dec*	10:30–4	M	T	W	T	F	S	S

*Closed 25 and 26 December.

Looking down on Boscastle Harbour, Cornwall

Carnewas and Bedruthan Steps

Bedruthan, near Padstow, Cornwall PL27 7UW

Map ① C8   1930

This is one of the most popular destinations on the Cornish coast. Spectacular clifftop views stretch across Bedruthan Beach (not National Trust). The Trust has rebuilt the steep cliff staircase to the beach, but visitors need to be aware of the risk of being cut off by the tide. **Note**: unsafe to bathe at any time. Toilet not always available.

Eating and shopping: National Trust shop and café (National Trust-approved concession) with adjoining clifftop tea-garden.

Making the most of your day: children's quiz/trail, walks leaflet and information panel. Play area beside picnic site. Bunkhouse and holiday cottages. Combine with a visit to Trerice (approximately 9 miles away). **Dogs**: allowed.

Access for all:
Car park and cliff top

Getting here: see website for details.

Finding out more: 01637 860563 or carnewas@nationaltrust.org.uk

Carnewas and Bedruthan Steps		M	T	W	T	F	S	S
Shop								
15 Feb–23 Feb	11–4	M	T	W	T	F	S	S
1 Mar–9 Mar	11–4	·	·	·	·	·	S	S
15 Mar–4 Apr	11–4	M	T	W	T	F	S	S
5 Apr–2 Nov	10:30–5	M	T	W	T	F	S	S
Café								
15 Feb–4 Apr	11–4	M	T	W	T	F	S	S
5 Apr–2 Nov	10:30–5	M	T	W	T	F	S	S
8 Nov–14 Dec	11–4	·	·	·	·	·	S	S
26 Dec–31 Dec	11–4	M	T	W	·	F	S	S

Cliff staircase closed from 3 November to mid-February. Telephone 01637 860701 to confirm café opening times in winter.

Above right, dramatic Bedruthan Steps, Cornwall

Godrevy

Gwithian, near Hayle, Cornwall TR27 5ED

Map ① B9   1939

Long sandy beaches on St Ives Bay with wildlife-rich cliffs and walks. Godrevy café in dunes (Trust-approved concession). **Note**: unstable cliffs and incoming tides. Toilets open in main season; car-park space limited during and following wet weather.

Finding out more: 01872 552412 or godrevy@nationaltrust.org.uk

The unspoilt Polly Joke cove lies between Holywell and Crantock, Cornwall

Holywell and Crantock

North Cornwall coast, near Newquay, Cornwall

Map ① C8 [icons] 1951

Close to Newquay, this feels like a different Cornwall: two classic north coast beaches with expanses of golden sand, great for sandcastles and surfing. Footpaths inland and around the coast invite you to discover wildlife-rich dunes and sandy grassland, a quiet estuary, cliffs carpeted with wild flowers, unspoilt coves and caves.

Eating and shopping: refreshments available nearby at Holywell, Crantock, Cubert and West Pentire. Fern Pit café (not National Trust), across the Gannel Estuary from Crantock beach, is accessible by ferryboat at high tide during main season or by footbridge at low tide.

Making the most of your day: surf schools and board hire at Crantock and Holywell. Rock-pooling at Holywell. Seals and rare butterflies to spot. Polly Joke Beach and summer wild flowers at West Pentire to discover.
Dogs: welcome under control everywhere, including beaches.

Access for all: [icons]

Getting here: see website for details.
Parking: Crantock car park (height restriction barrier when unmanned): SW 789 607; Holywell car park SW 767 586; Treago Mill (for Polly Joke, also known as Porth Joke) SW 776 599.

Finding out more: 01208 863046 or holywellandcrantock@nationaltrust.org.uk

Lizard Point and Kynance Cove

The Lizard, near Helston, Cornwall TR12 7NT

Map ① C10 [icons] 1935

Lizard Point, mainland Britain's most southerly point, offers dramatic coastal walks, rare wild flowers and interesting geological features. Two miles north lies Kynance Cove, considered one of the most beautiful beaches in the world. Marconi's historic wireless experiments are celebrated at the Lizard Wireless Station at Bass Point. **Note**: toilets in Kynance car park closed during winter.

Eating and shopping: café at Kynance Cove (March to October, dependent on weather through winter), café at Lizard Point (open all year) – both Trust-approved concessions.

Making the most of your day: Cornish choughs, colourful wildflower displays and basking sharks can be seen in spring and early summer. To make the most of the beach at Kynance, visit at low tide. **Dogs**: seasonal day-time dog bans on some beaches, including Kynance (Easter to 31 October).

Access for all: 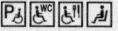 Lizard Point

Getting here: see website for details.
Parking: at Lizard Point and Kynance.

Finding out more: 01326 561407 (property office). 01326 291174 (Rangers) or lizard@nationaltrust.org.uk

The Lizard

Telephone for opening times of the Lizard Wireless Station at Bass Point.

Kynance Cove near Lizard Point, Cornwall

Kayaking at Mullion Cove in Cornwall

Mullion Cove and Poldhu Cove

Mullion, near Helston, Cornwall TR12 7JB

Map (1) C10  1945

Mullion Cove is home to a historic working harbour, with turquoise calm water in the summer and towering Atlantic waves in the winter. Nearby Poldhu is a family-friendly sandy beach with dunes. The Marconi Centre celebrates Poldhu as the site of the first transatlantic wireless signal. **Note**: car park and toilets not National Trust.

Eating and shopping: cafés at Mullion during summer, café at Poldhu open all year (none National Trust).

Making the most of your day: hire a kayak at Mullion Harbour and explore hidden bays and caves. The surf school at Poldhu offers lessons for all the family. Camping at Teneriffe Farm campsite near Mullion. **Dogs**: welcome, except for seasonal day-time dog ban on Poldhu beach.

Access for all: Mullion harbour

Getting here: see website for details.
Parking: nearest 300 yards (not National Trust).

Finding out more: 01326 291174 or mullioncove@nationaltrust.org.uk

Penrose

Penrose, Helston, Cornwall TR13 0RD

Map ① B10
1974

Home to Loe Pool (below), Cornwall's largest freshwater lake, Penrose is surrounded by beautiful woods, farmland and coastline, so there is plenty to explore. There are numerous places to walk, including the dramatic coast path, as well as safe off-road cycle routes. At Gunwalloe, a medieval church divides two beaches.

Eating and shopping: newly opened Stables Café in stables courtyard. Picnics welcome in walled garden.

Making the most of your day: new cycle routes (downloadable outdoors guide available). **Dogs**: welcome everywhere, but seasonal dog ban at Gunwalloe Church Cove.

Access for all: [Pd][Dd] Parkland [⛔][➡][♿]

Getting here: see website for details.
Sat Nav: use TR13 0RD for Penrose Hill car park; TR12 7QE for Gunwalloe (Church and Dollar Coves). **Parking**: free around parkland. For the stables use Penrose Hill car park. Also pay and display car park at Gunwalloe.

Finding out more: 01326 561407 or penroseestate@nationaltrust.org.uk

Penrose		M	T	W	T	F	S	S
Stables Café								
12 Apr–20 Jul	10–4:30						S	S
26 Jul–3 Sep	10–4:30	M	T	W	T	F	S	S
6 Sep–2 Nov	10–4:30						S	S

St Agnes and Chapel Porth

Chapel Porth, St Agnes, Cornwall TR5 0NS

Map ① C9 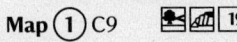 1956

This breathtaking coastal landscape is a walker's paradise, with sweeping expanses of rare coastal heath – which turn a dazzling purple and yellow in late summer – huge skies and views, an ancient beacon site and dramatic mine ruins (below). As if that were not enough, there is a popular surf beach that opens up into a vast expanse of sand at low tide. **Note**: toilets at Chapel Porth are seasonal.

Eating and shopping: pubs, cafés and shops (not National Trust) at St Agnes. Chapel Porth Beach café open daily summer and most winter weekends (01872 552487). Picnics welcome.

Making the most of your day: explore the landscape and discover the World Heritage Site mine buildings at Wheal Coates and Trevellas and the legend of Giant Bolster. **Dogs**: welcome everywhere, except on Chapel Porth Beach from Easter Sunday to 30 September inclusive.

Access for all: [Pd][Dd][wc][ll][ʎ]

Getting here: see website for details.
Parking: at Wheal Coates: SW 703 500; St Agnes Head: SW 699 512; St Agnes Beacon: SW 704 503; Towan Cross: SW 703 483; Chapel Porth: SW 697 495 (very busy in the summer).

Finding out more: 01872 552412 or chapelporth@nationaltrust.org.uk

Exmoor

Where moorland meets the sea: a National Park with high moorland, ancient woods, rushing river valleys, remote farms and cliffs plunging into the Bristol Channel.

Heddon Valley

Parracombe, Barnstaple, Devon EX31 4PY

Map ① F5 🚻🏛️📷♿🅿️ 1963

The dramatic West Exmoor coast, favourite landscape of the Romantic poets, offers not only the Heddon Valley, but also Woody Bay and the Hangman Hills to explore. There are spectacular coastal and woodland walks, as well as a car park, shop and information centre in the Heddon Valley.

Heddon Valley, North Devon, leads to the sea at Heddon's Mouth

Eating and shopping: shop selling walking equipment and clothing, maps, postcards, local history books, Exmoor products, gifts and ice-cream.

Making the most of your day: two all-terrain children's buggies and an all-terrain mobility scooter available to borrow from shop. Barbecues are free to borrow. **Dogs**: welcome.

Access for all:
Countryside ➡️ ⛰️

Getting here: see website for details.
Parking: opposite shop.

Finding out more: 01598 763402 or heddonvalley@nationaltrust.org.uk

Heddon Valley		M	T	W	T	F	S	S
Shop								
1 Apr–17 Apr	10:30–4:30	M	T	W	T	F	S	S
18 Apr–30 Sep	10:30–5	M	T	W	T	F	S	S
1 Oct–31 Oct	10:30–4:30	M	T	W	T	F	S	S

Holnicote Estate

near Minehead, Somerset

Map ① G5 ✝️🏛️♿🚶🐾🅿️ 1944

Set within Exmoor National Park, Holnicote was part of the Acland bequest, one of the largest estates donated to the Trust. There are 20 square miles of spectacular landscape to explore, with five picturesque villages and vast tracts of moorland, including Dunkery Beacon, Somerset's highest point and within the first European Dark Sky Reserve. Ancient Horner Wood has many species of bat, fungi and lichen. With more than 100 miles of paths, including the South West Coast Path, this is a fantastic area for walking, horse-riding, cycling and orienteering. Wildlife highlights include red deer, Exmoor ponies and the heath fritillary butterfly. **Note**: toilets at Bossington and Horner car parks; also at Selworthy (not National Trust).

Eating and shopping: Periwinkle tea-room on Selworthy Green serves light lunches or cream teas. Shop selling gifts and information on exploring the estate. Barbecues welcome in picnic field at Bossington car park.

The Holnicote Estate, Somerset: view from Dunkery Hill towards Selworthy, in the heart of Exmoor National Park

Making the most of your day: Selworthy and Horner orienteering trails. Downloadable walks or walk packs available from shop. Wild Wednesdays for children during school holidays. **Dogs**: welcome on leads.

Access for all: [WC] Grounds [access icons]

Getting here: see website for details.
Sat Nav: use TA24 8TP (Selworthy).
Parking: Bossington and Horner, pay and display (free to members), additional parking at Allerford, Dunkery, North Hill, Selworthy and Webbers Post.

Finding out more: 01643 862452 or holnicote@nationaltrust.org.uk

Holnicote Estate		M	T	W	T	F	S	S
Tea-room								
22 Mar–20 Jul	10:30–5		T	W	T	F	S	S
21 Jul–7 Sep	10:30–5	M	T	W	T	F	S	S
9 Sep–2 Nov	10:30–5		T	W	T	F	S	S
Shop								
22 Mar–2 Nov	12–5			W	T	F	S	S

Tea-room and shop open Bank Holiday Mondays; shop has extended opening times in summer. Opening hours for the tea-room and shop can vary according to weather conditions. Estate office open Monday to Friday, 8:30 to 5.

Watersmeet

Watersmeet Road, Lynmouth, Devon EX35 6NT

Map ① F5   [icons] 1955

This area, where the lush valleys of the East Lyn and Hoar Oak Water tumble together, is a haven for wildlife and offers excellent walking. At the heart sits Watersmeet House, a 19th-century fishing lodge, which is now a tea-garden, shop and information point. **Note**: deep gorge with steep walk down to house.

Eating and shopping: tea-garden serving hot and cold food and drinks in a magnificent wooded setting. Shop selling Exmoor produce and gifts, walking gear and maps.

Making the most of your day: Exmoor Spotter chart for families and *Exmoor Coast of Devon* walks leaflet available. **Dogs**: allowed on leads in tea-garden.

Access for all: Building Grounds [icon]

Getting here: see website for details.
Parking: pay and display (not National Trust), steep walk to house. Free car parks at Combe Park and Countisbury.

Finding out more: 01598 752648 or watersmeet@nationaltrust.org.uk

Watersmeet		M	T	W	T	F	S	S
Tea-room and tea-garden								
15 Feb–23 Feb	11–3	M	T	W	T	F	S	S
15 Mar–17 Apr	10:30–4:30	M	T	W	T	F	S	S
18 Apr–30 Sep	10:30–5	M	T	W	T	F	S	S
1 Oct–2 Nov	10:30–4:30	M	T	W	T	F	S	S

Watersmeet House shop opens 30 minutes after tea-room and tea-garden except for 15 to 23 February when shop is closed.

Watersmeet House, Devon, beside a rushing Exmoor river

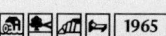

Jurassic Coast

England's first natural World Heritage Site: 95 miles of Dorset/Devon coastline, a thrilling geological 'walk through time' spanning 185 million years of Earth's history.

Branscombe

Seaton, Devon EX12 3DB

Map ① H7   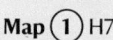 1965

Branscombe Beach, Devon: a good spot for swimming and picnics

Nestling in a valley that reaches down to the sea on East Devon's dramatic Jurassic Coast, the village of Branscombe is surrounded by picturesque countryside with miles of tranquil walking through woodland, farmland and beach. In addition, there is a working forge and a restored watermill. **Note**: nearest toilets at information point, village hall and beach car park.

Eating and shopping: Old Bakery tea-room (National Trust-approved concession) serving homemade soups, ploughman's, sandwiches and cream teas (seasonal opening: for details call 01297 680333). Quality ironwork on sale from the Old Forge.

Making the most of your day: extensive network of paths. Manor Mill a restored water-powered mill and Old Forge, a working forge. **Dogs**: on leads in garden, Old Bakery garden, information point, orchard and wider countryside.

Access for all: 🚾♿ **Building** 🦽🦼
Mill 🦽👫 **Grounds** 🦼

Getting here: see website for details.
Parking: limited next to Old Forge (donations welcome); car park behind village hall (not National Trust: donation); beach car park, not National Trust (charge including members).

Finding out more: 01752 346585 (South and East Devon Countryside Office) or branscombe@nationaltrust.org.uk

Branscombe		M	T	W	T	F	S	S
Manor Mill								
6 Apr–29 Jun	2–5	·	·	·	·	·	·	S
2 Jul–31 Aug	2–5	·	·	W	·	·	·	S
7 Sep–26 Oct	2–5	·	·	·	·	·	·	S
Old Forge								
Open all year	10–5*	M	T	W	T	F	S	S

*Telephone 01297 680481 to confirm forge opening times.

Burton Bradstock

near Bridport, Dorset

Map ① I7 🏖️📶 1973

One of the main gateways to Dorset's Jurassic Coast, with easy access to spectacular sandstone cliffs and miles of unspoilt beaches. Hive Beach is a hugely popular family destination, part of Chesil Beach – the largest shingle ridge in the world. Nearby, Burton Cliff glows bright gold in the sunlight.

Eating and shopping: Hive Beach Café (National Trust tenancy) on Chesil Bank serves local seafood.

Making the most of your day: events through the year. Family activities, including paddling in the sea and hunting for fossils. Circular and clifftop walks. Hive Beach popular for diving and angling. **Dogs**: welcome. Dog-free zone on Hive Beach 1 June to 30 September.

Spectacular cliffs at Burton Bradstock, Dorset

Access for all: ♿P

Getting here: see website for details.
Sat Nav: use DT6 4RF. **Parking**: pay and display (charge for non-members).

Finding out more: 01297 489481 or burtonbradstock@nationaltrust.org.uk

Visit

Golden Cap

Golden Cap Estate, Morcombelake,
Bridport, Dorset

Map ① I7  1961

Spectacular countryside estate on the Jurassic
Coast – England's only natural World Heritage
Site. The great rocky shoulder of Golden Cap
is the south coast's highest point, with
breathtaking views in all directions. Stonebarrow
Hill is a good starting point for discovering the
25 miles of footpaths around the estate.

Eating and shopping: small volunteer-run shop
and information centre, with toilets and
bunkhouse, in the old radar station at
Stonebarrow car park, Charmouth.

Making the most of your day: play trail on
Langdon Hill. Smugglers' trail on Stonebarrow
Hill. Family activities and events all year.
St Gabriel's Beach for fossils and traces of
185 million years of Earth's history.
Dogs: welcome.

Getting here: see website for details.
Sat Nav: for Stonebarrow car park and shop use
DT6 6RA. For Langdon Hill car park use DT6 6EP.
Parking: Stonebarrow Hill and Langdon Hill.

Finding out more: 01297 489481 or
goldencap@nationaltrust.org.uk

Ringstead Bay

Ringstead, near Weymouth, Dorset DT2 8NQ

Map ① J7 1949

This quiet, unspoilt stretch of the Jurassic
Coast in West Dorset is like the seaside of
childhood memories: a perfect sweep of
shingle beach with rock pools inviting you to
explore, backed by farmland and cliffs covered
with flowers and butterflies. The seawater is
incredibly clear and safe for bathing.

Eating and shopping: picnics welcome at the
Trust car park at the top of the hill, with its
views of the Jurassic Coast World Heritage Site.
Shop and café at the beach car park (not
National Trust).

Making the most of your day: the clifftops are
perfect for kite-flying or why not walk out to the
chalk headland of White Nothe, where there are
spectacular views of the bay and across to the
Isle of Portland? **Dogs**: welcome everywhere,
especially on the South West Coast Path.

Access for all: 🦽

Getting here: see website for details.
Parking: on the farmland at Southdown Farm
(SY 757 825) and at beach car park
(not National Trust).

Finding out more: 01297 489481 or
ringsteadbay@nationaltrust.org.uk

Sweeping coastline at Golden Cap in Dorset

Dorset's Ringstead Bay is like the seaside of childhood memories, with gentle waves and rock pools to explore

Coastal and countryside car parks in the South West

Cornwall

Morwenstow	SS	205 154
Duckpool	SS	202 117
Sandymouth	SS	203 100
Northcott Mouth	SS	204 084
Strangles Beach	SX	134 952
Glebe Cliff, Tintagel	SX	050 884
Port Quin	SW	972 805
Lundy Bay	SW	953 796
Pentireglaze	SW	942 799
Park Head	SW	853 707
Crantock	SW	789 607
Treago Mill (Polly Joke)	SW	778 601
Holywell Bay	SW	767 586
St Agnes Beacon	SW	704 503
Wheal Coates	SW	703 500
Chapel Porth	SW	697 495
Reskajeage Downs	SW	623 430
Derrick Cove	SW	620 429
Fishing Cove	SW	599 427
Trencrom	SW	517 359
Carn Galver	SW	422 364
Botallack	SW	366 334
Cape Cornwall	SW	353 318
Cot Valley	SW	358 308
Penrose	SW	639 259
Chyvarloe	SW	653 235
Gunwalloe	SW	660 207
Predannack	SW	669 162
Poltesco	SW	725 157
Bosveal (Durgan)	SW	775 276
St Anthony Head	SW	847 313
Porth Farm		
(Towan Beach)	SW	867 329
Pendower Beach	SW	897 384
Carne Beach	SW	905 384
Nare Head	SW	922 379
Penare (Dodman)	SW	998 404
Lamledra (Vault Beach)	SW	011 411
Coombe Farm	SX	110 512
Pencarrow Head	SX	150 513
Frogmore	SX	157 517
Lansallos	SX	174 518
Hendersick	SX	236 520

Devon

Countisbury	SS	747 497
Combe Park	SS	740 477
Woody Bay	SS	676 486
Trentishoe Down	SS	635 480
Torrs Walk, Ilfracombe	SS	512 476
Hartland:		
Brownsham	SS	285 259
Exmansworthy	SS	271 266
and East Titchberry	SS	244 270
Stoke	SX	558 466
Ringmore	SX	649 457
East Soar	SX	713 376
Snapes Point	SX	739 404
Prawle Point	SX	775 354
Little Dartmouth	SX	874 492
Higher Brownstone	SX	905 510
Coleton Camp	SX	909 513
Scabbacombe	SX	912 523
Man Sands	SX	913 531
Salcombe Hill	SY	148 889
Branscombe	SY	197 887
Plymbridge Woods	SX	524 585
Cadover Bridge	SX	533 636
Shaugh Prior	SX	554 645

Dorset

Cogden, West Dorset	SY	503 883
Stonebarrow Hill	SY	383 933
Langdon Hill	SY	413 931
Burton Bradstock	SY	491 888
Ringstead Bay	SY	760 822
Spyway	SY	996 785
Studland: Shell Bay	SZ	035 864
Knoll Beach	SZ	035 836
Middle Beach	SZ	037 828
South Beach	SZ	038 825

Gloucestershire

Haresfield: Cripplegate	SO	832 086
and Ash Lane	SO	824 066
Rodborough Common:		
Hill Fort	SO	852 035
Minchinhampton:		
Reservoir	SO	855 013
Mayhill	SO	691 221

Somerset

Sand Point	ST	330 660

A la Ronde

Summer Lane, Exmouth, Devon EX8 5BD

Map (1) G7   🏠♿🍴 1991

This unique 16-sided house, described by Lucinda Lambton as having 'a magical strangeness that one might dream of only as a child', was built for two spinster cousins, Jane and Mary Parminter, on their return from a European grand tour in the late 18th century. It contains many objects and mementoes of their travels, and the extraordinary interior decoration includes a feather frieze from many species of birds, including game birds, fowl, jays and parrots, laboriously stuck down with isinglass. The fragile shell-encrusted gallery, said to contain nearly 25,000 shells, is viewed via a 360-degree touchscreen virtual tour. **Note**: small, fragile rooms. Allow at least an hour to visit. Non-flash photography welcome. Shop or tea-room voucher for visitors arriving by green transport.

Eating and shopping: shop selling gifts, local produce, plants and ice-cream. Award-winning licensed tea-room with open-air seating and sea views (Trust-approved concession). Orchard picnic area. Second-hand book sales.

Making the most of your day: events, workshops, exhibitions, nature walks and school holiday craft activities. Self-guided themed tours, house family trail. Garden games. Tick off some *50 things to do before you're aged 11¾*. **Dogs**: welcome on leads throughout garden and grounds. Complimentary dog biscuits in shop.

Access for all: 🅿️🅳♿🚻🔆📷🖼️🎧·🅰️
House 🔆♿🚶 Grounds ♿➡️

Getting here: see website for details.
Parking: free. Caravans and trailers telephone in advance.

Finding out more: 01395 265514 (office). 01395 278552 (tea-room) or alaronde@nationaltrust.org.uk

A la Ronde		M	T	W	T	F	S	S
4 Jan–2 Feb*	12–4						S	S
8 Feb–23 Feb	11–5	M	T	W	T	F	S	S
1 Mar–2 Nov	11–5	M	T	W	T	F	S	S
8 Nov–14 Dec*	12–4						S	S

Grounds and shop open 30 minutes earlier and close 30 minutes later. Tea-room opens 30 minutes earlier; last orders at 5 and closes as shop and grounds. *4 January to 2 February and 8 November to 14 December house shown 'put to bed' by guided tours only (last tour 3:15). Main season: last admission to house 4.

Shells galore at A la Ronde in Devon

Portraits preside over the warm and inviting panelled Library at Antony in Cornwall

Antony

Torpoint, Cornwall PL11 2QA

Map ① E8   🏰 ❀ ⚓ 1961

Still the family home of the Carew Poles after hundreds of years, the beautiful early 18th-century house has fine collections of paintings, furniture and textiles. The landscape garden offers sweeping views and includes a formal garden with topiary, a knot garden, sculptures and the National Collection of Daylilies.
Note: members admitted free to Woodland Garden (not National Trust) only when house is open.

Eating and shopping: self-service tea-room offering light lunch or afternoon tea. Gift shop with souvenirs, plants and local produce.

Making the most of your day: garden and family events. Modern sculpture throughout gardens. Croquet on lawn. Quizzes and trails.

Dogs: assistance dogs only.

Access for all: 🅿️ Dₛ 🚻 ♿ 🏛 📷 🖼 ‥
House 🏰♿ Grounds 🏰➡♿

Getting here: see website for details.
Parking: free, 250 yards.

Finding out more: 01752 812191 or antony@nationaltrust.org.uk

Antony		M	T	W	T	F	S	S
1 Apr–29 May	12–5*	·	**T**	**W**	**T**	·	·	·
1 Jun–31 Aug	12–5*	·	**T**	**W**	**T**	·	·	**S**
2 Sep–30 Oct	12–5*	·	**T**	**W**	**T**	·	·	·
Woodland Garden (not National Trust)								
1 Mar–30 Oct	11–5:30	·	**T**	**W**	**T**	·	**S**	**S**

*House opens at 1. Open Good Friday, Easter Sunday and Bank Holiday Monday, Sunday 4 May and Bank Holiday Monday, Sunday 25 May and Bank Holiday Monday. Timed ticket entry to house. Bath Pond House interior can only be seen by written application to the property manager, on days house is open.

Arlington Court and the National Trust Carriage Museum

Arlington, near Barnstaple, Devon EX31 4LP

Map ① F5　🏠✝🐚✿⚓🐕 1949

An unexpected jewel, Arlington incorporates history and nature in a remarkable setting. The home of the Chichester family for more than 600 years, the collections displayed reflect the passions of the last heiress, Miss Rosalie Chichester, along with ships and shells. The interactive Carriage Museum in the original stable block brings coaching history to life. In the historic kitchen garden, our gardeners grow produce for the tea-room; the conservatory's exotic plantings tell of the Chichester family's world travels. There are lovely walks through the estate, which is abundant with wildlife. Two woodland play areas are perfect for exploring with children.

Eating and shopping: chutneys and preserves made from Arlington-grown produce. Tea-room serving estate produce (reduced menu November to March).

Making the most of your day: daily family activities (main school holidays). May Fair and Christmas Fair. Bird hide for viewing wildlife, plus heronry and bat camera. Meet the gardeners every Tuesday and Wednesday. **Dogs**: welcome on leads in garden, Carriage Museum and wider estate.

Access for all: 🅿🚲♿🚻🧸📷📖🎦📱
😊🔵 House 🔽♿🔖 Museum 🔖♿🔖
Grounds ➡🔖🔖

Getting here: see website for details.
Sat Nav: from South Molton, don't turn left into unmarked lane (deliveries only).
Parking: free, 150 yards.

Finding out more: 01271 850296 or arlingtoncourt@nationaltrust.org.uk

Arlington Court		M	T	W	T	F	S	S
15 Feb–23 Feb	11–4	M	T	W	T	F	S	S
15 Mar–2 Nov	11–5**	M	T	W	T	F	S	S
8 Nov–21 Dec*	11–4	.	.	.	.	.	S	S

Garden, shop and tea-room open 1 January, 11 to 4. Limited access to house and Carriage Museum in February, November and December. *Entrance by guided tours only, please call for timings and to book. **Garden, shop and tea-room open 10:30. Grounds open dawn till dusk, all year.

Ashleworth Tithe Barn

Ashleworth, Gloucestershire GL19 4JA

Map ① J2　🏠 1956

Barn, with immense stone-tiled roof, picturesquely situated close to the River Severn. **Note**: sorry no toilet.

Finding out more: 01452 814213 or ashleworth@nationaltrust.org.uk

Family day out at Arlington Court, Devon

Avebury

near Marlborough, Wiltshire

Map ① K4　🏚✝🍷🏛✼🛥🛏 | 1943 |

In the 1930s the pretty village of Avebury, partially encompassed by the stone circle of this World Heritage Site, witnessed archaeologist Alexander Keiller's excavations. In re-erecting many of the stones that make up the largest prehistoric stone circle in the world, Keiller uncovered the true wonder of one of Europe's most important megalithic monuments. His finds are on display in the Alexander Keiller Museum, housed in the 17th-century threshing barn and stables, where interactive displays and children's activities bring the landscape to life. Avebury Manor was transformed in a partnership between the National Trust and the BBC, creating a hands-on experience that celebrates and reflects the lives of the people who once lived here. **Note**: English Heritage holds guardianship of Avebury Stone Circle, owned and managed by the National Trust.

Discovering Avebury, Wiltshire, above and below

Eating and shopping: Circles Café and the Manor tea-room. Shop selling local gifts, including Avebury honey and books on the archaeology and mythology of the area.

Making the most of your day: guided tours of the stone circle all year. Specialist talks and guided tours of the landscape and manor. Family activities in Barn and events during holidays. Hunt for the golden hare at Easter or for witches' cats at Hallowe'en. Seasonal produce available from new kitchen garden. **Dogs**: assistance dogs only in house, garden and café. Elsewhere dogs on leads welcome.

Access for all: ⏏♿♿♿♿♿♿♿♿♿♿♿
Buildings ♿♿ Grounds ♿♿➡

Getting here: see website for details.
Sat Nav: use SN8 1RD. **Parking**: on A4631, 300 yards. Pay and display (non-members). Overnight parking prohibited. Please respect the community and do not park on the village streets.

Above, a corner of Avebury Manor garden, Wiltshire

Finding out more: 01672 539250 or avebury@nationaltrust.org.uk. National Trust Estate Office, High Street, Avebury, Wiltshire SN8 1RF

Avebury		M	T	W	T	F	S	S
Manor house and garden								
15 Feb–31 Mar	11–4	M	T	·	T	F	S	S
1 Apr–25 Oct	11–5	M	T	·	T	F	S	S
26 Oct–23 Dec	11–4*	M	T	·	T	F	S	S
Museum, shop and Circles Café								
1 Jan–31 Mar	10–4	M	T	W	T	F	S	S
1 Apr–25 Oct	10–6**	M	T	W	T	F	S	S
26 Oct–31 Dec	10–4*	M	T	W	T	F	S	S
Stone circle								
Open all year	Dawn–dusk	M	T	W	T	F	S	S

Last entry to manor house one hour before closing. Timed entry tickets to manor available on arrival and online. Manor closed 20 to 22 June. During winter only part of garden open. *Close dusk if earlier. **Shop and Circles Café close at 5:30. All except stone circle closed 24 to 26 December. Barn Gallery may close in cold weather.

Barrington Court

Barrington, near Ilminster, Somerset TA19 0NQ

Map ① I6   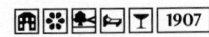 1907

Colonel Lyle, whose family firm became Tate & Lyle, realised his ambition of creating an idyllic country estate when he restored Barrington Court in the 1920s. This beautiful and empty manor house, owned by the National Trust since 1907, is nothing less than a hidden gem. Set within delightful flower gardens and apple orchards and surrounded by rolling parkland, Colonel Lyle's idea of a medieval estate remains for us to enjoy today. With its superb restaurant, playing fountains and friendly welcome, Barrington Court is a haven of peace and tranquillity. **Note**: craft workshops independently run (opening times may vary).

Eating and shopping: Beagles Café serving light refreshments and Art Deco-inspired Strode House Restaurant for more formal dining. Gift shop selling Barrington Court's award-winning cider and juice.

Making the most of your day: constantly changing programme of daily activities, ranging from historic dancing and special tours of hidden places to family trails. For details of special events, see website. **Dogs**: assistance dogs only in garden. Shaded parking available.

Access for all: 🅿🅳♿🚾♿♿📷♿🔊♿
Building ♿   Grounds ♿▶♿♿

Getting here: see website for details.
Sat Nav: incorrectly directs visitors to rear entrance – please follow brown tourist signs.
Parking: free.

Finding out more: 01460 241938 or barringtoncourt@nationaltrust.org.uk

Barrington Court		M	T	W	T	F	S	S
House, garden, parkland, shop, Strode House Restaurant								
4 Jan–16 Feb	11–3						S	S
17 Feb–2 Nov	11–5*	M	T	W	T	F	S	S
8 Nov–28 Dec	11–3						S	S
Beagles Café								
17 Feb–2 Nov	10–5	M	T	W	T	F	S	S

*Garden, park and shop open 10 to 5; restaurant open 12 to 3.

Barrington Court, Somerset, offers a great day out for families

Bath Assembly Rooms

Bennett Street, Bath, Somerset BA1 2QH

Map ① J4　🏛🔔🍽 1931

The Assembly Rooms were at the heart of fashionable Georgian society. The Fashion Museum is on the lower ground floor. **Note**: limited visitor access during functions. The Fashion Museum is run by Bath and North East Somerset Council. Entry charge for The Fashion Museum (including members).

Finding out more: 01225 477789 or bathassemblyrooms@nationaltrust.org.uk

Blaise Hamlet

Henbury, Bristol BS10 7QY

Map ① I3　🏠 1943

Delightful hamlet of nine picturesque cottages, designed by John Nash in 1809 for Blaise Estate pensioners. **Note**: access to green only; cottages not open. Sorry no toilet.

Finding out more: 01275 461900 or blaisehamlet@nationaltrust.org.uk

Bradley

Totnes Road, Newton Abbot, Devon TQ12 6BN

Map ① G8　🏛✝✿ 1938

Unspoilt and fascinating medieval manor house, still a relaxed family home, in a green haven among riverside meadows and woodland. Many charming original features, such as the medieval cat hole and gargoyles. The quiet and peaceful chapel was licensed for services in 1428. **Note**: sorry no toilet. Parking from 10:30 on open days.

Bradley, Devon: a relaxed family home

Eating and shopping: table-top shop selling honey, souvenirs, gifts and postcards.

Making the most of your day: open-air theatre and countryside craft events. Walks around the surrounding countryside. For a truly medieval experience, also visit nearby Compton Castle. **Dogs**: welcome in meadows and woodland. Assistance dogs only in garden and house.

Access for all: 🅿♿🖼🚶♿🅰
Building 🚶♿🏃　Grounds 🚶♿➡

Getting here: see website for details.
Sat Nav: TQ12 1LX directs to gate lodge (follow driveway for parking). **Parking**: in meadow. For designated parking call 01626 354513.

Finding out more: 01803 661907 or bradley@nationaltrust.org.uk

Bradley		M	T	W	T	F	S	S
1 Apr–25 Sep	11–5		**T**	**W**	**T**			

Brownsea Island

Poole Harbour, Poole, Dorset BH13 7EE

Map ① K7  1962

Brownsea Island, a protected wildlife area and Site of Special Scientific Interest (SSSI), is dramatically located in Poole Harbour with spectacular views across to the Purbeck Hills. Thriving natural habitats – including woodland, heathland and a lagoon – create a haven for wildlife. There are rare red squirrels and a wide variety of birds to spot. The island also has a rich history, for as well as boasting daffodil farming and pottery works, it was the birthplace of the Scouting and Guiding movement. **Note**: no public access to castle. Small entry fee to Dorset Wildlife Trust Nature Reserve (including members).

Eating and shopping: coffee bar and Villano Café. Gift and souvenir shop, also selling Brownsea Island outdoors range, old-fashioned sweets and ice-cream.

On the beach at Brownsea Island, Dorset, above, and deer-spotting, below

Making the most of your day: seasonal family activities and trails. Tracker Packs. Events. Wildlife walks and talks. Open-air theatre. Outdoor and visitor centres. Introductory walks and guided buggy tours for less mobile visitors (booking advised). **Dogs**: assistance dogs only.

Access for all: 🚻🚾🍴🔎♿🚫
Building 🏢   Grounds 🏢➡️

Getting here: half-hourly boat service from 10 (not National Trust). **Sat Nav**: Sandbanks Jetty, BH13 7QJ and Poole Quay, BH15 1HP.
Parking: close to Sandbanks and Poole Quay, not National Trust (charge including members) – see Borough of Poole website.

Finding out more: 01202 707744 or brownseaisland@nationaltrust.org.uk

Brownsea Island		M	T	W	T	F	S	S
Boats from Sandbanks Jetty only								
8 Feb–16 Mar*	10–4						S	S
Full boat service from Poole Quay and Sandbanks								
22 Mar–2 Nov	10–5	M	T	W	T	F	S	S
Limited opening for booked groups only								
2 Jan–21 Mar	10–4	M	T	W	T	F	S	S
3 Nov–21 Dec	10–4	M	T	W	T	F	S	S

Shop and Villano Café open until last boat. *Special weekend openings: boats leave every 30 minutes from Sandbanks only; shop, café and visitor centre will all be open.

Buckland Abbey, Garden and Estate

Yelverton, Devon PL20 6EY

Map ① E8 🏠✝♣🚣🛏🍴 1948

So much to explore at Buckland Abbey, Garden and Estate in Devon, above and below

Hundreds of years ago, Cistercian monks chose this tranquil valley as the perfect spot in which to worship, farm their estate and trade. The Abbey, later converted into a house, today combines furnished rooms with museum galleries bringing to life the story of how seafaring adventurers Sir Richard Grenville and Sir Francis Drake changed the shape of Buckland Abbey and the fate of England. Outdoors, the Cider House Garden includes a walled kitchen garden and wild garden; there are community growing areas, orchards and the impressive Great Barn, as well as woodland walks with far-reaching views and late spring bluebells. **Note**: Abbey interior presented in association with Plymouth City Museum.

Eating and shopping: Ox Yard Restaurant (available to hire) serves freshly cooked local produce, often using ingredients grown in the kitchen garden. Picnics welcome in grounds. Shop selling gifts and plants. Ox Yard Bookshop and Ox Yard Gallery. Holiday cottage.

Making the most of your day: new Rembrandt self-portrait exhibition. Willow Patch family area, family pack (not available year round) and information sheets. Numerous events, estate walks and letterbox trail. **Dogs**: welcome on leads on designated walks only.

Access for all: 🅿️♿🚻♿♿🎞🖼♿📷 ⊠
Abbey ♿♿ **Reception** ♿
Grounds ♿♿➡♿

Getting here: see website for details.
Parking: free, 150 yards.

Finding out more: 01822 853607 or bucklandabbey@nationaltrust.org.uk

Buckland Abbey		M	T	W	T	F	S	S
15 Feb–7 Mar	11:30–4:30*	M	T	W	T	F	S	S
8 Mar–2 Nov	10:30–5:30*	M	T	W	T	F	S	S
7 Nov–30 Nov	11:30–4:30*					F	S	S
5 Dec–21 Dec	11:30–4:30*	M	T	W	T	F	S	S

*Abbey opens 30 minutes later and closes 30 earlier. Ox Yard Gallery opening times may vary.

Castle Drogo

Drewsteignton, near Exeter, Devon EX6 6PB

Map ① F7  1974

Join us on an exciting journey as we continue to turn Castle Drogo 'Inside Out', undertaking conservation on a grand scale which will make the castle watertight – for the first time in its history. On the inside, the rooms have been completely redisplayed with theatrical installations, open storage areas and opportunities to get up close to the building works. On the outside, there is the chance to see men at work on the scaffold from a specially constructed viewing platform. Discover the beautiful Lutyens-designed terraced garden, the highest in the care of the Trust, with dramatic views of Dartmoor.
Note: access to castle occasionally restricted due to building works.

Eating and shopping: large café (available for functions) with indoor and open-air seating, public wi-fi and outdoor play area. Picnics welcome in garden or wild areas of the grounds. Shop selling local products, gifts and plants inspired by Castle Drogo's history and garden.

Making the most of your day: peaceful gardens and waymarked countryside walks. Family quizzes, trails and events. Croquet (small fee, details at visitor reception).
Dogs: assistance dogs only in gardens; welcome on leads in wider estate.

Access for all: 🅿 🅿 🚜 ♿ 🔊 🅰 📖 ✍ ⓐ
Building 🔊🦽♿ Grounds 🔊🦽🦽➡

Getting here: see website for details.
Parking: free, 400 yards.

Finding out more: 01647 433306 or castledrogo@nationaltrust.org.uk

Castle Drogo		M	T	W	T	F	S	S
Estate								
Open all year	Dawn–dusk	M	T	W	T	F	S	S
Garden, visitor centre, café and shop								
1 Jan–7 Mar*	11–4:30	M	T	W	T	F	S	S
8 Mar–2 Nov	9:30–5:30	M	T	W	T	F	S	S
3 Nov–31 Dec**	11–4:30	M	T	W	T	F	S	S
Castle and project viewing platform								
15 Feb–23 Feb	11–4	M	T	W	T	F	S	S
1 Mar–2 Mar	11–4	·	·	·	·	·	S	S
8 Mar–2 Nov	11–5	M	T	W	T	F	S	S
8 Nov–21 Dec	11–4	·	·	·	·	·	S	S

*Closed 13 to 31 January. **Closed 24 to 26 December. During restoration project the visitor route may change. Opening of the project viewing platform is subject to weather conditions.

Castle Drogo, Devon, as you have never seen it before

Chedworth Roman Villa

Yanworth, near Cheltenham,
Gloucestershire GL54 3LJ

Map ① K2 1924

This year we are celebrating the 150th anniversary of the Victorian discovery of Chedworth Roman Villa – one of the grandest villas in Roman Britain and one of the best-preserved Roman sites in the country. A new conservation building, opened in 2012, provides better-than-ever access to extensive mosaic floors, hypocaust systems and bathhouse rooms. The newly refurbished museum houses a range of finds and artefacts from the Villa, and the tranquil setting, within a wonderfully rich wildlife haven, provides an opportunity to wander among the Roman ruins while enjoying idyllic rural views.

Chedworth Roman Villa, Gloucestershire, above: one of the best-preserved Roman sites in the country

Eating and shopping: café serving light lunches, cakes, hot drinks and ice-creams, with indoor and open-air seating. Shop offering Roman-themed souvenirs, books and games, as well as seasonal plants and gifts.

Making the most of your day: new guidebook and audio guides. Roman dressing-up box for children, costumed interpreters and living history events. Children's activities, trails and quizzes on weekends and school holidays. **Dogs**: assistance dogs only.

Access for all: 🅿🚻♿🚹🔎📷🖼♿
Reception ♿🚻 **West Range** ♿⬆♿
Grounds ♿♿➡♿

Getting here: see website for details.
Parking: on lane at entrance, plus woodland (overflow) from March to October. Motor homes and caravans advised to arrive early.

Finding out more: 01242 890256 or chedworth@nationaltrust.org.uk

Chedworth Roman Villa		M	T	W	T	F	S	S
15 Feb–29 Mar	10–4	M	T	W	T	F	S	S
30 Mar–25 Oct	10–5	M	T	W	T	F	S	S
26 Oct–30 Nov	10–4	M	T	W	T	F	S	S

The Church House

Widecombe-in-the-Moor, Newton Abbot,
Devon TQ13 7TA

Map ① F7   1933

Fine example of a 16th-century church house,
originally used for parish festivities or 'ales'.
Note: used by local community. Please check
with National Trust shop next door to see if
you can visit. Sorry no toilet.

Finding out more: 01364 621321 or
churchhouse@nationaltrust.org.uk

Clevedon Court

Tickenham Road, Clevedon,
North Somerset BS21 6QU

Map ① I4 🏛️ ❄️ 1961

Clevedon Court, North Somerset:
remarkable medieval survival

Home to the lords of the manor of Clevedon for
centuries, the core of the house is a remarkable
survival from the medieval period. The house
was bought by Abraham Elton in 1709 and it is
still the much-loved family home of his
descendants today. **Note**: the Elton family
opens Clevedon Court for the National Trust.

Eating and shopping: kiosk serving cream teas
and soft drinks.

Making the most of your day: family guide
and children's quiz/trail. **Dogs**: assistance
dogs only.

Access for all: 🅿️ 👁️ ♿ 🏛️ 📷 🎞️ ⠿ 🅰️
Building ♿🚶 Grounds ♿

Getting here: see website for details.
Parking: free, 50 yards. Unsuitable for trailer
caravans or motor caravans. Alternative
parking 100 yards east of entrance in
cul-de-sac.

Finding out more: 01275 872257 or
clevedoncourt@nationaltrust.org.uk

Clevedon Court		M	T	W	T	F	S	S
2 Apr–28 Sep	2–5	·	·	**W**	**T**	·	·	**S**

Car park open 1:15. House entry by timed ticket, not
bookable. Open Bank Holiday Mondays.

Clouds Hill

Wareham, Dorset BH20 7NQ

Map (1) J7   🏠 | 1937

This tiny isolated brick and tile cottage in the heart of Dorset was the peaceful retreat of T. E. Lawrence ('Lawrence of Arabia'). The austere rooms are much as he left them and reflect his complex personality and close links with the Middle East, as detailed in a fascinating exhibition. **Note**: sorry no toilet.

Eating and shopping: shop selling books, gifts and Lawrence memorabilia.

Making the most of your day: combine your visit with a trip to Max Gate and Hardy's Cottage – the Dorchester homes of writer Thomas Hardy, friend of T. E. Lawrence. **Dogs**: welcome on leads in grounds only.

Access for all: 👁️   Building 🚶‍♿   Grounds 🚶

The Book Room at Clouds Hill in Dorset, below left, and the kitchen at Coleridge Cottage, Somerset

Getting here: see website for details.
Parking: free.

Finding out more: 01929 405616 or cloudshill@nationaltrust.org.uk

Clouds Hill		M	T	W	T	F	S	S
12 Mar–26 Oct	11–5		·	W	T	F	S	S
29 Oct–2 Nov	11–4		·	W	T	F	S	S

Open Bank Holiday Mondays. No electric light, so last admission at dusk.

Coleridge Cottage

35 Lime Street, Nether Stowey, Bridgwater, Somerset TA5 1NQ

Map (1) H5   🏠  1909

A visit to the former home of Samuel Taylor Coleridge offers the opportunity to immerse oneself in the sights, sounds and smells of an 18th-century cottage. Coleridge's poetry is brought to life in this simple house, the birthplace of the literary Romantic Movement, and its garden.

Eating and shopping: light refreshments on offer in the tea-room and shop selling gifts reflecting Coleridge's life and work.

Making the most of your day: regular events, special tours, family activities and trails. Visitors can hear poetry in the garden, draw water from the well and get hands-on in the kitchen.

Access for all: ⬚⬚⬚ Building ⬚⬚
Garden ⬚➡

Getting here: see website for details.
Parking: pub car park opposite, or village car park in Castle Street, 500 yards (neither National Trust).

Finding out more: 01278 732662 (Infoline). 01643 821314 or coleridgecottage@nationaltrust.org.uk

Coleridge Cottage		M	T	W	T	F	S	S
8 Mar–2 Nov	11–5	**M**	.	.	**T**	**F**	**S**	**S**

Art Deco elegance: the Saloon at Coleton Fishacre in Devon, was the scene of many an evening's entertainment

Coleton Fishacre

Brownstone Road, Kingswear, Devon TQ6 0EQ

Map ① G9   🏠❄⛴🏰🛏🍵 1982

This evocative 1920s Arts and Crafts-style country house, with its elegant Art Deco interior, perfectly encapsulates the spirit of the Jazz Age. The former home of the D'Oyly Carte family, it has a light, joyful atmosphere and inspiring views. Discover a glimpse of life 'upstairs and downstairs' and try on 1920s clothing in our popular handling room. In the garden, paths weave through glades and past tranquil ponds and rare tender plants from New Zealand and South Africa; many exotic plants thrive beneath the tree canopy. You can also walk down to the coastal viewpoint through the valley garden. **Note**: narrow approach lane requires some reversing at busy times (especially between 1 and 2:30).

Eating and shopping: Café Coleton serving light lunches, cakes and cream teas. Art Deco-inspired shop selling china, music, gifts and plants seen in this RHS-accredited garden.

Making the most of your day: daily guided garden walk, led by member of the garden team. Events including theatre in the garden and garden workshops. Family activities, such as pond-dipping, during school holidays.
Dogs: welcome on leads around garden perimeter (map available from reception).

Access for all:
Building 🚶 🏛 ♿ Grounds 🚶 ➡ ♿

Getting here: see website for details.
Parking: 20 yards from reception; overflow parking 150 yards.

Finding out more: 01803 842382 or coletonfishacre@nationaltrust.org.uk

Coleton Fishacre		M	T	W	T	F	S	S
15 Feb–30 Oct	10:30–5	M	T	W	T	.	S	S
1 Nov–22 Dec	11–4	M	.	.	.	.	S	S
27 Dec–31 Dec	11–4	M	T	W	.	.	S	S

Open Good Friday 18 April.

Compton Castle

Marldon, Paignton, Devon TQ3 1TA

Map ① G8   🏛 ✝ ✿ 🎫 🛏 1951

A rare survivor, this medieval fortress with high curtain walls, towers and two portcullis gates, set in a landscape of rolling hills and orchards, is a bewitching mixture of romance and history. Home for nearly 600 years to the Gilbert family, including Sir Humphrey Gilbert, half-brother to Sir Walter Ralegh.
Note: hall, sub-solar, solar, medieval kitchen, scullery, guard room and chapel open. Credit cards not accepted.

Compton Castle, Devon: classic medieval fortress

Eating and shopping: Castle Barton restaurant (not National Trust) opposite. Table-top shop selling souvenirs, gifts and postcards. Guidebooks and seasonal plants for sale.

Making the most of your day: history and squirrel trails for children. Picnics in our adjacent orchard welcome.
Dogs: assistance dogs only.

Access for all: 📱 💻 ♿ 👓   Building 🚶 🏛
Grounds 🚶 🏛

Getting here: see website for details.
Parking: free, 30 yards. Additional parking at Castle Barton opposite entrance, 100 yards.

Finding out more: 01803 661906 or comptoncastle@nationaltrust.org.uk

Compton Castle		M	T	W	T	F	S	S
1 Apr–30 Oct	10:30–4:30	.	T	W	T	.	.	.

Open Bank Holiday Mondays: 21 April, 5 May, 26 May and 25 August.

Corfe Castle

The Square, Corfe Castle, Wareham, Dorset BH20 5EZ

Map ① K7   🏛 🎫 🛏 1982

One of Britain's most iconic and evocative survivors of the English Civil War, the castle was partially demolished in 1646 by the Parliamentarians. A favourite haunt for adults and children alike, the romantic ruins, with their breathtaking views across Purbeck, are totally captivating. There are 1,000 years of history as a royal palace and fortress to discover and, with fallen walls and secret places, 'murder holes' and arrow loops, every corner has a tale to tell of treachery and treason. More recently, a wide variety of wildlife has made its home here.
Note: steep, uneven slopes; steps; sudden drops. All/parts of castle may close in high winds.

Eating and shopping: 18th-century tea-room serving cream teas. Summer garden with unrivalled castle views and an open log fire in winter. Shop in village square, offering products ranging from pocket-money treats to luxury locally made gifts. Visitor centre at the car park.

Members may have to pay on special events days

Making the most of your day: daily family trail. Monthly themed events, with activities every weekend and all school holidays April to September. Highlights include medieval archery, falconry, re-enactments, open-air theatre and cinema. **Dogs**: welcome on short leads.

Access for all: ♿ 🅿 🄳 👶 ♿ 🚻 🔊 📶 💷 🅰
Grounds 👟

Getting here: see website for details.
Parking: at foot of castle (800 yards walk uphill). Norden park and ride (½-mile walk) and West Street (in the village), neither National Trust and both pay and display.

Finding out more: 01929 481294 (ticket office). 01929 480921 (shop). 01929 481332 (tea-room) or corfecastle@nationaltrust.org.uk

Corfe Castle		M	T	W	T	F	S	S
1 Jan–28 Feb	10–4	M	T	W	T	F	S	S
1 Mar–31 Mar	10–5	M	T	W	T	F	S	S
1 Apr–30 Sep	10–6	M	T	W	T	F	S	S
1 Oct–31 Oct	10–5	M	T	W	T	F	S	S
1 Nov–31 Dec	10–4	M	T	W	T	F	S	S

Shop and tea-room: close at 5:30 April to September. Tea-room: closed for refurbishment 6 to 10 January. Shop closed 8 January. Castle, shop and tea-room: closed 6 March and 25 to 26 December.

Corfe Castle in Dorset: magnificent and romantic ruin with 1,000 years of history

Cotehele

St Dominick, near Saltash, Cornwall PL12 6TA

Map (1) E8 🏰 ✝ 🏛 ♣ 🛏 ⛵ ▦ **1947**

This rambling granite and slatestone Tudor house, with medieval origins, nestles in the Tamar Valley. With no electric lighting, time stands still in this former home of the Edgcumbe family. The Hall, adorned with arms and armour, provides an impressive gateway to the warren of tapestry-festooned rooms beyond, embellished with carved oak furniture, embroideries, pewter and ceramics. The garden includes formal and informal plantings, orchards and a famed annual display of daffodils. The Valley Garden features a medieval stewpond and dovecote with a breathtaking view of the river and Calstock Viaduct.

Eating and shopping: Barn Restaurant near house and The Edgcumbe on Cotehele Quay. Cornish food and gift shop as well as garden shop selling plants, garden furniture and accessories. Second-hand bookshop. West Country art and craft available in Cotehele Gallery. Seven holiday cottages.

The lawn in front of Cotehele in Cornwall is perfect for a spot of croquet, above, before exploring the mill, opposite

Making the most of your day: enjoy this year's theme: 'A Grand Tour of Cotehele'. Seasonal changes in the garden, events and activities year round. Children's trails and 'no-adults-allowed' room in the house. **Dogs**: dog-friendly walks throughout the estate. Assistance dogs only in formal garden.

Access for all: 🅿️ ♿ 🚻 ... 📷 💻 ...
Building ♿ 🔆 ♿ Grounds ♿ 🔆 ➡️

Getting here: see website for details.
Sat Nav: ignore from Tavistock, follow brown signs. **Parking**: free.

Finding out more: 01579 351346 (office). 01579 352711 (Barn Restaurant). 01579 352713 (shop) or cotehele@nationaltrust.org.uk

Cotehele		M	T	W	T	F	S	S
House								
15 Mar–2 Nov	11–4	M	T	W	T	·	S	S
3 Nov–31 Dec*	11–4	M	T	W	T	F	S	S
Garden and estate								
Open all year	Dawn–dusk	M	T	W	T	F	S	S
The Edgcumbe								
4 Jan–14 Feb	11–4	M	T	W	T	F	S	S
Barn Restaurant, The Edgcumbe, shop, plant sales, gallery								
15 Feb–14 Mar	11–4	M	T	W	T	F	S	S
15 Mar–2 Nov	11–5**	M	T	W	T	F	S	S
3 Nov–31 Dec	11–4	M	T	W	T	F	S	S

House open Good Friday and special CSI-Friday openings in August (bring a torch). *Hall of house and garland only. Everything closed 25 and 26 December, except garden and estate. **Barn Restaurant opens 10:30 main season.

Getting here: see website for details.
Parking: by arrangement only. Shuttle bus from Cotehele house.

Finding out more: 01579 350606 (mill). 01579 351346 (property office) or cotehele@nationaltrust.org.uk

Cotehele Mill		M	T	W	T	F	S	S
15 Mar–30 Sep	11–5	M	T	W	T	F	S	S
1 Oct–2 Nov	11–4:30	M	T	W	T	F	S	S

The Courts Garden

Holt, near Bradford on Avon,
Wiltshire BA14 6RR

Map (1) J4   ⌘ 1943

This hidden garden gem, with a different feel throughout the seasons, is sure to provide inspiration. In this intimate, friendly and relaxing retreat you will find herbaceous borders, quirky topiary, a kitchen garden, naturally planted spring bulbs, peaceful water gardens and arboretum.

Eating and shopping: Rose Garden tea-room (not National Trust) offers refreshments, lunch and afternoon tea. Property-grown plants, guidebooks and gifts on sale. Second-hand bookshop. 'trust' gallery shop in the nearby Glove Factory studios (studios not National Trust) selling unique gifts and art.

The Courts Garden, Wiltshire: full of variety

Cotehele Mill

St Dominick, near Saltash, Cornwall PL12 6TA

Map (1) E8    1947

After admiring the restored sailing barge *Shamrock*, moored at Cotehele Quay, you can take a short walk alongside the Morden stream to 19th-century Cotehele Mill to watch the wheel turn and enjoy a demonstration of corn being ground into flour. A hydroelectric scheme is located beyond the waterwheel. **Note**: toilets and parking at Cotehele Quay (not at mill).

Eating and shopping: Cotehele wholemeal flour, apple juice and gifts for sale. Light refreshments and lunches served at the Edgcumbe tea-room on Cotehele Quay. Pasties and ice-cream available from kiosk on quay.

Making the most of your day: costume and baking fun days. Daily tours at 3. Family trails and bakery demonstrations. Traditional chairmaker and pottery workshops. Two holiday cottages. **Dogs**: welcome, but assistance dogs only in workshops.

Access for all: [icons]
Building [icon]   Grounds [icon]

Making the most of your day: events, exhibitions, trails and friendly gardeners happy to offer tips. Combine with a visit to nearby Great Chalfield Manor and Garden (walk maps available at reception). **Dogs**: assistance dogs only.

Access for all: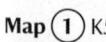
Garden

Getting here: see website for details.
Parking: free (not National Trust), 80 yards, in village hall car park opposite, on B3107. Additional overflow parking: follow signs. Please respect the community and avoid parking on the village streets.

Finding out more: 01225 782875 or courtsgarden@nationaltrust.org.uk

The Courts Garden	M	T	W	T	F	S	S
Garden and tea-room							
1 Feb–2 Mar	11–5:30*	·	·	·	·	·	S	S
3 Mar–2 Nov	11–5:30	M	T	·	T	F	S	S
Shop: 'trust' at the Glove Factory Studios**							
4 Jan–2 Mar	11–4	·	·	W	T	F	S	S
3 Mar–2 Nov	11–5	M	T	W	T	F	S	S
5 Nov–21 Dec	11–4	·	·	W	T	F	S	S

Tea-room last orders 4:45. Garden access out of season by appointment only. *Garden closed at dusk in winter if required.**Shop off site, approximately 150 yards from garden entrance.

Dinton Park and Philipps House

Dinton, Salisbury, Wiltshire SP3 5HH

Map (1) K5  1943

Neo-Grecian house in a tranquil park, designed by Jeffry Wyatville for William Wyndham in 1820. **Note**: sorry no toilet. Park is open daily all year. For house opening arrangements visit website or telephone.

Finding out more: 01672 538014 or sw.customerenquiries@nationaltrust.org.uk

Dunster Castle

Dunster, near Minehead, Somerset TA24 6SL

Map (1) G5 1976

Dramatically sited on top of a wooded hill, a castle has existed here since at least Norman times. Its impressive medieval gatehouse and ruined tower are a reminder of its turbulent history. However, the castle that you see today, owned by the Luttrell family for more than 600 years, became an elegant country home during the 19th century. The sunny terraced gardens are home to a variety of Mediterranean and subtropical plants, while the tranquil, riverside wooded gardens below feature a natural play area. There are stunning panoramic views over the surrounding countryside and moorland from the keep.

Dunster Castle, Somerset: drama outside and comfort within

Finding out more: 01643 823004 (Infoline). 01643 821314 or dunstercastle@nationaltrust.org.uk

Dunster Castle		M	T	W	T	F	S	S
Castle								
8 Mar–2 Nov	11–5	M	T	W	T	F	S	S
Garden, park and shop*								
8 Mar–2 Nov	10–5	M	T	W	T	F	S	S
3 Nov–31 Dec	11–4	M	T	W	T	F	S	S

Last entry to castle one hour before closing (except 18 July to 1 September). 'Dunster by Candlelight': castle open 5 to 9, Friday 5 and Saturday 6 December. *Shop: open 1 January and then weekends only in January; closed 25 and 26 December.

Eating and shopping: 17th-century stables shop selling local and regional gifts and guidebooks. Light refreshments available on site; riverside tea-room at Dunster Working Watermill and a selection of places to eat in Dunster village.

Making the most of your day: interactive exhibitions and 'Chapters' bring the stories of Dunster Castle to life. Guided tours of the Victorian kitchens. Events, open-air theatre and behind-the-scenes tours and re-enactments, many costumed, throughout season. **Dogs**: welcome in parkland and garden on leads.

Access for all: 🅿️ 🚻 ♿ 🏢 📷 ✏️ ⋯ 📷
Castle ♿ 🖼️ Stables 🖼️ Grounds 🖼️ ➡️ 📷

Getting here: see website for details.
Parking: 300 yards, shuttle to entrance available. Enter from A39.

Dunster Working Watermill

Mill Lane, Dunster, near Minehead, Somerset TA24 6SW

Map ① G5   🏚️ 1976

A restored and operational 18th-century watermill built on the site of a mill mentioned in the Domesday Survey of 1086. **Note**: the mill is a private business. Admission charge (including members).

Finding out more: 01643 821759 (mill). 01643 821314 (Dunster Castle) or dunstercastle@nationaltrust.org.uk

Dyrham Park

Dyrham, near Bath,
South Gloucestershire SN14 8ER

Map (1) J4   🏛✝❀⚓ 1961

There are more than 110 hectares (270 acres) of ancient parkland at Dyrham Park, where a historic herd of 185 fallow deer roam freely and magnificent trees and breathtaking views abound. At this beautiful late 17th-century home, which once belonged to hard-working civil servant William Blathwayt, you can discover how fashions changed over the centuries – from the original 17th-century Dutch-inspired interiors and formal garden, to the very different style of Victorian country squire Colonel Blathwayt. The elegant West Garden, with its splendid borders, ancient ponds and a perry pear orchard, is perfect for a quiet, relaxing stroll.

Eating and shopping: tea-room serving lunch, cakes and refreshments. In the summer and on busy days, the courtyard kiosk or the garden kiosk (with outdoor seating) offers drinks, ice-creams and snacks. The shop sells beautiful plants, books, local products and crafts.

Making the most of your day: events and activities all year, guided tours of the park and garden, dry-stone walling courses, croquet, jazz on the lawn, open-air theatre (summer) and Christmas festivities. Families can discover Old Lodge in the park, with its small natural play area and indoor and outdoor picnic tables, plus there are Tracker Packs to explore nature and regular children's nature trails. The Cotswold Way passes the property for walking further afield. Nearby Prior Park Landscape Garden offers great views and access to The Bath Skyline, where you can enjoy a six-mile circular walk encompassing beautiful woodlands, meadows and historic features. **Dogs**: welcome in car park only (exercise area at far end of car park).

Access for all: 🅿️♿🚽♿📖♿
House ♿ ♿♿   Grounds ♿➡️

Getting here: see website for details.
Sat Nav: use SN14 8HY and enter via A46.

Parking: free for use of Dyrham Park visitors only. Last entry one hour before closing and closes 5.30 or dusk when earlier.

Finding out more: 0117 937 2501 or dyrhampark@nationaltrust.org.uk

Dyrham Park		M	T	W	T	F	S	S
House								
8 Mar–29 Jun	11–5	M	T			F	S	S
30 Jun–31 Aug	11–5	M	T	W	T	F	S	S
1 Sep–25 Oct	11–5	M	T			F	S	S
26 Oct–2 Nov	11–4	M	T	W	T	F	S	S
Historic kitchen, garden, shop and tea-room								
15 Feb–25 Oct	10–5	M	T	W	T	F	S	S
26 Oct–2 Nov	10–4	M	T	W	T	F	S	S
8 Nov–14 Dec	10–4						S	S
Park								
Open all year*	10–5	M	T	W	T	F	S	S

Last admission one hour before closing. Closes dusk when earlier than 5. House open every day during Easter holidays (7 to 20 April) and May half-term (26 May to 1 June). Whole place closed until 1 on 3 and 17 September, 5 and 19 November, 3 December and 14 January. *Closed 25 December.

  Parking charges for non-members may apply

Dyrham Park, South Gloucestershire, clockwise from above: fallow deer, fun on giant stepping stones and the east front

East Pool Mine

Pool, near Redruth, Cornwall

Map ① C9   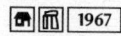 1967

East Pool celebrates the extraordinary lives of the people who worked at the very heart of the Cornish Mining World Heritage Site. With two great beam engines, preserved in their towering engine houses, this is a great place for all the family to discover the dramatic story of Cornish mining. **Note**: Trevithick Cottage, home of the celebrated Cornish engineer Richard Trevithick, is nearby at Penponds.

Eating and shopping: small shop selling gifts, including local minerals, mining and Cornish history books, plus hot drinks and snacks.

Making the most of your day: family activities and trails. Free guided tours. Hands-on exhibits and working models. **Dogs**: welcome in outdoor areas.

Michell's Engine House at East Pool Mine, Cornwall

Access for all: 🅿♿🚻👶🔎🎧🚶♿
Taylor's Engine House 🧎
Michell's Engine House 🧎 👭   Grounds ➡

Getting here: see website for details.
Sat Nav: use TR15 3NH. For Trevithick Cottage use TR14 0QG. **Parking**: free parking in Morrisons superstore (far end). Parking also at Michell's Engine House off A3047.

Finding out more: 01209 315027 or eastpool@nationaltrust.org.uk. Trevithick Road, Pool, Cornwall TR15 3NP

East Pool Mine				M	T	W	T	F	S	S
East Pool Mine and Taylor's Engine House										
18 Mar–1 Nov	10:30–5			·	T	W	T	F	S	·
Michell's Engine House										
18 Mar–1 Nov	12–4			·	T	W	T	F	S	·

Open Bank Holiday Mondays and Bank Holiday Sundays (March to October). Trevithick Cottage opening hours vary, please contact East Pool Mine for details.

Finch Foundry

Sticklepath, Okehampton, Devon EX20 2NW

Map ① F7   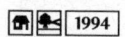 1994

Last remaining water-powered forge in England. The foundry gives a unique insight into 19th-century village life and a family-run business. At its peak, it made 400 tools a day, including sickles, scythes and shovels for farmers and miners. **Note**: narrow entrance to car park – height restrictions.

The tilt hammer in action at Finch Foundry in Devon

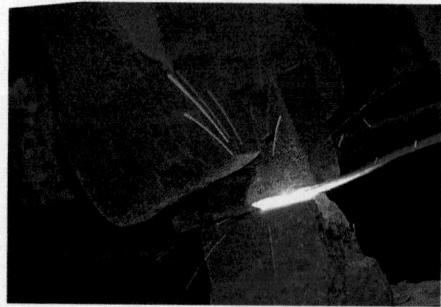

Eating and shopping: small tea-room serving snacks, cakes, tea and coffee. Small gift shop.

Making the most of your day: family activities. Stories, demonstrations and tours of machinery. Live blacksmithing event on St Clement's Day (22 November). Great starting point for moorland walks. **Dogs**: welcome in all areas except tea-room, shop and foundry during demonstrations.

Access for all: ⬚♿🏠♿🚻🔊 ⬚
Foundry ♿🏃 Grounds ♿

Getting here: see website for details.
Parking: free.

Finding out more: 01837 840046 or finchfoundry@nationaltrust.org.uk

Finch Foundry		M	T	W	T	F	S	S
15 Mar–2 Nov	11–5	**M**	**T**	**W**	**T**	**F**	**S**	**S**

Foundry and shop open for St Clement's Day, 22 November (patron saint of blacksmiths).

Glendurgan Garden

Mawnan Smith, near Falmouth,
Cornwall TR11 5JZ

Map ① C9   🏠✳♿🚣🏠 | 1962 |

Glendurgan Garden was described by its creators, the Quakers Alfred and Sarah Fox, as a 'small peace [sic] of heaven on earth'. Visitors can find out why it proved to be just this for the Foxes and their 12 children by exploring Glendurgan's three valleys, running down to the sheltered beach at Durgan on the Helford River. There is a puzzling maze, created by Alfred and Sarah to entertain the family. Enjoy camellias, magnolias and primroses in early spring followed by rhododendrons and bluebells in May. Lose yourself in the exotic greens of summer or dramatic autumn colour later on.

Eating and shopping: tea-house (Trust-approved concession) serving light lunches, including daily changing specials and afternoon tea. Ice-cream on sale at the beach in good weather. Shop and plant centre.

Beautiful puzzle: maze at Glendurgan Garden, Cornwall

Making the most of your day: Durgan Beach on Helford River. Durgan Fish Cellar provides local information and children's activities. **Dogs**: assistance dogs only in garden.

Access for all: ♿🚻♿🔊🚻🔊📖
Garden entrance ♿♿

Getting here: see website for details.
Parking: free.

Finding out more: 01326 252020 or glendurgan@nationaltrust.org.uk

Glendurgan Garden		M	T	W	T	F	S	S
8 Feb–3 Aug	10:30–5:30	·	**T**	**W**	**T**	**F**	**S**	**S**
4 Aug–31 Aug	10:30–5:30	**M**	**T**	**W**	**T**	**F**	**S**	**S**
2 Sep–2 Nov	10:30–5:30	·	**T**	**W**	**T**	**F**	**S**	**S**

Garden closes dusk if earlier. Open Bank Holiday Mondays.

Godolphin

Godolphin Cross, Helston, Cornwall TR13 9RE

Map ① B9 🎫🏛️📷❄️🛏️🛌 2000

Time seems to have stood still in this ancient and tranquil place. The Side Garden layout is largely unchanged since the 16th century, and the King's Garden provides a sheltered and relaxing place to sit. The whole estate is part of the Cornish Mining World Heritage Site, and its rich archaeology provides the perfect habitat for rare plants and wildlife. A walk up Godolphin Hill will reward you with panoramic coast-to-coast views, or you could just stroll through the woods. Why not stay in Godolphin House (a National Trust holiday home) and experience the splendour that mining riches bought? **Note**: limited house opening – check dates before you visit.

Timeless Godolphin, Cornwall, above and below

Eating and shopping: Piggery serving tea, coffee, biscuits, sandwiches and cakes. Souvenirs and postcards available. Blankets available to borrow from the Piggery for picnics in the orchard, garden or estate.

Making the most of your day: free guided tours of grounds and estate. Family trails, walks booklet. Gardener's potting shed has information on flora and fauna. Events, activities and exhibitions all year. Trengwainton Garden nearby. **Dogs**: welcome outdoors on short leads.

Access for all: 🅿️🔄♿🚻🧷🛗🚪👨‍🦽👫
Garden 🚶‍♿🚶‍♿

Getting here: see website for details.
Parking: free.

Finding out more: 01736 763194 or godolphin@nationaltrust.org.uk

Godolphin		M	T	W	T	F	S	S
Estate								
Open all year		M	T	W	T	F	S	S
Garden								
1 Jan–31 Jan	10–4	M	T	W	T	F	S	S
1 Feb–2 Nov	10–5	M	T	W	T	F	S	S
3 Nov–31 Dec	10–4	M	T	W	T	F	S	S
House								
1 Feb–6 Feb	10–5	M	T	W	T	·	S	S
1 Mar–6 Mar	10–5	M	T	W	T	·	S	S
5 Apr–10 Apr	10–5	M	T	W	T	·	S	S
3 May–8 May	10–5	M	T	W	T	·	S	S
7 Jun–12 Jun	10–5	M	T	W	T	·	S	S
5 Jul–10 Jul	10–5	M	T	W	T	·	S	S
6 Sep–11 Sep	10–5	M	T	W	T	·	S	S
4 Oct–9 Oct	10–5	M	T	W	T	·	S	S
29 Nov–14 Dec	10–4	M	T	W	T	F	S	S

Garden closed 24 and 25 December.

Great Chalfield Manor and Garden, Wiltshire: this fine moated medieval manor is set in peaceful countryside

Great Chalfield Manor and Garden

near Melksham, Wiltshire SN12 8NH

Map ① J4 　🏚️✝️❀🎴 1943

Moated medieval manor set in peaceful countryside with fine oriel windows and rooftops adorned with soldiers, griffins and monkeys. The romantic garden, with terraces, topiary houses, gazebo, lily pond, roses and spring-fed fishpond, can be enjoyed throughout the seasons. Charming surroundings, featuring barns, gatehouse and beautiful church (not National Trust). **Note**: home to donor family tenants, who manage it for the National Trust. Members attending annual plant fair before normal opening times pay for admission.

Eating and shopping: help yourself to tea and coffee in the Motor House (not National Trust). Guidebook and postcards available. Plants on sale.

Making the most of your day: guided tour of the manor rooms. Annual plant fair. Country walk to nearby Courts Garden (map available).

Access for all: 🅿️♿🚻📷🎫♿♿
Manor ♿🏠♿ 　Garden ♿➡️

Getting here: see website for details.
Parking: free, 100 yards, on grass verge outside manor gates.

Finding out more: 01225 782239 or greatchalfieldmanor@nationaltrust.org.uk

Great Chalfield		M	T	W	T	F	S	S
Manor								
1 Apr–30 Oct	*		.	T	W	T	.	.	S
Garden								
1 Apr–30 Oct	11–5		.	T	W	T	.	.	
6 Apr–26 Oct	2–5		.	.	.	.	.	S

*Admission to manor house by 45-minute guided tour only (places limited, not bookable). Tuesday, Wednesday and Thursday: at 11, 12, 2, 3 and 4. Sunday: at 2, 3 and 4. Additional timed manor tickets may be available on Sundays and other busy days.

Greenway

Greenway Road, Galmpton, near Brixham,
Devon TQ5 0ES

Map ① G8 🏠 ❄ 🍴 🛏 🔔 🍷 2000

Greenway offers an extraordinary glimpse into
the holiday home of the famous author Agatha
Christie and her family. The relaxed and
atmospheric house is set in the 1950s and
contains many of the family's collections,
including archaeology, Tunbridge ware, silver,
botanical porcelain and books. Outside there is
a large and romantic woodland garden, with
restored vinery and peach house, which drifts
down the hillside towards the sparkling Dart
Estuary and the boathouse. Please consider
'green ways' to get here: for example, ferry
(shuttle service available up from the quay),
bus, steam train, cycling or walking.
Note: booking essential for car parking. Steam
train halt approximately ½ mile away (walk
through woodland).

View from Greenway, Devon, above, and vintage bus, below

Eating and shopping: licensed Barn Café
serving lunches, pasties, cakes and cream teas.
House Kitchen serving two-course lunches
(booking advised). Tack-room for takeaway
options open at peak times. Agatha Christie-
inspired shop selling books, DVDs, music, local
food, gifts and plants.

Making the most of your day: afternoon
guided garden tours. Events including twilight
tours, garden workshops and theatre in the
garden. Family croquet, clock golf, trails and
quizzes. Arrive on Barnaby, the 1950s vintage
bus. **Dogs:** welcome in garden on leads
(tethering rings available in courtyard).
Dog bin at reception.

Access for all: 🅿 🐕 ♿ 🚻 🔄 📷 🏠 📺 ♫
👓 🖼 **Buildings** 🏠🏠🏠 **Garden** 🏠🏠

Getting here: ferry from Dartmouth, Totnes,
Brixham or Torquay. **Parking:** spaces must be
booked (telephone infoline or visit website) –
same-day booking possible by telephone.
No parking on Greenway Road or Galmpton.

Finding out more: 01803 842382 (Infoline).
01803 882811 (ferry and vintage bus).
01803 555872 (steam train) or
greenway@nationaltrust.org.uk

Greenway		M	T	W	T	F	S	S
8 Mar–6 Apr	10:30–5	·	·	W	T	F	S	S
8 Apr–20 Apr	10:30–5	·	T	W	T	F	S	S
23 Apr–20 Jul	10:30–5	·	·	W	T	F	S	S
22 Jul–20 Aug	10:30–5	·	T	W	T	F	S	S
21 Aug–2 Nov	10:30–5	·	·	W	T	F	S	S
6 Dec–21 Dec	11–4	·	·	·	·	·	S	S
27 Dec–31 Dec	11–4	M	T	W	·	·	S	S

Open Bank Holiday Mondays 21 April, 5 May, 26 May and
25 August.

We welcome dogs assisting visitors with disabilities

Hailes Abbey

near Winchcombe, Cheltenham,
Gloucestershire GL54 5PB

Map (1) K1   ✝ 🏛 1937

Once a Cistercian abbey, founded in 1246 by
Richard of Cornwall. Pilgrims visited and
financed 'the Holy Blood of Hailes'.
Note: financed, managed and maintained by
English Heritage (0117 975 0700).

Finding out more: 01242 602398 or
hailesabbey@nationaltrust.org.uk

Hardy's Cottage

Higher Bockhampton, near Dorchester,
Dorset DT2 8QJ

Map (1) J7   🏠 ✿ 1948

Thomas Hardy was born in 1840 in this small
cob and thatch cottage, which was built by his
great-grandfather and is little altered since the
family left. His early novels *Under the
Greenwood Tree* and *Far from the Madding Crowd*
were written here. **Note**: sorry no toilet.

Eating and shopping: Thomas Hardy's books
for sale, postcards and small gifts.

Making the most of your day: why not
combine your visit with a trip to Max Gate,
Hardy's later home in Dorchester, just a couple
of miles away? **Dogs**: welcome on leads in
garden only.

Access for all: 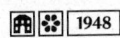
Building 🔼 **Grounds** 🚶➡

Getting here: see website for details.
Parking: free (not National Trust),
approximately 700 yards.

Hardy's Cottage, Dorset: cob and thatch charm

Finding out more: 01305 262366 or
hardyscottage@nationaltrust.org.uk

Hardy's Cottage			M	T	W	T	F	S	S
12 Mar–2 Nov	11–5		·	·	**W**	**T**	**F**	**S**	**S**
Open Bank Holiday Mondays.									

Heelis

Kemble Drive, Swindon, Wiltshire SN2 2NA

Map (1) K3   🏠 ▼ 2005

The Trust's award-winning central office is a
remarkable example of an innovative and
sustainable building.

Finding out more: 01793 817575 or
heelis@nationaltrust.org.uk

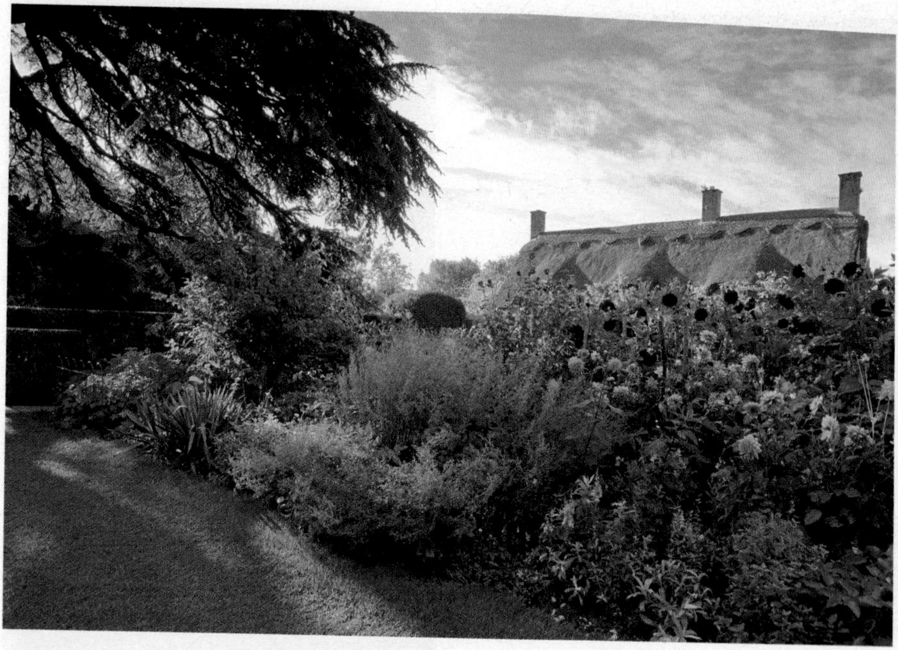

The gardens at Hidcote, Gloucestershire, are inspirational whatever the time of year

Hidcote

Hidcote Bartrim, near Chipping Campden, Gloucestershire GL55 6LR

Map ① L1   ❀ ⛰ ⛾ 1948

Memories don't get any better than this. At Hidcote, one of the country's great gardens, you can experience for yourself the fulfilment of a quiet American's English fantasy. There are exquisite garden rooms, each with its own unique character, with rare shrubs and trees, herbaceous borders and unusual plants from around the world. The garden changes in harmony with the seasons, from vibrant spring bulbs to autumn's spectacular Red Border. Nestled in the Cotswolds with sweeping views across the Vale of Evesham, a visit to Hidcote is inspirational at any time of year.

Eating and shopping: Barn Café, plus Winthrop's Café and conservatory. Largest Trust plant centre. Shop selling exclusive Hidcote souvenirs.

Making the most of your day: daily introductory talks. Exclusive evening Head Gardener tours and open-air theatre events. Themed family activities and workshops. **Dogs**: assistance dogs only.

Access for all: ♿ ♿ ♿ ♿ ♿ ♿ ♿ ♿
Visitor reception ♿ ♿ **Grounds** ♿ ➡ ♿ ♿

Getting here: see website for details.
Parking: free, 100 yards.

Finding out more: 01386 438333 or hidcote@nationaltrust.org.uk

Hidcote		M	T	W	T	F	S	S
15 Feb–9 Mar	11–4						S	S
15 Mar–27 Apr	10–6	M	T	W			S	S
28 Apr–31 Aug	10–7	M	T	W	T	F	S	S
1 Sep–28 Sep	10–6	M	T	W	T	F	S	S
29 Sep–2 Nov	10–5	M	T	W			S	S
8 Nov–21 Dec	11–4						S	S

Open Good Friday. Last admission to garden one hour before closing. Barn Café closed during November and December.

Killerton

Broadclyst, Exeter, Devon EX5 3LE

Map ① G6 🏠✝🏛🏵🦋🛏🍴 1944

Would you give away your family home for your political beliefs? Sir Richard Acland did just this with his estate, which includes 20 farms and 250 cottages and is one of the largest in the Trust. Killerton House, built in 1779, brings to life generations of Aclands, one of Devon's oldest families. More of a family home than a grand house, it is a place you can imagine living in. This year's historic fashion exhibition is '*The Nature of Fashion*', which focuses on natural fibres. One of Killerton's highlights is the garden, created by Veitch. It is beautiful year-round, with rhododendrons, magnolias, unusual trees, flower borders, sweeping lawns and countryside views. Follow the dragon trail and walks around the parkland.

Killerton, Devon: a detail from the magnificent costume collection, above, and summer fun on the lawn, below

Eating and shopping: large shop selling award-winning Killerton cider, chutney, flour and honey, plus wide range of local gifts, food and books. Second-hand bookshop. Well-stocked plant centre. Food and drink available in the Killerton Kitchen, Stables Café and Thirsty Dragon kiosk. Picnics welcome.

Making the most of your day: visitors are welcome to play the piano, browse in the library or dress up in replica costume. There is a wide range of activities for families and children, including the mouse trail in the house, play trail and *50 things before you're 11 ¾* map. The Discovery Centre is open during school holidays. Outside, the garden has secret paths and a rustic summerhouse, where Tom, the pet bear, lived. There are family walks, including dog-friendly ones, cycle tracks and orienteering routes. Events include Easter Egg hunts, classic car, Vintage Weekend, summer plays, Wicked Wednesdays, Apple Weekend and Christmas. **Dogs**: welcome on leads in park and estate walks. Dog bowls and posts.

Access for all: House Grounds

Getting here: see website for details. **Sat Nav**: postcode leads to house, so follow brown signs once at property. **Parking**: free, 280 yards.

Finding out more: 01392 881345 or killerton@nationaltrust.org.uk

Killerton		M	T	W	T	F	S	S
Park and garden								
Open all year	10–7	**M**	**T**	**W**	**T**	**F**	**S**	**S**
House and Killerton Kitchen								
2 Jan–5 Jan	11–4	·	·	·	**T**	**F**	**S**	**S**
15 Feb–7 Mar	11–3*	**M**	**T**	**W**	**T**	**F**	**S**	**S**
8 Mar–2 Nov	11–5	**M**	**T**	**W**	**T**	**F**	**S**	**S**
22 Nov–31 Dec**	11–4	**M**	**T**	**W**	**T**	**F**	**S**	**S**
Stables Café								
1 Jan–14 Feb	11–4	**M**	**T**	**W**	**T**	**F**	**S**	**S**
15 Feb–31 Dec	10–5	**M**	**T**	**W**	**T**	**F**	**S**	**S**
Shop and plant sales								
2 Jan–5 Jan	11–4	·	·	·	**T**	**F**	**S**	**S**
11 Jan–9 Feb	11–4	·	·	·	·	·	**S**	**S**
15 Feb–31 Oct	11–5:30	**M**	**T**	**W**	**T**	**F**	**S**	**S**
1 Nov–31 Dec	11–5	**M**	**T**	**W**	**T**	**F**	**S**	**S**

*From 15 February (half-term week) and also at weekends until 2 March, the house will be open until 4. **Special Christmas opening 22 November to early January: house closed 24, 25 and 26 December and New Year's Day. Shop and Stables Café close at 3 on 26 December.

Colourful herbaceous border at Killerton in Devon

Clyston Mill, below, and a quiet corner of Marker's Cottage, top right: both part of the Killerton Estate, Devon

Killerton Estate: Budlake Post Office, Marker's and Clyston Mill

Killerton Estate, Broadclyst, Devon

Map ① G7  1944

Get a feel for life on the wider Killerton Estate by searching out Marker's, a modified medieval hall-house with unusual painted screen; the picturesque working watermill at nearby Clyston; and Budlake, a thatched cottage that once served as the village post office, with a pretty cottage garden. **Note**: nearest toilets by Broadclyst car park.

Eating and shopping: Clyston flour available at the mill or at the large gift shop at Killerton. Wide range of food and drink on offer at Killerton in the Killerton Kitchen, Stables Café or Thirsty Dragon kiosk.

Making the most of your day: unusual and quirky things to spot, from the red telephone box and two-seated privvy at Budlake. Flour ground at Clyston. Map available at Killerton. **Dogs**: on leads at Budlake and Clyston Mill. Assistance dogs only at Marker's.

Access for all:
Marker's 🔾 Clyston 🔾🔾➡

Getting here: see website for details.
Parking: for Marker's and Clyston use Broadclyst car park.

Finding out more: 01392 881345 or killerton@nationaltrust.org.uk

Budlake, Marker's and Clyston Mill	M	T	W	T	F	S	S
29 Mar–2 Nov 1–5	M	T	W	·	·	S	S

King John's Hunting Lodge

The Square, Axbridge, Somerset BS26 2AP

Map ① I4 🔾 1968

This early Tudor timber-framed wool merchant's house (*circa* 1500) provides a fascinating insight into local history.
Note: run as a local history museum by Axbridge and District Museum Trust. Entry charges apply (charge including members).

Finding out more: 01934 732012 or kingjohns@nationaltrust.org.uk

The opulent Spanish Room at Kingston Lacy, Dorset, above, contains many outstanding works of art. Opposite: a view of the striking exterior

Kingston Lacy

Wimborne Minster, Dorset BH21 4EA

Map ① K7   🏛️🏚️🌸♿🛏️⛺🍴 1982

Home of the Bankes family for more than 300 years, this striking 17th-century house is noted for its lavish interiors. The outstanding art collection includes paintings by Rubens, Van Dyck, Titian and Tintoretto, as well as the largest private collection of Egyptian artefacts in the UK. Outside, there are beautiful lawns, a restored Japanese tea-garden and several waymarked walks through the surrounding parkland, with its fine herd of North Devon cattle. The 3,443-hectare (8,500-acre) estate is dominated by the Iron Age hill fort of Badbury Rings, home to 14 varieties of orchid.

Eating and shopping: prize-winning scones, beef from the Kingston Lacy North Devon herd, regional and local foods and wines, plants, high-quality gifts and souvenirs for sale.

Making the most of your day: events and activities, including farmers' markets, open-air theatre, tractor-trailer tours, children's crafts, Hallowe'en spooktacular, 'Above and Below Stairs' days. Art collection, with works by Rubens, Titian and Tintoretto. Outside, you'll find no end of treats, including an

Edwardian-inspired Japanese Garden, a Winter Garden with magnificent snowdrop displays, the Egyptian obelisk and sarcophagus, a woodland play area and a working kitchen garden with colourful community allotments. Across the wider estate there are excellent walks and trails, including a riverside walk at Eyebridge, and the opportunity to explore the ancient Badbury Rings. **Dogs**: under close control in restaurant courtyard, park and woodlands only.

Access for all: 🅿️♿🚻♿♿📷🏠📺🚶
👓🔍 **Building** ♿ **Grounds** ♿➡️♿♿

Getting here: see website for details.
Sat Nav: unreliable, follow B3082 to main entrance. **Parking**: free. Charge at Badbury Rings on point-to-point race days.

Finding out more: 01202 883402 or kingstonlacy@nationaltrust.org.uk

Kingston Lacy		M	T	W	T	F	S	S
House								
1 Mar–2 Nov*	11–5	·	·	**W**	**T**	**F**	**S**	**S**
Garden, park, shop and restaurant								
1 Jan–28 Feb	10:30–4	**M**	**T**	**W**	**T**	**F**	**S**	**S**
1 Mar–2 Nov	10:30–6	**M**	**T**	**W**	**T**	**F**	**S**	**S**
3 Nov–23 Dec	10:30–4	**M**	**T**	**W**	**T**	**F**	**S**	**S**
27 Dec–31 Dec	10:30–4	**M**	**T**	**W**	·	·	**S**	**S**

Open Bank Holiday Mondays. Timed tickets may operate on Bank Holiday Sundays and Mondays. Last admission to house one hour before closing. *House Entrance Hall and Servants' Hall open and decorated for Christmas during December weekends (5 to 21 December). May close in poor weather.

Knightshayes

Bolham, Tiverton, Devon EX16 7RQ

Map ① G6　🏠🔭❄♿🛏🍽 | 1972 |

With acres of glorious gardens and parkland surrounding a spectacular Gothic Revival house, Knightshayes is a country estate on a grand scale. The house is a rare example of the work of William Burges, whose richly decorated interiors have always inspired extremes in opinion. The garden is among the finest in Devon, and its collection represents one of the most varied in the Trust. With more than 1,200 plant species unique to Knightshayes and riotous seasonal colour, it's always worth a visit. Don't miss the fully productive kitchen garden, which provides the café with fresh seasonal produce.

Richly decorated interior at Knightshayes in Devon

Eating and shopping: Stables café serving hot meals and light refreshments. Tea-room in the conservatory by the house serving hot drinks and cakes. Plant centre and gift shop selling local wares, along with fresh produce for sale from the kitchen garden.

Making the most of your day: newly opened kitchen area in the house. Waymarked trails and walks leaflets for gardens and parkland. Free introductory garden walks. Seasonal family events and activities. **Dogs**: on leads in parkland, off leads in wood.

Access for all: 🅿♿🚻♿♿♿♿♿📷♿
♿♿ House ♿♿♿ Stables ♿♿♿
Gardens ♿➡♿

Getting here: see website for details.
Sat Nav: do not use, instead on nearing Tiverton/Bolham follow signs. **Parking**: free.

Finding out more: 01884 254665 or knightshayes@nationaltrust.org.uk

Knightshayes		M	T	W	T	F	S	S
1 Feb–30 Mar	10–4*	M	T	W	T	F	S	S
31 Mar–2 Nov	10–5*	M	T	W	T	F	S	S
5 Nov–21 Dec	10–4*			W	T	F	S	S
22 Dec–31 Dec	10–4*	M	T	W		F	S	S

*House opens at 11. Selected rooms open in the house during winter months.

Lacock, Wiltshire: the village, above left, and Abbey cloisters, above right

Lacock Abbey, Fox Talbot Museum and Village

Lacock, near Chippenham, Wiltshire SN15 2LG

Map (1) K4  1944

Lacock is the birthplace of photography and a popular film location. Exploring the village feels like stepping back in time, or into a costume drama. Once a medieval nunnery, the Abbey sits at the heart of the village, surrounded by informal wooded grounds and gardens. You can imagine monastic life in the unusually intact ground-floor cloisters and rooms. Above, you will find intriguing furnished rooms where architecture and personal objects tell a fascinating 800-year story of change from nunnery to family home. In the South Gallery, you can stand on the spot where William Henry Fox Talbot – often described as the inventor of photography – changed our view of the world. The museum celebrates his achievements and shows changing photographic exhibitions. **Note**: furnished rooms of the Abbey are closed on Tuesdays and winter weekdays.

Eating and shopping: tea-room. Village and museum shops for gifts, homeware, Lacock souvenirs and plants. Second-hand bookshop in Abbey. There are many shopping and eating/drinking opportunities in the village (not National Trust). Picnics welcome in grounds.

Making the most of your day: there is so much to see that you could easily spend a whole day exploring the village, Abbey, gardens and museum. The level grounds offer lovely walks, changing seasonal interest and a great place to play. For families there is a changing programme of trails and special events, while our year-round programme of events caters for all interests and ages. Lacock is also a popular film location: past productions include *Harry Potter*, *Cranford* and *Pride and Prejudice*. This year, join us to celebrate Fox Talbot announcing to the world his invention of photography as we mark this 175-year anniversary. **Dogs**: welcome in Abbey grounds from 1 November to 31 March.

Access for all: 🅿️ 🐕 ⚲ 🚻 🔔 🖼️ 🎫 ..: 🅰️
Abbey 🔽 🔼   Museum 🔼 🔽 ♿
Grounds 🔼 🔽 ➡️ 🔽 ♿

Getting here: see website for details.
Parking: 220 yards (pay and display).
No visitor parking on village streets.

Finding out more: 01249 730459 or lacockabbey@nationaltrust.org.uk

Lacock Abbey		M	T	W	T	F	S	S
Village								
Open all year*		M	T	W	T	F	S	S
Cloisters, grounds, museum, exhibition, tea-room and shop								
2 Jan–14 Feb	11–4	M	T	W	T	F	S	S
15 Feb–2 Nov**	10:30–5:30	M	T	W	T	F	S	S
3 Nov–24 Dec	11–4	M	T	W	T	F	S	S
27 Dec–31 Dec†	11–4	M	T	W	.	.	S	S
Abbey rooms (first floor) – Great Hall only								
4 Jan–9 Feb††	12–4	.	.	.	.	.	S	S
20 Dec–28 Dec	12–4	.	.	.	.	.	S	S
Abbey rooms (first floor)								
15 Feb–2 Nov	11–5	M	.	W	T	F	S	S
8 Nov–14 Dec	12–4	.	.	.	.	.	S	S

Last admission 45 minutes before closing. *Village businesses open at various times. **15 February to 2 November: high street shop and tea-room open at 10. †Tea-room open 26 December. Cloisters and grounds may close at dusk in winter. ††Other Abbey rooms open when possible around essential winter cleaning.

Lanhydrock

Bodmin, Cornwall PL30 5AD

Map ① D8    1953

This year, for the first time, visitors are able to drive in through the 18th-century Double Lodges and along the restored carriage drive to Lanhydrock. The home of the Victorian Agar-Robartes family, the house appears as if they have just popped out for tea. There are more than 50 rooms to explore and it's easy to see the contrasts between the servants' life 'downstairs' and the elegant family rooms. The extensive garden is full of colour all year and there is plenty to discover across the estate, from ancient woodlands to tranquil riverside paths. There are off-road cycle trails, with special trails for families and novice riders, and you can even hire a bike from us.

Eating and shopping: Victorian Servants' Hall restaurant. Shop selling local foods and gifts. Second-hand bookshop. New this spring – café, plant centre and cycle hire.

Making the most of your day: indoors there is a remarkable ceiling in the Long Gallery, Victorian servants' quarters and extensive kitchens to explore. Outside there are garden tours, walks through the woodland, park and riverside paths, as well as a magnificent collection of magnolias, which flower all through spring. Children will love the new adventure playground and family-friendly off-road cycle trails (map available).
Dogs: assistance dogs only in garden (dog-friendly walks throughout estate).

Access for all:
House 🔣🔣🔣🔣🔣   Grounds 🔣🔣🔣🔣

Getting here: see website for details.
Sat Nav: use PL30 4AB (1 Double Lodges).
Parking: free, 600 yards.

Finding out more: 01208 265950 or lanhydrock@nationaltrust.org.uk

Lanhydrock, Cornwall, clockwise from above: view from the church tower over the parterre, the dairy and exploring outside

Lanhydrock		M	T	W	T	F	S	S
House								
1 Mar–30 Mar	11–5	·	T	W	T	F	S	S
1 Apr–30 Sep	11–5:30	·	T	W	T	F	S	S
1 Oct–2 Nov	11–5	·	T	W	T	F	S	S
Garden								
15 Feb–2 Nov	10–6	M	T	W	T	F	S	S
Estate and cycle trails								
Open all year	Dawn–dusk	M	T	W	T	F	S	S
Refreshments								
1 Jan–28 Feb	10–4	M	T	W	T	F	S	S
1 Mar–2 Nov	10–5:30	M	T	W	T	F	S	S
3 Nov–31 Dec*	10–4	M	T	W	T	F	S	S
Shop								
15 Feb–28 Feb	11–4	M	T	W	T	F	S	S
1 Mar–31 Mar	11–5	M	T	W	T	F	S	S
1 Apr–30 Sep	11–5:30	M	T	W	T	F	S	S
1 Oct–2 Nov	11–5	M	T	W	T	F	S	S
3 Nov–31 Dec*	11–4	M	T	W	T	F	S	S

House: also open Mondays 7, 14 and 21 April, 5 and 26 May, 21 and 28 July, all Mondays in August, 1 September and 27 October; entry is controlled (queuing at busy times). Plant centre and second-hand bookshop: open daily 1 March to 2 November. Cycle hire open from 15 February.
*Closed 25 and 26 December.

Lawrence House

9 Castle Street, Launceston, Cornwall PL15 8BA

Map ① E7   🏛 ✳ 1964

This Georgian town house, now a museum, hosts special exhibitions. Large display of costumes and a children's toy room.
Note: leased to Launceston Town Council.

Finding out more: 01566 773277 or lawrencehouse@nationaltrust.org.uk

Levant Mine and Beam Engine

Trewellard, Pendeen, near St Just, Cornwall TR19 7SX

Map ① A9   🏛 🖼 ⚙ 1967

Levant Mine and Beam Engine in Cornwall

Perched on a clifftop high above the Atlantic Ocean, Levant was one of Cornwall's 'champion' mines, the world's major producers of copper and tin. The heart of the site is the 1840 engine house, with its original steam winding engine, but you can also explore a dramatic ruined landscape.

Eating and shopping: light refreshments available. Small shop selling mining-related goods and books.

Making the most of your day: daily running of the steam engine and guided tours of the site. Hands-on rock breaking and washing area. Geocaching and map and compass trails. Downloadable walks to Geevor and Botallack.
Dogs: welcome on leads.

Access for all: 🅿♿🚾♿🏛🖼♿🔆♿
Building 🏛🏛➡♿

Getting here: see website for details.
Parking: free, 328 yards.

Finding out more: 01736 786156 or levant@nationaltrust.org.uk

Levant Beam Engine		M	T	W	T	F	S	S
3 Jan–14 Mar	10:30–4					**F**		
16 Mar–2 Nov	10:30–5	**M**	**T**	**W**	**T**	**F**		**S**
7 Nov–12 Dec	10:30–4					**F**		

Engine steaming from 11.

Little Clarendon

Dinton, Salisbury, Wiltshire SP3 5DZ

Map ① K5   🏠✝ 1940

Late 15th-century stone house with curious 20th-century chapel. **Note**: sorry no toilet.

Finding out more: 01985 843600 or littleclarendon@nationaltrust.org.uk

Lodge Park and Sherborne Estate

Aldsworth, near Cheltenham, Gloucestershire GL54 3PP

Map ① K/L2   🏠🛏️🔔🍽️ 1983

England's only surviving 17th-century deer course and grandstand, created in 1634 by John 'Crump' Dutton, inspired by his passion for gambling, banqueting and entertaining. The National Trust's first restoration project relying on archaeological evidence. Impressive views of the deer course and park (designed by Charles Bridgeman in the 1720s). **Note**: toilet at Lodge Park only.

Eating and shopping: small shop and courtyard café.

Making the most of your day: open-air theatre and opera. Outdoor events and living history. Walks through the surrounding Sherborne Estate. **Dogs**: welcome under close control.

Access for all: 🅿️🇩♿🚻🖥️👁️
Building ♿🔼

Getting here: see website for details.
Parking: free for Lodge Park. For Sherborne Estate use Ewe Pen Barn car park or Water Meadows (off A40 towards Sherborne).

Lodge Park, Gloucestershire

Finding out more: 01451 844130 or lodgepark@nationaltrust.org.uk

Lodge Park and Sherborne Estate		M	T	W	T	F	S	S
Lodge Park								
7 Mar–2 Nov	11–4					**F**	**S**	**S**
Sherborne Estate								
Open all year		**M**	**T**	**W**	**T**	**F**	**S**	**S**

Lodge Park opens Bank Holiday Mondays. Occasionally closes for weddings (telephone to confirm opening times).

Loughwood Meeting House

Dalwood, Axminster, Devon EX13 7DU

Map ① H7   ✝ 1969

Atmospheric 17th-century thatched Baptist meeting house dug into the hillside; open daily all year. **Note**: sorry no toilet.

Finding out more: 01752 346585 or loughwood@nationaltrust.org.uk

Lundy: wildlife-rich island in the Bristol Channel

Lundy

Bristol Channel, Devon

Map (1) D5
1969

Undisturbed by cars, this wildlife-rich island, designated the first Marine Conservation Area, encompasses a small village with an inn, Victorian church and the 13th-century Marisco Castle. **Note**: financed, administered and maintained by the Landmark Trust.
MS *Oldenburg* fares (including members), discounts available.

Eating and shopping: tavern serving hot and cold food and drinks. Shop selling souvenirs, Lundy stamps, snacks and ice-creams.

Making the most of your day: diving, walking, letterboxing, bird and wildlife-watching. Holiday cottages (not National Trust).
Dogs: assistance dogs only.

Access for all: 🅿♿♿♿ **Building** ♿
Grounds ♿

Getting here: ferry from Bideford or Ilfracombe. **Sat Nav**: Ilfracombe: EX34 9EQ. Bideford: EX39 2EY. **Parking**: at Bideford and Ilfracombe (pay and display).

Finding out more: 01271 863636 or lundy@nationaltrust.org.uk. The Lundy Shore Office, The Quay, Bideford, Devon EX39 2LY.

Lundy

MS *Oldenburg* sails from Bideford or Ilfracombe up to four times a week from the end of March until the end of October carrying both day and staying passengers. A helicopter service operates from Hartland Point from November to mid-March, Mondays and Fridays only, for staying visitors.

Lydford Gorge

Lydford, near Tavistock, Devon EX20 4BH

Map (1) F7 1947

This dramatic legend-rich river gorge (below), the deepest in the South West, offers a variety of exhilarating walks. Around every corner the River Lyd plunges, tumbles, swirls and gently meanders as it travels through the steep-sided, oak-wooded gorge. Throughout the seasons there is an abundance of wildlife and plants to see, from woodland birds to wild garlic in the spring and fungi in the autumn. **Note**: rugged terrain, vertical drops.

Eating and shopping: shop selling gifts, books, outdoor clothing and footwear. Two tea-rooms serving soup, sandwiches, cream teas, cakes and local ice-cream. Takeaway drinks and food available.

Places may occasionally close for conservation, safety or events

Making the most of your day: family events, wildlife-themed and bushcraft activities, children's play area, bird hide.
Dogs: welcome on leads.

Access for all:
Buildings 🏠 Gorge ⛰

Getting here: see website for details.
Parking: free.

Finding out more: 01822 820320 or lydfordgorge@nationaltrust.org.uk

Lydford Gorge		M	T	W	T	F	S	S
8 Mar–2 Nov*	10–5**	**M**	**T**	**W**	**T**	**F**	**S**	**S**

*Short walk to the Whitelady Waterfall open all year.
**Waterfall tea-room opens at 11.

Lytes Cary Manor

near Somerton, Somerset TA11 7HU

Map ① I5   🏛 ✝ 🍴 ❀ 🎋 🛏 1949

This intimate medieval manor house, with its beautiful Arts and Crafts-inspired garden, was originally the family home of Henry Lyte. Lytes Cary was lovingly restored in the 20th century by Sir Walter Jenner and is shown as it was in his time.

The garden rooms contain a magical collection of topiary and herbaceous borders, while tranquil walks on the estate take you alongside the River Cary. Our community allotments are bursting with creative and colourful designs.

Eating and shopping: refreshments available. Rustic shop selling garden accessories and plants.

Making the most of your day: estate walks and children's outdoor play area. Our garden team is always happy to offer inspiration and tips. The West Wing is available as a holiday rental (sleeps 14). **Dogs**: welcome on leads on estate walks only.

Access for all: 🅿 🄳 🚻 🔌 🔍 🚗 ⦂
Building ⛰ 🚹 ♿ Grounds ⛰ ♿

Getting here: see website for details.
Parking: free, 40 yards.

Finding out more: 01458 224471 or lytescarymanor@nationaltrust.org.uk

Lytes Cary Manor		M	T	W	T	F	S	S
House								
15 Mar–2 Nov	11–5	**M**	**T**	**W**	·	**F**	**S**	**S**
Garden, parkland, refreshments and shop								
15 Mar–2 Nov	10:30–5	**M**	**T**	**W**	**T**	**F**	**S**	**S**
Estate walks								
Open all year	Dawn–dusk	**M**	**T**	**W**	**T**	**F**	**S**	**S**

The beautiful Arts and Crafts-inspired garden at Lytes Cary Manor in Somerset

Market Hall

High Street, Chipping Campden,
Gloucestershire GL55 6AJ

Map ① K1 🏠 1942

Outstanding building, constructed nearly
400 years ago to give shelter to market traders.
Note: nearest toilet in town centre.

Finding out more: 01386 438333 or
markethall@nationaltrust.org.uk

Max Gate

Alington Avenue, Dorchester, Dorset DT1 2AB

Map ① J7 🏠 ✽ 1940

**Max Gate, Dorset: Thomas Hardy's
atmospheric home**

Max Gate, home to Dorset's most famous
author and poet, Thomas Hardy, was designed
by the writer himself in 1885. This atmospheric
Victorian home is where Hardy wrote some of
his most famous novels including *Tess of the
d'Urbervilles* and *Jude the Obscure*, as well as
most of his poetry.

Eating and shopping: Hardy books, souvenirs
and small gifts on sale. Tea and coffee available.

Making the most of your day: combine your
visit with a trip to Hardy's Cottage, the
thatched cottage in which the writer was born,
just a couple of miles away. **Dogs**: welcome on
leads in garden only.

Access for all: 🖼 ⦂ Ⓐ Building 👨‍🦽

Getting here: see website for details.
Sat Nav: unreliable, look for signs from A352.
Parking: free (not National Trust), restricted,
50 yards.

Finding out more: 01305 262538 or
maxgate@nationaltrust.org.uk

Max Gate		M	T	W	T	F	S	S
12 Mar–2 Nov	11–5		·	**W**	**T**	**F**	**S**	**S**
Open Bank Holiday Mondays.								

Mompesson House

The Close, Salisbury, Wiltshire SP1 2EL

Map ① K5  1952

When walking into the celebrated Cathedral Close in Salisbury, visitors step back into a past world, and on entering Mompesson House, featured in the award-winning film *Sense and Sensibility*, the feeling of leaving the modern world behind deepens. The tranquil atmosphere is enhanced by the magnificent plasterwork, fine period furniture and graceful oak staircase, which are the main features of this perfectly proportioned Queen Anne house. In addition, the Turnbull collection of 18th-century drinking glasses is of national importance. The delightful walled garden has a pergola and traditionally planted herbaceous borders.

Graceful Mompesson House, Wiltshire: perfectly proportioned

Eating and shopping: tea-room serving locally baked scones and cakes, light lunches and teas. National Trust shop only 60 yards away. Turnbull Glass Collection catalogue for sale.

Making the most of your day: exhibition of sculptures by Elisabeth Frink, Peter Randall-Page and others in house and garden throughout the season. Regular croquet sessions on the lawn and occasional live music, including Northumbrian Pipers.
Dogs: assistance dogs only.

Access for all: ⬚⬚⬚⬚⬚⬚⬚⬚⬚⬚
Building ⬚⬚ Grounds ⬚⬚

Getting here: see website for details.
Parking: 260 yards in city centre, pay and display (not National Trust).

Finding out more: 01722 420980 (Infoline). 01722 335659 or mompessonhouse@nationaltrust.org.uk

Mompesson House		M	T	W	T	F	S	S
15 Mar–2 Nov	11–5	M	T	W	.	.	S	S
Open Good Friday.								

Montacute House

Montacute, Somerset TA15 6XP

Map (1) I6 🏯 ✿ 🏖 🛏 🔔 🍷 | 1931 |

In the heart of the picturesque Ham stone village of Montacute, this magnificent golden mansion is surrounded by formal lawns, famous wobbly hedges, grand trees and garden pavilions. The Elizabethan house is full of oak-panelled rooms with period furniture and tapestries and the longest gallery in England. In partnership with the National Portrait Gallery, we exhibit more than 50 Tudor and Jacobean portraits from its collection. In the garden, spring colour changes to vivid flower and rose borders in summer. In winter, follow the crisp lines of the lawns and hedges and enjoy stunning views of the house.

Eating and shopping: a variety of lunches and delicious cakes available. Shop selling gifts and souvenirs. Plant sales.

Making the most of your day: introductory talks, activities, family trails, events, outdoor swings and parkland. New National Portrait Gallery exhibition, 'Pictured and Seen'. Combine with a visit to Tintinhull Garden or Barrington Court. **Dogs**: welcome under control in parkland. In winter, also welcome in the garden on leads.

Access for all: 🅿♿ 🚻 ♿ 🔍 🚶 ∴ 🅰
Building ♿ 🏠♿ 🔽 Grounds 🏠♿ ➡ 🔽

Getting here: see website for details.
Parking: free.

Finding out more: 01935 823289 or montacute@nationaltrust.org.uk

Montacute House		M	T	W	T	F	S	S
House								
4 Jan–9 Mar*	12–3	·	·	·	·	·	S	S
15 Mar–2 Nov	11–5	M	·	W	T	F	S	S
8 Nov–28 Dec*	12–3	·	·	·	·	·	S	S
Garden, parkland, café and shop								
1 Jan–14 Mar	11–4	·	·	W	T	F	S	S
15 Mar–2 Nov	10–5	M	T	W	T	F	S	S
5 Nov–28 Dec	11–4	·	·	W	T	F	S	S

*House open by guided tour only (last tour 2:30). Whole place closed for essential maintenance 22 to 24 January and closed 24 and 25 December.

Elizabethan Montacute House in Somerset: the west front, top, and young visitors, below

Newark Park

Ozleworth, Wotton-under-Edge,
Gloucestershire GL12 7PZ

Map (1) J3   🏠 ✿ 🍴 🛏 1949

You can always expect the unexpected at
Newark Park, which overlooks the splendid
Ozleworth Valley. From Tudor beginnings to
dramatic rescue by a 20th-century Texan,
Newark has a wonderful quirky character and
eclectic collections. The garden and estate
provide space to play and contemplate, with
new discoveries at every turn. **Note:** accessible
toilet only at house, other toilets in car park.

Eating and shopping: shop in visitor reception.
Light refreshments available.

Newark Park, Gloucestershire: expect the unexpected

Making the most of your day: waymarked
walks across estate. Children's Tracker Pack
available. Garden games and croquet on the
lawn. Rugs for hire and peacocks to keep
you company. **Dogs**: welcome on leads
(livestock grazing).

Access for all: 🅿️ ♿ 🚻 📺 ♿ ∴ 📷
Building ♿ ♿ Grounds ♿

Getting here: see website for details.
Sat Nav: only works from north, so follow
brown signs from Wotton-under-Edge and
A46. **Parking**: 100 yards.

Finding out more: 01793 817666 (Infoline).
01453 842644 or
newarkpark@nationaltrust.org.uk

Newark Park		M	T	W	T	F	S	S
15 Feb–23 Feb	11–4			**W**	**T**	**F**	**S**	**S**
5 Mar–2 Nov	11–5			**W**	**T**	**F**	**S**	**S**
6 Dec–7 Dec	11–4						**S**	**S**

Open Bank Holidays. Closes dusk if earlier.

The glorious view from Overbeck's, Devon, stretches for miles up the estuary and out along the coast

Overbeck's

Sharpitor, Salcombe, Devon TQ8 8LW

Map (1) F9  1937

A hidden paradise of subtropical plants, eclectic collections and the highly individual seaside home of inventor and scientist Otto Overbeck. Overbeck's is an exotic and fascinating gem of a place perched high on the cliffs above Salcombe, with glorious views over estuary and coast. This Edwardian house and garden is the perfect day out for anyone who enjoys exploring, or the keen gardener who wants to be inspired by the collection of rare plants. Don't miss Otto's 'rejuvenator', the sounds of the Polyphon – a giant music box – and Fred the ghost! This year we've opened a new woodland path. **Note**: entrance path and grounds are very steep in places.

Eating and shopping: lunch and cream teas served in the Billiards tea-room. Picnic hampers available. Shop selling gifts, books, local products and walking accessories. Plant sales.

Making the most of your day: self-guided garden trails: 'Japanese', 'Cooks', 'Historians' and 'Non-gardeners'. Museum and garden tours. Walks leaflet. **Dogs**: allowed in reception area and coastal walks only.

Access for all: ☒☒☒☒☒☒☒☒☒
Building ☒   Grounds ☒☒

Getting here: see website for details.
Sat Nav: follow brown signs on A381 into Salcombe and through Malborough.
Parking: small car park and limited spaces on approach lane. Additional parking at East Soar car park (1-mile walk along footpath). Approach lane very narrow in places.

Finding out more: 01548 842893 or overbecks@nationaltrust.org.uk

Overbeck's		M	T	W	T	F	S	S
15 Feb–2 Nov	11–5	**M**	**T**	**W**	**T**	**F**	**S**	**S**
Tea-room open until 4:45.								

Priest's House, Muchelney

Muchelney, Langport, Somerset TA10 0DQ

Map (1) I6 1911

Medieval hall-house, built in 1308, and little altered since the early 17th century.
Note: private home, but open 16 March to 28 September, Sunday and Monday, 2 to 5. Sorry no toilets.

Finding out more: 01458 253771 or priestshouse@nationaltrust.org.uk

Prior Park Landscape Garden

Ralph Allen Drive, Bath, Somerset BA2 5AH

Map ① J4   ❖ 1993

This magical landscape garden, perched on a hillside overlooking Bath, was created between 1735 and 1764 by Ralph Allen, a local entrepreneur. The garden is being restored to appear much as it did at the time of Allen's death in 1764. Discover Ralph Allen's story and why Prior Park is unlike many other gardens. Although there are few flowers and no formal beds, you will find winding paths leading to hidden retreats, a grotto, viewpoints with breathtaking views over Bath, cascades, tranquil lakes and an elegant Palladian Bridge – one of only four in the world. **Note:** house not accessible. Steep slopes, steps and uneven paths.

Palladian Bridge in Prior Park Landscape Garden, Somerset

Eating and shopping: Tea Shed by the lakes serving light snacks, cakes and refreshments. Small shop selling outdoor-related products and pocket-money gifts.

Making the most of your day: events and activities all year, free guided tours, natural play area and seasonal trails. Join the Bath Skyline 6-mile circular walk, just minutes from the garden. **Dogs:** welcome on short leads.

Access for all: 🅿️♿🚻♿♿♿♿♿
Grounds ♿♿

Getting here: see website for details.
Parking: for disabled visitors only. Car parks in city centre, 1 mile (steep, uphill walk). Frequent bus services from train station, Abbey and Dorchester Street (by bus station).

Finding out more: 01225 833422 or priorpark@nationaltrust.org.uk

Prior Park Landscape Garden		M	T	W	T	F	S	S
4 Jan–26 Jan	10–5						**S**	**S**
1 Feb–2 Nov	10–5:30	**M**	**T**	**W**	**T**	**F**	**S**	**S**
8 Nov–28 Dec	10–5						**S**	**S**

Last admission one hour before closing. Closes dusk if earlier than 5:30.

St Michael's Mount, Cornwall: this unique and magical island is reached by an ancient causeway from Marazion

St Michael's Mount

Marazion, Cornwall TR17 0HS

Map ① B9 🏛️ ✝️ ❀ 🏰 1954

This iconic rocky island, crowned by a medieval church and castle, is home to the St Aubyn family and a 30-strong community of islanders. Visitors can immerse themselves in history at the Mount, where the architecture dates back to the 12th century and legends – such as that of Jack the Giant Killer – abound. There is a subtropical terraced garden and spectacular views of Mount's Bay and the Lizard from the castle battlements. If the tide is in, you can take an evocative boat trip to the island or, at low tide, walk across the ancient causeway from Marazion. **Note**: steep climb to castle up uneven, cobbled pathway. St Aubyn family/National Trust partnership.

Eating and shopping: Island Café (licensed) serving Cornish pasties, sandwiches and cream teas. Sail Loft Restaurant (licensed) serving Newlyn fish, daily specials, cream teas and homemade cakes. Island Shop and Courtyard Shop selling local contemporary gifts, Cornish produce, jewellery, bags, arts and crafts.

Making the most of your day: children's castle quiz and garden trail. Tours (by arrangement). Events and exhibitions. Live music on the village green most Sundays. Sunday church services Whitsun to end September. **Dogs**: assistance dogs only in castle and garden.

Access for all: 🅿️ 🚌 🚻 ♿ 🏰 📷 🖼️
Castle ♿ Village ♿ ♿

Getting here: see website for details. **Parking**: numerous spaces in Marazion, opposite St Michael's Mount, not National Trust (charge including members).

Finding out more: 01736 710265/01736 710507 or stmichaelsmount@nationaltrust.org.uk. www.stmichaelsmount.co.uk. Estate Office, King's Road, Marazion, Cornwall TR17 0EL

St Michael's Mount		M	T	W	T	F	S	S
Castle								
30 Mar–29 Jun	10:30–5	M	T	W	T	F		S
30 Jun–31 Aug	10:30–5:30	M	T	W	T	F		S
1 Sep–2 Nov	10:30–5	M	T	W	T	F		S
Garden								
14 Apr–27 Jun	10:30–5	M	T	W	T	F		
3 Jul–29 Aug	10:30–5:30				T	F		
4 Sep–26 Sep	10:30–5				T	F		

Last admission 45 minutes before castle closes (enough time should be allowed for travel from the mainland). Castle winter opening, call Estate Office for details.

We welcome dogs assisting visitors with disabilities

Saltram

Plympton, Plymouth, Devon PL7 1UH

Map (1) F8   [icons] 1957

Saltram overlooks the River Plym and is set in a rolling landscape park that provides precious green space on the outskirts of Plymouth. Strolling along the riverside or through the woodland, you can almost forget that the city lies so close. Saltram was home to the Parker family from 1743, when an earlier mansion was remodelled to reflect the family's increasingly prominent position. It is magnificently decorated, with original contents including Chinese wallpapers and an exceptional collection of paintings (several by Sir Joshua Reynolds). It also has a superb country-house library and Robert Adam's Neo-classical Saloon. The garden is predominantly 19th-century, with a working 18th-century orangery and follies, beautiful shrubberies and imposing specimen trees providing year-round interest.

Saltram, Devon: pedal power, above, and the exterior, below, with its Greek revival portico

Eating and shopping: Park Café serving meals and snacks. Shops selling plants, gifts and local arts and crafts.

Making the most of your day: events and activities all year, including open-air theatre, family activities, guided walks and tours. Seasonal trails and paths lead through scented avenues, and the outdoor classroom (available to hire) hosts Forest School sessions. The park has numerous paths – perfect for walking, running or cycling. While in the house there are opportunities to dress up, as well as guided tours, themed trails and conservation in action. This year we are highlighting our impressive collection of books (below).

Dogs: welcome in woods and parkland.

Access for all: 🅿️🅳♿🚻🖐️🅰️📷💺
House 🏠♿ Grounds 🏠➡️🚾♿

Getting here: see website for details.
Sat Nav: enter Merafield Road not postcode.
Parking: free, 50 yards.

Finding out more: 01752 333500 or saltram@nationaltrust.org.uk

Saltram		M	T	W	T	F	S	S
Park								
Open all year	Dawn–dusk	M	T	W	T	F	S	S
House								
8 Mar–2 Nov	12–4:30*	M	T	W	T		S	S
Garden, Park Café and shop								
1 Jan–9 Mar	10–4**	M	T	W	T	F	S	S
10 Mar–2 Nov	10–5**	M	T	W	T	F	S	S
3 Nov–31 Dec	10–4**	M	T	W	T	F	S	S
Chapel arts and crafts								
10 Mar–2 Nov	11–5	M	T	W	T	F	S	S

House open Good Friday and first Friday of month during open season for tours. Last house admission 45 minutes before closing, timed ticket entry. *House opens 11:30 on Thursdays. **Garden opens at 11. Garden, café and shop closed 25 and 26 December. Chapel Gallery limited opening until 9 March, closes 4 in winter.

Shute Barton

Shute, near Axminster, Devon EX13 7PT

Map ① H7  🏠❄️🛏️🏘️ 1959

Medieval manor house, with later Tudor gatehouse and battlemented turrets – now a holiday cottage. **Note**: only open the third weekend in May, June, September and October.

Finding out more: 01752 346585 or shute@nationaltrust.org.uk

Snowshill Manor and Garden

Snowshill, near Broadway, Gloucestershire WR12 7JU

Map ① K1 🏠❄️🏘️ 1951

Charles Wade's passion for craftsmanship, colour and design led him to find and restore a quirky collection of objects of beauty, both everyday and extraordinary. Passionate about traditional skills and design, he started collecting as a child, eventually buying and renovating the Manor to house the thousands of treasures he acquired. His creation is an extraordinary 'Aladdin's Cave' of unexpected delights – not a museum – where craftsmanship can be explored in an intimate way. The Manor itself is set in a beautiful terraced garden, with lovely views over the surrounding countryside. Charles Wade's home, the humble Priest's House, is also open.

Eating and shopping: restaurant serving lunches, cream teas and homemade cakes. Shop selling gifts, plants and local produce. Second-hand bookshop.

Making the most of your day: Tracker Packs, indoor and outdoor children's trails. Introductory and garden talks. Events.
Dogs: assistance dogs only.

Access for all: ⬛⬛⬛⬛⬛⬛⬛⬛⬛⬛⬛⬛
Manor ⬛ Garden ⬛⬛

Getting here: see website for details.
Parking: free, 500 yards.

Finding out more: 01386 852410 or
snowshillmanor@nationaltrust.org.uk

Snowshill Manor and Garden		M	T	W	T	F	S	S
Manor and Priest's House								
29 Mar–6 Jul	12–5*		·	W	T	F	S	S
7 Jul–31 Aug	11:30–4:30*	M	·	W	T	F	S	S
3 Sep–2 Nov	12–5*		·	W	T	F	S	S
Garden, shop and restaurant							·	
29 Mar–6 Jul	11–5:30		·	W	T	F	S	S
7 Jul–31 Aug	11–5	M	·	W	T	F	S	S
3 Sep–2 Nov	11–5:30		·	W	T	F	S	S
8 Nov–30 Nov	10:30–3:30	·	·	·	·	·	S	S
Manor by guided tour only (additional charge)								
8 Nov–30 Nov	11–3	·	·	·	·	·	S	S

Manor admission is by limited timed tickets, issued on a
first-come, first-served basis. Tickets run out on peak days.
Last admission to Manor one hour before it closes.
Open all Bank Holidays between April and October.
*Priest's House opens at 11.

**Snowshill Manor and Garden, Gloucestershire: the Well
Court, top, and Charles Wade's bedroom, below**

Stembridge Tower Mill

High Ham, Somerset TA10 9DJ

Map ① I5   1969

Built in 1822, this is the last remaining thatched
windmill in England – the only survivor of five
in the area. **Note**: holiday cottage on site,
please respect the tenants' privacy. Sorry no
toilet. Parking limited.

Finding out more: 01935 823289 or
stembridgemill@nationaltrust.org.uk

Stoke-sub-Hamdon Priory

North Street, Stoke-sub-Hamdon,
Somerset TA14 6QP

Map ① I6   🏠 1946

Fascinating small complex of buildings,
formerly the home of priests serving the
Chapel of St Nicholas (now destroyed).
Note: sorry no toilet.

Finding out more: 01935 823289 or
stokehamdonpriory@nationaltrust.org.uk

Stourhead

near Mere, Wiltshire BA12 6QF

Map ① J5
1946

'A living work of art' is how a magazine described Stourhead when it first opened in the 1740s. The world-famous landscape garden has as its centrepiece a magnificent lake reflecting classical temples, mystical grottoes and rare and exotic trees. Stourhead House, set amid 'picnic perfect' lawns and parkland, contains a unique Regency library, Chippendale furniture and inspirational paintings, and offers an Italian 'Grand Tour' adventure. The garden and house are at the heart of a 1,072-hectare (2,650-acre) estate, where chalk downs, ancient woods, Iron Age hill forts and farmland are managed for people and wildlife.

Eating and shopping: one of the largest Trust gift shops, garden shop and plant centre. Farm shop. Award-winning restaurant and 18th-century Spread Eagle Inn. Ice-cream parlour serving takeaway snacks and refreshments. Art gallery. Picnics welcome.

Making the most of your day: this year we launch 'Harry's Story', allowing you to experience Stourhead through the eyes of Harry 'our only, and best of sons'. Join us on an emotional journey through memories of childhood, love, war and tragedy, and stories of family drama, restoration and survival.
Dogs: welcome in countryside all year and in landscape garden, on short fixed leads, daily after 4, March to November, and daily December to February.

Stourhead, Wiltshire, clockwise from above: Temple of Apollo, autumnal fun and the grand entrance to the house

Access for all: ⟨icons⟩
Building ⟨icons⟩ Grounds ⟨icons⟩

Getting here: see website for details.
Parking: 400 yards. King Alfred's Tower 50 yards.

Finding out more: 01747 841152 or stourhead@nationaltrust.org.uk. Stourhead Estate Office, Stourton, Warminster, Wiltshire BA12 6QD

Stourhead		M	T	W	T	F	S	S
House								
5 Jan–9 Mar*	11–3						S	S
15 Mar–2 Nov	11–4:30	M	T	W	T	F	S	S
8 Nov–23 Nov*	11–3						S	S
29 Nov–21 Dec**	11–3	M	T	W	T	F	S	S
Shop, garden and restaurant								
1 Jan–31 Mar	9–5†	M	T	W	T	F	S	S
1 Apr–30 Sep	9–7†	M	T	W	T	F	S	S
1 Oct–31 Dec	9–5†	M	T	W	T	F	S	S
King Alfred's Tower								
1 Mar–26 Oct	12–4						S	S

House limited winter opening: *5 January to 9 February and 8 to 23 November (weekends) 'Winter Warmers' – fire lit and board games in the Entrance Hall only; 15 February to 9 March (weekends) 'Conservation in action' – selected rooms.
**29 November to 21 December 'The Christmas House' – selected rooms open and decorated. †Shop opens at 10 all year and closes at 6, April to September. Stourhead closed 25 December.

The Hall in Tintagel Old Post Office, Cornwall

Finding out more: 01840 770024 or tintageloldpo@nationaltrust.org.uk

Tintagel Old Post Office		M	T	W	T	F	S	S
15 Feb–23 Feb	11–4	M	T	W	T	F	S	S
8 Mar–6 Apr	11–4	M	T	W	T	F	S	S
7 Apr–28 Sep	10:30–5:30	M	T	W	T	F	S	S
29 Sep–2 Nov	11–4	M	T	W	T	F	S	S

Tintinhull Garden

Farm Street, Tintinhull, Yeovil, Somerset BA22 8PZ

Map (1) I6  1953

The vision of the amateur gardener Phyllis Reiss lives on today in this delightful garden. Described as one of the most harmonious small gardens in Britain, the 'rooms' have secluded lawns, pools and colourful mixed borders, and the lovely kitchen garden provides vegetables for the restaurant at nearby Montacute House.

Eating and shopping: tea-room serving cakes and cream teas. Plant sales and small shop.

Making the most of your day: explorer sheet guide to village. Combine with a visit to Montacute House. The garden's manor house is available to rent as a holiday cottage. **Dogs**: assistance dogs only.

Access for all: ⳨⳨⳨⳨⳨⳨⳨⳨
Building ⳨⳨ Gardens ⳨⳨⳨

Tintinhull Garden, Somerset: harmony and elegance

Tintagel Old Post Office

Fore Street, Tintagel, Cornwall PL34 0DB

Map (1) D7 ⳨⳨ 1903

Built around 1380 as a farmhouse, this building never actually sold stamps but has had various uses across the centuries and was the Trust's first house in Cornwall. The homely rooms are mostly furnished with 16th-century furniture, whilst the cottage garden provides a peaceful retreat from the bustling high street.
Note: nearest toilet, 54 yards.

Eating and shopping: gift shop in Post Room offering local products. Picnics welcome in the cottage garden.

Making the most of your day: family trail, garden games and rag-rug making. Varied events during the season. **Dogs**: assistance dogs only.

Access for all: ⳨⳨⳨⳨⳨
Building ⳨⳨ Grounds ⳨⳨

Getting here: see website for details.
Parking: no parking on site. Pay and display (not National Trust). Nearest Trust parking at Glebe Cliff in Tintagel.

Getting here: see website for details.
Parking: free, 150 yards.

Finding out more: 01935 823289 or tintinhull@nationaltrust.org.uk

Tintinhull Garden		M	T	W	T	F	S	S
29 Mar–1 Jun	11–5		·	**W**	**T**	**F**	**S**	**S**
3 Jun–29 Jul	11–5		**T**	**W**	**T**	**F**	**S**	**S**
30 Jul–2 Nov	11–5		·	**W**	**T**	**F**	**S**	**S**

Open Bank Holiday Mondays.

Treasurer's House, Martock

Martock, Somerset TA12 6JL

Map (1) I6 1971

Completed in 1293, this medieval house includes a Great Hall, 15th-century kitchen and an unusual wall-painting. **Note**: private home, but open 16 March to 28 September, Sunday, Monday and Tuesday, 2 to 5. Sorry no toilets or parking.

Finding out more: 01935 825015 or treasurersmartock@nationaltrust.org.uk

Trelissick Garden

Feock, near Truro, Cornwall TR3 6QL

Map (1) C9  1955

On its own peninsula with ever-changing views of the estuary of the River Fal, Trelissick has one of the most amazing natural settings in the country. There has been a settlement here dating back to the Iron Age, and today there are more than 12 hectares (30 acres) of elevated garden to explore, with twisting paths that lead you through significant collections of hydrangeas, rhododendrons, camellias, ginger lilies and year-round exciting woodland plants. As well as the garden, the 121-hectare (300-acre) estate, with its countryside, woodlands and coast, makes for breathtaking walks.
Note: new this year, limited access to house.

Eating and shopping: Crofters self-service licensed café. The Barn opens for Sunday lunches; also available with the Courtyard Room for functions and events. Gift and plant shop, second-hand bookshop, Cornish art and craft gallery. Six holiday cottages.

View over the River Fal from Trelissick Garden, Cornwall

Making the most of your day: parkland and woodland walks with amazing views. Events all year. Spring and summer garden tours. Magical illuminated traditional Christmas with late-night openings. **Dogs**: welcome on parkland and woodland walks. Assistance dogs only in garden.

Access for all:
Reception ♿ 🅰 Stables ♿ 🅰
Garden ♿ ♿ ♿ ➡ 🦽 🅰

Getting here: see website for details.
Parking: 30 yards.

Finding out more: 01872 862090 or trelissick@nationaltrust.org.uk

Trelissick Garden		M	T	W	T	F	S	S
1 Jan–14 Feb	10:30–4	M	T	W	T	F	S	S
15 Feb–31 Oct	10:30–5:30	M	T	W	T	F	S	S
1 Nov–24 Dec	11–4	M	T	W	T	F	S	S
27 Dec–31 Dec	11–4	M	T	W	·	·	S	S

Garden closes dusk if earlier. Parts of garden lit up at night in run-up to Christmas.

Trengwainton Garden

Madron, near Penzance, Cornwall TR20 8RZ

Map ① B9   🌼 🦽 1961

A garden of special plants nurtured for generations by those with a passion for their beauty and extraordinary story. First to make their mark was Sir Rose Price in 1820, who built the walled kitchen garden to the dimensions of Noah's Ark. It was the Bolitho family though, investing in the plant-hunting expeditions of the 1920s, who gave the garden its special character: champion magnolias and award-winning rhododendrons, plus camellias, azaleas and stands of giant tree ferns. If you stroll uphill beside the stream to the Terrace, you will be rewarded with glorious sea views.

Eating and shopping: award-winning tea-room in its own lovely walled garden (Trust-approved concession). National Trust shop including local gifts and plants.

Making the most of your day: events, activities and family trails. Nearby Godolphin can be visited in the same day.
Dogs: welcome on leads.

Access for all: 🅿 🐕 ♿ ♿ ♿ ♿ ♿ ‼ 🅰
Reception ♿   Grounds ♿ ➡ 🅰

Getting here: see website for details.
Parking: free, 150 yards.

Finding out more: 01736 363148 or trengwainton@nationaltrust.org.uk

Trengwainton Garden		M	T	W	T	F	S	S
16 Feb–2 Nov	10:30–5	M	T	W	T	·	·	S
5 Dec–14 Dec	10:30–4	·	·	·	·	F	·	S

Open Good Friday. Tea-room opens at 10.

The stream garden at Trengwainton in Cornwall

Trerice, Cornwall: this intimate Elizabethan manor house bears the stamp of successive generations of inhabitants

Trerice

Kestle Mill, near Newquay, Cornwall TR8 4PG

Map ① C8  1953

This Elizabethan manor house lies in a secluded wooded valley, with rare examples of Dutch gables, fine plaster ceilings and a magnificent Great Hall window. There is so much to discover about the history of this unique manor house, the families who lived here, its architecture and restoration. The story of Trerice is brought to life by a wide range of events throughout the year.

Eating and shopping: self-service restaurant offering morning coffee, lunch made with local produce, Sunday roasts and a delicious selection of cakes and desserts. Shop selling a range of local products, souvenirs and plants.

Making the most of your day: Tudor-themed workshops, living history, costume days, introductory and garden talks, conservation events and atmospheric evenings. Family activities and trails, Cornish 'kayles' and other traditional games and replica armour to try on. **Dogs**: welcome in car park only.

Access for all: 🅿️♿🚻🔊📷🎧📖📶♿
House 🏠♿ Garden 🚶♿➡♿

Getting here: see website for details.
Parking: free, 300 yards.

Finding out more: 01637 875404 or
trerice@nationaltrust.org.uk

Trerice		M	T	W	T	F	S	S
House, garden, shop and tea-room								
15 Feb–2 Nov	10:30–5*	M	T	W	T	F	S	S
Great Hall, garden, shop, tea-room								
8 Nov–21 Dec	11–4	·	·	·	·	·	S	S

*House opens at 11. Atmospheric evening opening every Friday in March and October.

Tyntesfield

Wraxall, Bristol, North Somerset BS48 1NX

Map (1) I4   [icons] 2002

This ever-changing house and estate continues to reveal the fascinating history of four generations of the Gibbs family through their collection of more than 50,000 objects, displayed in 'From the ordinary to the extraordinary'. With a fortune gained from importing guano, the Gibbs filled the house and estate with an eclectic mix of everyday items and incredible treasures. Join us on our journey to conserve and bring to life this Victorian masterpiece. Surrounding the house is the extensive garden with flower-filled terraces and champion trees, as well as the productive walled kitchen garden. You'll also be able to stretch your legs and take in wonderful views in the wider estate and woodland.
Note: house tickets sell out very quickly during holiday periods.

Eating and shopping: the Cow Barn Kitchen restaurant and café at Home Farm serves dishes made with estate-grown ingredients. Large well-stocked shop, including plant sales and local products. The Pavilion Café provides a rest stop when exploring the garden.

Making the most of your day: year-round events and activities for all the family, including living history, workshops, open-air theatre, guided walks and talks with specialists. Food and craft market on the first Sunday of month from April to November. Free daily garden tours (check times on arrival). Christmas at Tyntesfield events include concerts, activities and fabulous food and shopping. Join us with your four-legged friend in the formal garden during the winter for 'Winter Walkies'.
Dogs: welcome on two woodland estate walks.

Access for all: [icons]
House [icons]   Grounds [icons]

Getting here: see website for details.
Parking: 50 yards from ticket office (which is 490 yards from house).

Members may have to pay on special events days

Tyntesfield, North Somerset: Victorian splendour indoors, left, and discovering the grounds, above

Finding out more: 0844 800 4966 (Infoline). 01275 461900 or tyntesfield@nationaltrust.org.uk

Tyntesfield		M	T	W	T	F	S	S
House and chapel								
15 Feb–28 Feb	11–3	M	T	W	·	F	S	S
8 Mar–2 Nov	11–5	M	T	W	·	F	S	S
1 Dec–21 Dec	11–3	M	T	W	·	F	S	S
Garden, estate, restaurant, café and shop*								
1 Jan–7 Mar	10–5	M	T	W	T	F	S	S
8 Mar–2 Nov	10–6	M	T	W	T	F	S	S
3 Nov–31 Dec**	10–5	M	T	W	T	F	S	S

Last admission to house 75 minutes before closing. Timed tickets to house (limited numbers). House ticket booking available via website. *Restaurant opens at 11; garden and estate close at 5 or dusk if earlier; restaurant, café and shop close 30 minutes before that. **Garden and estate closed 25 December. 24 and 31 December: close at 3.

Westbury College Gatehouse

College Road, Westbury-on-Trym, Bristol BS9 3EH

Map ① I3   1907

15th-century gatehouse to 13th-century College of Priests – former home of theological reformer John Wyclif. **Note**: access by key, available from Holy Trinity Parish chuch office. Sorry no toilet.

Finding out more: 01275 461900 or westburycollege@nationaltrust.org.uk

Westbury Court Garden

Westbury-on-Severn, Gloucestershire GL14 1PD

Map (1) J2 [⊞] 1967

Originally laid out between 1696 and 1705, this is the only restored Dutch water garden in the country (above). There are canals, clipped hedges, working 17th-century vegetable plots and many old varieties of fruit trees.

Making the most of your day: evening garden tours, Easter Egg trails, Apple Day.
Dogs: welcome on short leads at all times.

Access for all: [icons]
Grounds [icons]

Getting here: see website for details.
Parking: free, 300 yards.

Finding out more: 01452 760461 or westburycourt@nationaltrust.org.uk

Westbury Court Garden		M	T	W	T	F	S	S
12 Mar–29 Jun	10–5	·	·	**W**	**T**	**F**	**S**	**S**
1 Jul–31 Aug	10–5	**M**	**T**	**W**	**T**	**F**	**S**	**S**
3 Sep–26 Oct	10–5	·	·	**W**	**T**	**F**	**S**	**S**

Open Bank Holiday Mondays. Open other times by appointment.

Westwood Manor

Westwood, near Bradford-on-Avon, Wiltshire BA15 2AF

Map (1) J4 [⊞][✚][⊞] 1960

This beautiful small Jacobean manor house, virtually untouched since 1650, has a very personal feel: visitors find it easy to imagine living here. See decorative plasterwork, fine period furniture and tapestries and two rare early keyboard instruments, a spinet and virginal. There is a small modern topiary and pond garden. **Note**: Westwood Manor is a family home, administered by the tenant. There are no public toilets.

Eating and shopping: pick up a copy of our CD of Elizabethan music, recorded here on the recently restored virginal and spinet.

Making the most of your day: children's quizzes (house suitable for over-fives). After visiting Westwood, why not explore Great Chalfield and The Courts nearby?

Access for all: [icons]
Manor [icons] Garden [icons]

Getting here: see website for details.
Parking: free, 90 yards.

Finding out more: 01225 863374 or westwoodmanor@nationaltrust.org.uk

Westwood Manor		M	T	W	T	F	S	S
1 Apr–30 Sep	2–5	·	**T**	**W**	·	·	·	**S**

White Mill

Sturminster Marshall, near Wimborne Minster, Dorset BH21 4BX

Map (1) K6   1982

Corn mill with original wooden machinery in a peaceful riverside setting.

Finding out more: 01258 858051 or whitemill@nationaltrust.org.uk

South East

Famed throughout the world, the iconic White Cliffs of Dover in Kent have been a symbol of hope and freedom for centuries

Outdoors in the South East

The South East of England, while being one of the country's most densely populated areas, still boasts extensive and beautiful green spaces, waterways and miles of dramatic coastline. Here are some regional highlights of our great outdoors.

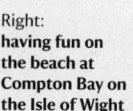

Right:
having fun on the beach at Compton Bay on the Isle of Wight

Coast and countryside on the Isle of Wight
The most southerly point of the region is the Isle of Wight. Here much of the finest countryside and coastline is owned by the National Trust, including the magnificent chalk downs of Ventnor, Tennyson Down and the Needles Headland. There are plenty of outdoor adventures to be had here, from surfing at Compton Bay, to walking and wildlife spotting. Then, after all this activity, enjoy a spot of relaxation on our beautiful beaches.

Escape London and head to the Surrey Hills
The rolling hills and green spaces of Surrey are a mere stone's throw from London, but a million miles away from city living. Get away from it all with cycling or walking and take in some of the region's best views. Or, for a relaxing water experience, hire a boat and enjoy the delights of the River Wey, the largest stretch of waterway that the National Trust cares for.

New Forest Northern Commons

The beauty of the New Forest's isolated wilderness, with its blazes of purple summer heather followed by rich autumn colour, is captivating. The regeneration of wildlife-rich landscapes at Bramshaw, shaped through historic rural practices that still thrive today, is inspirational. You can experience what the forest has to offer for both retreat and adventure by joining us on a journey of discovery, either on foot or horseback.

The picturesque Chiltern Hills

We look after a group of popular beauty spots in the picturesque Chiltern Hills, where there are many fabulous walking and cycling opportunities. Popular spots include Watlington Hill, West Wycombe Hill, Coombe Hill and Ivinghoe Beacon along the Chiltern escarpment. You can spend a pleasant day exploring this attractive landscape of woods, farms and hamlets, stopping for lunch at a pub then a walk among the 16th-century cottages and inns of West Wycombe village.

Kent – the Garden of England

Why not blow away the cobwebs at the iconic White Cliffs of Dover or enjoy a woodland walk at Toys Hill or at Petts Wood and Hawkwood? At Knole, there are a number of trails through the park, where walkers can spot the resident deer. Or you could visit Old Soar Manor, following the circular walk from Ightham Mote – the perfect spot to refuel with a cream tea. Alternatively, step back in time at beautiful Tudor Chiddingstone village.

South Downs – Britain's newest national park

Devil's Dyke, Slindon and the Woolbeding estates are part of the South Downs, which stretches for 70 miles across Sussex. It is a destination valued for its outdoor activities, rare habitats, stunning wildlife and ancient history. There is something for everyone: from bracing coastal walks to gentle strolls, and from zorbing or cycling, to kayaking and power kiting.

For more information on all our countryside and coastal places, please visit **www.nationaltrust.org.uk/southeast**

Above left and right: **Devil's Dyke on the South Downs** Right: **Toys Hill, Kent**

Outdoors in the South East

With leafy woodlands, leisurely waterways, open chalk downland, sweeping coastline and rolling views, the South East region offers an eclectic mix of nature's jewels.

Ashridge Estate

near Berkhamsted, Hertfordshire

Map ② E3 ⊞🏛🔄🦆 1926

Standing on the ridge of the Chiltern Hills, the Ashridge Estate is a product of 3,000 years of farming, forestry and conservation. The result, both a Site of Special Scientific Interest and an Area of Outstanding Natural Beauty, is a place where visitors can escape modern life and unwind. From the visitor centre, miles of footpaths meander through 2,000 hectares (5,000 acres) of ancient woodland, open parkland and chalk downland. There are carpets of bluebells in spring, herds of wild deer, and a climb up the Bridgewater Monument reveals panoramic views.
Note: toilets only available when café open.

Eating and shopping: shop offers an ever-changing choice of gifts, local produce, books, local maps and self-guided walk leaflets. Al fresco dining at the Brownlow Café (National Trust-approved concession).

Making the most of your day: events include guided wildlife walks and talks. Education programme and forest school clubs. Chilterns Countryside Festival in September.
Dogs: allowed under close control (deer roam freely).

Access for all: 📷🚾♿👢📷📷
Visitor centre 📷♿
Grounds 📷➡📷

Getting here: see website for details.
Sat Nav: use HP4 1LT for visitor centre.
Parking: free.

Bridgewater Monument on the Ashridge Estate, Hertfordshire

Finding out more: 01494 755557 (Infoline). 01442 851227 or ashridge@nationaltrust.org.uk

Ashridge Estate		M	T	W	T	F	S	S
Estate								
Open all year	Dawn–dusk	M	T	W	T	F	S	S
Visitor centre and shop								
15 Feb–21 Dec	10–5	M	T	W	T	F	S	S
Bridgewater Monument (weather dependent)								
5 Apr–2 Nov	11–4:30	.	.	.	.	.	S	S
Brownlow Café								
1 Jan–21 Mar	8–4	M	T	W	T	F	S	S
22 Mar–3 Nov	8–6	M	T	W	T	F	S	S
4 Nov–31 Dec	8–4	M	T	W	T	F	S	S

Visitor centre, shop and café may close at dusk if earlier. Last entry to monument 4:15. Monument open Bank Holiday Mondays. Café closed 25 December.

www.nationaltrust.org.uk/southeast

Note: toilets in Coleshill Estate office yard and next to village shop and tea-room in Buscot.

Eating and shopping: Buscot tea-room offering lunches and afternoon tea. Locally sourced produce served at Coleshill shop and tea-room and The Radnor Arms (award-winning ales and microbrewery).

Making the most of your day: guided walks throughout the year, including tours of the Second World War bunker. **Dogs**: on leads only.

Getting here: see website for details.
Parking: at Buscot village; Coleshill Estate office.

Finding out more: 01793 762209 or buscotandcoleshill@nationaltrust.org.uk

The Buscot and Coleshill Estates

Coleshill Watermill open second Sunday of the month: April to October, 2 to 5.

Discovering the Buscot and Coleshill Estates on the Oxfordshire/Wiltshire border

The Buscot and Coleshill Estates

Coleshill, near Swindon, Wiltshire SN6 7PT

Map ② C4   1956

These countryside estates on the western borders of Oxfordshire include the attractive, unspoilt villages of Buscot and Coleshill, each with a thriving tea-room. There are circular walks of differing lengths and a series of footpaths criss-crossing the estates, with breathtaking countryside and wildlife at Buscot Lock and Badbury Hill.

Cobham Wood and Mausoleum

near Cobham, Kent

Map (2) H5  2014

Once part of the Darnley family's estate, the woodland opens onto views of the atmospheric mausoleum, designed by James Wyatt. **Note**: no vehicle access or parking. Sorry no toilets.

Finding out more: 01732 810378 or cobham@nationaltrust.org.uk

Compton Bay and Downs

Compton, Isle of Wight PO30 4HB

Map (2) C9   1961

Compton Bay has all the elements of a great day out, a sandy beach with plenty of space for families, surfing and other non-motorised water sports. There is even a section of beach for dog walkers. The multi-coloured cliffs and coastal views provide a wonderful backdrop, and the geological history of the bay is fascinating, going back to the time of dinosaurs.

Eating and shopping: licensed van selling hot and cold snacks, drinks and ice-cream.

Sandy beach at Compton Bay, the Isle of Wight

Making the most of your day: one of the best spots on the Isle of Wight for swimming, surfing, fossil hunting, or just sitting around. **Dogs**: welcome on beach between Hanover Point and Brook Chine all year.

Access for all: 🔲

Getting here: see website for details.
Parking: pay and display (for non-members).

Finding out more: 01983 741020 or comptonbay@nationaltrust.org.uk

Runnymede

Windsor Road, Egham, near Old Windsor, Surrey TW20 0AE

Map (2) F5  1931

Picturesque open landscape nestling beside the Thames, site of King John's sealing of the Magna Carta nearly 800 years ago. **Note**: toilets available during tea-room opening hours only. Mooring and fishing (during fishing season) available for additional fee (including members).

Finding out more: 01784 432891 or runnymede@nationaltrust.org.uk

The White Cliffs of Dover

Langdon Cliffs, Upper Road, Dover, Kent CT16 1HJ

Map (2) K7  1968

There can be no doubt that The White Cliffs of Dover are one of this country's most spectacular natural features. They are an official icon of Britain and have been a symbol of hope for generations. You can appreciate their beauty and enjoy their special appeal through the seasons by taking one of the country's most dramatic clifftop walks, which offers unrivalled views of the busy English Channel

The White Cliffs of Dover, Kent: the clifftop walk has to be one of the most dramatic in England

and the French coast. While here, learn more about the fascinating military and penal history of The White Cliffs and savour the rare flora and fauna found only on this chalk grassland. **Note**: toilets available only when visitor centre is open.

Eating and shopping: shop selling gifts and outdoor goods. Coffee shop serving lunches and afternoon tea. Both with unrivalled views of the Port of Dover.

Making the most of your day: waymarked trail to the lighthouse. Spectacular viewpoints. Events and guided walks throughout year. **Dogs**: under close control at all times (stock grazing).

Access for all: 🅿️♿🚻♿♿🚶♿🅰️
Visitor centre ♿♿ **Countryside** ♿♿

Getting here: see website for details.
Sat Nav: use CT15 5NA.

Finding out more: 01304 202756 or whitecliffs@nationaltrust.org.uk

The White Cliffs of Dover		M	T	W	T	F	S	S
Visitor centre								
1 Jan–2 Mar	11–4	M	T	W	T	F	S	S
3 Mar–13 Jul	10–5	M	T	W	T	F	S	S
14 Jul–7 Sep	10–5:30	M	T	W	T	F	S	S
8 Sep–2 Nov	10–5	M	T	W	T	F	S	S
3 Nov–31 Dec	11–4	M	T	W	T	F	S	S
Car park								
1 Jan–2 Mar	8–6	M	T	W	T	F	S	S
3 Mar–2 Nov	8–7	M	T	W	T	F	S	S
3 Nov–31 Dec	8–6	M	T	W	T	F	S	S

Visitor centre and car park closed 24 and 25 December.

White Horse Hill

Uffington, Oxfordshire SN7 7UK

Map ② C4   🏛️♿♿ 1979

The oldest dated chalk figure in the country and an Iron Age hill fort. **Note**: archaeological monuments under English Heritage guardianship. Sorry no toilet.

Finding out more: 01793 762209 or whitehorsehill@nationaltrust.org.uk

South Downs

Wild coast, varied wildlife, remarkable history – enjoy our top spots in Britain's newest National Park.

Birling Gap and the Seven Sisters

East Dean, near Eastbourne,
East Sussex BN20 0AB

Map ② H9 🖼🏄⛰🍷 1931

Stretching between Birling Gap and Cuckmere Haven are the world famous Seven Sisters chalk cliffs, one of the longest stretches of unspoilt coastline on the south coast. Here you can enjoy spectacular views along the coast, intricate wave-cut platforms, a stunning beach ideal for seaside picnics and networks of rock pools. Inland, there are lovely quiet walks across ancient chalk downland, rich in butterflies and flowers.

Birling Gap is a delightful place to start your walk, with a National Trust café and shop perched on the edge of the cliffs.

Eating and shopping: café serving breakfast, lunch, teas, homemade cakes, snacks and locally sourced fish and chips. Brand new shop selling local and seasonal items. Picnics welcome.

Making the most of your day: events and activities for all ages, information point at busy times. Chyngton Farm, Frog Firle Farm, Alfriston Clergy House and Monk's House nearby. **Dogs**: welcome, but on leads near livestock and in some parts of café.

Access for all: 🅿♿🚾♿🚻♿♿
Café 🦽 Shop 🦽

Getting here: see website for details.
Parking: at Birling Gap (pay and display for non-members).

Finding out more: 01323 423197 or birlinggap@nationaltrust.org.uk

Birling Gap and the Seven Sisters
Café and shop open 10 to 4 with extended hours in summer; closed 24 and 25 December.

Making a discovery at Birling Gap, East Sussex

www.nationaltrust.org.uk/southeast

Looking north from Devil's Dyke, East Sussex

Devil's Dyke

near Brighton, East Sussex

Map ② G8  1995

At nearly a mile long, the Dyke Valley is the longest, deepest and widest 'dry valley' in the UK. Legend has it that the Devil dug this chasm to drown the parishioners of the Weald. On the other hand, scientists believe it was formed naturally just over 10,000 years ago in the last ice age. The walls of the Iron Age hill fort can be seen when you walk around the hill, and there is a carpet of flowers and a myriad of colourful insects to discover in the valley.

Eating and shopping: Devil's Dyke pub (not National Trust) beside car park.

Making the most of your day: self-guided walks leaflet, orienteering course map and family Discovery Packs available from information trailer (open April to September, weekends and some weekdays). Numerous bridleways offer great cycling.

Access for all:

Getting here: see website for details.
Sat Nav: use BN1 8YJ. **Parking**: large car park.

Finding out more: 01273 857712 or devilsdyke@nationaltrust.org.uk

Ditchling Beacon

near Ditchling, Westmeston, East Sussex

Map ② G8  1953

Just seven miles north of Brighton, at 248 metres above sea level, Ditchling Beacon is the highest point in East Sussex and offers commanding 360-degree views from its summit. You can look south out to sea, north across the Weald or east–west across the Downs. The site also has the remains of an Iron Age hill fort.

Eating and shopping: picnics welcome.

Making the most of your day: great for bracing walks with some of the best scenery on the South Downs. Traces of the rampart and ditch of the hill fort to discover. Why not visit nearby Ditchling Down? **Dogs**: welcome but must be kept on leads at all times.

Access for all:

Getting here: see website for details.
Sat Nav: use BN6 8XG. **Parking**: car park on Ditchling Road. Payment for non-members by Ringo (pay by mobile).

Finding out more: 01323 423197 or ditchlingbeacon@nationaltrust.org.uk

Ditchling Beacon is the highest point in East Sussex

Saddlescombe Farm and Newtimber Hill

near Brighton, West Sussex

Map (2) G8  1937

Saddlescombe Farm is a hidden gem on the South Downs Way, only five miles from Brighton. Documented in the Domesday Book, this unique example of a downland farm shows what life was really like throughout the last 1,000 years. Newtimber Hill is one of the finest examples of chalk grassland in the country and is home to many varieties of downland flowers and much wildlife, as well as ancient lime trees and 19th-century graffitied beech trees in the woodland. **Note**: Saddlescombe is a working farm and is fully open only on special open days.

Eating and shopping: Hiker's Rest café (not National Trust) serving teas, cakes and light lunches (closed Wednesdays, and throughout January and February).

Making the most of your day: circular route to Devil's Dyke and walks up Newtimber Hill through ancient woodland. Cycling along the South Downs Way. Open days and events throughout the year. **Dogs**: welcome, on leads where livestock grazing.

Access for all: Buildings

Getting here: see website for details.
Sat Nav: use BN45 7DE. **Parking**: very limited lay-by parking opposite farm entrance (no parking in farm) or park at Devil's Dyke.

Finding out more: 01273 857712 or saddlescombe@nationaltrust.org.uk

Slindon Estate

Slindon, near Arundel, West Sussex BN18 0RG

Map (2) E8

The ancient Slindon Estate covers 1,400 hectares (3,459 acres) of woodland, downland, farmland and parkland. It boasts countless historic landscape features as well as an unspoilt Sussex village. Visitors can discover sun-dappled woodlands and meadows rich in flowers and wildlife, while the expansive views take in the Weald and the South Downs, continuing across the coastal plain to the sea.

Eating and shopping: The Forge in Slindon village stocks everything from locally baked bread, deli items, fruit and vegetables, to sandwiches, biscuits and cakes. Fresh coffee and tea, beer, light breakfasts, lunches and afternoon tea are also available.

Making the most of your day: there are 24 miles of rights of way to explore. Why not take some time to discover the village as well? **Dogs**: welcome under close control.

Access for all:

Getting here: see website for details.
Parking: three car parks: Park Lane, SU 960076; Duke's Road, SU 953073 and Bignor Hill, SU 973129.

Finding out more: 01243 814730 or slindonestate@nationaltrust.org.uk

Wildlife-rich Newtimber Hill, left, and the ancient Slindon Estate, below, are both in West Sussex

Surrey Hills

This Area of Outstanding Natural Beauty offers some of South East England's most beautiful and accessible countryside, from rolling chalk downs and flower-rich grasslands, to heaths and woodlands.

Box Hill

Tadworth, Surrey

Map ② F6      1914

A great place for family adventures: exploring the woods, braving the natural play trail, finding the tower or paddling in the River Mole at the stepping stones. On a clear day you can see for miles from the top of Box Hill, so if you're hiking up, the view is well worth it. You can pick up free walks guides from the visitor centre and café or find your own way along our many footpaths. This year is the 100th anniversary of Box Hill being bequeathed to the National Trust and we will have various special events to celebrate.

Eating and shopping: the Box Hill café, with its vintage crockery, has indoor and outdoor seating and serves light lunches, snacks and afternoon teas. Servery offers take-away hot drinks, cakes, sandwiches and the famous revival flapjack!

Making the most of your day: school holiday activities and walks guides. Anniversary events. Perfect starting point for a longer walk over to Leith Hill or Polesden Lacey. **Dogs**: under close control where livestock is grazing.

Access for all: 🅿️ 🚻 ♿ 🏞️
Building ♿ 🦽   Grounds ➡️

Getting here: see website for details.
Sat Nav: use KT20 7LB.
Parking: £4 non-members.

Finding out more: 01372 220640 or boxhill@nationaltrust.org.uk

Box Hill		M	T	W	T	F	S	S
Shop, café, discovery zone and servery								
1 Jan–30 Mar	10–4	M	T	W	T	F	S	S
31 Mar–26 Oct	9–5	M	T	W	T	F	S	S
27 Oct–31 Dec	10–4	M	T	W	T	F	S	S

During bad weather the servery, shop, café and discovery zone may close early. Closed on 25 December.

Setting off on a snowy adventure at Box Hill, Surrey

Denbies Hillside

near Dorking, Surrey

Map ②F6 ⊞ 1963

Denbies Hillside is a dramatic chalk escarpment with panoramic views of Leith Hill, the highest point in south-east England. It is a great spot for walking, picnics and wildlife-watching – you may even spot such chalk downland species as the Adonis blue and chalkhill blue butterflies.

Eating and shopping: picnic area with benches in Steers Field.

Making the most of your day: self-guided trail, spectacular views and several Second World War pillboxes to discover. Why not visit nearby Hackhurst Downs? **Dogs**: welcome on leads when livestock are grazing.

Access for all: ⊞ ⊞

Getting here: see website for details.
Sat Nav: use RH5 6SR. **Parking**: at Ranmore West car park and Denbies Hillside.

Finding out more: 01306 887485 or denbieshillside@nationaltrust.org.uk

Panoramic view from Denbies Hillside, Surrey

On top of the world at the Devil's Punch Bowl viewing point at Hindhead Commons in Surrey

Hindhead Commons and the Devil's Punch Bowl

London Road, Hindhead, Surrey GU26 6AB

Map ②E7 ⊞ 1906

Spectacular views from Hindhead Commons and uninterrupted walks to the Devil's Punchbowl make this an unforgettable place to relax and take in some of the best countryside in the South East. Since the opening of the A3 tunnel, paths, cycle routes and bridleways have been reconnected and natural contours restored. Peace and calm now reign and the glorious landscape, with its carpets of purple heather in the summer and grazing Highland cattle, is there to enjoy. There's plenty of space for family adventures and lovely spots for picnics.

Leith Hill

near Coldharbour village, Dorking, Surrey

Map ② F7  1923

There are unbeatable views from the top of the tower; at 1,000 feet above sea level, you can see all the way from London to the seaside. Don't miss the wonderful walks, or Rhododendron Wood and Leith Hill Place, childhood home of composer Ralph Vaughan Williams. **Note**: sorry no toilet at tower.

Eating and shopping: teas, coffees, hot and cold food available at tower (not National Trust). Tea, coffee and cakes available at Leith Hill Place, courtesy of baking volunteers. Picnics welcome, but barbecues prohibited.

Making the most of your day: Leith Hill Place soundscape tour, entrance by free timed ticket. Trail guides available from tower, Leith Hill Place and car parks. Other activities, tours and events. **Dogs**: on leads on heathland (April to July) and in Leith Hill Place, under control elsewhere.

Access for all: Tower ⬚

Getting here: see website for details.
Sat Nav: for Rhododendron Wood use RH5 6LU. For Leith Lane use RH5 6LY.

The tower at Leith Hill, Surrey

Eating and shopping: café serving hot home-cooked food, as well as sandwiches and cakes – indoor and outdoor seating. Picnics welcome.

Making the most of your day: events throughout year. Walks leaflets. **Dogs**: under very close control during bird-nesting season (March to October).

Access for all: ⬚⬚⬚⬚
Café and shop ⬚ Grounds ➡

Getting here: see website for details.
Parking: £4 non-members.

Finding out more: 01428 681050 (Rangers). 01428 608771 (café) or hindhead@nationaltrust.org.uk

Hindhead Commons		M	T	W	T	F	S	S
Café								
1 Jan–28 Mar	9–4	M	T	W	T	F	S	S
29 Mar–26 Oct	9–5*	M	T	W	T	F	S	S
27 Oct–31 Dec	9–4	M	T	W	T	F	S	S

*Café open until 6 at weekends; closed on 25 December.

Parking: designated areas along road at foot of hill (no vehicle access to summit). Leith Hill Place parking in Rhododendron Wood (£4 a car for non-members), then 437-yard walk across sloping field. Limited blue badge parking at house (on Leith Hill Lane).

Finding out more: 01306 712711 or leithhill@nationaltrust.org.uk

Leith Hill		M	T	W	T	F	S	S
Leith Hill Place								
4 Apr–2 Nov	11–5	M	·	·	·	F	S	S

Tower and tea kiosk open 10 to 3 (extended opening during fine weather), closed 25 December.

Reigate Hill and Gatton Park

near Reigate, Surrey

Map ② G6   [≡] 1912

A peaceful moment of contemplation on the North Downs Way at Gatton Park in Surrey

Reigate Hill is a spectacular escarpment with sweeping views across the Weald. It is a great spot for walking, family picnics and wildlife-watching. A short walk away is Reigate Fort – a 19th-century defensive fort. To the east is Gatton Park, designed by Lancelot 'Capability' Brown. **Note**: areas of Gatton Park open once a month by the Gatton Trust.

Eating and shopping: picnics welcome. Tea kiosk (not National Trust).

Making the most of your day: self-guided circular trail around Gatton Park – free leaflet available from the information boards. On your walk, you may spot rare chalk downland species such as the Adonis blue butterfly. **Dogs**: welcome, on leads when livestock grazing.

Access for all: [♿][♿]

Getting here: see website for details. **Sat Nav**: use RH2 OHX. **Parking**: free at Wray Lane car park.

Finding out more: 01372 220640 or reigate@nationaltrust.org.uk

Idyllic Alfriston Clergy House, East Sussex

Alfriston Clergy House

The Tye, Alfriston, Polegate,
East Sussex BN26 5TL

Map ② H8  1896

This rare 14th-century Wealden 'hall-house'
was the first building to be acquired by the
National Trust, in 1896. The thatched,
timber-framed house is in an idyllic setting,
with views across the River Cuckmere, and is
surrounded by a tranquil cottage garden full of
wildlife. **Note**: nearest toilet in village car park.

Eating and shopping: shop selling souvenirs.

Making the most of your day: children's
quizzes and trails. Varied events all year.
Short circular walks and longer distance
hikes over South Downs.

Access for all:
Building 🔽🏛 Grounds 🔽🏛

Getting here: see website for details.
Parking: 500 yards across village
(not National Trust).

Finding out more: 01323 871961 or
alfriston@nationaltrust.org.uk

Alfriston Clergy House		M	T	W	T	F	S	S
1 Mar–16 Mar	10:30–5						S	S
17 Mar–2 Nov	10:30–5	M	T	W			S	S
3 Nov–21 Dec	11–4	M	T	W			S	S

Open Good Friday.

Ascott

Wing, near Leighton Buzzard,
Buckinghamshire LU7 0PR

Map ② E3  1949

This half-timbered Jacobean farmhouse,
transformed by the de Rothschilds towards
the end of the 19th century, now houses an
exceptional collection of paintings, fine
furniture and superb oriental porcelain.
The extensive gardens are an attractive mix
of formal and natural, with specimen trees,
shrubs and beautiful herbaceous borders.

Making the most of your day: unusual
features to spot in the gardens.
Dogs: assistance dogs only.

Access for all: 🅰♿🅿⋯🄰
Building 🔽🔽🔽 Grounds 🔽🔽➡

Getting here: see website for details.
Parking: free, 220 yards.

Finding out more: 01296 688242 or
ascott@nationaltrust.org.uk

Ascott		M	T	W	T	F	S	S
25 Mar–1 Jun	2–6		T	W	T	F	S	S
3 Jun–24 Jul	2–6		T	W	T			
29 Jul–12 Sep	2–6		T	W	T	F	S	S

Open Bank Holiday Mondays and Good Friday.
Last admission one hour before closing. Gardens open in
aid of National Gardens Scheme on 5 May and 25 August
(charges including members).

Main avenue leading to Ascott, Buckinghamshire

Ashdown House, Berkshire: this unique former hunting lodge was built for the Queen of Bohemia

Ashdown House

Lambourn, Newbury, Berkshire RG17 8RE

Map ② C5 🏛️ 🏚️ ❄️ 🎣 1956

Unique 17th-century chalk-block hunting lodge, with doll's-house appearance, built for the Queen of Bohemia by the Earl of Craven. The guided tour, which reveals an intriguing family history, leads up the staircase hung with fine 17th-century paintings. Outstanding rooftop views across three counties.
Note: access to roof via 100-step staircase. Property is tenanted, so check opening times before visiting.

Making the most of your day: guided tour.
Dogs: on leads in woodland only.

Access for all: 🚻 📷 📖 📩
Building 🔼 Grounds ♿

Getting here: see website for details.
Sat Nav: follow local brown signs.
Parking: in main estate car park, 437 yards.

Finding out more: 01494 755569 (Infoline).
01793 762209 or
ashdownhouse@nationaltrust.org.uk

Ashdown House		M	T	W	T	F	S	S
House								
2 Apr–29 Oct	2–5	·	·	**W**	·	·	**S**	·
Woodland								
Open all year		**M**	**T**	**W**	**T**	·	**S**	**S**

Admission by guided tour only to house at 2:15, 3:15 and 4:15 (places limited).

Basildon Park

Lower Basildon, Reading, Berkshire RG8 9NR

Map ② D5  1978

Visiting Basildon Park is a great experience for the whole family. Be sure to see our newly opened 1950s Laundry and enjoy family activities in the Old Kitchen. You can also picnic in the gardens and explore our extensive historic parkland. The Basildon Park you see today is a re-creation and restoration of the 18th-century mansion, brought back to life in the 1950s as the country home of Lord and Lady Iliffe. Inspired by the original designs of the architect John Carr, the Iliffes collected important 18th- and 19th-century paintings and antiques especially for the interiors of Basildon Park. **Note**: entrance to main show rooms of mansion on first floor – 21 steps from ground level.

Eating and shopping: mansion tea-room serves light lunches between 12 and 2:30, with homemade cakes and cream teas available all day. The Parlour in the stableyard offers tasty treats and drinks from 10. The shop sells books, plants, local food, ice-creams and much more.

Making the most of your day: guided house tours and parkland walks. Events. Outdoor play areas and Wild Wood Walk for families. Piano for visitors to play. Greys Court, Nuffield Place and The Vyne are nearby. **Dogs**: welcome on leads.

Access for all: [icons] Mansion [icons] Grounds [icons]

Getting here: see website for details.
Sat Nav: use RG8 9NU for main entrance on A329. **Parking**: free, 400 yards from mansion.

Finding out more: 0118 984 3040 or basildonpark@nationaltrust.org.uk

Basildon Park		M	T	W	T	F	S	S
Grounds, shop and tea-room								
1 Feb–28 Feb	10–4	M	T	W	T	F	S	S
1 Mar–2 Nov	10–5	M	T	W	T	F	S	S
3 Nov–31 Dec	10–4	M	T	W	T	F	S	S
House								
1 Feb–28 Feb*	12–3	M	T	W	T	F	S	S
1 Mar–2 Nov**	12–5	M	T	W	T	F	S	S
3 Nov–28 Nov*	12–3	M	T	W	T	F	S	S
29 Nov–31 Dec	11–4	M	T	W	T	F	S	S

*House tours only. **House tours daily from 11 to 12. Closed 24 and 25 December.

Stately Basildon Park in Berkshire: a great experience for the whole family

Bateman's

Bateman's Lane, Burwash,
East Sussex TN19 7DS

Map ② H7 🏠🖼️❄️🍴☂️ 1940

Rudyard Kipling loved this place; it was his personal paradise, and somewhere he could enjoy family life. Surrounded by the wooded landscape of the Sussex Weald, this 17th-century house, with mullioned windows, pretty secluded garden and acres of countryside, provided a tranquil sanctuary. The atmospheric oak-beamed rooms remain much as he left them. Outside, winding paths take in manicured lawns, a wildflower meadow and Kipling's 1928 Rolls-Royce Phantom 1, while beside the river sits a working 17th-century watermill. This year, the house is open from 1 March until 31 December (excluding 24 and 25 December).

Catching the wind at Bateman's in East Sussex

Eating and shopping: shop selling Kipling books and souvenirs. Restaurant.

Making the most of your day: family fun days, storytelling, re-enactment weekends, garden and countryside walks. Children's quizzes and trails. Scotney Castle and Bodiam Castle nearby. **Dogs**: on leads in car park and countryside paths only. Dog crèche available.

Access for all: 🅿️♿♿🚻♿♿📷🔊♿:⬛🅰️
Building 🏠♿♿ Grounds ♿➡️♿

Getting here: see website for details.
Parking: free, 30 yards.

Finding out more: 01435 882302 or batemans@nationaltrust.org.uk

Bateman's		M	T	W	T	F	S	S
House								
1 Mar–2 Nov	11–5	M	T	W	T	F	S	S
3 Nov–31 Dec	11:30–3:30	M	T	W	T	F	S	S
Garden, shop and restaurant								
1 Mar–2 Nov	10–5:30*	M	T	W	T	F	S	S
3 Nov–31 Dec	11–4	M	T	W	T	F	S	S

*Restaurant closes at 5. Closed 24 and 25 December. Mill grinds corn most Wednesdays and Saturdays at 2.

Bembridge Fort

Bembridge Down, near Bembridge,
Isle of Wight PO36 8QY

Map ② D9  1967

In a commanding position on top of Bembridge Down, this derelict Victorian fort is open for volunteer-run guided tours. **Note**: sorry no toilets. Access by guided tour, booking essential, £3.50 charge (including members).

Finding out more: 01983 741020 or bembridgefort@nationaltrust.org.uk. c/o Longstone Farmhouse, Strawberry Lane, Mottistone, Isle of Wight PO30 4EA

Finding out more: 01983 873945 or bembridgemill@nationaltrust.org.uk

Bembridge Windmill		M	T	W	T	F	S	S
15 Mar–2 Nov	10:30–5	**M**	**T**	**W**	**T**	**F**	**S**	**S**

Closes dusk if earlier. Conducted school groups and special visits March to end October by written appointment.

Bembridge Windmill on the Isle of Wight

Bembridge Windmill

High Street, Bembridge,
Isle of Wight PO35 5SQ

Map ② D9  1961

This little gem, the only surviving windmill on the Isle of Wight, is one of its most iconic images. Built around 1700 and last operated in 1913, it still has most of its original machinery intact. Climb to the top and follow the milling process back down its four floors.

Eating and shopping: ice-cream kiosk, hot and cold drinks, including tea, hot chocolate and various coffees. Postcards, sweets, gifts and souvenirs. Picnic table in grounds.

Making the most of your day: walks, including the start of Culver Trail. Nature trails (school holidays). Bembridge Fort (booking essential) nearby. **Dogs**: on leads welcome in grounds. Assistance dogs only in windmill.

Access for all: 🅿️🚻♿️🏠🌳•.•
Building ♿🏛♿

Getting here: see website for details.
Sat Nav: do not use postcode, look for brown signs. **Parking**: free (not National Trust), 100 yards in lay-by.

Boarstall Duck Decoy

Boarstall, near Bicester,
Buckinghamshire HP18 9UX

Map ② D3  1980

One of the very few remaining decoys in the country, providing a fascinating insight into a rare aspect of rural life.

Finding out more: 01280 817156 or boarstalldecoy@nationaltrust.org.uk

Boarstall Tower

Boarstall, near Bicester,
Buckinghamshire HP18 9UX

Map ② D3  1943

Charming 14th-century moated gatehouse set in beautiful gardens, retaining original fortified appearance. Many rooms remain virtually unchanged. Grade I listed. **Note**: access to upper levels is via a spiral staircase.

Finding out more: 01280 817156 or boarstalltower@nationaltrust.org.uk

Bodiam Castle

Bodiam, near Robertsbridge,
East Sussex TN32 5UA

Map ② I7   🏰🏠👪🍴 1926

One of Britain's most picturesque and evocative castles set in the heart of the High Weald. There are spiral staircases, battlements and look-outs, where you can imagine arrows raining down over the original portcullis. Colourful castle characters and fascinating snippets of medieval castle life can be discovered as you wander through the ruined courtyard and the tower chambers. With stunning countryside views, the only limitation to your visit is your imagination. We're now open all year, so the castle can be enjoyed in every season. **Note**: toilets in car park only. Property often used by educational groups during term.

Eating and shopping: shop selling gifts, castle-themed products and local produce. Tea-room serving homemade lunches, teas, snacks and ice-cream. Seasonal snack kiosk.

Bodiam Castle in East Sussex, above and below, could have stepped straight out of a fairy tale

Making the most of your day: castle character talks and children's trails and activities. Events include medieval-themed weekend and Christmas events. Family activities throughout school holidays. Bateman's and Scotney Castle nearby. **Dogs**: welcome on leads in grounds only.

Access for all: 🅿🅳♿🚻🚼🔊👜📷💻♨ 👓🅰 Castle 🚶🏛♿♿ Grounds ➡♿

Getting here: see website for details.
Parking: 400 yards.

Finding out more: 01580 830196 or bodiamcastle@nationaltrust.org.uk

Bodiam Castle		M	T	W	T	F	S	S
4 Jan–9 Feb	11–4						**S**	**S**
15 Feb–31 Dec*	10–5	**M**	**T**	**W**	**T**	**F**	**S**	**S**

*Castle opens 10:30 to 5 or dusk if earlier.
Closed 24 and 25 December.

Buckingham Chantry Chapel

Market Hill, Buckingham,
Buckinghamshire MK18 1JX

Map ② D2   ✝🍴 1912

Atmospheric 15th-century chapel, restored by Sir Gilbert Scott in 1875. Today it is a thriving second-hand bookshop and coffee shop.

Finding out more: 01280 817156 or buckinghamchantry@nationaltrust.org.uk

Buscot Old Parsonage

Buscot, Faringdon, Oxfordshire SN7 8DQ

Map ② C4 🏠 ❀ 1949

Beautiful early 18th-century house with small walled garden, on the banks of the Thames.
Note: administered by a tenant (booking essential). Sorry no toilets.

Finding out more: 01793 762209 or buscot@nationaltrust.org.uk

Buscot Park

Faringdon, Oxfordshire SN7 8BU

Map ② C4 🏠 ❀ ♨ 1949

Lord Faringdon and his family live in the house, maintain its interior, curate its contents on behalf of the Trustees of The Faringdon Collection and manage and develop the grounds and gardens. This unusual arrangement for a National Trust property gives it an idiosyncratic air and a different take on taste and presentation. As a result the whole entity becomes more fluid and more surprising. New works of art mingle with the old within the house, and new alleys and vistas stride out within the grounds. Paintings, statuary and objects by contemporary artists reinvigorate the whole – refreshing the spirit.
Note: administered on behalf of the National Trust by Lord Faringdon.

Eating and shopping: tea-room (not National Trust). Local honey, peppermints, cider, plants and kitchen garden produce (when available). Ice-cream available.

Making the most of your day: occasional events in grounds and theatre (available for hire). Picnics. **Dogs**: in Paddock (overflow car park) only.

Access for all: 🅿️🐕♿🚻👶📷♿
House 🔆📶 Grounds 🔆🔆🔆➡️🔆🔆

Buscot Park in Oxfordshire: the Peto Water Garden

Getting here: see website for details.
Parking: free.

Finding out more: 01367 240932 (Infoline). 01367 240786 or buscotpark@nationaltrust.org.uk. www. buscotpark.com

Buscot Park		M	T	W	T	F	S	S
Grounds only								
1 Apr–30 Sep	2–6	M	T					
House, grounds and tea-room								
2 Apr–26 Sep*	2–6			W	T	F		

*House, grounds and tea-room weekend opening: 5, 6, 19 and 20 April, 3, 4, 10, 11, 24 and 25 May, 14, 15, 28 and 29 June, 12, 13, 26 and 27 July, 9, 10, 23 and 24 August, 13, 14, 27 and 28 September 2 to 6 (tea-room 2 to 5:30). Last admission to house one hour before closing. Open Bank Holidays and Good Friday.

Chartwell

Mapleton Road, Westerham, Kent TN16 1PS

Map ② G6 🏠❄️🖼️🔔🍷 1946

The Churchill family loved Chartwell. It was a home and a place that truly inspired Sir Winston. The house is still much as it was when the family lived here, with pictures, books and personal mementoes evoking the career and wide-ranging interests of this influential family. The studio is home to the largest single collection of Churchill's paintings. The gardens reflect Churchill's love of the landscape and nature. They include the lakes he created, the kitchen garden and the Marycot, a playhouse designed for his youngest daughter Mary. The woodland estate offers family walks, trails, den building, Canadian camp and opportunities to blow away the cobwebs and stretch your legs. New temporary exhibition open in the winter. **Note**: house entrance by timed ticket only (no booking available).

Eating and shopping: self-service restaurant offering Churchill-inspired meals and produce from the kitchen garden. Shop stocks Churchill memorabilia, home and garden ranges and local products. Extended plant centre.

Making the most of your day: woodland trail, offering spectacular views of house, connects with the hilly five-mile circular Weardale Walk to Emmetts Garden. Free talks and tours on selected days, including guided garden tours through Churchill's family garden and daily studio talks about Sir Winston and his love of painting. Regular special events in the restaurant and tastings in the shop. Other events include themed weekends. Children's trails and activities, get muddy in our new woodland play area. Why not combine with a visit to Quebec House, only two miles away? **Dogs**: welcome on woodland walks; on short leads in gardens only.

Access for all: 🅿️ 🚧 ♿ 🚽 ♿ 📷 🏛️ VT ♿ 👁️ 🖐️ **Building** ♿ ♿ ♿ **Grounds** ♿ ♿ ♿

Getting here: see website for details.
Parking: pay and display.

Chartwell, Kent, clockwise from main picture: south front in spring, enjoying the gardens and Lady Churchill's Rose Garden

Finding out more: 01732 868381 or chartwell@nationaltrust.org.uk

Chartwell		M	T	W	T	F	S	S
House								
1 Mar–2 Nov	11–5	M	T	W	T	F	S	S
Garden, exhibition, shop and restaurant								
1 Jan–28 Feb	11–4	M	T	W	T	F	S	S
1 Mar–2 Nov	10–5	M	T	W	T	F	S	S
3 Nov–31 Dec	11–4	M	T	W	T	F	S	S

The studio opens daily, times vary, closed in January. The exhibition closes for short periods to change the display. Admission to house by timed ticket (places limited), obtain on arrival from the visitor centre. Last admission 45 minutes before closing. Closes dusk if earlier. All winter opening weather permitting. Closed 24 and 25 December.

Chastleton House

Chastleton, near Moreton-in-Marsh, Oxfordshire GL56 0SU

Map ② C3 🏠 ❀ 🚪 1991

A rare gem of a Jacobean country house and garden, Chastleton was created between 1607 and 1612 by a prosperous wool merchant as an impressive statement of wealth and power. Owned by the same, increasingly impoverished, family until 1991, it has remained essentially unchanged for more than 400 years, with the interiors and contents gradually succumbing to the ravages of time. With virtually no intrusion from the 21st century, this fascinating place exudes an informal and timeless atmosphere in a gloriously unspoilt setting. **Note:** timed ticket system will be introduced in busy periods.

Eating and shopping: plants and garden produce for sale (subject to availability). Second-hand bookshop. Local publications and souvenirs. Refreshments available from local church (not National Trust) most days. Picnics welcome (in car park only).

Making the most of your day: free family explorer packs, croquet on the lawn, garden tours and conservation in action. Themed events. Out-of-hours and taster tours on request. **Dogs:** welcome on leads in car park and field opposite house only.

Access for all: 🅿️ 🅓 🚾 ♿ 🏛️ 🎧 👁️‍🗨️ 🅰️
Building ♿🔼 Garden ♿

Getting here: see website for details.
Sat Nav: follow brown signs. **Parking:** free, 270 yards (short steep hill).

Finding out more: 01494 755560 (Infoline). 01608 674981 or chastleton@nationaltrust.org.uk

Chastleton House		M	T	W	T	F	S	S
5 Mar–30 Mar	1–4	·	·	**W**	**T**	**F**	**S**	**S**
2 Apr–28 Sep	1–5	·	·	**W**	**T**	**F**	**S**	**S**
1 Oct–2 Nov	1–4	·	·	**W**	**T**	**F**	**S**	**S**
29 Nov–14 Dec	1–4	·	·	·	·	·	**S**	**S**

Last entry one hour before closing. Timed-ticket system on arrival, places limited. Closed Bank Holiday Mondays.

Chastleton House, Oxfordshire, has remained virtually unchanged for more than 400 years, sinking into a gentle decline

Making the most of your day: children's trails, events, attic tours (selected Sundays) and lecture lunches. Surrey Infantry Museum. Combine with a visit to nearby Hatchlands Park. Clandon's First World War military hospital remembered. **Dogs**: assistance dogs only.

Access for all: 🅿️ 🐕 🔧 🔔 🖐️ 🏛️ 💻 🎧 👓 📷

Building 🔧 ⬆️ ♿ Grounds 🔧 ♿

Getting here: see website for details.
Sat Nav: misleading, ensure you enter from A247. **Parking**: free, 250 yards.

Finding out more: 01483 222482 or clandonpark@nationaltrust.org.uk

Clandon Park		M	T	W	T	F	S	S
House, garden, museum, shop and restaurant*								
2 Mar–6 Jul	10:30–5	·	T	W	T	·	·	S
7 Jul–1 Sep	10:30–5	M	T	W	T	·	·	S
2 Sep–2 Nov	10:30–5	·	T	W	T	·	·	S
Shop and restaurant								
4 Nov–30 Nov	12–4	·	T	W	T	·	·	S
1 Dec–23 Dec**	12–4	M	T	W	T	·	·	S
Restaurant								
1 Dec–23 Dec**	7–11	M	T	W	T	·	·	S
Surrey Infantry Museum†								
4 Nov–18 Dec	12–4	·	T	W	T	·	·	

*House opens at 11. **December restaurant booking essential. †Museum open Mondays 1, 8, 15 December and by appointment on Sundays in November and December. Activities during January and February. Family-friendly offer February half-term. Open Bank Holiday Mondays, Good Friday and Easter Saturday.

Clandon Park, Surrey, above and below: built to impress

Clandon Park

West Clandon, Guildford, Surrey GU4 7RQ

Map ② F6   🏠 ❀ 🔔 🍷 | 1956 |

Designed to impress and entertain, Clandon Park was built around 1730 for the 2nd Lord Onslow by Venetian architect Giacomo Leoni, and is one of England's most complete examples of a Palladian mansion. It contains a superb collection of 18th-century furniture, porcelain and textiles, mostly acquired in the 1920s by connoisseur Mrs Gubbay. The intimate gardens are home to the only Maori meeting house in the UK – brought from New Zealand in 1892. The wider parkland is privately owned by the Onslows – a family with a great political history and unique in providing three Speakers of the House of Commons. **Note**: lift availability restricted (booking essential).

Eating and shopping: shop in 19th-century kitchen. Undercroft restaurant (National Trust-approved concession). Picnic area.

Claremont Landscape Garden

Portsmouth Road, Esher, Surrey KT10 9JG

Map (2) F6 ❖ 1949

Hidden in the heart of Surrey, but within easy reach of London, Claremont is not a typical garden of herbaceous borders; instead it is a green oasis, with ever-changing views and secret glades. A delightful landscape garden where you can escape everyday life and enjoy simple pleasures with family and friends. Once the garden of some of the richest and most powerful people in the country, today the grounds are open for everyone to explore. Unexpected features are a serpentine lake overlooked by an impressive turf amphitheatre and grotto, as well as the camellia terrace, skittle alley and children's play areas.
Note: limited parking during busy times. Please park considerately to maximise spaces available.

Two views of the impressive turf amphitheatre at Claremont Landscape Garden, Surrey

Eating and shopping: café (licensed) serving lunches and homemade cakes, biscuits and scones freshly baked every morning. Outside terraced seating area overlooking lake. Café is outside the pay barrier and situated close to the car park at the main entrance. Free wi-fi.

Making the most of your day: events throughout the year, including children's trails, crafts and activities during school holidays. Guided walks. Belvedere Tower open on selected dates (April to October).
Dogs: welcome on leads between 1 November and 31 March only.

Access for all: 🅿️ 🦮 🚾 ♿ 🪑 👓 📷
Grounds ♿ ➡️ ♿

Getting here: see website for details.
Sat Nav: unreliable, instead follow brown signs from Cobham and Esher. **Parking**: free. Main car park at entrance. Limited at busy times – use car park in West End Lane opposite.

Finding out more: 01372 467806 or claremont@nationaltrust.org.uk

Claremont Landscape Garden		M	T	W	T	F	S	S
1 Jan–31 Jan	10–4*	M	T	W	T	F	S	S
1 Feb–31 Mar	10–5*	M	T	W	T	F	S	S
1 Apr–31 Oct	10–6*	M	T	W	T	F	S	S
1 Nov–24 Dec	10–4*	M	T	W	T	F	S	S
26 Dec–31 Dec	10–4*	M	T	W		F	S	S

*Café and shop close 30 minutes earlier than garden.
Closed 25 December. Belvedere Tower open 1 January, 11 to 2, and first weekend of month April to October, 2 to 4.
Late night opening 7 June until 9.

Claydon

Middle Claydon, near Buckingham,
Buckinghamshire MK18 2EY

Map (2) D3 🏛️➕✳️⚓🔔⛲ 1956

Nestled in peaceful parkland, with tranquil lake walks, this Georgian home hides a lavish interior that left the 18th-century Verney family facing financial ruin. Rococo carvings frame portraits of interesting characters, from Civil War heroes to Barbary buccaneers. This inspirational place is where Florence Nightingale, sister of Lady Parthenope Verney, spent her summers. **Note**: gardens (not National Trust) opened by permission of the Verney family. Garden entry charges apply (including members).

Eating and shopping: second-hand bookshop and small gift shop. Courtyard shops, seasonal kitchen garden produce, restaurant and tea-room (not National Trust). Picnics welcome.

Making the most of your day: talking pictures, children's trails, 17th-century Verney family costume exhibition, replica costume to try on, family school holiday activities and lake walks. Waddesdon Manor and Stowe both nearby.
Dogs: welcome in park on leads.

Access for all: 🅿️♿️🚻♿️🔍📷💺🖼️VT♿️👓
House ♿️♿️♿️ Grounds ♿️♿️➡️

Getting here: see website for details.
Parking: free.

Finding out more: 01296 730349 or claydon@nationaltrust.org.uk

Claydon			M	T	W	T	F	S	S
15 Mar–2 Nov	11–5		**M**	**T**	**W**	·	·	**S**	**S**

For garden opening times call 01296 730252.
Restaurant open 12 to 3. Open Good Friday.

Surrounded by parkland and with a lake in front, the setting of Claydon in Buckinghamshire could hardly be bettered. Inside, the cost of creating the lavish interiors almost ruined the Verney family

Cliveden

Cliveden Road, Taplow, Maidenhead, Buckinghamshire SL6 0JA

Map (2) E5 1942

Set high above the River Thames with far-reaching views, these gardens capture the grandeur of a bygone age. A glittering hub of society for more than 300 years, Cliveden was renowned for hosting glamorous parties and exclusive political gatherings – especially when home to Nancy and Waldorf Astor in the early 20th century. Today you can stroll through a series of impressive gardens, each with vibrant seasonal planting. Miles of walks, many open throughout the year, meander through the majestic woodlands and along picturesque riverbank paths. For families it's a special place to explore, with a giant maze and storybook-themed play area. A short guided tour of part of the house (now a hotel) is available on certain days. **Note**: mooring charge on Cliveden Reach, £8 per 24 hours (including members), does not include entry.

Eating and shopping: Dovecote Coffee House serving morning coffee and afternoon tea. Lunch (12 to 2:30) and snacks available at the Orangery Café. Doll's House (café and shop), beside play area, designed especially for families. Shop, including plant sales. Picnics welcome.

Making the most of your day: highlights for families include the storybook-themed play area, yew tree maze and free seasonal trails, as well as the woodland play trail and den-building area.

The gardens at Cliveden, Buckinghamshire, capture the grandeur of a bygone age

The introductory film *Cliveden: Camelot on Thames* sets the scene. Events, including open-air theatre, family fun days and guided walks. Summertime boat trips on the Thames (additional charge). Greys Court and Hughenden are nearby. **Dogs**: welcome under close control in woodlands only.

Access for all:
House **Garden**

Getting here: see website for details.
Sat Nav: use Cliveden Road and SL1 8NS.
Parking: free.

Finding out more: 01628 605069 or cliveden@nationaltrust.org.uk

Cliveden		M	T	W	T	F	S	S
Woodland								
1 Jan–14 Feb	10–4	M	T	W	T	F	S	S
Garden, shop, café and woodland*								
15 Feb–26 Oct	10–5:30	M	T	W	T	F	S	S
27 Oct–31 Dec	10–4	M	T	W	T	F	S	S
House (part), chapel								
3 Apr–26 Oct	3–5:30	·	·	·	T	·	·	S

*Shop closed 25 to 31 December. Admission to house by timed ticket only. Property closed 25 December.

Dorneywood Garden

Dorneywood, Dorney Wood Road, Burnham,
Buckinghamshire SL1 8PY

Map ②E5   ✿ 1942

Ministerial residence with country garden.
Afternoon teas. Open selected afternoons
(dates may change at short notice).
Note: no photography. Booking essential.
Visitor details recorded for security reasons.

Finding out more:
dorneywood@nationaltrust.org.uk

Emmetts Garden

Ide Hill, Sevenoaks, Kent TN14 6BA

Map ②H6   ✿🏊 1965

Emmetts is an Edwardian estate once owned
by Frederic Lubbock and influenced by
William Robinson. The idyllic hillside garden
was laid out in the late 19th century and
contains many exotic and rare plants from
around the world. We are best known for
our amazing spring colour and bluebell
display and vibrant autumn foliage but there
is something to see all year round. There are
fantastic walks, with spectacular views,
around the neighbouring countryside which
start at Emmetts.

A sea of bluebells, above, at Emmetts Garden in Kent, and
the Rose Garden fountain, below

Eating and shopping: Stable tea-room serving
sandwiches and cakes. Shop selling a variety of
plants, gifts, food and drink.

Making the most of your day: events all year.
Garden tours (selected days). Children's
activities. Walk guides for the surrounding
countryside. **Dogs**: on short leads only.

Access for all: 🅿️♿🚻🦽📷♿
Grounds 🦽➡️♿

Getting here: see website for details.
Parking: free, 100 yards.

Finding out more: 01732 750367 or
emmetts@nationaltrust.org.uk

Emmetts Garden		M	T	W	T	F	S	S
1 Mar–31 Dec	10–5	M	T	W	T	F	S	S

Last admission 45 minutes before closing. Closes dusk if
earlier. Closed 24 and 25 December.

Members may have to pay on special events days

Great Coxwell Barn

Great Coxwell, Faringdon, Oxfordshire SN7 7LZ

Map ② C4   🏠 1956

Former 13th-century monastic barn, a favourite of William Morris, who would regularly bring his guests to wonder at its structure.
Note: sorry no toilet; narrow access lanes leading to property.

Finding out more: 01793 762209 or greatcoxwellbarn@nationaltrust.org.uk

Greys Court

Rotherfield Greys, Henley-on-Thames, Oxfordshire RG9 4PG

Map ② D5   🏠❋🛏 1969

An intimate family home and peaceful estate set in the rolling hills of the Chilterns. This picturesque 16th-century mansion and tranquil gardens were home to the Brunner family until recent years. The house exudes a welcoming atmosphere, with a well-stocked kitchen and homely living rooms. The series of walled gardens stands out as a patchwork of colour amid the medieval ruins. Other buildings from earlier eras include the 12th-century Great Tower and a rare Tudor donkey wheel, still in use until the early 20th century.

Eating and shopping: new tea-room serving morning coffee, afternoon tea, lunches and snacks. Family-inspired shop. Seasonal organic produce from gardens (when available).

Making the most of your day: new outdoor children's play area. Open-air events and wider estate walks. Family activities, including explorer packs and garden and house trails. Nuffield Place nearby. **Dogs**: welcome on estate walk.

Access for all: 🅿♿🚻♿👜🐾📷📖Ⓐ
House 🅶 Tea-room 🅶 Grounds 🅶♿

Getting here: see website for details.
Parking: free, 220 yards.

Finding out more: 01494 755564 (Infoline). 01491 628529 or greyscourt@nationaltrust.org.uk

Greys Court		M	T	W	T	F	S	S
3 Mar–2 Nov	10–5*	M	T	W	T	F	S	S
3 Nov–31 Dec**	10–4*	M	T	W	T	F	S	S

*House opens at 11, entry by guided tour between 11 and 1.
**November house entry by guided tour only. Limited number of tickets available at property. Closes dusk if earlier. Property closed 7 September, 24 and 25 December.

Greys Court, Oxfordshire: the School Room, above, and the kitchen, below

Hartwell House Hotel, Restaurant and Spa

Oxford Road, near Aylesbury, Buckinghamshire HP17 8NR

Map ② E3 🏠❄️♿🛏️🔔🍷 2008

Elegant Grade I listed stately home with magnificent grounds, including ruined church, lake, bridge and 36 hectares (90 acres) of parkland. **Note**: access is for paying guests of the hotel, including for luncheon, afternoon tea and dinner. Held on a long lease from the Ernest Cook Trust.

Finding out more: 01296 747444.
01296 747450 (fax) or
info@hartwell-house.com
www.hartwell-house.com

Hatchlands Park

East Clandon, Guildford, Surrey GU4 7RT

Map ② F6 🏠❄️♿ 1945

Hatchlands Park was built in the 1750s for Admiral Boscawen, a Georgian naval hero. The mansion is set in informal grounds, with one parterre garden designed by Gertrude Jekyll. The extensive surrounding parkland provides waymarked walks in a tranquil setting, including a beautiful display of bluebells in the ancient woodland. Today the mansion is a family home, containing tenant Alec Cobbe's superb collection of paintings. The six ground-floor rooms also display the Cobbe Collection, Europe's largest collection of keyboard instruments associated with famous composers such as J. C. Bach, Chopin and Elgar. **Note**: National Gardens Scheme (NGS) quiet garden open for the first time.

Eating and shopping: tea-room (National Trust-approved concession) in the original kitchen. Gift shop.

Hatchlands Park, Surrey: a detail of the Adam fireplace

Making the most of your day: children's trails and adventure area, events, cellar tours (selected days), exhibition in the Old Stable, Cobbe Collection Trust concerts. Guided mansion tours most Thursdays. Clandon Park only 2 miles away. **Dogs**: welcome under close control in designated parkland areas only.

Access for all: 📸♿🚻🦽🧸📷🎧👜👓
Building 🚶‍♀️🦽♿ Grounds �▶️🚶

Getting here: see website for details.
Sat Nav: can be misleading – follow brown signs to main entrance on A246.
Parking: free, 300 yards.

Finding out more: 01483 222482 or hatchlands@nationaltrust.org.uk

Hatchlands Park		M	T	W	T	F	S	S
House and garden*								
1 Apr–31 Jul	2–5:30	·	T	W	T	·	·	S
1 Aug–31 Aug	2–5:30	·	T	W	T	F	·	S
2 Sep–30 Oct	2–5:30	·	T	W	T	·	·	S
Park walks and NGS quiet garden								
1 Apr–2 Nov	10:30–6	M	T	W	T	F	S	S
Shop and tea-room**								
1 Apr–2 Nov	10:30–5:30	·	T	W	T	·	S	S

*Garden open 10:30 to 6 on house open days. **Shop and tea-room open Mondays and Fridays in August. Open Bank Holiday Mondays. Timed tickets may be used at busy periods.

Hinton Ampner

Hinton Ampner, near Alresford,
Hampshire SO24 0LA

Map ② D7 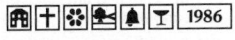 1986

This elegant country house and tranquil garden sit so harmoniously within the landscape that one would be lost without the other. The house was lovingly rebuilt by its last owner, Ralph Dutton, after a catastrophic fire in 1960, and its beautifully proportioned rooms house his exquisite collection of ceramics and art. Each window looks out onto the delightful views beyond; manicured lawns lead the eye down avenues of topiary, past borders full of fragrant roses, to breathtaking views across the South Downs. Newly opened parkland, dotted with ancient oaks, creates a pastoral idyll in which to roam.

Eating and shopping: Stables tea-room serving seasonal dishes, homemade cakes and cream teas, made using produce grown in our walled garden. Shop selling many locally sourced products, including estate-grown plants.

Hinton Ampner, Hampshire, above: a tranquil garden surrounds the elegant house containing an exquisite collection of art and ceramics

Making the most of your day: open all year, new estate walking trails and free seasonal garden walks. Conservation demonstrations (Wednesday). Children's trails and events programme. Uppark House and Garden and Winchester City Mill nearby. **Dogs**: welcome on leads in parkland, estate walks and tea-room courtyard.

Access for all: 🅿️♿🚾🏠🔊🗣️📷🏛️🎧👶🅰️
Building ♿🅱️ Grounds ♿➡️🅱️

Getting here: see website for details.
Parking: free.

Finding out more: 01962 771305 or hintonampner@nationaltrust.org.uk

Hinton Ampner		M	T	W	T	F	S	S
Marble Hall*								
1 Jan–26 Jan	10–4	M	T	W	T	F	S	S
27 Dec–31 Dec	10–4	M	T	W	.	.	S	S
House								
1 Feb–28 Feb**	10–4	M	T	W	T	F	S	S
1 Mar–2 Nov	11–5	M	T	W	T	F	S	S
3 Nov–2 Dec	10–4	M	T	W	T	F	S	S
6 Dec–14 Dec*	10–4	M	T	W	T	F	S	S
Estate, garden, shop and tea-room								
Open all year	10–4†	M	T	W	T	F	S	S

*Exhibition only. **1 to 14 February 30-minute guided tours of selected rooms only, entry by timed ticket available on day. 15 to 28 February free-flow. †From 1 March to 2 November, shop and tea-room open until 5:30, estate and garden open until 6. Whole property closed 24 and 25 December.

The Homewood

Portsmouth Road, Esher, Surrey KT10 9JL

Map ② F6   🏠 ✻ 1999

Extraordinary Modernist house and landscape garden, designed in 1938 by the architect Patrick Gwynne. **Note**: administered on behalf of the National Trust by a tenant. Sorry no toilet. Additional charge for minibus and guided tour (including members).

Finding out more: 01372 476424 or thehomewood@nationaltrust.org.uk. c/o Claremont Landscape Garden, Portsmouth Road, Esher, Surrey KT10 9JG

Handsome Hughenden in Buckinghamshire: the perfect place to relax and unwind

Hughenden

High Wycombe, Buckinghamshire HP14 4LA

Map ② E4   🏠 ✝ ✻ 🐾 ⊤ 1947

It's hardly surprising that the colourful Victorian Prime Minister Benjamin Disraeli fell in love with Hughenden. This handsome home, set in a timeless Chiltern valley with fine views and woodland walks, is still the perfect place to relax and unwind today. His hillside hideaway later became the HQ for a top-secret, Second World War operation that put Hughenden high on Hitler's hit list. A replica air-raid shelter, 1940s living room and ice-house bunker bring wartime Britain to life. With red kites soaring over ancient woods and views over rolling parkland, Hughenden is a truly magical place.

Eating and shopping: Stableyard café selling locally sourced hot meals, sandwiches, cakes and drinks. Gift shop stocks local produce, such as ales and honey, as well as Disraeli and 'Hillside' memorabilia. Second-hand bookshop and home-grown plants.

Making the most of your day: morning guided tour of manor. Free introductory talks throughout the day. Children's trails in the manor and walled garden.

Woodland walks (maps available). West Wycombe Park, Village and Hill nearby. **Dogs**: welcome in orchard, park and woodland. Assistance dogs only in formal gardens.

Access for all: 🅿️♿🚗♿🚻♿🖐♿📷💻🔎 ··🅿️
Manor ♿🏠♿   Grounds ♿♿

Getting here: see website for details.
Parking: free.

Finding out more: 01494 755565 (Infoline). 01494 755573 or hughenden@nationaltrust.org.uk

Hughenden		M	T	W	T	F	S	S
Manor, garden, shop and restaurant								
1 Jan–14 Feb*	11–3	M	T	W	T	F	S	S
15 Feb–31 Dec	10–5:30**	M	T	W	T	F	S	S
Park								
Open all year	Dawn–dusk	M	T	W	T	F	S	S

*Special winter indoor offer, telephone or see website for details and times. **Manor open at 11 and closes at 5. Closes dusk if earlier. Closed 24 and 25 December.

Ightham Mote

Mote Road, Ivy Hatch, Sevenoaks,
Kent TN15 0NT

Map ② H6   🏠 ✿ 🖼 🛏 ⊤ | 1985 |

Hidden deep in the Kent countryside, a sense
of magic surrounds this romantic, medieval
moated manor house. Spanning centuries, if
walls could talk it would have a lot to say; the
crypt of a medieval knight, the painted ceiling
of a Tudor courtier, a Victorian gentleman's
billiard-room and an American's take on an
English country paradise. The tranquil garden
features lakes, an orchard and flower borders,
whilst the wider estate, with its secret glades
and wonderful views, is breathtaking.
Note: very steep slope from reception
(lower drop-off point available).

Eating and shopping: Mote Restaurant serving
hot lunches, sandwiches, cream teas, cakes and
hot, cold, alcoholic and non-alcoholic beverages.
Shop selling gifts, local produce and plants.

Making the most of your day: events
throughout the year, including theatre
productions, themed restaurant evenings,
behind-the-scenes events, arts and crafts
courses, countryside walks, outdoor activities
and family fun days. **Dogs**: welcome on estate
and restaurant patio area.

**With a history spanning centuries, romantic moated
Ightham Mote in Kent has many stories to tell**

Access for all: 🅿️🐕🦽♿🚹🔛🅿️📷💻📹🚶
👁️🅰️ Building 🪜🧗♿🚹🚻 Grounds ♿➡️

Getting here: see website for details.
Parking: 200 yards.

Finding out more: 01732 810378 or
ighthammote@nationaltrust.org.uk

Ightham Mote		M	T	W	T	F	S	S
Shop, restaurant and garden								
1 Feb–23 Feb	11–3	·	·	·	·	·	S	S
House, shop, restaurant and garden								
1 Mar–2 Nov	10:30–5*	M	T	W	T	F	S	S
3 Nov–31 Dec**	11–3	M	T	W	T	F	S	S
Estate								
Open all year	Dawn–dusk	M	T	W	T	F	S	S

*House opens at 11. **November: admission to house on
complimentary tours only. December: ground floor of house
open and dressed for Christmas, hard-path garden open.
Closed 24 and 25 December.

King's Head

King's Head Passage, Market Square, Aylesbury,
Buckinghamshire HP20 2RW

Map ② E3   🏠 ⊤ | 1925 |

Historic public house dating back to 1455, with
a pleasant family atmosphere. This is one of
England's best-preserved coaching inns.
Note: Farmers' Bar leased by Chiltern Brewery.

Finding out more: 01296 718812
(Farmers' Bar). 01280 817156 (National Trust)
or kingshead@nationaltrust.org.uk

![Knole house viewed across the grounds with trees]

Knole

Sevenoaks, Kent TN15 0RP

Map ② H6  1946

This year, we begin our mission to transform this beautiful place. Built as a palace in a medieval deer-park, Knole was owned by the Archbishops of Canterbury, the Tudor dynasty and the Sackville family, who live here still. Although quietly gleaming, the house bears the marks of six centuries of history, and now stands on the brink of an exciting project, during which we plan to refurbish the show rooms and open the attics and tower rooms. We are also starting to build Knole Studios, creating a new conservation studio, learning centre and café. Even though we have a significant project underway, we want to share Knole for longer, so we are opening the park and Brewhouse Café Outdoors year-round.

Eating and shopping: limited refreshments served outdoors while our café is being built. Picnic in Green Court (on blankets) or enjoy the park at our picnic tables. Shop selling local produce, books, gifts and pocket-money toys.

Making the most of your day: our Estate Office, with its typewriter, adding machine, estate documents and traditional furniture, tells a story of Knole in the 20th century and life pre-dating the electronic age. Changing art exhibitions in the Orangery. Guided walks in our parkland, a Site of Special Scientific Interest (find out more in our Park Experience Room). Conservation talks and tours. Family holiday events, including park activities, Tudor dressing-up days and trails in the showrooms and courtyards. Show rooms accessed via steps; please ask us how we can help you access our spaces. Ightham Mote, Chartwell, Emmetts Garden, Scotney Castle and Sissinghurst Castle nearby. **Dogs**: welcome in park on leads.

Access for all: 🅿️🦽♿🚻🧷🧸🎒📷📹♿
👁️🐕 Show rooms ♿♿♿ Orangery ♿♿♿
Garden/park ♿♿➡️♿

Already fascinating, Knole in Kent is being transformed, with plans to open new rooms and refurbish old ones

Getting here: see website for details.
Sat Nav: use TN13 1HU and follow brown signs to park entrance. **Parking**: 60 yards, available when Knole is open, otherwise parking in nearby town centre.

Finding out more: 01732 462100 or knole@nationaltrust.org.uk

Knole		M	T	W	T	F	S	S
Show rooms								
8 Mar–2 Nov	12–4	·	T	W	T	F	S	S
Visitor centre, Orangery, Estate Office, shop, courtyards								
8 Mar–2 Nov	10:30–5	·	T	W	T	F	S	S
5 Nov–21 Dec	11–4	·	·	W	T	F	S	S
Outdoor Café								
Open all year*	10:30–5	M	T	W	T	F	S	S
Garden								
1 Apr–30 Sep	11–4	·	T	·	·	·	·	·

Open Bank Holiday Mondays (garden excluded). Open on Mondays 7, 14 April, 28 July, 4, 11, 18 August, 1 September and 27 October (showrooms and garden excluded). Timed tickets may be in operation. *January, February, November and December café open 11 to 4; closed 24 and 25 December. Car park open year round, 10:15 to 6; closed 24 and 25 December. Park open daily for pedestrians and cyclists.

Lamb House

West Street, Rye, East Sussex TN31 7ES

Map ② J8    1950

Georgian house with walled garden in picturesque Rye, home to Henry James, E. F. Benson and other celebrated writers. **Note**: open Tuesday and Saturday afternoons. Maintained on the National Trust's behalf by a tenant. Sorry no toilets.

Finding out more: 01580 762334 or lambhouse@nationaltrust.org.uk

Long Crendon Courthouse

Long Crendon, Aylesbury, Buckinghamshire HP18 9AN

Map ② D4   1900

Superb example of a 14th-century courthouse with a wealth of local history – the second building acquired by the Trust. **Note**: extremely steep stairs. Sorry no toilet.

Finding out more: 01280 817156 or longcrendon@nationaltrust.org.uk

Monk's House

Rodmell, Lewes, East Sussex BN7 3HF

Map ② G8    1980

Novelist Virginia Woolf's country home and retreat, a charming weatherboarded cottage – featuring the room where she created her best-known works.

Finding out more: 01273 474760 or monkshouse@nationaltrust.org.uk

Mottisfont

near Romsey, Hampshire SO51 0LP

Map (2) C7 🏠🌼🍴🍸 1957

Once across the crystal-clear river, visitors enter a piece of paradise. Ancient trees, babbling brooks and rolling lawns frame this lovely old house. An 18th-century home with a medieval priory at its heart, Mottisfont inspired a 1930s dream of creativity. Artists came here to relax and create works, some of which are still visible in our historic rooms. This tradition continues today, along with major exhibitions in our top-floor gallery. Outside, carpets of spring bulbs, a walled rose garden, rich autumn leaves and a colourful winter garden make Mottisfont a feast for the senses all year round. **Note**: National Collection of Old-fashioned Roses (usually flowering June).

Eating and shopping: Kitchen Café serving meals and cakes. Ice-cream parlour. Spacious shop. Second-hand books. Plant sales.

Mottisfont in Hampshire, below and opposite: a piece of paradise which inspired a 1930s dream of creativity

Making the most of your day: open-air theatre and events throughout the year. Free daily guided walks and talks. Family fun activities, including building dens, make-and-take days and a new wild play area. Changing exhibitions in the art gallery. New this summer: Quentin Blake comes to Mottisfont, with an exhibition of classic children's illustrations and a new creative family trail. Seasonal variety in the Winter Garden, with 60,000 spring bulbs and late summer borders. Wider estate to explore on foot or by bike. **Dogs**: welcome on short leads in most of grounds and garden.

Access for all: 🅿️♿🚻♿♿📷📺🎫👓📷
Building 🏢🏢♿ Grounds ♿➡️

Getting here: see website for details.
Sat Nav: use SO51 0LN. **Parking**: free.

Finding out more: 01794 340757 or mottisfont@nationaltrust.org.uk

Mottisfont		M	T	W	T	F	S	S
Garden, shop, café and art gallery								
Open all year	10–5*	M	T	W	T	F	S	S
House								
1 Mar–2 Nov	11–5	M	T	W	T	F	S	S

*Art gallery opens at 11. Gallery closes for short periods to change exhibitions. Closed 24 and 25 December. Closes at dusk if earlier. Late opening during rose season in June and July (except house and café), subject to weather.

Always remember your current membership card

Mottistone Gardens

Mottistone, near Brighstone,
Isle of Wight PO30 4EA

Map ② C9 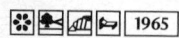 1965

Set in a sheltered valley, this magical garden is full of surprises, with shrub-filled banks, hidden pathways and colourful herbaceous borders. Surrounding an attractive Elizabethan manor house (tenanted so not open), this 20th-century garden is experimenting with a Mediterranean-style planting scheme to take advantage of its southerly location. Other surprises include a young olive grove, a small organic kitchen garden and a traditional tea-garden set alongside The Shack, a unique cabin retreat designed as their summer drawing office by architects John Seely (2nd Lord Mottistone) and Paul Paget. There are also delightful walks across the adjoining Mottistone Estate. **Note**: manor house open two days a year.

Eating and shopping: shop selling gifts, books, cards and postcards. Plant stall. Second-hand books. Tea-garden serving ice-cream, hot and cold drinks, soup, sandwiches, cake and light refreshments (not National Trust). Picnic table.

Making the most of your day: family events and garden tours. Flowerpot trail and estate walks. Newtown Old Town Hall and The Needles Old Battery and New Battery nearby. **Dogs**: welcome on leads.

Access for all: ⏚ ⏚ ⏚ ⏚ ⏚ ⏚ ⏚ ⏚ ⏚ ⏚
The Shack ⏚ ⏚ Garden ⏚ ⏚ ➡ ⏚

Getting here: see website for details.
Parking: free, 50 yards.

Finding out more: 01983 741302 or mottistonegardens@nationaltrust.org.uk

Mottistone Gardens			M	T	W	T	F	S	S
16 Mar–30 Oct	11–5		M	T	W	T	·	·	S

Closes dusk if earlier. Manor House open two days only: Sunday 25 May (members only), guided tours 9:30 to 12 by timed ticket (available on day), free-flow 1 to 5; Monday 26 May open 11 to 5 (additional charges apply).

Colourful 20th-century Mottistone Gardens on the Isle of Wight

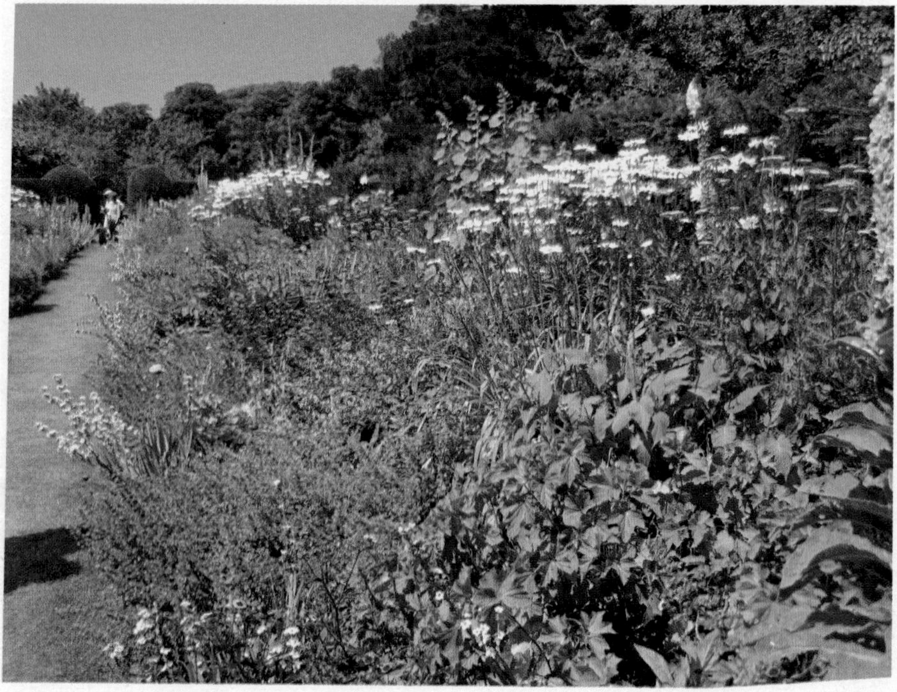

The Needles Old Battery on the Isle of Wight

The Needles Old Battery and New Battery

West High Down, Alum Bay,
Isle of Wight PO39 0JH

Map ② C9  1975

Perched high above The Needles, amid acres of unspoilt countryside, is The Needles Old Battery, a Victorian fort built in 1862 and used throughout both World Wars. The Parade Ground has two original guns, and the fort's fascinating military history is brought to life with displays and models, plus a series of vivid cartoons by acclaimed comic book artist Geoff Campion. An underground tunnel leads to a searchlight emplacement with dramatic views over The Needles rocks. The New Battery, further up the headland, has an exhibition on the secret British rocket tests carried out there during the Cold War. **Note**: steep paths and uneven surfaces. Spiral staircase to tunnel. Toilet at Old Battery only.

Eating and shopping: clifftop tea-room serving soup, sandwiches, cakes and light refreshments. Picnic tables (Parade Ground).

Guardroom shop selling postcards, gifts and souvenirs. Refreshments, snacks and ice-cream available at New Battery kiosk.

Making the most of your day: family events. Family activity packs, inspector trail and soldier trail. Clifftop walks to Tennyson Monument and beyond. **Dogs**: welcome on leads, although assistance dogs only in tea-room.

Access for all: 🅿🚾♿🖐📷🖼🚶♿
Old Battery 🖼♿🚶♿ New Battery 🖼

Getting here: see website for details.
Parking: no parking on site. Limited disabled parking by arrangement. Alum Bay ¾ mile (not National Trust, minimum £4). Freshwater Bay 3½ miles (not National Trust), or Highdown (SZ325856) 2 miles, both across Downs.

Finding out more: 01983 754772 or needlesoldbattery@nationaltrust.org.uk

The Needles Batteries		M	T	W	T	F	S	S
Tea-room								
4 Jan–2 Mar	11–3	·	·	·	·	·	S	S
15 Feb–23 Feb	11–3	M	T	W	T	F	S	S
8 Nov–14 Dec	11–3	·	·	·	·	·	S	S
New Battery, Old Battery and tea-room								
15 Mar–2 Nov	10:30–5*	M	T	W	T	F	S	S

*New Battery open 11 to 4. Old Battery closes dusk if earlier. Property closes in high winds. 11 May: no disabled vehicular access due to Walk the Wight. 21 June: Old Battery early opening (6:30) for Round the Island Yacht Race.

Quirky Newtown Old Town Hall, Isle of Wight

Newtown Old Town Hall

Newtown, near Shalfleet,
Isle of Wight PO30 4PA

Map ② C9 🏠 ♨ 🏛 ✦ 1933

Tucked away in a tiny hamlet adjoining the National Nature Reserve, this small and quirky 17th-century building is the only remaining evidence of Newtown's former importance. It's hard to believe that this tranquil corner of the island once held what were often turbulent elections before sending two Members to Parliament. **Note**: nearest toilet in car park.

Eating and shopping: postcards and souvenirs available.

Making the most of your day: children's quiz sheet. Exhibitions by local artists. Walks around adjoining National Nature Reserve. Outdoor family activities (bookable) run by Newtown Ranger from nearby Visitor Point (01983 531622).

Access for all: 🚻♿📷🏛♿♿📷 Building ♿

Getting here: see website for details.
Parking: free, 15 yards.

Finding out more: 01983 531785 or oldtownhall@nationaltrust.org.uk

Newtown Old Town Hall		M	T	W	T	F	S	S
16 Mar–29 Jun	2–5	·	T	W	T	·	·	S
30 Jun–31 Aug	2–5	M	T	W	T	·	·	S
2 Sep–23 Oct	2–5	·	T	W	T	·	·	S

Last admission 15 minutes before closing. Closes dusk if earlier. Open Bank Holiday Mondays.

We welcome dogs assisting visitors with disabilities

Nuffield Place

Huntercombe, near Henley-on-Thames,
Oxfordshire RG9 5RY

Map (2) D5   🏛 ❀ 2011

Finding out more: 01491 641224 or
nuffieldplace@nationaltrust.org.uk

Nuffield Place				M	T	W	T	F	S	S
2 Apr–2 Nov	11–5					W	T	F	S	S

Open Bank Holiday Mondays. Closed Sunday 27 April and
Sunday 29 June. Timed tickets may be used on certain days.

Home of Britain's greatest philanthropist,
William Morris, Lord Nuffield, the founder of
Morris Motor Cars and one of the richest men
in the world. The house and collection provide
a glimpse into the lifestyle of this modest
millionaire. Comprising everyday objects,
it reflects the tastes of the 1930s.

Eating and shopping: tea-room serving
light lunches and afternoon tea. Shop selling
unique Nuffield Place products, gifts, books
and postcards.

Making the most of your day: children's
house guide, quizzes, woodland trails and
gardens. Greys Court nearby. **Dogs**: on leads
in woodland.

Access for all: 🅿♿   **Building** 🚶   **Grounds** 🚶

Getting here: see website for details.
Parking: free.

Nuffield Place, Oxfordshire, below, and Lord Nuffield's
well-stocked tool cupboard, above, which was housed in
his bedroom wardrobe

Nymans

Handcross, near Haywards Heath,
West Sussex RH17 6EB

Map ② G7 🏠 ❀ 🎠 🛏 🔔 🍸 1954

In the late 19th century, Ludwig Messel bought
the Nymans Estate in the High Weald to make a
dream family home. Inspired by the beautiful
wooded surroundings, he created a stunning
garden with plants collected from around the
world. Here this incredibly creative family
entertained friends and family and enjoyed
relaxing, playing and picnicking in the garden
and woods. Today Nymans is still a garden
lovers' home – a place to relax all year round
and enjoy a peaceful country garden. Partially
destroyed by fire in 1947, the romantic ruins of
a fairytale Gothic mansion remain alongside
the surviving Messel Family Rooms. Nymans is
one of the Trust's greenest properties and aims
to inspire a more sustainable way of living.

Eating and shopping: large shop, plant and
garden centre offering Nymans' collection
of plants. Redesigned café serving a choice of
fresh, seasonal food. 'Grab and go' kiosk in
the tea-garden. Woodland craft sales.
Second-hand bookshop.

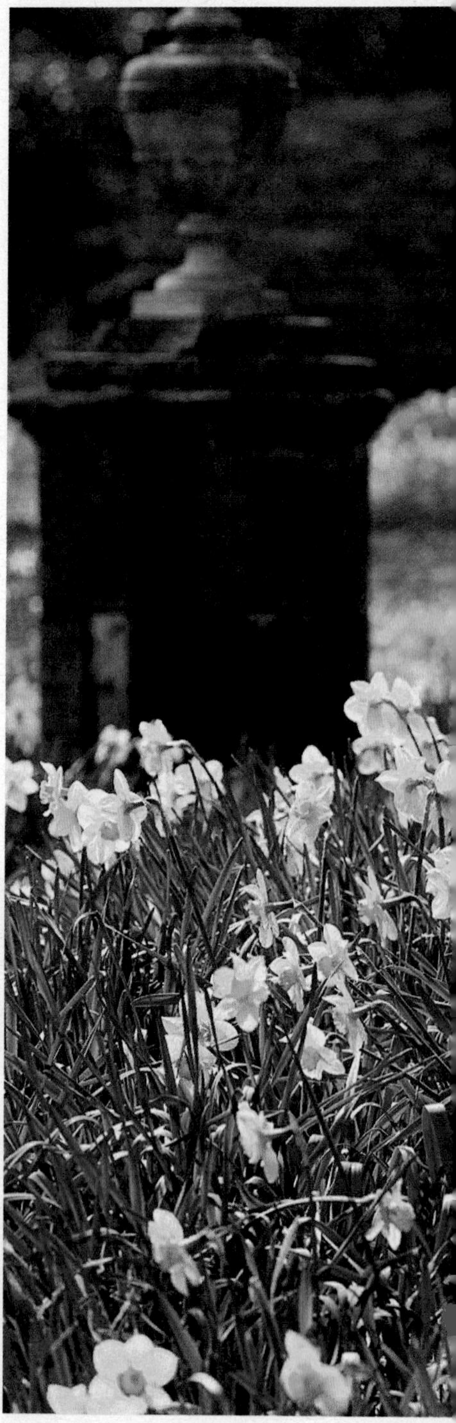

Two views of Nymans in West Sussex: the stunning garden was created by Ludwig Messel and contains plants collected from around the world

Making the most of your day: daily guided walks and talks in the garden or woods. Small gallery in the house with changing exhibitions every season. Mobility buggy tours of the garden or woods. Children will love our natural play trail, geocaching in the garden and woods, as well as the pick-up and go activities and school holiday trails. We also have art and craft workshops and gardening workshops throughout the year. **Dogs**: in woodland only, on leads during bird nesting season (1 March to 31 July).

Access for all: [symbols]
House [symbols]   Garden [symbols]

Getting here: see website for details.
Parking: free.

Finding out more: 01444 405250 or nymans@nationaltrust.org.uk

Nymans		M	T	W	T	F	S	S
Garden, woods, gallery, café and shops								
Open all year	10–5*	M	T	W	T	F	S	S
Messel Family Rooms								
1 Mar–31 Oct	11–3	M	T	W	T	F	S	S

*Gallery closes 30 minutes earlier and for short periods during the year to change exhibitions. Closed 25 and 26 December. November to February closes at 4. For more information and for any other changes, please see our website.

Oakhurst Cottage

Hambledon, near Godalming, Surrey GU8 4HF

Map ② E7   [symbols] [1952]

Quaint 16th-century cottage with contents spanning 400 years, with a delightful cottage garden. **Note**: sorry no toilet. Nearest visitor facilities at Winkworth Arboretum (4 miles approximately). Access by booked guided tour only and limited to a maximum of six visitors in the cottage at any one time.

Finding out more: 01483 208936 or oakhurstcottage@nationaltrust.org.uk

Old Soar Manor

Plaxtol, Borough Green, Kent TN15 0QX

Map (2) H6  1947

Dating from 1290, the remaining rooms of this knight's house offer a glimpse back to the time of Edward I. **Note**: sorry no toilet or restaurant. Narrow lanes, limited off-road parking.

Finding out more: 01732 810378 or oldsoarmanor@nationaltrust.org.uk

Owletts

The Street, Cobham, Gravesend, Kent DA12 3AP

Map (2) H5 1938

Dating back to the reign of Charles II, Owletts became the family home of the renowned architect Sir Herbert Baker.

Finding out more: 01732 810378 or owletts@nationaltrust.org.uk

Petworth House and Park

Petworth, West Sussex GU28 0AE

Map (2) E7  1947

Shaped by a family of collectors over the past 800 years, this 17th-century 'house of art' inspired countless artists, including England's greatest landscape painter J. M. W. Turner. The finest collection of art and sculpture in the National Trust, including world-famous paintings by Van Dyck, Reynolds, Blake and Turner himself, is displayed in the opulent staterooms and North Gallery. 'Below stairs', the Servants' Quarters tell a very different story, as the lives of cooks, maids and butlers are brought to life. Outdoors is a woodland Pleasure Ground and acres of 'Capability' Brown landscape park, with views over the South Downs National Park. Additional private rooms open on weekdays by kind permission of Lord and Lady Egremont. **Note**: additional charge for Christmas Fair and Winter Art Exhibition (including members).

Eating and shopping: Servants' Hall coffee shop and Audit Room restaurant. Gift shop selling presents, and children's books and toys.

Making the most of your day: events and activities, including talks, guided walks and behind-the-scenes tours. Family multimedia guide and trails, plus children's activities in the house. Multimedia tours and downloadable app. **Dogs**: under close control in Petworth Park. Assistance dogs only in Pleasure Ground.

Access for all: ⬚⬚⬚⬚⬚⬚⬚⬚⬚⬚⬚ ⬚⬚ **Building** ⬚⬚⬚

Getting here: see website for details. **Sat Nav**: use GU28 9LR. **Parking**: on A283, 700 yards. Charge for non-members. Separate car park for Petworth Park.

Finding out more: 01798 342207 or petworth@nationaltrust.org.uk

The west front of Petworth House and Park, West Sussex, above, and the opulent Grand Staircase, below

Petworth House and Park		M	T	W	T	F	S	S
House*								
15 Mar–5 Nov	11–5	M	T	W	·	·	S	S
Pleasure Ground, shop and restaurant								
11 Jan–14 Mar	10:30–3:30	M	T	W	T	F	S	S
15 Mar–5 Nov	10:30–5	M	T	W	T	F	S	S
6 Nov–31 Dec**	10:30–3:30	M	T	W	T	F	S	S

*On Thursdays and Fridays the house is closed, but Snapshot Tours are available, places limited. Extra rooms shown weekdays from 1: Monday (not Bank Holiday Mondays), White and Gold Room and White Library; Tuesday and Wednesday, three bedrooms on first floor.
**Closed 24 and 25 December.

Pitstone Windmill

Ivinghoe, Buckinghamshire

Map ② E3   ⬚ ⬚ 1937

One of the oldest windmills in the UK, with stunning views of the Chilterns. **Note**: sorry no toilet. At the end of a rough track.

Finding out more: 01442 851227 or pitstonemill@nationaltrust.org.uk

Polesden Lacey

Great Bookham, near Dorking, Surrey RH5 6BD

Map (2) F6  1942

'This is a delicious house…' remarked Queen Elizabeth, the Queen Mother on her honeymoon at Polesden Lacey. This country retreat, with glorious views across the rolling Surrey Hills and acres of countryside, was home to famous Edwardian hostess Mrs Greville, who entertained royalty and the celebrities of her time. The house has stunning interiors and contains Mrs Greville's fabulous collection of art and ceramics. The beautiful gardens have something to delight every season, including climbing roses, herbaceous borders and a winter garden. There are four waymarked walks around the estate offering a variety of features, including ancient woodland. Geocaching is a great way of enjoying the outdoors and is popular with all ages. **Note**: Christmas events – additional charge (including members).

Eating and shopping: restaurant and coffee shop offering home cooking, drinks and snacks made using fresh, seasonal and local produce. Gorgeous home and giftware, souvenirs and plants available to buy. All located outside the pay perimeter. Second-hand bookshop in the grounds.

Making the most of your day: free daily garden tours. Children will love dressing up, playing puff billiards or following the themed trail in the house, as well as having a go at clock golf in the gardens. The popular Glorious Glimpse house tours (weekends) return in January, February and November. We also have a wide variety of events, including family activities in the school holidays, live jazz every Sunday (June to August). If you fancy relaxing with friends and family, then just pull up one of our complimentary deckchairs. Why not stay longer? We have a charming three-bedroom holiday cottage available to rent. **Dogs**: on leads in designated areas, under close control on landscape walks, estate and farmland.

Access for all: ⭒⭒⭒⭒⭒⭒⭒⭒⭒⭒⭒
House ⭒⭒⭒ **Grounds** ⭒⭒⭒

Polesden Lacey in Surrey, home to indefatigable hostess Mrs Greville, far right. Right, one of the stunning interiors

For all enquiries telephone 0844 800 1895 (seven days a week)

Getting here: see website for details.
Parking: 200 yards (pay and display).

Finding out more: 01372 458203 (Infoline).
01372 452048 or
polesdenlacey@nationaltrust.org.uk

Polesden Lacey		M	T	W	T	F	S	S
House								
1 Mar–2 Nov*	11–5	**M**	**T**	**W**	**T**	**F**	**S**	**S**
Gardens, restaurant, shop and coffee shop**								
Open all year	10–5	**M**	**T**	**W**	**T**	**F**	**S**	**S**

*House can only be visited by guided tour weekdays from 11 to 12:30. Winter weekends: house open only for events, booking required on arrival. Charges apply for Christmas (including members). **Closed 25 February, 24 and 25 December. Facilities close at 4 in January, November and December. Car park open all year, 7:30 to 7:30.

Priory Cottages

1 Mill Street, Steventon, Abingdon,
Oxfordshire OX13 6SP

Map (2) C5   1939

Now converted into two houses, these former monastic buildings were gifted to the National Trust by the famous Ferguson's Gang.
Note: Priory Cottage South only open. Administered by a tenant (booking essential). Sorry no toilet.

Finding out more: 01793 762209 or
priorycottages@nationaltrust.org.uk

Quebec House

Quebec Square, Westerham, Kent TN16 1TD

Map (2) G6 🏠 ❀ ☂ | 1918 |

This small but charming house was General James Wolfe's childhood home, and gives a glimpse into family life in the 1730s. In our exhibition you can relive the dramatic battle that won North America but tragically ended in General Wolfe's death.

Eating and shopping: tea-room in the Coach House serving light refreshments.

Making the most of your day: events, including special talks, children's activities, living history and family trails. Exhibition.

Access for all: 🔤♿🚽🦻🔊🖼🎵👁🦽

Building ♿🦽 Grounds ♿▶🦽

Getting here: see website for details.
Parking: on A25, 80 yards via footpath.

Finding out more: 01959 567430 or quebechouse@nationaltrust.org.uk

Quebec House		M	T	W	T	F	S	S
1 Mar–31 Oct	11–5*			W	T	F	S	S
1 Nov–21 Dec	1–4						S	S

*The house opens one hour later at 12. Open Bank Holiday Mondays. Closes at dusk if earlier.

Quebec House in Kent: small and charming

River Wey and Godalming Navigations and Dapdune Wharf

Navigations Office and Dapdune Wharf, Wharf Road, Guildford, Surrey GU1 4RR

Map (2) F6 🏠♿☂ | 1964 |

A hidden haven where you can take a boat trip, explore a restored barge, or enjoy scenic walks. Dapdune Wharf in Guildford brings to life stories of this historical waterway, along 20 miles of waterside towpath. A great place for children to have fun – and raid our dressing-up box. **Note**: boat trip charges, mooring and fishing fees apply to members.

Eating and shopping: small tea-room serving sandwiches, cakes, ice-cream and drinks. Small shop with plant sales. Picnic areas at Dapdune Wharf.

Making the most of your day: year-round events, including events for children at Dapdune and guided walks along towpath and beyond. Guildford Festival Boat Gathering in July. Overnight moorings available. **Dogs**: on leads at Dapdune Wharf and lock areas; elsewhere under control.

Access for all: 🅿♿🚽🦻🔊👁🦽
Grounds 🦽

Peaceful spot on the River Wey, Surrey

Getting here: see website for details.
Parking: at Dapdune Wharf.

Finding out more: 01483 561389 or
riverwey@nationaltrust.org.uk

River Wey and Dapdune Wharf		M	T	W	T	F	S	S
Dapdune Wharf								
15 Mar–25 May	11–5	M	·	·	T	F	S	S
26 May–1 Jun	11–5	M	T	W	T	F	S	S
2 Jun–27 Jul	11–5	M	·	·	T	F	S	S
28 Jul–31 Aug	11–5	M	T	W	T	F	S	S
1 Sep–26 Oct	11–5	M	·	·	T	F	S	S
27 Oct–2 Nov	11–4	M	T	W	T	F	S	S

River trips from Dapdune Wharf 11 to 4 (conditions permitting). Access to towpath during daylight hours all year.

St John's Jerusalem

Sutton-at-Hone, Dartford, Kent DA4 9HQ

Map ② H5 ✚ ✷ 1943

13th-century chapel surrounded by a tranquil moated garden, once part of the former Commandery of the Knights Hospitallers.
Note: occupied as a private residence, maintained and managed by a tenant on behalf of the National Trust.

Finding out more: 01732 810378 or
stjohnsjerusalem@nationaltrust.org.uk

Sandham Memorial Chapel

Harts Lane, Burghclere, near Newbury, Hampshire RG20 9JT

Map ② C6 ✚ ✷ 1947

An outstanding series of large-scale paintings by acclaimed artist Stanley Spencer is usually housed in this modest red-brick building (below), which is closed for conservation works until late summer. During that time, a selection of the paintings can be seen on tour. **Note**: visit website for exhibition venues and dates.

Eating and shopping: books, postcards, locally made gifts and home-grown plants for sale. Picnics welcome in garden.

Making the most of your day: reference folders, children's quiz and handling kit available. **Dogs**: in grounds on leads only.

Access for all: 🅿️🎨🚶‍♀️👓📷
Building 🔵🔵 Grounds 🔵🔵

Getting here: see website for details.
Parking: in lay-by opposite, on road between church and village hall or village car park (¼ mile).

Finding out more: 01635 278394 or
sandham@nationaltrust.org.uk

Sandham Memorial Chapel		M	T	W	T	F	S	S
28 Jul–31 Oct*	10–4	M	T	W	T	F	S	S

*Property closed until late summer. Please check website for opening times and arrangements.

Scotney Castle, Kent: fairy-tale mix of country house, moated castle and romantic garden

Members may have to pay on special events days

Scotney Castle

Lamberhurst, Tunbridge Wells, Kent TN3 8JN

Map ② I7  1970

A country house, romantic garden and 14th-century moated castle – all set in a beautiful wooded estate. The homely Victorian mansion is filled with stories of country life, while the fairytale castle provides the perfect backdrop for the picturesque garden. There's something to discover every season, with beautiful summer displays of rhododendrons and azaleas, and vibrant autumn colour. The estate trails are open all year and take in the stunning Kent landscape, woodlands with carpets of spring bluebells and a traditional farm that provides hops for the shop's Scotney Ale.

Eating and shopping: tea-room offering lunch, sandwiches and cream teas. Kiosk in picnic area serving light refreshments. Scotney Ale and honey available. Plant sales.

Making the most of your day: wide range of activities and events throughout the year, including open-air theatre, music, lecture lunches and family activities. Estate and wildlife walks. **Dogs**: welcome on leads around estate. Assistance dogs only in garden.

Access for all: 🅿️ 🐕 ♿ 🔄 📷 🎥 🚶
House ♿♿♿ Grounds ♿➡️♿

Getting here: see website for details.
Parking: 130 yards (limited spaces), overflow parking 440 yards.

Finding out more: 01892 893820 (Infoline). 01892 893868 or scotneycastle@nationaltrust.org.uk

Scotney Castle		M	T	W	T	F	S	S
House, garden, Old Castle, shop and tea-room								
15 Feb–2 Nov	10–5*	M	T	W	T	F	S	S
3 Nov–31 Dec	10–3**	M	T	W	T	F	S	S
Estate walks								
Open all year		M	T	W	T	F	S	S

*House opens at 11. **Shop and tea-room close at 3:30.
House and garden last admission one hour before closing.
All visitors require timed ticket to visit house (places limited, early sell-outs possible). Property may close during adverse weather. Closed 24 and 25 December.

Shalford Mill

Shalford, near Guildford, Surrey GU4 8BS

Map ② E6   1932

You can feel the evocative stories of the past in the very structure of the mill, although the machinery no longer works. The wonderful story of the Ferguson's Gang is waiting for you – eccentric girls from the 1930s, determined to save the fabric of England for the future. **Note**: sorry no toilet.

Making the most of your day: regular guided tours. **Dogs**: assistance dogs only.

Access for all: 🎥 ⠿ Building ♿

Getting here: see website for details.
Parking: none on site.

Finding out more: 01483 561389 or shalfordmill@nationaltrust.org.uk

Shalford Mill		M	T	W	T	F	S	S
30 Mar–2 Nov	11–5	·	·	W	·	·	·	S

Open Bank Holiday Mondays and Saturdays on Bank Holiday weekends.

Shalford Mill in Surrey: so many stories to discover

Sheffield Park and Garden

Sheffield Park, East Sussex TN22 3QX

Map ② G7 ❖ ♨ 1954

This informal landscape garden was laid out in the 18th century by 'Capability' Brown, then enhanced early in the 20th century by its owner, Arthur G. Soames. The four larger lakes form the centrepiece, reflecting the careful composition of trees, shrubs, waterfalls and sky. In spring, there are colourful shows of daffodils and bluebells, while the rhododendrons and azaleas are beautiful during the early summer. Autumn brings lovely foliage colours from the many trees and shrubs, some quite rare, and winter walks can also be enjoyed in this garden for all seasons. South Park and East Park are areas of historic parkland, with views, wildlife havens, a disused lock and meandering river.

Eating and shopping: Coach House tea-room serving specialist coffee, homemade cakes, sandwiches, hot lunches and cream teas. Catering buggy usually in garden. Shop selling local, garden-related and outdoor products. Large plant sales area. New this year: second-hand bookshop.

Sheffield Park and Garden, East Sussex: laid out in the 18th century by 'Capability' Brown, this informal landscape garden has four large lakes as its centrepiece, which reflect the colourful shrubs and trees surrounding them. Left, young visitors admire the water lilies

Making the most of your day: family fun activities all year, with extra activities daily in the school holidays. Garden tours on Tuesday and Thursday. Pulham Falls cascade 12 to 1 (Tuesday and Friday). Don't miss the Ringwood Toll play trail in South Park for climbing, den-building, balance beams and much more. Cricket matches take place most weekends from May to September. Why not make a day of it with the nearby Bluebell Railway? It now connects through East Grinstead station to London, Croydon and all mainline stations (weekend bus link operates spring and summer). **Dogs**: welcome in South or East Park. Assistance dogs only in garden.

Access for all: 🅿️♿🚻♿🖼️🔄🚶👓🅰️
Reception ♿♿ Garden ♿▶♿♿

Getting here: see website for details.
Parking: free.

Finding out more: 01825 790231 or sheffieldpark@nationaltrust.org.uk

Sheffield Park and Garden		M	T	W	T	F	S	S
1 Jan–1 Mar	10:30–4	M	T	W	T	F	S	S
2 Mar–9 Nov	10:30–5:30	M	T	W	T	F	S	S
10 Nov–31 Dec	10:30–4	M	T	W	T	F	S	S

Parkland open dawn to dusk. Garden, shop and tea-room closed 25 December. Last admission into the garden is one hour before closing. Tea-room opens at 10.

Sissinghurst Castle

Biddenden Road, near Cranbrook,
Kent TN17 2AB

Map ② I7  1967

Historic, poetic, iconic: a refuge dedicated to beauty, Sissinghurst is an Elizabethan manor house gently seated in the Weald of Kent. Among the pink crumbling brickwork, Vita Sackville-West and Harold Nicolson created a renowned garden, which embraces every season. You can also discover the wider landscape with the help of our walking trails, which lead through the vegetable garden, working farmland and historic lakes and woodlands. **Note**: access to library, tower and gardens only.

Eating and shopping: Granary Restaurant serving lunch and coffee shop offering afternoon tea, made with produce from our vegetable garden and farm. Shops selling gifts and plants grown in the Sissinghurst nursery.

Making the most of your day: exhibitions and events all year, including open-air theatre and late-night summer garden opening. Activities, including dawn chorus walks and Ranger-led nature trails. Acres of ancient woodland. Panoramic views across the Wealden countryside from the tower. The Library contains the Trust's most significant collection of 20th-century literature and visitors can learn how we conserve it. Exploring equipment for children available to borrow. Smallhythe Place, Lamb House and Stoneacre nearby.

A froth of roses at Sissinghurst Castle in Kent, below and right: a garden of timeless quality

Places may occasionally close for conservation, safety or events

Dogs: welcome on estate. Assistance dogs only in garden and vegetable garden.

Access for all: ☐☐☐☐☐☐☐☐☐☐☐ **Building** ☐☐☐ **Grounds** ☐☐☐

Getting here: see website for details.
Parking: 315 yards.

Finding out more: 01580 710700 or sissinghurst@nationaltrust.org.uk

Sissinghurst Castle		M	T	W	T	F	S	S
Garden								
15 Mar–31 Dec	11–5:30*	M	T	W	T	F	S	S
Shop and restaurant								
15 Mar–31 Dec	10–5:30	M	T	W	T	F	S	S
Estate								
Open all year	Dawn–dusk	M	T	W	T	F	S	S

*Summer opening 17 May to 30 June until 7 on Mondays, Wednesdays and Fridays. Last garden entry 45 minutes before closing. Due to its fragile nature we can't allow children's buggies in the garden, carriers are provided. 1 November to 31 December guided property tours, half price admission. Closed 24 and 25 December.

Pretty half-timbered Smallhythe Place, Kent

Smallhythe Place

Smallhythe, Tenterden, Kent TN30 7NG

Map ② I7    1939

Nestled in the beautiful Weald of Kent, this small early 16th-century cottage is imbued with the vibrant spirit of the adored Victorian actress, Ellen Terry, and contains her fascinating theatrical collection. Voices of famous names who have graced the stage, echo through our thatched Barn Theatre in the garden.

Eating and shopping: vintage-style tea-room (licensed) attached to Barn Theatre selling soups, sandwiches, cakes and drinks.

Making the most of your day: wide range of indoor plays and music in the Barn Theatre and open-air theatre in the garden. Smallhythe Music and Beer Festival. Sissinghurst Castle, Lamb House and Stoneacre nearby.
Dogs: allowed on leads in grounds.

Access for all: 🏷️🖼️🎞️∴🅰️
Building 🏚️🏛️ Grounds 🏛️➡️

Getting here: see website for details.
Parking: free (not National Trust), 50 yards.

Finding out more: 01580 762334 or smallhytheplace@nationaltrust.org.uk

Smallhythe Place		M	T	W	T	F	S	S
1 Mar–29 Oct	11–5*	M	T	W	·	·	S	S

*Tea-room opens 11:30 to 4:30. Open Good Friday. Closes dusk if earlier.

South Foreland Lighthouse in Kent

South Foreland Lighthouse

The Front, St Margaret's Bay, Dover, Kent CT15 6HP

Map ② K6   🏠♿🏰🛏️🍽️ 1989

This historic landmark, dramatically situated on the White Cliffs, guided ships past the infamous Goodwin Sands and has a fascinating tale to tell. It was the first lighthouse powered by electricity and the site of the first international radio transmission.
Note: no access for cars.

Eating and shopping: loose-leaf tea and homemade cakes served in Mrs Knott's tea-room. Shop selling ice-cream, cold drinks and gifts.

Making the most of your day: tours with knowledgeable guides, interactive and hands-on displays. Family fun in the grounds with kite-flying and outdoor games.
Dogs: allowed in grounds only.

Access for all: 🏷️🖼️🎞️📺🎞️∴🅰️
Lighthouse 🏚️🚶 Tea-room 🏛️🚶

Getting here: see website for details.
Parking: no parking on site. Nearest at White Cliffs, 2-mile clifftop walk, or St Margaret's 1 mile.

Finding out more: 01304 853281 or southforeland@nationaltrust.org.uk

South Foreland Lighthouse		M	T	W	T	F	S	S
Tea-room								
1 Feb–9 Mar	11–3	·	·	·	·	·	S	S
Lighthouse and tea-room								
10 Mar–6 Apr	11–5:30	M	·	·	·	F	S	S
7 Apr–20 Apr	11–5:30	M	T	W	T	F	S	S
21 Apr–25 May	11–5:30	M	·	·	·	F	S	S
26 May–1 Jun	11–5:30	M	T	W	T	F	S	S
2 Jun–20 Jul	11–5:30	M	·	·	T	F	S	S
21 Jul–7 Sep	11–5:30	M	T	W	T	F	S	S
8 Sep–26 Oct	11–5:30	M	·	·	·	F	S	S
27 Oct–2 Nov	11–3	M	T	W	T	F	S	S

Lighthouse and tea-room open 1 January, 11 to 3.

Standen

West Hoathly Road, East Grinstead,
West Sussex RH19 4NE

Map ② G7 🏠🌼♿🛏🍽 1973

Standen tells the story of family life during the 1920s in a unique setting. The late Victorian house, designed by Philip Webb and decorated by the firm of Morris & Co., is filled with decorative art and shows the Arts and Crafts Movement at its best. Mrs Beale's gardens are being restored to their former glory in our 'Standen Revival' project. On the wider estate, footpaths and self-guided walks lead out into our beautiful woodlands and the High Weald Area of Outstanding Natural Beauty.
Note: tours to top of water tower, charge (including members).

Eating and shopping: Barn Café serving fresh kitchen garden produce. Shop selling gifts inspired by William Morris. Plant sales, including Standen Collection.

Arts and Crafts Standen, West Sussex, inside and out

Making the most of your day: free daily talks and tours. Events all year. Children's activities and woodland family play area. **Dogs**: welcome in woodlands, and in garden on short leads.

Access for all: 🅿️🐶♿🧏🦽📷🚂👓🖐️🎨
House 🦽♿ ♿ Gardens 🦽➡️♿

Getting here: see website for details.
Parking: free, 200 yards.

Finding out more: 01342 323029 or standen@nationaltrust.org.uk

Standen		M	T	W	T	F	S	S
House, garden, café and shop*								
15 Feb–2 Nov	10–5**	M	T	W	T	F	S	S
3 Nov–31 Dec	10–4**	M	T	W	T	F	S	S
Estate								
Open all year		M	T	W	T	F	S	S

*Access to house by guided tour only at certain times, free-flow at all other times. **House opens at 11 and closes 30 minutes before the times stated above. Closed 24 and 25 December. Access to car park only during opening hours. Closes at dusk if earlier.

Stoneacre

Otham, Maidstone, Kent ME15 8RS

Map (2) I6   🏠 ❀ 1928

15th-century Wealden timber-framed house surrounded by garden, orchard, rolling meadows and woodland. Home to famous designer and critic Aymer Vallance.
Note: open Saturdays only, March to October, by tenants on behalf of the National Trust.

Finding out more: 01622 863247 or stoneacre@nationaltrust.org.uk

Stowe

Buckingham, Buckinghamshire MK18 5EQ

Map (2) D2   🏠 ❀ 🚣 🔔 🍷 1990

At Stowe, visitors can follow in the footsteps of 18th-century tourists, immersing themselves in our stunning, informal landscape. A short walk down the drive and an impressive vista opens up, with a breathtaking view across the lake. With more than 40 historic temples and monuments, each with its own story, Stowe incorporates history, nature and beauty in majestic surroundings. The sheer size and space make the garden perfect for those who love the outdoors and enjoy walking. Whatever the weather or the season, there is something here to enjoy. Activities, events and a wide range of walks and trails make Stowe an ideal day out for the family throughout the year.

Eating and shopping: café serving homemade seasonal light lunches, cakes, soups and scones. Shop selling gifts, jewellery, plants and local products, including Stowe Ale. Picnics welcome in wildflower paddock outside New Inn.

Making the most of your day: seasonal events, walks and trails and family activities throughout the year. Farmhouse kitchen garden. Restored 18th-century parlour rooms in New Inn. Stowe House's staterooms (not National Trust) are also worth a visit. Family cycle trail. Specially themed leaflets to help you make the most of your day.
Dogs: welcome on leads.

Access for all:
Visitor centre **Grounds**

Getting here: see website for details.
Parking: free, 545 yards.

Finding out more: 01280 817156 or stowe@nationaltrust.org.uk

Stowe		M	T	W	T	F	S	S
Gardens, shop, café and parlour rooms								
1 Jan–2 Mar	10–4	**M**	**T**	**W**	**T**	**F**	**S**	**S**
3 Mar–2 Nov*	10–6	**M**	**T**	**W**	**T**	**F**	**S**	**S**
3 Nov–31 Dec	10–4	**M**	**T**	**W**	**T**	**F**	**S**	**S**
Parkland								
Open all year	Dawn–dusk	**M**	**T**	**W**	**T**	**F**	**S**	**S**

Last entry to the gardens is recommended 90 minutes before closing or dusk if earlier. *Landscape gardens closed 24 May, but visitor centre, parkland, café and shop open. Closed 25 December.

The stunning informal landscape at Stowe, Buckinghamshire, contains lakes, far left and below, as well as temples galore, left. There are 40 temples altogether, each telling a different story

Uppark House and Garden

South Harting, Petersfield,
West Sussex GU31 5QR

Map ② E8 🏛️❄️♿🍽️ 1954

Set in gardens inspired by the work of landscape designers 'Capability' Brown and Humphry Repton, this house of faded Georgian grandeur contains beautiful interiors and a Grand Tour collection that includes a magnificent 18th-century dolls'-house. Over the years, Uppark has been home to parties, scandal and fame, featuring many famous names, such as the Prince Regent, Emma Hamilton and even a young H. G. Wells. With space to relax and enjoy the stunning views across the countryside to the sea, Uppark House and Garden is the perfect destination for a day out.

Elegant Uppark House and Garden, West Sussex

Eating and shopping: shop selling local products and peat-free plants. Restaurant (licensed) serving homemade food.

Making the most of your day: house introductory talks and trails. Garden trails and free garden tours every Thursday. Lecture lunch programme (March and November). Petworth House and Hinton Ampner nearby. **Dogs**: on leads on woodland walk only. Please note: no shaded parking.

Access for all: 🅿️♿🚻♿♿♿📺♿📶♿
House ♿♿👫♿ Gardens ♿♿➡️♿

Getting here: see website for details.
Parking: free, 300 yards.

Finding out more: 01730 825857 (Infoline). 01730 825415 or uppark@nationaltrust.org.uk

Uppark House and Garden		M	T	W	T	F	S	S
House, garden, shop and restaurant*								
16 Mar–2 Nov	11–4:30**	M	T	W	T	·	·	S
9 Nov–21 Dec	11–3	·	·	·	·	·	·	S

*Taster tours only to part of the house from 11 to 12:30, numbers limited (free-flow on Bank Holiday Mondays, Good Friday and Easter Sunday). **Last entry to house at 4. Open Good Friday. Garden tours every Thursday from April to October. Print Room open first Wednesday of each month (times as house). Open Saturday 6 December.

The Vyne in Hampshire: illustrious connections

The Vyne

Vyne Road, Sherborne St John, Basingstoke, Hampshire RG24 9HL

Map ② D6 ⬚✝✿🏞️⬚🍽️ 1956

Once an important Tudor palace, this atmospheric mansion has some illustrious connections, from Henry VIII to Jane Austen and J. R. R. Tolkien. Rare 16th-century interiors mix with elaborate 18th-century architecture, and there are rooms filled with treasures, including an ancient cursed ring and jewel-encrusted casket. Outside, acres of wildlife-rich gardens, meadows and woods create a wonderful space for relaxation and exploration, and a unique 'Hidden Realm' play space gives children freedom to let their imaginations take them on fantasy adventures. Sweeping lawns offer lakeside picnicking, and a short stroll reveals a cosy bird hide overlooking the water meadows. **Note**: occasional room closures for essential conservation work and filming.

Eating and shopping: tea-room serving soup and sandwiches, cakes and scones. Gift shop. Second-hand bookshop and plant sales. Picnics welcome.

Making the most of your day: events all year, including open-air theatre, exhibitions and themed days. Seasonal garden tours, trails and woodland walks. Inspirational 'Hidden Realm' children's playground. **Dogs**: welcome on short leads in woodlands and most of gardens.

Access for all: ⬚⬚⬚⬚⬚⬚⬚⬚⬚⬚ ⬚⬚ Building ⬚⬚ Grounds ⬚⬚

Getting here: see website for details.
Sat Nav: not reliable, follow brown tourist signs. **Parking**: free.

Finding out more: 01256 883858 or thevyne@nationaltrust.org.uk

The Vyne		M	T	W	T	F	S	S
2 Jan–31 Dec	10–5*	**M**	**T**	**W**	**T**	**F**	**S**	**S**

*House closes at 4:30. Guided tours only between 10 and 12. Limited winter offer 2 January to 28 February. Gardens open until 6 from 30 June to 31 August. Closed 24 and 25 December.

Waddesdon Manor

Waddesdon, near Aylesbury,
Buckinghamshire HP18 0JH

Map ② D3   🏠 🍴 ❀ ⚲ 🔔 🍷 1957

Baron Ferdinand de Rothschild started building Waddesdon Manor in 1874 to display his outstanding collection of art treasures and entertain the fashionable world. The highest quality 18th-century French decorative arts are displayed alongside magnificent English portraits and Dutch Old Master paintings, while outside is one of the finest Victorian gardens in Britain, famous for its parterre and ornate working aviary. Today, the Manor continues its great tradition of entertainment and hospitality with a range of events celebrating food and wine. There are also opportunities to explore its history, collections and gardens through changing exhibitions and special interest days. **Note**: managed by a Rothschild family charitable trust. House entrance by timed tickets only.

Eating and shopping: three licensed restaurants (not National Trust). Snacks and drinks available at the Summerhouse or Coffee Bar. Shops, plant centre and old-fashioned sweet shop at the Stables.

Making the most of your day: wide range of free activities on aspects of the house, collection and special exhibitions with experts. Guided walks in the gardens, Wildlife Explorer Trails and talks about the work of the aviary. Rolling presentations on the Rothschilds and Waddesdon. Special interest days, wine tastings, family events, jazz evenings, car days and food markets and fairs.
Dogs: assistance dogs only.

Access for all: 🅿 ♿ 🚻 🔧 📷 🔊 ♿
Building 🏠♿ Grounds 🏠➡♿

Getting here: see website for details.
Parking: ¾ mile (transfer available).

Finding out more: 01296 653226 or waddesdonmanor@nationaltrust.org.uk

Waddesdon Manor in Buckinghamshire, above and right, contains an outstanding collection of art treasures

Waddesdon Manor		M	T	W	T	F	S	S
Gardens, aviary, woodland playground, shops, restaurants								
4 Jan–23 Mar	10–5						S	S
15 Feb–23 Feb	10–5	M	T	W	T	F	S	S
29 Oct–9 Nov	10–5			W	T	F	S	S
Gardens, house, wine cellars, shops, restaurants								
26 Mar–24 Oct	12–4			W	T	F		
29 Mar–26 Oct	11–4						S	S
12 Nov–31 Dec	11–4			W	T	F	S	S
Bachelors' Wing								
26 Mar–24 Oct	12–4			W	T	F		

Recommended last admission to house one hour before closing. Open Bank Holiday Mondays. Open 22 and 23 December and 1 January 2015. Closed 24 to 26 December. House operates by timed-ticket system (including members), available from ticket office or online at www.waddesdon.org.uk (tickets limited). To guarantee entry during busy periods, especially over Christmas and Bank Holidays, please book house entry tickets. Admission to house must include a gardens ticket.

Wakehurst Place

Ardingly, Haywards Heath,
West Sussex RH17 6TN

Map (2) G7 🏛️❄️🚣🌱🔔🍷 1964

The country estate of the Royal Botanic Gardens, Kew, this beautiful garden is the National Trust's most visited property. It is internationally significant, not only for its collections but also for its scientific research and plant conservation. The glorious gardens, wetland and woodland contain plants from around the world and you may even spot kingfishers in their natural habitat at the Loder Valley Nature Reserve and meadowland. A wide range of activities and events take place throughout the year and a 'must see' is Kew's Millennium Seed Bank, a unique venue where science and horticulture work side-by-side to deliver Kew's mission, saving plants from around the world.

Note: funded and managed by the Royal Botanic Gardens, Kew. National Trust UK members free. International membership cards are not accepted. Car-parking charges apply (including members).

Eating and shopping: Stables restaurant. Seed Café serving sandwiches and cakes. Gift shop (not National Trust). Plant centre.

Making the most of your day: free guided tour and informative walk around botanical gardens. Events and activities, including courses and talks, bat evenings, seasonal soup and stroll, photography workshops, as well as kingfisher and badger watching (charge applies). Loder Valley Nature Reserve with wetland and meadowland (admission limited). Natural play areas and Adventurous Journeys trail for children and families. Winter festival events, with the country's tallest living Christmas tree, carols evening and Santa's Winter Wonderland. **Dogs**: assistance dogs only.

Access for all: 🅿️♿🚻♿♿♿
Building ♿♿♿ **Grounds** ♿➡️♿♿

Wakehurst Place in West Sussex, below and above right: the country estate of the Royal Botanic Gardens, Kew

Getting here: see website for details.
Parking: 50 yards.

Finding out more: 01444 894066 or
wakehurst@kew.org. www.kew.org

Wakehurst Place		M	T	W	T	F	S	S
1 Jan–28 Feb	10–4:30*	M	T	W	T	F	S	S
1 Mar–31 Oct	10–6*	M	T	W	T	F	S	S
1 Nov–31 Dec	10–4:30*	M	T	W	T	F	S	S

*Mansion and Millennium Seed Bank close one hour earlier.
Seed Café and shop close 5:30 March to October, 4:15
November to 1 January, 4 from 2 January to February. Stables
restaurant closes 5 from March to October, 3:45 November to
February. Property closed 24 and 25 December. Shop closed
Easter Sunday. UK National Trust members free (reciprocal
agreements made between the Trust and other parties do
not apply).

West Green House Garden

West Green, Hartley Wintney,
Hampshire RG27 8JB

Map ② D6 🔲 1957

Nationally acclaimed gardens created by writer
and designer Marylyn Abbott, with celebrated
potager, parterres, follies and lavish perennial
borders. **Note**: maintained on behalf of the
National Trust by Marylyn Abbott. Facilities
not National Trust.

Finding out more: 01252 844611 or
westgreenhouse@nationaltrust.org.uk

West Wycombe Park, Village and Hill

West Wycombe, Buckinghamshire HP14 3AJ

Map ② E4 🔲 1943

Alongside this historic village lies an exquisite
country mansion. This lavish home and serene
landscape garden reflect the wealth and
personality of its creator, the infamous Sir
Francis Dashwood, founder of the Hellfire Club.
Still home to the Dashwood family and their
fine collection, it remains a busy, private estate.
Note: opened in partnership with the
National Trust.

West Wycombe in Buckinghamshire

Exploring the grounds at West Wycombe Park

Eating and shopping: refreshments available at George and Dragon public house, Village Community Library, West Wycombe Garden Centre and Hellfire Caves (none National Trust). Variety of shops in National Trust village. Picnics welcome on West Wycombe Hill.

Making the most of your day: centuries-old village high street with historic cottages, coaching inns and courtyards. Nearby West Wycombe Hill: wildflower meadows, iconic Golden Ball and Mausoleum, far-reaching views and woodland walks. **Dogs**: welcome on West Wycombe Hill. Assistance dogs only in Park.

Access for all: 🅿️ 🏬 🚻 🎧 🚶 ••
Building 🔆 ♿

Getting here: see website for details.
Parking: 250 yards.

Finding out more: 01494 755571 (Infoline). 01494 513569 or westwycombe@nationaltrust.org.uk

West Wycombe			M	T	W	T	F	S	S
Grounds only									
1 Apr–29 May	2–6		**M**	**T**	**W**	**T**	·	·	**S**
House and grounds									
1 Jun–31 Aug	2–6		**M**	**T**	**W**	**T**	·	·	**S**

Last admission 45 minutes before closing. Entry to the house on weekdays is by guided tour/timed ticket in June, July and August. A free-flow system operates on Sundays and Bank Holidays.

Winchester City Mill

Bridge Street, Winchester, Hampshire SO23 0EJ

Map ② D7  1929

For centuries, this ancient working watermill in the heart of historic Winchester has used the power of the River Itchen to mill stone-ground flour. A tranquil haven, it attracts plenty of wildlife, from trout and water voles, to visiting otter families, which can be viewed on CCTV. **Note**: nearest toilet 220 yards (not National Trust).

Eating and shopping: shop selling local produce, gifts and books and our freshly milled wholemeal flour.

Winchester City Mill, Hampshire

Making the most of your day: events and activities for families and children (school holidays). Milling and baking demonstrations and workshops. **Dogs**: assistance dogs only.

Access for all: 🅿♿🎠📷📱🔊👓📷
Building 🏛

Getting here: see website for details.
Sat Nav: do not use. **Parking**: Chesil car park or park and ride (St Catherine's to Winchester route).

Finding out more: 01962 870057 or winchestercitymill@nationaltrust.org.uk

Winchester City Mill		M	T	W	T	F	S	S
1 Jan–16 Feb	11–4	M	T	W	T	F	S	S
17 Feb–30 Nov	10–5	M	T	W	T	F	S	S
1 Dec–24 Dec	10:30–4	M	T	W	T	F	S	S
27 Dec–31 Dec	12–4	M	T	W	·	·	S	S

Winkworth Arboretum

Hascombe Road, Godalming, Surrey GU8 4AD

Map ② F7   ❀📷 1952

The National Trust's only arboretum, Winkworth is a collection of more than 1,000 different trees and plants set within the glorious Surrey countryside. Created by Dr Wilfrid Fox in the early 20th century, the extraordinary planting combinations will inspire you with their texture, colour and fragrance. In spring the brilliant carpets of old English bluebells vie for attention with the impressive displays of azaleas and magnolias. Ideal for a family day out or picnic in summer, in autumn the arboretum is ablaze with stunning foliage, while the rich and stark winter landscape has attractions all of its own.
Note: steep slopes; banks of lake and wetlands only partially fenced.

Eating and shopping: small tea-room offers freshly baked scones, cakes and light lunches.

Making the most of your day: events and guided walks throughout the year.
Dogs: welcome on leads.

Glorious colours at Winkworth Arboretum, Surrey

Access for all: 🅿♿🚻🍴 Grounds ♿➡

Getting here: see website for details.
Parking: free, 100 yards.

Finding out more: 01483 208477 or winkwortharboretum@nationaltrust.org.uk

Winkworth Arboretum		M	T	W	T	F	S	S
1 Jan–31 Jan	10–4*	M	T	W	T	F	S	S
1 Feb–31 Mar	10–5*	M	T	W	T	F	S	S
1 Apr–31 Oct	10–6*	M	T	W	T	F	S	S
1 Nov–31 Dec	10–4*	M	T	W	T	F	S	S

*Tea-room closes 30 minutes earlier than Arboretum.
Car-park gates locked at 6. Closed 25 December.

Woolbeding Gardens

Midhurst, West Sussex GU29 9RR

Map ② E7/8 ✿ 1956

Described by Disraeli as 'the greenest valley with the prettiest river in the world', Woolbeding is a modern masterpiece, with colour-themed garden rooms and a landscape garden. Stunning views over the River Rother and beautiful floral displays are just a few of the surprises at this horticultural haven. **Note: booking essential**. Access by park and ride minibus only.

Eating and shopping: our new Coffee Bar serves sandwiches, cakes and hot and cold drinks. Shop selling gardening books, gifts and plants.

Making the most of your day: introductory talks, enchanted grotto and croquet lawn. Nearby properties include Petworth House and Park, Uppark House and Garden, and Hinton Ampner. **Dogs**: assistance dogs only.

Access for all: P♿ ♿WC ⓘ
Reception ♿♿ Garden ♿➡♿

Getting here: see website for details.
Parking: no local parking or on site. Access by park and ride minibus only.

Finding out more: 0844 249 1895 or woolbedinggardens@nationaltrust.org.uk

Woolbeding Gardens		M	T	W	T	F	S	S
24 Apr–26 Sep	10:30–4:30	·	·	·	**T**	**F**	·	·

Booking essential. Access by park and ride only.

Woolbeding Gardens, West Sussex, is a modern masterpiece with colour-themed 'rooms' and beautiful displays of flowers

London

Osterley Park and House in Middlesex:
a country estate within the capital

Carlyle's House

24 Cheyne Row, Chelsea, London SW3 5HL

Map ② F5   ⊞ ✿ 1936

This Victorian writer's home, near the Thames in Chelsea, is in remarkably authentic condition, with an unusually large collection of original furniture and artefacts and full of fascinating information. With six rooms plus a small garden – this could be the only house in Chelsea still with an outside privy.

Access for all: 🔈 ♿ 👁
Building 🔼👫 **Grounds** 🔼

Getting here: see website for details.
Parking: limited metered street parking.

Finding out more: 020 7352 7087 or carlyleshouse@nationaltrust.org.uk

Carlyle's House	M	T	W	T	F	S	S
8 Mar–2 Nov 11–4:30			·	W	T	F	S	S

Open Bank Holiday Mondays.

Carlyle's House in Chelsea: contemporary drawing

Eastbury Manor House

Eastbury Square, Barking, Essex IG11 9SN

Map ② G5   ⊞ ✿ 🔔 1918

The Tudor Eastbury Manor House in Barking, Essex

Brick-built Tudor house, completed around 1573 and little altered since. Early 17th-century wall-paintings, showing fishing scenes and a cityscape, grace the former Great Chamber. There are exposed timbers in the attic, a fine original spiral oak staircase in the turret, soaring chimneys, cobbled courtyard and peaceful walled garden with bee-boles.
Note: managed by the London Borough of Barking and Dagenham.

Eating and shopping: garden tea-room serving drinks, sandwiches, snacks and light meals. Sales point selling books, toys and more.

Making the most of your day: guided tours and heritage days, costumed guides, authors' talks, food sampling, children's activities and candlelit tours. **Dogs**: in grounds only on leads.

Access for all: 🅿 ♿ 🚻 ♿ ♿ 🔈 📺 ♿ 👁 ♿
Building 🔼↕🔽 **Courtyard** 🔼🔽 **Grounds** 🔼

Getting here: see website for details.
Parking: limited, on adjacent streets (telephone for details).

Finding out more: 020 8227 5216 or eastburymanor@nationaltrust.org.uk

Eastbury Manor House		M	T	W	T	F	S	S
3 Feb–18 Dec*	10–4**	M	T	W	T	·	·	·
1 Jun–28 Sep	12–5**	·	·	·	·	·	·	S

*Open Saturdays on 8 February, 1 March, 8 March, 5 April and Sunday 7 December. **Tea-room and shop closes 30 minutes earlier. Closed Bank Holiday Mondays. Candlelit tours from 7:30 on Tuesday 25 February, 25 March, 28 October, 25 November and 16 December.

Fenton House and Garden

Hampstead Grove, Hampstead, London NW3 6SP

Map ② G4    1952

A cabinet of curiosities, this 1686 town house is filled with world-class decorative and fine art collections of musical instruments, ceramics, paintings, textiles and furniture. The ever-changing horticultural gem that is our garden, includes an orchard, kitchen garden, rose garden, formal terraces and lawns, and never fails to delight.

Eating and shopping: small shop area selling local and National Trust items, garden plants and produce. Simple catering is available for tea, coffee and light snacks.

Making the most of your day: garden events, including annual Apple Weekend. Joint tickets with 2 Willow Road available. Combine with a visit to one of Hampstead's National Trust Partner attractions. **Dogs**: assistance dogs only.

Access for all: 🔲🔲🔲🔲
Building 🔲🔲🔲   Grounds 🔲

Getting here: see website for details.
Parking: no parking on site.

Finding out more: 020 7435 3471 or fentonhouse@nationaltrust.org.uk

Fenton House and Garden		M	T	W	T	F	S	S
1 Mar–2 Nov	11–5	·	·	W	T	F	S	S
29 Nov–21 Dec	11–4	·	·	·	·	·	S	S

Open Bank Holiday Mondays.

George Inn

The George Inn Yard, 77 Borough High Street, Southwark, London SE1 1NH

Map ② G5   🔲🔲 1937

This public house, dating from the 17th century, is London's last remaining galleried inn. **Note**: leased to a private company. No table bookings (telephone for details).

Finding out more: 020 7407 2056 or georgeinn@nationaltrust.org.uk

The Shudi and Broadwood harpsichord in the dining-room at Fenton House and Garden, Hampstead

Ham House and Garden

Ham Street, Ham, Richmond, Surrey TW10 7RS

Map (2) F5 1948

This rare and atmospheric Stuart house sits on the banks of the River Thames in Richmond. The house is internationally recognised for its superb collection of paintings, furniture and textiles, largely acquired 400 years ago. It is reputed to be one of the most haunted houses in Britain. Outside, the restored 17th-century garden includes a productive kitchen garden containing many heritage crops, the formal 'Wilderness', complete with summerhouses and many beautiful spots perfect for a picnic. **Note**: to protect our fragile textiles, some rooms in the house have low light levels.

The atmospheric Ham House and Garden in Richmond, above and below, on the banks of the Thames

Eating and shopping: the recently refurbished Orangery Café serves light lunches and teas, using much of the produce from the walled kitchen garden. The Tea Shed sells refreshments (seasonal). Picnics welcome. Gift shop, including plant sales. Second-hand bookshop.

Making the most of your day: events throughout the year, including ghost tours. Interactive basement. Family art activities. House and garden trails. Free garden tours. Downloadable trails from local Underground and Overground stations to Ham.
Dogs: assistance dogs only.

Access for all:
House
Café
Grounds

Getting here: see website for details.
Sat Nav: takes you to stables on Ham Street nearby. **Parking**: free in car park, 380 yards (not National Trust) and on street.

Finding out more: 020 8940 1950 or hamhouse@nationaltrust.org.uk

Ham House and Garden		M	T	W	T	F	S	S
House								
15 Feb–6 Mar	11–4*	**M**	**T**	**W**	**T**	·	**S**	**S**
8 Mar–2 Nov	11–4**	**M**	**T**	**W**	**T**	·	**S**	**S**
Garden, below stairs, shop and café								
4 Jan–9 Feb	10–4	·	·	·	·	·	**S**	**S**
15 Feb–2 Nov	10–5	**M**	**T**	**W**	**T**	**F**	**S**	**S**
3 Nov–31 Dec	10–4	**M**	**T**	**W**	**T**	**F**	**S**	**S**

*Guided tours of selected rooms, last tour 3:30 (places limited), no free-flow. **Short talks between 11 and 12, last talk 11:45 (places limited). House opens for free-flow at 12. House open 18 April. Closed 25 and 26 December.

Members may have to pay on special events days

Morden Hall Park: serene oasis in South London

Morden Hall Park

Morden Hall Road, Morden, London SM4 5JD

Map ② G5 🏠🚻🌼🦌🐕🍷 1942

Hidden behind Grade II listed walls in the heart of suburbia, lies this serene oasis. This tranquil former deer-park is one of the few remaining estates that lined the River Wandle during its industrial heyday. Meandering through the park, the river creates a haven for a variety of wildlife. At the heart of the park is an interesting cluster of buildings linked to the estate's historical past, including snuff mills, one now a Learning Centre, as well as a charming Victorian stableyard which has been restored and opened as a unique sustainable visitor centre, powered using renewable energy. **Note**: May Fair and other special events, admission charges apply (including members).

Eating and shopping: Riverside café for hot meals and afternoon tea, Stableyard café for hot drinks, snacks and local ice-creams. Gift shop with an excellent range, second-hand bookshop in the stables, crafts and garden centre (not National Trust). Picnics welcome.

Making the most of your day: exciting events throughout the year. A variety of walks and trails. Family activities and natural play area. Rose garden. **Dogs**: welcome on leads around buildings and mown grass, including rose garden. Within sight elsewhere.

Access for all: 🅿️ᴅ🚻♿🔊🔉📷👨‍🦽:• ♿
Snuff Mill ♿♿🚹♿
Visitor centre, cafés and shop ♿ Grounds ♿➡️♿

Getting here: see website for details.
Parking: next to the Garden Centre (charge for non-members).

Finding out more: 020 8545 6850 or mordenhallpark@nationaltrust.org.uk

Morden Hall Park	Open every day all year

Car park and rose garden open 8 to 6, shop and café open 10 to 5. Car park, shop and café closed 25 and 26 December. Stableyard café opening dependent on weather.

Osterley Park and House

Jersey Road, Isleworth, Middlesex TW7 4RB

Map ② F5 🏠✳🏊🔔🍴 1949

Surrounded by gardens, park and farmland, Osterley is one of the last surviving country estates in London. Created in the 18th century by architect Robert Adam as a party house for the Child family to entertain their friends, it continues to impress today. Our iTouch guides or downloadable iPhone app bring the stunning interiors to life. The restored 18th-century gardens and parkland are a tranquil retreat from urban life; perfect for picnics and leisurely strolls. In summer, you can snooze in deckchairs on the Temple Lawn and throughout winter, enjoy brisk walks through the vibrant Winter Garden.

Eating and shopping: Stables tea-room and tea-terrace. Gift shop. Plant sales. Second-hand bookshop. Lakeside ice-cream and snack kiosk (National Trust-approved concession). Picnics welcome in park.

Grand interior, below, and outdoor fun, above, at Osterley Park and House, Middlesex

Making the most of your day: family activities, including dressing-up and tours. Family trails. Park and lake walks (free leaflet). Cycling in park (shared paths). Closer-to-nature wildlife walks. **Dogs**: allowed on leads in park only.

Access for all: 🅿️♿🚌♿🚻🔤👓🎧📖📹♿
👓🅰️ House 🔣♿ Garden ♿➡♿♿

Getting here: see website for details.
Sat Nav: use TW7 4RD. **Parking**: 400 yards.

Finding out more: 020 8232 5050 or osterley@nationaltrust.org.uk

Osterley Park and House		M	T	W	T	F	S	S
House, garden, café, shop and second-hand bookshop*								
1 Mar–4 Apr	12–4**	M	T	W	T	F	S	S
5 Apr–30 Sep	11–5**	M	T	W	T	F	S	S
1 Oct–31 Oct	12–4**	M	T	W	T	F	S	S
Garden and café								
1 Nov–31 Dec	12–4**	M	T	W	T	F	S	S
Shop and second-hand bookshop								
1 Nov–14 Dec	12–4						S	S
House								
29 Nov–14 Dec	12–4						S	S
Park and car park								
1 Jan–4 Apr	8–6	M	T	W	T	F	S	S
5 Apr–30 Sep	8–7:30	M	T	W	T	F	S	S
1 Oct–31 Dec†	8–6	M	T	W	T	F	S	S

*House: basement floor only every Monday and Tuesday, 1 March to 31 October. Last entry one hour before stated closing time. **Café opens one hour earlier. †Park and car park open 25 and 26 December and 1 January, 11 to 4.

Rainham Hall

The Broadway, Rainham, Havering, London RM13 9YN

Owing to a major restoration project, Rainham Hall will be closed this year.

Red House

Red House Lane, Bexleyheath, Kent DA6 8JF

Map ② H5  2003

The only house commissioned, created and lived in by William Morris, founder of the Arts and Crafts Movement, Red House is a building of extraordinary architectural and social significance. When it was completed in 1860, it was described by Edward Burne-Jones as 'the beautifullest place on earth'. **Note**: house is unfurnished, but contains original features and furniture by Morris, Webb and Burne-Jones.

Eating and shopping: shop selling Morris-related gifts and souvenirs. Second-hand bookshop. Coach House tea-room serving light refreshments. Picnics welcome in orchard.

Making the most of your day: events, including Easter Fun, summer arts and crafts fair, autumn Apple Day and carols at Christmas. Family fun (school holidays). Games in garden. Exhibition. **Dogs**: assistance dogs only.

Access for all: 🅿️♿🔊🦽🖐️📷📖🔁
Building 🔽 Grounds ♿➡️

Getting here: see website for details.
Sat Nav: use DA6 8HL – Danson Park car park.
Parking: Danson Park, 1 mile. Charge at weekends and Bank Holidays (including members).

Detail of Red House in Bexleyheath

Finding out more: 020 8304 9878 or redhouse@nationaltrust.org.uk

Red House	M	T	W	T	F	S	S
19 Feb–2 Nov	11–5	·	·	**W**	**T**	**F**	**S**	**S**
7 Nov–21 Dec	11–4:30	·	·	·	·	**F**	**S**	**S**

Free-flow 1:30 to 5 (booking not required). Admission by guided tour only at 11, 11:30, 12, 12:30 and 1 (booking essential). Last admission 45 minutes before closing. Last serving in tea-room 4:30 (4 in winter). Open Bank Holiday Mondays.

Sutton House

2 and 4 Homerton High Street, Hackney, London E9 6JQ

Map ② G4  1938

Tudor comfort at Sutton House in Hackney

A Tudor courtier's house in thriving modern-day Hackney. With linenfold oak panelling, 17th-century wall-paintings and a tranquil courtyard, this is a haven in the heart of the city and a window onto London's history. Newly refurbished café and second-hand bookshop.

Eating and shopping: tea-room serving cream tea on vintage crockery. Second-hand books for sale in the dining-room.

Making the most of your day: Georgian panels can be opened to reveal Tudor arches. Family treasure chests to delve into and Tudor kitchen. Family days, craft fairs and cinema nights. **Dogs**: assistance dogs only.

Access for all: ♿🔊🖐️🦽📷📖🚻👓📷
Building 🔽♿♿♿

Getting here: see website for details. Parking: no parking on site. Limited metered parking nearby.

Finding out more: 020 8986 2264 or suttonhouse@nationaltrust.org.uk

Sutton House		M	T	W	T	F	S	S
5 Feb–19 Dec	10:30–5	·	·	W	T	F	·	·
8 Feb–21 Dec	12–5	·	·	·	·	·	S	S
7 Apr–15 Apr	10:30–5	M	T	·	·	·	·	·
28 Jul–26 Aug	10:30–5	M	T	·	·	·	·	·

Open Bank Holiday Mondays and Good Friday. Open daily during Easter and summer holidays. Property is regularly used by local community groups, the rooms will always be open as advertised, but call if you would like to visit during a quiet time. Occasional 'Museum Lates' opening.

575 Wandsworth Road

575 Wandsworth Road, Lambeth, London SW8 3JD

Map ② G5 2010

Modest terraced house (above), transformed into a work of art, with a breathtaking hand-carved fretwork interior.
Note: sorry no toilets. Access by guided tour only (booking fee for non-members).

Access for all: House 🖼️🖼️

Getting here: see website for details.
Parking: no parking on site.

Finding out more: 0844 249 1895 (bookings). 020 7720 9459 (enquiries) or 575wandsworthroad@nationaltrust.org.uk

575 Wandsworth Road		M	T	W	T	F	S	S
1 Mar–2 Nov	times vary	·	·	W	·	F	S	S

Admission by guided tour only, booking essential (places limited). Evening tours only on Wednesdays. House closed the last Sunday of every month.

2 Willow Road

Hampstead, London NW3 1TH

Map ② G5  1994

This late 1930s house, an architect's vision of the future, paints a vivid picture of the creative and social circles in which Ernö and Ursula Goldfinger moved. Today you can explore the intimate and evocative interiors, innovative designs, intriguing personal possessions and impressive 20th-century art collection. Note: nearest toilet at local pub.

Eating and shopping: a small table in the entrance hall has property-related items available for sale.

Making the most of your day: events, including late openings, walks and tours. Fenton House nearby (joint tickets available). Combine your visit to include one of Hampstead's National Trust Partners. Dogs: assistance dogs only.

Access for all: 🅿️ 🅳 🖼️ 🖼️ 🖼️ 🖼️
Building 🖼️🖼️

Getting here: see website for details.
Parking: very limited parking nearby, pay and display (charge including members).

Finding out more: 020 7435 6166 or 2willowroad@nationaltrust.org.uk

2 Willow Road		M	T	W	T	F	S	S
1 Mar–2 Nov	11–5	·	·	W	T	F	S	S

Open Bank Holiday Mondays. Entry by guided tour only at 11, 12, 1 and 2 (places limited with tickets available only on the day). Wednesday to Friday tours at 11 are occasionally booked by groups. 3 to 5, self-guided viewing (timed entry when busy).

The upper landing at 2 Willow Road in Hampstead

National Trust
Partner

London partners

'National Trust Partner' is an exciting new venture between the National Trust and a selection of small, independent heritage attractions and museums within London. The Partnership aims to bring enhanced benefits to National Trust members living in London or for those visiting the capital for a day out, helping to provide increased opportunities to explore our rich and diverse heritage.

Entry charges: 50 per cent discount for members on presentation of a valid membership card. For full visiting information (and access), please see individual National Trust Partner websites.

Benjamin Franklin House

The world's only remaining home of Benjamin Franklin, featuring a unique 'Historical Experience'.

Underground: Charing Cross or Embankment.
Train: Charing Cross.

Finding out more: 020 7925 1405 or www.benjaminfranklinhouse.org

Bevis Marks Synagogue

Dated 1701, Britain's oldest surviving synagogue contains Cromwellian and Queen Anne furniture.

Underground: Liverpool Street or Aldgate.
Train: Liverpool Street.

Finding out more: 020 7626 1274 or www.bevismarks.org.uk

Danson House

Beautiful Georgian villa with sumptuous interiors built for pleasure and entertaining.

Train: Bexleyheath.

Finding out more: 020 8303 6699 or www.dansonhouse.org.uk

The Fan Museum

Unique collection of more than 4,000 fans, housed in elegant Georgian buildings.

Train: Cutty Sark (DLR) or Greenwich.

Finding out more: 020 8305 1441 or www.thefanmuseum.org.uk

Dr Johnson's House

Late 17th-century town house, once home to lexicographer and wit Samuel Johnson.

Underground: Chancery Lane or Blackfriars.
Train: Blackfriars.

Finding out more: 020 7353 3745 or www.drjohnsonshouse.org

Foundling Museum

Nationally important collection of 18th-century art, interiors, social history and music.

Underground: Russell Square, King's Cross St Pancras or Euston.
Train: King's Cross, St Pancras or Euston.

Finding out more: 020 7841 3600 or www.foundlingmuseum.org.uk

Freud Museum London

The final home of pioneering psychoanalysts Sigmund Freud and his daughter Anna.

Underground: Finchley Road.
Train: Finchley Road & Frognal.

Finding out more: 020 7435 2002 or www.freud.org.uk

Handel House Museum

Home of composer Handel and where he wrote many masterpieces, including *Messiah*.

Underground: Bond Street or Oxford Circus.

Finding out more: 020 7495 1685 or www.handelhouse.org

Hall Place and Gardens

Stunning Tudor house with magnificent gardens.

Train: Bexley.

Finding out more: 01322 526574 or www.hallplace.org.uk

Keats House

House where Romantic poet John Keats lived from 1818 to 1820.

Underground: Hampstead or Belsize Park.
Train: Hampstead Heath.

Finding out more: 020 7332 3868 or www.cityoflondon.gov.uk/keatshousehampstead

Leighton House Museum

Restored home of Victorian painter Lord Leighton, with priceless Islamic tile collection.

Underground: High Street Kensington or Holland Park.

Finding out more: 020 7602 3316 or www.leightonhouse.co.uk

The Old Operating Theatre Museum

Unique, atmospheric museum, hidden in the timbered Herb Garret of St Thomas's Church.

Underground: London Bridge.
Train: London Bridge.

Finding out more: 020 7188 2679 or www.thegarret.org.uk

Museum of Brands

Intense experience of consumer culture: journey from Victorian times to your childhood.

Underground: Notting Hill Gate.

Finding out more: 020 7908 0880 or www.museumofbrands.com

Strawberry Hill House

Horace Walpole's beautifully restored Gothic-revival castle by the Thames in Twickenham.

Train: Strawberry Hill.

Finding out more: 020 8744 1241 or www.strawberryhillhouse.org.uk ·

East of England

Norfolk's striking Horsey Windpump stands tall within the mysterious broadland landscape

Outdoors in the East of England

Here in the East of England, we benefit from wonderful unspoilt scenery; and with so many different landscapes, there are many spectacular views to enjoy. Each place has its own charm, character and history, and offers something special for everyone. We care deeply about these places and work hard to protect the rich diversity of life that they support.

Every compass point has its gems, ranging from forgotten landscapes in the west, secret military history in the east and iconic wildlife in the north, to dramatic hunting forests in the south. Depending on your mood, you can be as active or as relaxed as you like in the great outdoors. Where will you discover your special place?

Above: **Blakes Wood, Essex,** in spring
Right: **cycling on the Blickling Estate, Norfolk**

In the East of England, you are spoilt for coast and countryside choices. So whether you want to go outdoors to play, enjoy the beauty of the landscape and nature or just get away from it all, the variety of places means that the only difficulty you'll have is in deciding where to start.

Walking

One of the best ways to discover the great outdoors has to be on foot, and we have endless routes to explore. Choices include a half-mile stroll along the boardwalk at Wicken Fen, a short climb up to Sharpenhoe Clappers, or a long coastal walk at Blakeney Point on the Norfolk coast. You can join our expert guides, download a self-led trail or even join one of our regular health or Nordic walks.

Adventure for all

If you enjoy a faster pace of life, how about a two-wheeled adventure? There are plenty of routes to discover. Hatfield Forest is just one place which now offers cycle-hire. From bikes and helmets to trailers and child seats, we've got everything you need for a great family day out.

Alternatively, think of our beautiful places as your very own outdoor gym – train outside and feel great inside. Park runs take place every weekend at Sheringham Park and on the Wimpole Estate, while Dunstable Downs hosts an adrenaline warrior race for fitness fanatics.

For those preferring life on the water, we offer guided boat trips along the Wicken Fen Lode and activity holidays at Brancaster Activity Centre on the Norfolk coast, an ideal family adventure.

Above:
Sheringham Park in Norfolk
Below: **children covered in mud at Brancaster, Norfolk**

Wildlife wows

Throughout the seasons, our places are a blanket of colour as a succession of flowers comes into bloom. Spectacular displays of bluebells at Blakes Wood and an abundance of buttercups at Hatfield Forest never fail to lift spirits. While wildlife, such as the beautiful butterflies at West Runton, amazes and delights.

If you want complete peace, why not head to the highest hill in Norfolk at Roman Camp, West Runton, where you can feel on top of the world? Or you may enjoy a spectacular sunset or a spot of star-gazing along the Norfolk coast.

Our places support a wonderfully rich diversity of life, both flora and fauna, and provide endless opportunities for adventure and exploration for everyone. What will you discover?

Outdoors in the East of England

Whether you love getting active, prefer a gentler pace, or simply want to be wowed by wildlife, you will be spoilt for choice in this spectacular region.

Finding out more: 01263 740241 or blakeneypoint@nationaltrust.org.uk

Blakeney		M	T	W	T	F	S	S
Lifeboat House (Blakeney Point)								
31 Mar–2 Nov	Dawn-dusk	M	T	W	T	F	S	S

Lifeboat House and toilets (Blakeney Point) open dawn to dusk. Refreshment kiosk (not National Trust) and Information Centre at Morston Quay open according to tides and weather.

Blakeney National Nature Reserve

Morston Quay, Quay Road, Morston, Norfolk NR25 7BH

Map (3) I3  1912

Wide open spaces and uninterrupted views of this unspoilt coastline make for an inspiring visit, at any time of year. The reserve (above) is an internationally important nature reserve hosting a range of flora and fauna; most notably the spectacular displays of the breeding seal and tern colony on Blakeney Point. **Note:** nearest toilet at Morston Quay and Blakeney Quay (not National Trust).

Eating and shopping: refreshments and seafood stall (not National Trust) at Morston Quay. Seafood, including Morston mussels from local suppliers (not National Trust). Nearby pubs and hotels (not National Trust) offering locally themed menus.

Making the most of your day: visitor centres at Morston Quay and Lifeboat House on Blakeney Point. Coastal walks on the Norfolk Coast Path. Guided walks available. Ferry trips (not National Trust) to Blakeney Point. **Dogs**: some restrictions (particularly Blakeney Point), 1 April to mid-August.

Access for all: WC VT **Information centre** Lifeboat House

Getting here: see website for details.
Parking: pay and display (members free) at the Green Way Stiffkey Saltmarshes, Morston Quay and Blakeney Quay (not National Trust).

Brancaster Estate

Beach Road, Brancaster, Norfolk

Map (3) H3  1923

The estate encompasses Branodunum, an intriguing Scheduled Ancient Monument, and the golden sands at Brancaster Beach – ideal for sand castles. **Note:** nearest toilet Brancaster Beach. Scolt Head Island National Nature Reserve managed by Natural England.

Finding out more: 01263 740241 or brancaster@nationaltrust.org.uk

Copt Hall Marshes

Copt Hall Lane, Little Wigborough, Essex CO5 7RD

Map (3) I9 1989

Working farm on the remote and beautiful Blackwater Estuary – a fantastic birdwatching spot, important for overwintering species.

Finding out more: 01376 562226 or copthall@nationaltrust.org.uk

Danbury Commons and Blakes Wood

near Danbury, Essex

Map ③ H9  1953

Varied countryside, ranging from the lowland heath of Danbury Common to ancient woodland with stunning spring flowers at Blakes Wood. **Note**: sorry no toilets. Danbury Common main car park closes at dusk.

Finding out more: 01245 227662 or danbury@nationaltrust.org.uk

Dunstable Downs, Chilterns Gateway Centre and Whipsnade Estate

Dunstable Road, Dunstable, Bedfordshire LU6 2GY

Map ③ E8  1928

Acres of space to enjoy with fabulous views over the Vale of Aylesbury and along the Chiltern Ridge.

Dunstable Downs is in an Area of Outstanding Natural Beauty, famous for its chalk grassland, rich in wildlife. There are many ideas for walks and family days out at the Gateway Centre. **Note**: Chilterns Gateway Centre is owned by Central Bedfordshire Council and managed by the National Trust.

Eating and shopping: seasonal and regional products, kites and children's toys and activities for sale. Café serving locally produced food to eat in or take away – including the famous Bedfordshire Clanger.

Making the most of your day: events, including annual Kite Festival in July. Nature trail and playscape in Chute Wood. Waymarked routes. **Dogs**: under close control, on leads near livestock and ground-nesting birds.

Access for all: ⃞⃞⃞⃞⃞⃞
Chilterns Gateway Centre ⃞⃞
Dunstable Downs ➡

Getting here: see website for details.
Sat Nav: for older equipment use LU6 2TA.
Parking: Dunstable Downs, off B4541 (pay and display); Whipsnade crossroads (Whipsnade Heath), junction of B4541 and B4540.

Finding out more: 01582 500920 or dunstabledowns@nationaltrust.org.uk

Dunstable Downs
Chilterns Gateway Centre open 10 to 5, closes earlier in winter and open later in summer (August 9 to 6). Closed 24 and 25 December.

Fabulous view from Dunstable Downs, Bedfordshire

Heather carpets the rare and precious habitat of Dunwich Heath in Suffolk

Dunwich Heath and Beach

Dunwich, Saxmundham, Suffolk IP17 3DJ

Map (3) K6   🖼🏖♿🛏🍽 1968

Tucked away on the Suffolk coast, Dunwich Heath offers peace and quiet and a true sense of being at one with nature. A rare and precious habitat, the heath is in an Area of Outstanding Natural Beauty and home to species such as the Dartford warbler and nightjar. Quiet and serene, wild and dramatic, this is an inspiring visit whatever the time of year. From July to September, the heath is alive with colour – its patchwork of pink and purple heather and coconut-scented gorse is an unmissable experience. **Note**: parking restrictions may operate at times of extreme fire risk.

Eating and shopping: clifftop tea-room serving breakfast, lunch, homemade cakes (gluten-free available) and ice-cream. Coastal-themed shop selling a selection of local products and Dunwich-branded items.

Making the most of your day: self-guided trails and guided walks. Family activities, including geocaching and nature trails. SeaWatch building with telescopes and wildlife identification charts. Children's play area. **Dogs**: welcome. On leads at certain periods.

Access for all: 🅿🅳♿🚾🍽♿♿
Buildings 🏠♿   Grounds ➡♿

Getting here: see website for details.
Parking: 150 yards (pay and display).

Finding out more: 01728 648501 or dunwichheath@nationaltrust.org.uk

Dunwich Heath and Beach		M	T	W	T	F	S	S
Heath								
Open all year	Dawn–dusk	M	T	W	T	F	S	S
Tea-room and shop								
4 Jan–16 Feb	10–4						S	S
19 Feb–30 Mar	10–4			W	T	F	S	S
31 Mar–28 Sep	10–5	M	T	W	T	F	S	S
1 Oct–2 Nov	10–4			W	T	F	S	S
8 Nov–14 Dec	10–4						S	S
15 Dec–21 Dec	10–4	M	T	W	T	F	S	S
Tea-room								
1 Jan–3 Jan	10–4			W	T	F		
26 Dec–31 Dec	10–4	M	T	W		F	S	S

Tea-room: service limited in early and late season; may stay open later in summer.

Hatfield Forest

near Bishop's Stortford, Essex

Map ③ G8  1924

When Henry I established a royal hunting forest here in 1100, little could he have guessed that almost a millennium later it would be the best survival of its kind in the world. The fine ancient trees are still managed using once-forgotten techniques, and beneath them, descendants of the original herd of fallow deer still roam. Ride horseback in the style of the Norman nobility and enjoy the wide open plains that continue to be grazed by cows. Come and celebrate the 90th year of opening to the public by revelling in the freedom of this special place.

Eating and shopping: shop selling local gifts, our new guidebook as well as Hatfield Forest venison and Red Poll beef. Café (licensed) selling a wide range of hot and cold refreshments.

Hatfield Forest, Essex: an arboreal challenge

Making the most of your day: events. Trail bike and rowing boat hire. Download our mobile app (iTunes/android) before you visit or borrow a preloaded device. **Dogs**: welcome. On leads in lake area and near livestock.

Access for all: Pᗩ ᗩ ᗩ ᗩ ᗩ ᗩ ᗩ
Grounds ᗩ ➡ ᗩ ᗩ

Getting here: see website for details.

Finding out more: 01279 874040 (Infoline). 01279 870678 or hatfieldforest@nationaltrust.org.uk

Hatfield Forest		M	T	W	T	F	S	S
Elgins and Shell House car parks								
4 Jan–16 Mar	10–3:30						S	S
24 Mar–31 Oct	10–5	M	T	W	T	F		
22 Mar–2 Nov	9–5						S	S
8 Nov–28 Dec	10–3:30						S	S
Café								
1 Jan–23 Mar	10–3:30			W	T	F	S	S
24 Mar–2 Nov	9–5	M	T	W	T	F	S	S
5 Nov–31 Dec	10–3:30			W	T	F	S	S
Shop								
4 Jan–23 Mar	10–3:30						S	S
24 Mar–2 Nov	10–5	M	T	W	T	F	S	S
8 Nov–28 Dec	10–3:30						S	S

Café and shop open daily 10 to 3:30 during February and December school holidays. Car parks open from 9 daily during summer school holidays and Bank Holidays. Café closed 25 December. Shop closed 25 and 26 December.

Heigham Holmes

Martham Staithe, Ferrygate Lane, Martham, Norfolk

Map ③ K5  1987

Remote island nature reserve, with grazing marshes and ditches, supporting the wildlife of this internationally important and vast broadland landscape. **Note**: admission limited to guided visits (booking essential), due to restricted access via floating river crossing. Charge applicable (including members).

Finding out more: 01493 393450 or heighamholmes@nationaltrust.org.uk

Orford Ness National Nature Reserve, Suffolk

Northey Island

Maldon, Essex CM9 6PP

Map (3) I9 [icons] 1978

A peaceful retreat in the Blackwater Estuary, important for overwintering birds, Northey is also the oldest recorded battlefield in Britain. **Note**: access by causeway, so restricted by tides. Telephone in advance to arrange your visit.

Finding out more: 01621 853142 or northeyisland@nationaltrust.org.uk

Orford Ness National Nature Reserve

Orford, Woodbridge, Suffolk

Map (3) K7 [icons] 1993

This is Suffolk's secret coast, only reached by National Trust ferry. Wild, remote and exposed, the 'Island' contains the ruined remnants of a disturbing past. Ranked among the most important shingle features in the world, rare and fragile wildlife thrives where weapons, including atomic bombs, were once tested and perfected. **Note**: limited tickets. Steep, slippery steps, long distances. Hazardous debris. Limited access: 'pagodas' only on tours. Members pay a charge for ferry crossing.

Eating and shopping: cafés and pubs in village. Fresh fish available at quay. Local smokehouses.

Making the most of your day: guided tours and photography tours give safe access to Atomic Weapons Research Establishment site (booking essential for all tours). **Dogs**: assistance dogs only.

Access for all: [icons] **Buildings** [icons]
Trails

Getting here: see website for details.
Sat Nav: IP12 2NU. **Parking**: Quay Street pay and display (not National Trust), 150 yards to National Trust office on Orford Quay to purchase ferry ticket.

Finding out more: 01728 648024 (infoline). 01394 450900 (tour bookings) or orfordness@nationaltrust.org.uk

Orford Ness		M	T	W	T	F	S	S
19 Apr–28 Jun	10–2	·	·	·	·	·	S	·
1 Jul–4 Oct	10–2	·	T	W	T	F	S	·
11 Oct–1 Nov	10–2	·	·	·	·	·	S	·

The only access is by National Trust ferry from Orford Quay, with boats crossing regularly to the Ness between 10 and 2 only, the last ferry leaving the Ness at 5. Main visitor trail (Red Route) always available, other routes open seasonally.

Rayleigh Mount

Rayleigh, Essex

Map (3) I10   1923

Medieval motte and bailey castle site, with adjacent windmill housing historical exhibition. **Note**: exhibition in windmill operated by Rochford District Council.

Finding out more: 01284 747500 or rayleighmount@nationaltrust.org.uk

Sharpenhoe

Sharpenhoe Road, Streatley, Bedfordshire

Map ③ F8    1939

Reputedly haunted, this classic chalk grassland escarpment is crowned with beech woodland and traces of an Iron Age hill fort.

Finding out more: 01582 873663 or sharpenhoe@nationaltrust.org.uk

Sheringham Park

Upper Sheringham, Norfolk NR26 8TL

Map ③ J4    1987

There are breathtaking views of the North Norfolk coast to be enjoyed from Sheringham Park – created 200 years ago by the visionary landscape gardener Humphry Repton. More than 80 species of rhododendron and azalea can be found here, providing colour through most of the year – peaking in May and June. The woodland, parkland and clifftop habitats provide the opportunity to observe a wide variety of wildlife and wild flowers. You can easily spend a day exploring the numerous trails on this 405-hectare (1,000-acre) estate, while listening to birdsong or watching a passing steam train on the local Poppy Line.

Note: Sheringham Hall is privately occupied. April to September: limited access by written appointment with leaseholder.

Eating and shopping: gift shop selling souvenirs. Plant sales, including rhododendrons. Courtyard Café serving bacon rolls, chips, baps, cream teas and ice-cream. Picnics welcome in a number of areas.

Making the most of your day: the Gazebo viewing tower offers unrivalled views of the Norfolk coastline. Tracker Packs for children. GPSs available for Geocaching. Programme of guided walks. **Dogs**: on leads near livestock and visitor facilities.

Access for all:
Building   Grounds

Getting here: see website for details.
Parking: 60 yards, pay and display (£4.90 for non-members).

Finding out more: 01263 820550 or sheringhampark@nationaltrust.org.uk

Sheringham Park		M	T	W	T	F	S	S
Park								
Open all year	Dawn–dusk	M	T	W	T	F	S	S
Visitor centre and Courtyard Café								
4 Jan–9 Mar	11–4						S	S
15 Mar–28 Sep	10–5	M	T	W	T	F	S	S
29 Sep–2 Nov	10–5	M			T	F	S	S
8 Nov–28 Dec	11–4						S	S

Visitor centre and Courtyard Café: open daily 15 to 23 February and 25 October to 2 November, 10 to 5; 27 to 31 December, 11 to 4.

A gentle ride at Sheringham Park, Norfolk

West Runton and Beeston Regis Heath

Roman Camp, West Runton,
Norfolk NR27 9ND

Map ③ J4  1925

A lovely place to walk among heath and woods, with fine views of the North Norfolk coast. **Note**: sorry no toilets.

Finding out more: 01263 820550 or westrunton@nationaltrust.org.uk

Whipsnade Tree Cathedral

Whipsnade, Dunstable, Bedfordshire LU6 2LQ

Map ③ E8 1960

Peaceful place, with trees planted in the shape of a medieval cathedral. Created after First World War for fallen comrades. **Note**: National Trust owned, administered by Trustees of Whipsnade Tree Cathedral. Dogs allowed under close control. Small car park. Open all year, 9 to 5. Donations welcome.

Finding out more: 01582 872406 or whipsnadetc@nationaltrust.org.uk

Wicken Fen National Nature Reserve

Lode Lane, Wicken, Ely,
Cambridgeshire CB7 5XP

Map ③ G6 1899

Wicken Fen, with its vast skies above flowering meadows, sedge and reedbeds, is a window onto a lost landscape. As Britain's oldest nature reserve and one of Europe's most important wetlands, it supports an amazing variety of wildlife, with more than 8,500 species of plants, birds and dragonflies, including such rare species as hen harriers and bitterns. The landscape feels wild, though people have managed it for years; as revealed by the fenman's yard, windpump and cottage. The past meets the future in the Wicken Fen Vision, an ambitious landscape-scale conservation project, opening up new areas for wildlife and you to explore. Grazing herds of Highland cattle and Konik ponies help create a diverse range of new habitats.

Eating and shopping: shop in the visitor centre selling wildlife and outdoor books, as well as local food and crafts. Café serving Newmarket sausage sandwiches, homemade soup, light lunches and afternoon teas. Picnics welcome.

Making the most of your day: there are many ways to explore: on foot, by bike or boat. Our walking trails will suit every need, from the all-weather boardwalk to longer routes taking

Vast skies and meadows at Wicken Fen National Nature Reserve in Cambridgeshire, above and opposite

you into the far corners of the Fen. Trips in our open boat offer you a new way to see the landscape and wildlife, or cycle the Lodes Way across the wider reserve and on to Anglesey Abbey; we even have cycle hire. Discover seasonal wildlife highlights from our observation hides. Visit the fenman's yard, workshop and cottage to uncover the fascinating history of the local fenmen. Family events run through the year. **Dogs**: welcome on leads on reserve and in visitor centre.

Access for all: 🅿️♿🅳♿🚻♿♿📷⦂♿

Building ♿♿ Grounds ♿♿

Getting here: see website for details.
Parking: 120 yards.

Finding out more: 01353 720274 or wickenfen@nationaltrust.org.uk

Wicken Fen		M	T	W	T	F	S	S
Reserve, visitor centre and shop								
Open all year	10–5	M	T	W	T	F	S	S
Café								
1 Jan–16 Feb	10:30–4:30	·	·	W	T	F	S	S
17 Feb–2 Nov	10–5	M	T	W	T	F	S	S
5 Nov–31 Dec	10:30–4:30	·	·	W	T	F	S	S
Fen Cottage and cycle hire								
29 Mar–2 Nov	11:30–4:30*	M	T	W	T	F	S	S

Closed 25 December. Access to reserve dawn to dusk. Visitor centre closes dusk in winter. Boat trips run on cycle hire open days, weather permitting. *Cycle hire from 10 to 5, last cycle hire 3:30.

Anglesey Abbey, Gardens and Lode Mill

Quy Road, Lode, Cambridge,
Cambridgeshire CB25 9EJ

Map ③ G7 🏚️🏛️♣️🔔🌲🍸 1966

Lord Fairhaven, with his passion for English tradition and style, renovated Anglesey Abbey into a sumptious country home, from where he could pursue his love for horse racing at nearby Newmarket. Visitors stepping into his elegant home will journey back to a golden age of country-house living. A generous host, his guests, including royalty, were treated to a luxurious stay. The celebrated garden, with its sweeping avenues, classical statuary and flower borders, offers captivating views, vibrant colours and delicious scents in every season. Explore our historic working watermill, wildlife discovery area and famous Winter Garden.

Anglesey Abbey, above, and its gardens, below, in Cambridgeshire

Eating and shopping: Redwoods restaurant serving seasonal menu with dishes made using local produce. Shop selling local products and gifts. Historic watermill selling freshly milled wholemeal flour. Plant centre selling plants and garden furniture. Second-hand bookshop.

Making the most of your day: family activities. Weekday garden tours. New Domestic Wing opens this summer. Winter lights: garden illuminated at night, December weekends.
Dogs: assistance dogs only. Dog walking routes nearby.

Access for all: 🅿️♿🚾🦽👪↻🎞️♿👁️◐
Abbey and mill 🦽♿ Grounds ♿▶️🦽🦽

Getting here: see website for details.
Parking: free, 50 yards.

Finding out more: 01223 810080 or angleseyabbey@nationaltrust.org.uk

Anglesey Abbey		M	T	W	T	F	S	S
House								
12 Mar–20 Jul	11–5			W	T	F	S	S
22 Jul–7 Sep	11–5		T	W	T	F	S	S
10 Sep–2 Nov	11–5			W	T	F	S	S
House (guided tours)								
11 Mar–15 Jul	11:30–2:30		T					
9 Sep–28 Oct	11:30–2:30		T					
4 Nov–23 Dec	12–1:30		T	W	T	F		
Lode Mill								
1 Jan–28 Dec	11–4			W	T	F	S	S
Garden, restaurant, shop and plant centre								
1 Jan–30 Mar	10:30–4:30	M	T	W	T	F	S	S
31 Mar–2 Nov	10–5:30	M	T	W	T	F	S	S
3 Nov–31 Dec	10:30–4:30	M	T	W	T	F	S	S

Mill and house open on Bank Holiday Mondays. Timed tickets to house on busy days. Last entry to house and bookshop 4. House tours: summer, every 30 minutes 11:30 to 2:30; winter, 12 and 1:30. Property closed 24 to 26 December. Snowdrop season: 1 February to 9 March.

Blickling Estate

Blickling, Aylsham, Norfolk NR11 6NF

Map (3) J4 🏠🍴✽♿🛏🔔🍷 1940

Nobody ever forgets their first sight of Blickling. The turreted red-brick Jacobean mansion and cherished yew hedges sit at the heart of a beautiful garden, serene lake and 202-hectare (500-acre) historic park. Widely accepted as the birthplace of Anne Boleyn, stories of the estate's complex family history are many and varied – and include tales of king's mistresses, political intrigue and social ambition. Experience the atmospheric Long Gallery; housing the most important book collection in the National Trust, it showcases the significance of the printed word. Don't leave without exploring the estate by bike or on foot. With its working farms, woodland and narrow lanes, you'll find a landscape that is quintessentially 'Norfolk'.

Eating and shopping: two cafés and restaurant. Large second-hand bookshop. Stamp shop, gift shop, plant centre and pub (not National Trust).

Making the most of your day: events and activities for all ages. Changing local art, craft and photography exhibitions. Living history performances. Open-air theatre and music concerts. RAF Oulton Museum. Free house and garden tours. Fishing. Waymarked parkland walks (guides available from visitor reception). Pyramid mausoleum. Cycle hire and marked routes. Felbrigg Hall nearby. Stay for longer in one of the estate holiday cottages.

Blickling Estate, Norfolk, above and below: so much to explore

Cycling at Blickling in Norfolk

Dogs: welcome on leads in park and courtyard café. Assistance dogs welcome in formal garden.

Access for all: 🅿️🅳♿🔉♿📖♿
House ♿♿♿♿
Gardens ♿➡️♿

Getting here: see website for details.
Parking: 400 yards.

Finding out more: 01263 738030 or blickling@nationaltrust.org.uk

Blickling Estate		M	T	W	T	F	S	S
Historic park and woodland								
Open all year	Dawn–dusk	**M**	**T**	**W**	**T**	**F**	**S**	**S**
Gardens, shop and cafés								
2 Jan–6 Jan	10:15–4	**M**	·	·	**T**	**F**	**S**	**S**
9 Jan–14 Feb	10:15–3	·	·	·	**T**	**F**	**S**	**S**
15 Feb–2 Nov	10:15–5:30	**M**	**T**	**W**	**T**	**F**	**S**	**S**
6 Nov–21 Dec	10:15–4	·	·	·	**T**	**F**	**S**	**S**
House								
15 Feb–23 Feb	11–3:30	**M**	**T**	**W**	**T**	**F**	**S**	**S**
1 Mar–16 Mar	11–3	·	·	·	·	·	**S**	**S**
17 Mar–2 Nov	12–5	**M**	·	**W**	**T**	**F**	**S**	**S**
8 Nov–30 Nov	11–2	·	·	·	·	·	**S**	**S**
6 Dec–21 Dec	11–5	·	·	·	·	·	**S**	**S**

Last entry to house one hour before closing. House also open on Tuesday 8, 15 and 22 April, 27 May, 29 July, 5, 12, 19 and 26 August, 2 September, 28 October. Cycle hire available at weekends and daily during school holidays. House open for 'backstage' tours only in November.

Bourne Mill

Bourne Road, Colchester, Essex CO2 8RT

Map ③ I8   🏛️ 1936

Delightful piece of late Elizabethan playfulness built for banquets and converted into a mill, still with working waterwheel. **Note**: sorry no toilet. Limited parking in mill grounds.

Finding out more: 01206 572422 or bournemill@nationaltrust.org.uk

Brancaster Activity Centre

Dial House, Harbour Way, Brancaster Staithe, Norfolk PE31 8BW

Map ③ H3   🏠♿🚌🛏️🍴 1984

A residential activity centre suitable for a wide range of groups including schools and families. Our adventurous activities and field studies can also be enjoyed by day visitors. A great venue for meetings and training sessions, as well as an ideal base for exploring the North Norfolk coast and countryside. **Note**: please contact the centre for more information on residential group bookings, courses and activities. Prices vary according to activity.

Eating and shopping: meals for residents are prepared fresh on site, using locally sourced produce whenever possible (some grown in our garden). Small gift shop selling local and ethical products available for guests.

Making the most of your day: range of coastal discovery activities and adventurous pursuits. Special interest workshops. Family fun weeks. Guided tours of Brancaster Estate and local area. **Dogs**: please contact the centre.

Access for all: Activity Centre 🏘️👨‍👩‍👧

Getting here: see website for details.
Parking: limited within Harbour Way, Brancaster Staithe (not National Trust).

Finding out more: 01485 210719 or brancaster@nationaltrust.org.uk

Brancaster	M	T	W	T	F	S	S

Please contact the centre for more information on residential group bookings, courses and activities.

An adventure at Brancaster Activity Centre, Norfolk

Coggeshall Grange Barn

Grange Hill, Coggeshall, Colchester, Essex CO6 1RE

Map ③ I8    **1989**

One of the largest medieval timber-framed buildings in Europe, with oak timbers soaring into a cathedral-like roof spanning eight centuries.

Finding out more: 01376 562226 or coggeshall@nationaltrust.org.uk

Elizabethan House Museum

4 South Quay, Great Yarmouth, Norfolk NR30 2QH

Map ③ K5   **1943**

An amazing hands-on museum that will enthrall and fascinate all ages. The museum reflects the life and times of the families who lived in this 16th-century quayside building, from Tudor right through to Victorian times. **Note**: house managed by Norfolk Museums and Archaeology Service.

Eating and shopping: small shop.

Making the most of your day: activity-packed toy room for children and hands-on activities, including Tudor dressing-up costumes.

Access for all: 📷🖼️🔲📺🎵👁️ Building 🔲🏘️

Getting here: see website for details.
Parking: free at South Quay or town centre (pay and display), not National Trust.

Finding out more: 01493 855746 or elizabethanhouse@nationaltrust.org.uk

Elizabethan House Museum		M	T	W	T	F	S	S
1 Apr–31 Oct	10–4	M	T	W	T	F		S

Felbrigg Hall, Gardens and Estate

Felbrigg, Norwich, Norfolk NR11 8PR

Map ③ J4 🏠 ✝ ❀ 🎬 🛏 1969

This 'bountiful estate' really lives up to its name. Felbrigg Hall is full of delights, a surprising mixture of opulence and homeliness where every room has something to feed the imagination. The decorative and productive walled garden traditionally provided fruit and vegetables for the kitchens of the Hall and now provides inspiration to visitors, flowers for the Hall and, occasionally, produce to the tea-room. The rolling landscape park with a lake, 211 hectares (520 acres) of woods and miles of waymarked trails, is a great place to explore nature, spot wildlife or just to get away from it all.

Eating and shopping: tea-room offers homemade and locally sourced cakes and snacks. Gift shop with wide range of goods and plants. Well-stocked second-hand bookshop.

Making the most of your day: children's trails. Events, including Chilli Fiesta, Honey Fair, the Hall at Harvest and Hall at Christmas.

Dogs: on leads in parkland when stock grazing, under close control in woodland.

Access for all: 🅿️♿ Dℐ♿ 🚻 👢♿ 🏠♿ ⦂♿ 🅰️
Hall 🏠♿ 🅱️   Grounds 🏠♿ 🚶♿ ➡️ ♿

Getting here: see website for details.
Sat Nav: gives poor directions, follow brown signs.

Finding out more: 01263 837444 or felbrigg@nationaltrust.org.uk

Felbrigg Hall		M	T	W	T	F	S	S
House and bookshop								
1 Mar–26 Oct	11–5	M	T	W	·	·	S	S
21 Jul–29 Aug*	11–5	M	T	W	T	F	S	S
27 Oct–2 Nov	11–4	M	T	W	·	·	S	S
Gardens								
1 Mar–26 Oct	11–5:30	M	T	W	T	F	S	S
27 Oct–2 Nov	11–4	M	T	W	T	F	S	S
Refreshments and shop								
1 Mar–2 Nov	10:30–5:30	M	T	W	T	F	S	S
27 Dec–31 Dec	11–3	M	T	W	·	·	S	S
Gardens, refreshments, shop and bookshop								
6 Nov–21 Dec	11–3	·	·	·	T	F	S	S
Refreshments, shop and bookshop								
4 Jan–23 Feb	11–3	·	·	·	·	·	S	S
Parkland								
Open all year	Dawn–dusk	M	T	W	T	F	S	S

House and bookshop open Good Friday, times as above.
*21 July to 29 August: access to some areas of house may be limited on Thursdays and Fridays.

A waterfall of wisteria at Felbrigg Hall in Norfolk

Flatford: Bridge Cottage, Suffolk: set in a landscape which inspired Constable so many years ago, it is just as alluring today

Flatford: Bridge Cottage

Flatford, East Bergholt, Suffolk CO7 6UL

Map ③ I8   🏠 ⭐ 1943

In an idyllic location by the River Stour, the quiet hamlet of Flatford sits surrounded by beautiful Dedham Vale countryside. A short walk from Bridge Cottage are the locations which inspired many of Constable's iconic paintings. You can stand in the very same places that Constable stood so many years ago and enjoy views that he would recognise. Our small exhibition will give you an insight into Constable's paintings, then you could explore the countryside on foot or hire a boat and row along the river to immerse yourself in the history and beauty of Flatford. **Note**: no public access inside to Field Studies Council – Flatford Mill, Valley Farm and Willy Lott's house.

Eating and shopping: riverside tea-room serving homemade cakes and light lunches. Shop selling plants, gifts and souvenirs.

Making the most of your day: volunteer guides offer tours sharing their passion for Constable and show some of the locations he used. Waymarked countryside walks and family trails around Flatford. **Dogs**: welcome, but be aware of livestock.

Access for all: 🅿️🅳♿🚻♿♿📷♿:•🅰️
Bridge Cottage ♿♿   Grounds ♿♿♿

Getting here: see website for details.
Parking: 200 yards.

Finding out more: 01206 298260 or flatfordbridgecottage@nationaltrust.org.uk

Flatford: Bridge Cottage		M	T	W	T	F	S	S
4 Jan–2 Mar	10:30–3:30						S	S
5 Mar–30 Mar	10:30–5			W	T	F	S	S
31 Mar–27 Apr	10:30–5	M	T	W	T	F	S	S
28 Apr–28 Sep	10:30–5:30	M	T	W	T	F	S	S
29 Sep–26 Oct	10:30–5	M	T	W	T	F	S	S
29 Oct–21 Dec	10:30–3:30			W	T	F	S	S

Striking Horsey Windpump, Norfolk, offers stunning views

Horsey Windpump

Horsey, Great Yarmouth, Norfolk NR29 4EF

Map ③ K4 　🏕🦆🏰🐾🛏 1948

This striking windpump offers stunning views over Horsey Mere and the mysterious broadland landscape, full of exceptional wildlife. Here you'll find a great introduction to the Broads – whether you want to go for a walk, visit the beach or just enjoy a cup of tea. **Note**: surrounded by Horsey Estate – managed by the Buxton family. Building work to replace stock/sails.

Eating and shopping: Horsey Staithe Stores (next to Horsey Windpump) serving light refreshments and selling local gifts, souvenirs and books.

Making the most of your day: walking routes to Horsey Mere and to the beach, refreshments are available at Horsey Staithe Stores.

Boat trips (not National Trust) across Horsey Mere (holiday periods only). **Dogs**: welcome (on leads near wildlife and livestock).

Access for all: 🅿♿🚻🧷🛋📷📷🚶♿
Windpump 🦽♿♿　Grounds ♿➡

Getting here: see website for details.
Parking: 50 yards, pay and display.

Finding out more: 01493 393450 or horseywindpump@nationaltrust.org.uk. Norfolk Coast Office, Friary Farm, Cley Road, Blakeney, Norfolk NR25 7NW

Horsey Windpump		M	T	W	T	F	S	S
Horsey Windpump								
1 Mar–30 Mar	10–4:30	·	·	·	·	·	S	S
31 Mar–2 Nov	10–4:30	M	T	W	T	F	S	S
Horsey Staithe Stores								
1 Mar–30 Mar	10–4:30	·	·	·	·	·	S	S
31 Mar–2 Nov	10–4:30	M	T	W	T	F	S	S
8 Nov–30 Nov	10–4:30	·	·	·	·	·	S	S

Car park open all year, dawn to dusk.

We welcome dogs assisting visitors with disabilities

Houghton Mill

Houghton, near Huntingdon,
Cambridgeshire PE28 2AZ

Map ③ F6   🏛️♿🏕️ [1939]

In a stunning riverside setting, surrounded by meadow walks, Houghton Mill is the oldest working watermill on the Great Ouse. There are hands-on activities for all the family, as well as milling demonstrations, and you can buy our flour, ground in the traditional way by our French burr millstones.

Eating and shopping: riverside tea-room serving snacks, cakes and scones made with our traditional stoneground flour. Small shop selling freshly ground Houghton Mill wholemeal flour, souvenirs and second-hand books.

Getting hands-on at Houghton Mill, Cambridgeshire

Making the most of your day: milling demonstrations, family events, open-air theatre and baking days. Children's trails, activities and summer holiday events. Access to surrounding meadows via public footpaths. Riverside caravan and campsite.
Dogs: welcome in grounds.

Access for all: 🅿️♿🚾🦽🖐️📷🎦🎧♿
Building 🚶🚶 Grounds ➡️

Getting here: see website for details.
Parking: 20 yards, pay and display.

Finding out more: 01480 301494 or houghtonmill@nationaltrust.org.uk

Houghton Mill		M	T	W	T	F	S	S
Mill and tea-room								
15 Mar–1 Oct	11*–5	M	T	W	·	·	S	S
4 Oct–26 Oct	11–5	·	·	·	·	·	S	S

*Mill open 1 to 5 weekdays. Open Bank Holiday Mondays and Good Friday 11 to 5. Caravan and campsite: open March to October; managed by the Caravan Club (01480 466716). Car park closes 8 or dusk if earlier. Toilets: as tea-room but closed Thursday and Friday.

Ickworth

The Rotunda, Horringer, Bury St Edmunds,
Suffolk IP29 5QE

Map ③ H7

A grand place for a truly entertaining day out.
Ickworth's impressive Rotunda – a magnificent
showcase commissioned by the 4th Earl of
Bristol to house his priceless treasures
collected on tours around Europe in the 18th
century – is an architectural marvel. For 200
years, the eccentric, and sometimes infamous,
Hervey family added to the treasures inside
and out, also creating the earliest Italianate
garden in England. The exquisite craftsmanship
of the finest Huguenot silversmiths is
breathtaking, and you can follow the family's
history through outstanding portraits by
Gainsborough, Hogarth and Reynolds. After
walking in the tranquil parkland, experience
1930s domestic service in the restored
servants' basement, sharing the real stories and
memories of former staff who kept this country
estate running. **Note:** for wedding, conference
and banqueting facilities telephone 01284
735957; Ickworth Hotel 01284 735350.

Eating and shopping: West Wing table-service
restaurant. Porter's Lodge outdoor café
serving light snacks and refreshments.
Gift shop. Second-hand bookshop.
Plant and garden centre.

Making the most of your day: events and
activities all year, including snowdrops,
heritage daffodils and Easter Egg trails.
'Ickworth Lives' exhibition and 1930s Living
History days. Open-air theatre, cooking
workshops, Wood Fair and family Christmas
weekends. Paintings by Titian, Velázquez,
Reynolds and Gainsborough, as well as
Georgian silver collection and Italian porcelain.
Guided and waymarked walks. Cycle routes.
Geocache sites, children's play area and trim
trail. **Dogs:** welcome on leads near livestock
and close to house. Assistance dogs only in
Italianate gardens.

Access for all: 🅿️ 🅳️ ♿ 🚽 🏠 📷 🎥 ✍️
House ♿ ⬆ 🚶 **West Wing** ♿ ⬆ 🚶 ♿
Grounds 🚶 ♿ ♿ ♿

Getting here: see website for details.
Parking: in main car park.

Finding out more: 01284 735270 or
ickworth@nationaltrust.org.uk

Two views of the impressive Rotunda at Ickworth, Suffolk, opposite and below. Above, daily domestic tasks are brought to life in the kitchen

Ickworth		M	T	W	T	F	S	S
House								
14 Mar–2 Nov*	11–5	M	T	.	.	F	S	S
20 Mar–30 Oct	12–3	.	.	.	T	.	.	.
23 Jul–27 Aug	12–3	.	.	W	.	.	.	.
8 Nov–21 Dec**	11–4	.	.	.	.	.	S	S
West Wing reception, shop and restaurant								
1 Jan–13 Mar	10:30–4	M	T	W	T	F	S	S
14 Mar–2 Nov	10:30–5	M	T	W	T	F	S	S
3 Nov–31 Dec	10:30–4	M	T	W	T	F	S	S
Parkland, woods and children's playground								
Open all year	8–8	M	T	W	T	F	S	S
Italianate Gardens								
Open all year	9–5:30	M	T	W	T	F	S	S
Plant and garden shop								
15 Mar–2 Nov	11:30–5:30	M	T	W	T	F	S	S
Porter's Lodge outdoor café								
4 Jan–28 Dec	10–4	.	.	.	.	.	S	S
15 Mar–2 Nov	10–5	M	T	.	T	F	S	S
4 May–1 Sep	10–5	M	T	W	T	F	S	S

*Free guided tours only until 1 when house open, booking on the day. Free-flow only on Thursdays, Sundays and Bank Holidays. **Entrance hall and basement only weekends in December. Last entry to house one hour before closing. Closed 25 December. Gardens and plant shop opening times may be reduced outside summertime. Parkland closes 8 or dusk if earlier.

Lavenham Guildhall

Market Place, Lavenham, Sudbury,
Suffolk CO10 9QZ

Map ③ I7    1951

Set at the very heart of the lovely village of
Lavenham, the Guildhall of Corpus Christi tells
the story of one of the best-preserved and
wealthiest towns in Tudor England. When you
step inside this fine timber-framed building,
you will discover the story of the Guild and
Lavenham's famous blue cloth, as well as the
people who have used the Guildhall through
history. Be sure to treat yourself to one of our
delicious homemade cakes before exploring
the picturesque streets of Lavenham, lined with
more than 320 buildings of historic interest.
Note: parts of property may close for
refurbishment in March and April.

Eating and shopping: tea-room serving light
lunches, cream teas, and hot and cold drinks.

Lavenham Guildhall in Suffolk sits at the very heart
of this lovely village

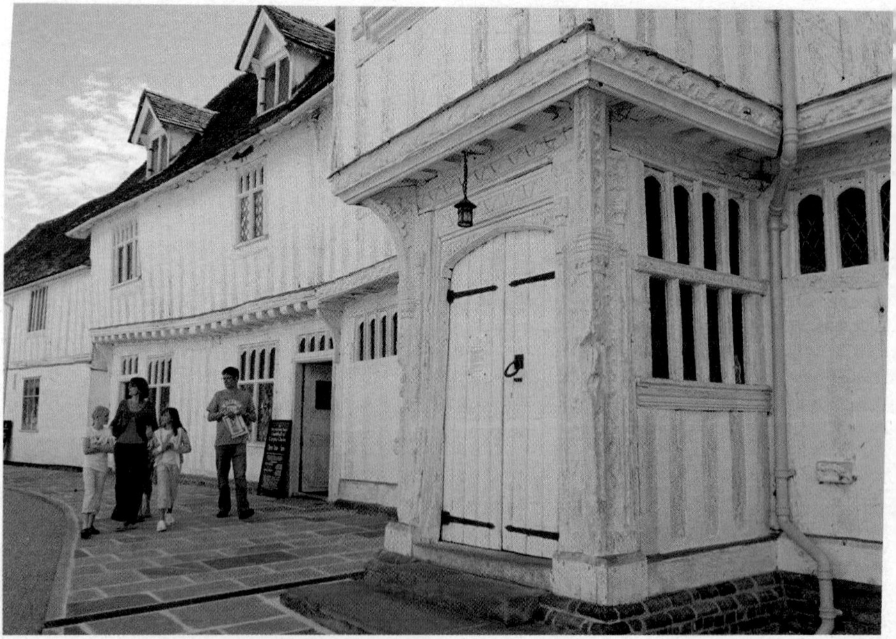

Shop selling local gifts, souvenirs,
books and plants.

Making the most of your day: children's
activities, including house trails and Tudor
dressing-up costumes. Guided walks and talks
(summer). Events. Local history exhibition.

Access for all: ♿ 🚻 🏷 🖥 📷 👁 🅿
Guildhall ♿ 🏷   Garden ♿ 🏷

Getting here: see website for details.
Parking: free in village.

Finding out more: 01787 247646 or
lavenhamguildhall@nationaltrust.org.uk

Lavenham Guildhall		M	T	W	T	F	S	S
Guildhall, tea-room and shop								
8 Mar–30 Mar	11–4	·	·	W	T	F	S	S
31 Mar–31 Oct	11–5	M	T	W	T	F	S	S
1 Nov–30 Nov	11–4	·	·	·	·	·	S	S
Shop								
4 Jan–2 Mar	11–4	·	·	·	·	·	S	S
1 Nov–21 Dec	11–4	·	·	·	T	F	S	S
Tea-room								
1 Nov–21 Dec	11–4	·	·	·	T	F	S	S

During spring some parts of the building may not
be accessible due to our Heritage Lottery-funded
re-presentation project of the whole museum.

Melford Hall

Long Melford, Sudbury, Suffolk CO10 9AA

Map ③ I7   🏠 ✿ 🖼 | 1960 |

For almost five centuries the picturesque turrets of Melford Hall have dominated Long Melford's village green. Melford Hall is an eclectic mixture of old and new, and its architecture and furnishings chart the changing tastes and fashions of the successive generations who called Melford Hall home. Above all though, Melford is a story of love, determination and survival after it was almost destroyed in both 1642 and 1942. Today it remains a welcoming family home where you can follow in the footsteps of Beatrix Potter and royalty and experience the hospitable charm that this wonderful Suffolk gem has always offered.

Picturesque Melford Hall in Suffolk, right and below, remains a warm family home, where visitors are welcome to picnic and play games on the lawn

Eating and shopping: small tea-room or Park Room serving sandwiches and cream teas. Gatehouse shop selling souvenirs, gifts, second-hand books, souvenir story books and plants.

Making the most of your day: walks, talks and family events. Children's spot-it quiz and trail. **Dogs**: on leads in car park and park walk only.

Access for all: 🅿️♿🚻🍴🏠🔄📷
Building ♿🏠📷🅿️   Grounds ♿🏠

Getting here: see website for details.
Parking: free.

Finding out more: 01787 376395 (Infoline). 01787 379228 or melford@nationaltrust.org.uk

Melford Hall		M	T	W	T	F	S	S
2 Apr–31 Oct	1–5	·	·	**W**	**T**	**F**	**S**	**S**

Open Bank Holiday Mondays.

Oxburgh Hall

Oxborough, near Swaffham, Norfolk PE33 9PS

Map ③ H5 ⊞✝❀⊤ 1952

No one ever forgets their first sight of Oxburgh. This romantic, moated manor house was built by the Bedingfeld family in the 15th century and they have lived here ever since. Inside, visitors can learn about the family's Roman Catholic history, including the secret priest's hole. There is also astonishing needlework by Mary, Queen of Scots, and a display of historic wallpaper samples. You can climb the original spiral stairs to the gatehouse roof and enjoy panoramic views, and the family chapel is also open. Outside, there is a woodcarving trail in the gardens and woodlands to explore.

Eating and shopping: tea-room in old Kitchen and Servants' Hall. The Pantry is a seasonal kiosk serving light refreshments. Picnic area. Gift shop selling local East Anglian products. Plant sales. Second-hand bookshop.

Making the most of your day: free daily guided garden tours and winter weekend snowdrop walks. Free children's trails in house and garden. Year-round events. Woodland walks and nature trails. **Dogs**: assistance dogs only.

Access for all: 🅿♿🚻♿♿🎦📷📖🎦♿
Hall ♿♿🚼♿ Chapel ♿ Garden ♿➡♿

Getting here: see website for details.
Parking: free.

Finding out more: 01366 328258 or oxburghhall@nationaltrust.org.uk

Romantic moated Oxburgh Hall in Norfolk, home to the Bedingfeld family since the 15th century, contains many stories and secrets

Oxburgh Hall		M	T	W	T	F	S	S
Garden, shop and tea-room								
4 Jan–16 Feb	11–4	·	·	·	·	·	S	S
17 Feb–26 Feb	11–4	M	T	W	·	·	S	S
27 Oct–2 Nov	11–4	M	T	W	T	F	S	S
8 Nov–21 Dec	11–4	·	·	·	·	·	S	S
House timed tours								
15 Feb–26 Feb	12–2:30	M	T	W	·	·	S	S
House, garden, shop and tea-room								
1 Mar–6 Apr*	11–5	M	T	W	·	·	S	S
7 Apr–20 Apr*	11–5	M	T	W	T	F	S	S
21 Apr–25 May*	11–5	M	T	W	·	·	S	S
26 May–1 Jun*	11–5	M	T	W	T	F	S	S
2 Jun–30 Jul*	11–5	M	T	W	·	·	S	S
31 Jul–31 Aug*	11–5	M	T	W	T	F	S	S
1 Sep–1 Oct*	11–5	M	T	W	·	·	S	S
4 Oct–2 Nov	11–4	M	T	W	·	·	S	S

*Admission to garden, shop and tea-room from 10:30.

Paycocke's House and Garden

25 West Street, Coggeshall, Colchester, Essex CO6 1NS

Map ③ I8    **1924**

Exquisitely carved half-timbered Tudor cloth merchant's house (below), with a beautiful and tranquil cottage garden. Visitors can follow the changing fortunes of the house over its 500 years of history, as it went from riches to rags, and see how it was saved from demolition and restored to its former glory.

Eating and shopping: coffee shop serving cream teas, coffee and cakes. Garden room shop selling local products, crafts and gifts. Second-hand bookshop. Plants available at our garden stall. Picnics welcome.

Making the most of your day: children's activities, including trail, costumes and garden games. Events all year, including walks, exhibitions and open-air cinema. Why not combine with a visit to Coggeshall Grange Barn nearby? **Dogs**: welcome in garden only.

Access for all: 🐶🚻🏬♿📷🎧🅿
Building 🏠 **Grounds** 🏠

Getting here: see website for details.
Parking: at Grange Barn, ½ mile (1 to 4:30).
Free car park at Stoneham Street, ¼ mile (not National Trust). Limited roadside parking.

Finding out more: 01376 561305 or paycockes@nationaltrust.org.uk

Paycocke's		M	T	W	T	F	S	S
26 Mar–2 Nov	11–5*	·	·	W	T	F	S	S

*Garden opens at 10:30, coffee shop closes 4:30.
Open Bank Holiday Mondays.

Peckover House and Garden

North Brink, Wisbech, Cambridgeshire PE13 1JR

Map ③ G5 [icons] 1943

Peckover House is a secret gem, an oasis hidden away in an urban environment. A classic Georgian merchant's town house, it was lived in by the Peckover family for 150 years. The Peckovers were staunch Quakers, which meant they had a very simple lifestyle, yet at the same time they ran a successful private bank. Both facets of their life can be seen as you wander through the house and gardens. The very large garden is an outstanding sensory delight, with newly restored Orangery, summerhouses, croquet lawn, herbaceous borders and more than 60 varieties of roses.

Eating and shopping: tea-room in the barn. Gift shop in old banking wing. Second-hand bookshop. Plant sales.

A blaze of colour in the garden at Peckover House, Cambridgeshire: an oasis hidden away in an urban environment

Making the most of your day: Bechstein piano to play. Free garden tours. Croquet (summer). Children's handling collection and trails. Behind-the-scenes tours (selected days). Octavia Hill's birthplace nearby.
Dogs: assistance dogs only.

Access for all: [icons]
House [icons] Garden [icons]

Getting here: see website for details.
Sat Nav: use PE13 1RG for nearest car park.
Parking: free in town, nearest is Chapel Road, 300 yards (not National Trust).

Finding out more: 01945 583463 or peckover@nationaltrust.org.uk

Peckover House and Garden		M	T	W	T	F	S	S
4 Jan–23 Feb*	12–4						S	S
1 Mar–6 Apr	12–5	M	T	W			S	S
7 Apr–20 Apr	12–5	M	T	W	T	F	S	S
21 Apr–25 May	12–5	M	T	W			S	S
26 May–1 Jun	12–5	M	T	W	T	F	S	S
2 Jun–29 Jun	12–5	M	T	W			S	S
30 Jun–6 Jul	12–5	M	T	W	T	F	S	S
7 Jul–26 Oct	12–5	M	T	W			S	S
27 Oct–2 Nov	12–5	M	T	W	T	F	S	S
6 Dec–14 Dec	12–5						S	S

*4 January to 23 February, admission to house by timed conservation tour only, 1:30 and 3. 1 March to 2 November, house open at 1, shop closes at 4:30. 2 to 5 July, garden opens 11, house 12.

Ramsey Abbey Gatehouse

Abbey School, Ramsey, Huntingdon, Cambridgeshire PE26 1DH

Map ③ F6　🐘 1952

This fascinating medieval gatehouse along with the Lady Chapel are all that remain of the great Benedictine abbey at Ramsey. **Note:** exterior open all year. Gatehouse and Lady Chapel in Abbey open first Sunday of month, April to September (1 to 5). Sorry no toilets.

Finding out more: 01284 747500 or ramseyabbey@nationaltrust.org.uk

St George's Guildhall

29 King Street, King's Lynn, Norfolk PE30 1HA

Map ③ H5　🐘 1951

The largest surviving medieval guildhall in England, with many original features – now a theatre. **Note:** managed by King's Lynn and West Norfolk Borough Council and King's Lynn Arts Centre Trust.

Finding out more: 01553 779095. 01553 764864 (box office) or stgeorgesguildhall@nationaltrust.org.uk

Shaw's Corner

Ayot St Lawrence, near Welwyn, Hertfordshire AL6 9BX

Map ③ F9　🐘 ❁ 1944

You can follow in the footsteps of one of the world's greatest playwrights, George Bernard Shaw, as you explore his fascinating home and enjoy the beauty and tranquillity of his inspiring garden.

Shaw's Corner, Hertfordshire: the great man's writing shed

Note: access roads very narrow.

Eating and shopping: souvenir shop. Second-hand bookshop. Ice-cream and soft drinks available in garden. Pre-1950s varieties of plants for sale.

Making the most of your day: events, including open-air performances of George Bernard Shaw's plays (summer). **Dogs:** assistance dogs only.

Access for all: 🅿️♿ 🖼️ 🎧 ⠿ 🅰️
House 🔆 ♿ 👪 ♿　Grounds 🔆 ♿ ♿

Getting here: see website for details.
Parking: free, 30 yards.

Finding out more: 01438 829221 (Infoline). 01438 820307 or shawscorner@nationaltrust.org.uk

Shaw's Corner		M	T	W	T	F	S	S
22 Mar–2 Nov	12–5:30*	·	·	**W**	**T**	**F**	**S**	**S**

*House open 1 to 5. Open Bank Holiday Mondays.

Sutton Hoo

Tranmer House, Sutton Hoo, Woodbridge, Suffolk IP12 3DJ

Map ③ J7 🏠 🏛 ♿ 🚶 ☂ 1998

Undisturbed for 1,300 years, an Anglo-Saxon king and his treasured possessions were unearthed days before the outbreak of the Second World War, changing our perceptions of the past for ever. The atmospheric ancient burial mounds, breathtaking replica treasure, original finds and reconstruction of the king's burial chamber bring this fascinating story to life. Edith Pretty's Arts and Crafts country house takes you back to that remarkable discovery, while sitting and relaxing in true 1930s style. Beautiful seasonal colours and wildlife can be seen all year on the estate walks.

Eating and shopping: café serving locally sourced and homemade food. Gift shop selling exclusive ceramics and jewellery. Second-hand bookshop.

Making the most of your day: events and family activities all year. 'Let's Dig It!' archaeology trench, Anglo-Saxon festivals and encampments, living history, children's play area as well as wildlife and nature walks. **Dogs**: welcome on leads in park and café terrace area only.

Access for all: 🅿️ ♿ ♿ ♿ ♿ ♿ ♿ ♿ ••
Buildings ♿ ♿   Grounds ♿ ➡ ♿ ♿

Getting here: see website for details.
Parking: 30 yards (pay and display when exhibition closed).

Finding out more: 01394 389700 or suttonhoo@nationaltrust.org.uk

Sutton Hoo		M	T	W	T	F	S	S
1 Jan–5 Jan	11–4	·	·	**W**	**T**	**F**	**S**	**S**
11 Jan–9 Feb	11–4	·	·	·	·	·	**S**	**S**
15 Feb–23 Feb	11–4	**M**	**T**	**W**	**T**	**F**	**S**	**S**
1 Mar–9 Mar	11–4	·	·	·	·	·	**S**	**S**
15 Mar–2 Nov	10:30–5	**M**	**T**	**W**	**T**	**F**	**S**	**S**
8 Nov–28 Dec	11–4	·	·	·	·	·	**S**	**S**
29 Dec–31 Dec	11–4	**M**	**T**	**W**	·	·	·	·

Open Bank Holiday Mondays. Estate walks open daily all year, 9 to 6 (except for some Thursdays, November to end December).

Sutton Hoo, Suffolk: a reconstructed warrior's helmet gives a flavour of the many treasures unearthed at this atmospheric Anglo-Saxon burial site

Members may have to pay on special events days

The Theatre Royal Bury St Edmunds, Suffolk, is the only surviving Regency playhouse in Britain

Theatre Royal Bury St Edmunds

Westgate Street, Bury St Edmunds,
Suffolk IP33 1QR

Map ③ I7 🏠🔔🍴 1974

This Grade I listed theatre, one of the country's most significant theatre buildings and the only surviving Regency playhouse in Britain, will give you an intimate and unique theatrical experience. We offer year-round tours and open-door sessions. **Note**: managed by Bury St Edmunds Theatre Management Ltd. Admission charges apply to live shows and selected guided tours (including members).

Eating and shopping: gifts and souvenirs on sale. Light snacks available in Greene Room.

Making the most of your day: tours and self-guided visits.

Access for all: ♿🚻 **Building** 🏛♿

Getting here: see website for details.
Parking: free on Westgate Street or at Swan Lane, 546 yards.

Finding out more: 01284 769505 or theatreroyal@nationaltrust.org.uk

Theatre Royal Bury St Edmunds		M	T	W	T	F	S	S
1 Feb–10 May	10:30–1	·	·	·	·	·	S	·
4 Feb–15 May	2–4	·	T	·	T	·	·	·
17 May–2 Aug*	11–5	·	·	·	·	·	S	S
6 Aug–16 Aug**	11:30–3:30	·	·	W	T	F	S	S
2 Sep–13 Nov	2–4	·	T	·	T	·	·	·
6 Sep–15 Nov	10:30–1	·	·	·	·	·	S	·

Guided tours: February to May and September to November, Tuesdays and Thursdays at 2, Saturdays at 11. *'Backstage Past': guided tours, Saturdays and Sundays at 11:30 and 3. **'Backstage Past': performance-led tours, Wednesday to Sunday, 11:30, 2 and 3:30. Call before visiting. As a working theatre, opening times may vary – see www.theatreroyal.org

Willington Dovecote and Stables

Willington, Church End, near Bedford,
Bedfordshire MK44 3PX

Map ③ F7 🏠 1914

A hidden gem in a tranquil setting, these outstanding Tudor stone buildings were built for Henry VIII's 1541 visit. **Note**: sorry no toilet. Open last Sunday of month (April to September) and other times by appointment with the voluntary custodian, Mrs J. Endersby, 01234 838278.

Finding out more: 01284 747500 or willingtondovecote@nationaltrust.org.uk

Wimpole Estate

Arrington, Royston, Cambridgeshire SG8 0BW

Map ③ G7

1976

A unique working estate, with an impressive mansion at its heart. We will tell you the stories of the people who shaped Wimpole, while you soak up the atmosphere and take in the spectacular views. Inside the hall, the smaller, more intimate rooms contrast with the equally beautiful but grander Georgian interiors. While outside, there are pleasure grounds and a walled garden, bursting with seasonal produce and glorious herbaceous borders. At Home Farm, you can contrast the traditional farmyard with the noisy modern piggery and cattle sheds, while our stockman explains about our rare breeds, your food and our farming.
Note: half-price entry to Home Farm for members (under-fives free).

Wimpole Estate, Cambridgeshire: the impressive mansion, below, and making friends with a local resident, above

Eating and shopping: Old Rectory Restaurant and Farm Café serving dishes made with walled garden and Home Farm produce. Shop selling local pottery, gifts, Wimpole rare-breed meat and eggs. Plant sales. Second-hand bookshop.

Making the most of your day: guided walks, bat and wildlife walks, free family trails and Tracker Packs. Daily farm activities. Events, including lambing time, open-air theatre, craft fair and Christmas events. **Dogs**: welcome on leads in park.

Access for all: 🅿️♿🚻👶♿🖐️📷🎧📷♿
Hall ♿ Farm ♿ Gardens ♿➡️♿

Getting here: see website for details.
Parking: 275 yards.

Finding out more: 01223 206000 or wimpole@nationaltrust.org.uk

Wimpole Estate		M	T	W	T	F	S	S
Garden, Old Rectory Restaurant and stable block								
1 Jan–14 Feb	11–4	M	T	W	T	F	S	S
15 Feb–2 Nov	10–5	M	T	W	T	F	S	S
3 Nov–31 Dec	11–4	M	T	W	T	F	S	S
Home Farm and Farm Café								
4 Jan–9 Feb	11–4	·	·	·	·	·	S	S
15 Feb–2 Nov	10:30–5	M	T	W	T	F	S	S
8 Nov–28 Dec	11–4	·	·	·	·	·	S	S
Hall								
1 Mar–2 Nov	11–5	M	T	W	T	·	S	S
Hall (guided basement tour)								
8 Nov–21 Dec	11–3	·	·	·	·	·	S	S
Park								
Open all year	Dawn–dusk	M	T	W	T	F	S	S

Home Farm open 1 to 6 January and 27 to 31 December, daily, 11 to 4. Estate closed 25, 26 December except park and stable block (servery and gift shops) open 26 December 11 to 4. Bookshop as shop, but closed Monday mornings.

Midlands

Journey through time at the Birmingham Back to Backs, to discover what it was like to live between the 1840s and 1970s

Outdoors in the Midlands

At the very heart of England, the Midlands offers a stunning variety of natural landscapes just waiting to be explored. From the wild beauty of the Shropshire Hills and dramatic views of the Peak District, to the open parkland of Clumber Park and panoramic views of Clent Hills, there is so much to enjoy. For an area with many urban communities and major cities, including Birmingham and Nottingham, the amount of green space is remarkable, making the outdoors and nature truly accessible for all.

Right: **Dark Peak in the Peak District, Derbyshire**

We have a wealth of activities, to suit all ages and energy levels, which will help you connect with the outdoors.

Wonderful walking
We are spoilt for choice when it comes to walking. So whether it be a gentle amble or a long ramble, the Midlands has the walk for you. Many of our estates have pleasant circular routes – at Brockhampton in Herefordshire there's a one and a half-mile route which is perfect for the family. Or, if you prefer a good ramble, the 'Long Mynd' (Long Mountain) in Shropshire has an ancient track, known as the Portway, which extends for ten miles and is home to a wide variety of flora and fauna.

Outdoor play

What better way to encourage children to connect with the great outdoors than by play? And it's so much fun. Throughout the Midlands our places offer plenty of space to let young imaginations run wild. Why not explore the new natural play areas at Baddesley Clinton in Warwickshire and Kinver Edge in Staffordshire? Or, at Longshaw in Derbyshire, let the magical characters, the Boggarts, bring the natural play area to life.

Pedal power

Cycling is a great way to be active and enjoy the outdoors. We have routes to cater for all abilities. For a heart rate-raising experience, explore the mountain bike trails at Carding Mill Valley in Shropshire or, for a more gentle pace, hire bikes for the family at Clumber Park in Nottinghamshire and take your pick from more than 20 miles of cycle routes.

Camping

A camping holiday is the perfect way to spend quality time with the family. In the Peak District we have a campsite at Upper Booth Farm in Edale, so you can pitch your tent and enjoy the spectacular scenery. For an alternative camping experience, staying in one of the camping pods or yurt at Clumber Park in Nottinghamshire can't be beaten.

Above:
**Dudmaston
Estate,
Shropshire**
Right: **Dovedale,
Derbyshire**

Wildlife spotting

Whether you want to wind down from everyday life or teach your children to identify different butterflies, wildlife spotting is good for the soul. You can glimpse deer at Calke Abbey in Derbyshire and Attingham Park in Shropshire, while our new bird hides at Croome in Worcestershire and Carding Mill Valley in Shropshire are ideal for watching birds.

Or just relax…

If a relaxed pace is more your thing, you can still experience the outdoors in this lovely area.

Stroll through the enchanting wooded parkland at the Dudmaston Estate in Shropshire or enjoy the perfect picnic at Hardwick Hall in Derbyshire, where you can spread out a blanket on the green within the Stableyard.

Outdoors in the Midlands

With a huge variety of landscapes and places to enjoy, the Midlands offers countryside on your doorstep that is waiting to be explored.

Carding Mill Valley and the Shropshire Hills

Church Stretton, Shropshire

Map ④ H5 🏚🍴🔖🐕🍵 1965

With 2,000 hectares (4,942 acres) of heather-covered hills featuring iconic views of the Shropshire Hills Area of Outstanding Natural Beauty. An important place for wildlife, geology, landscape and archaeology, with excellent visitor facilities and information in Carding Mill Valley.

Eating and shopping: Chalet Pavilion tea-room serves local food, including hot lunches, drinks and ice-cream. The shop sells gifts, souvenirs, maps and pond nets.

Making the most of your day: events all year. Free walks cards available in Carding Mill Valley. **Dogs**: under close control (grazing livestock).

Access for all: 🅿♿🇩♿🚻♿❗♿🎵
Building ♿ Grounds ♿

Getting here: see website for details.
Sat Nav: use SY6 6JG. **Parking**: 50 yards (pay and display).

Finding out more: 01694 725000 or cardingmill@nationaltrust.org.uk

Carding Mill Valley		M	T	W	T	F	S	S
Tea-room and shop*								
1 Jan–3 Jan	10–4			W	T	F		
4 Jan–16 Feb	10–4						S	S
17 Feb–2 Nov	10–5	M	T	W	T	F	S	S
3 Nov–22 Dec	10–4	M				F	S	S
23 Dec–31 Dec	10–4	M	T	W		F	S	S

*Shop opens at 11 on weekdays. Tea-room and shop close at dusk if earlier. Tea-room and shop closed on 24 and 25 December. Toilets and information hut open 9 to 7, March to October; 9 to 4:15 November to February.

Carding Mill Valley and the Shropshire Hills, Shropshire: unique peace can be enjoyed in this outstandingly beautiful place

Breathtaking Clent Hills in Worcestershire: the perfect place for a refreshing walk or picnic

Clent Hills

near Romsley, Worcestershire

Map ④ J6  1959

Set on the edge of Birmingham and the Black Country, this green oasis with panoramic views is the perfect place for a refreshing walk or a picnic in breathtaking surroundings. Families can create their own adventures – building dens, hunting for geocaches or simply getting closer to nature. **Note**: nearest facilities at Nimmings Wood entrance.

Eating and shopping: café (not National Trust) at Nimmings Wood car park serving light meals and refreshments.

Making the most of your day: waymarked routes and monthly guided rambles (bookable). Natural play area. **Dogs**: welcome but please do be considerate of other visitors.

Access for all:

Getting here: see website for details.
Sat Nav: use B62 0NL for Nimmings Wood entrance. **Parking**: at Nimmings Wood; additional parking at Adam's Hill and Walton Hill.

Finding out more: 01562 712822 or clenthills@nationaltrust.org.uk

---
Clent Hills

Nimmings Wood car-park gates open 8 and close 5 winter, 9 in summer. Closed 25 December.

Duffield Castle

Milford Road, Duffield, Derbyshire DE56 4DW

Map ③ C4 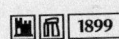 1899

Remains of one of England's largest 13th-century castles. **Note**: sorry no toilets. Steep steps.

Finding out more: 01332 844052 or duffieldcastle@nationaltrust.org.uk

---

Ulverscroft Nature Reserve

Ulverscroft, Copt Oak, near Loughborough, Leicestershire

Map ③ D5 1945

Part of the ancient forest of Charnwood, Ulverscroft is especially beautiful during the spring – with heathland and woodland habitats. **Note**: assistance dogs only. Sorry no toilet. Access by permit only from Leicestershire and Rutland Wildlife Trust (0116 272 0444) – apply several days before visit.

Finding out more: 01332 863822 or ulverscroftnaturereserve@nationaltrust.org.uk

Peak District

The Peak District has stunning scenery and breathtaking landscapes for you to enjoy throughout the year.

Dark Peak

near Hope Valley, Derbyshire

Map ③ B2 🏛 📷 ♨ ✈ ⚓ 1936

Kinder Scout, iconic plateau and home of the 1932 Mass Trespass, continues to provide exhilarating walks with glimpses of rare moorland wildlife. Footpaths and bridleways stretch across the moors from Bleaklow to Derwent Edge, while at Mam Tor, you can choose between the short trail to the ancient hilltop fortress or join part of a longer ridge walk along the Hope Valley. Winnats Pass cuts through the limestone crags from Mam Tor to Castleton – riddled with caves and ghost stories – and at Odin Mine, hidden beneath the Mam Tor landslip, you can spot remains of the old lead mining industry. **Note**: nearest toilet in adjacent villages and at visitor centres at Ladybower Reservoir, Edale and Castleton.

Eating and shopping: Penny Pot in Edale, serving cooked breakfasts, soup, sandwiches and cakes, teas and coffees. Seating and bike racks outside, sofas and log burner inside.

Making the most of your day: downloadable leaflet with walks and geocache details. Information barns. Stay longer at our Edale bunkhouse. **Dogs**: on leads at all times from early March to end July.

Access for all: 👶♿ ⚿ ♨

Getting here: see website for details.
Parking: at Mam Nick, by Mam Tor, pay and display. Also at Edale, Castleton, Bowden Bridge Hayfield, Sett Valley Hayfield and Upper Derwent Valley, all pay and display (none National Trust).

Astonishing rock formations at Dark Peak in Derbyshire

Finding out more: 01433 670368 or peakdistrict@nationaltrust.org.uk

Dark Peak		M	T	W	T	F	S	S
Penny Pot Café								
3 Jan–16 Mar	10–4					F	S	S
18 Mar–2 Nov	10–4:30		T	W	T	F	S	S
30 Jun–7 Sep	10–4:30	M	T	W	T	F	S	S
3 May–28 Sep	8:30–4:30						S	S
7 Nov–21 Dec	10–4					F	S	S
27 Dec–31 Dec	10–4	M	T	W			S	S

Open all year: information shelters at Lee Barn (SK096855) and Dalehead (SK101843) in Edale; South Head (SK060854) at Kinder; Edale End (SK161864); Grindle Barns above Ladybower Reservoir (SK189895). Mam Nick car park (SK123832). Dalehead Bunkhouse (01433 670368); camping and bed and breakfast available at some farms.

White Peak

Ilam, Ashbourne, Derbyshire

Map ③ B3 🏛🏚🛗✿🎎👣🖼⛺
1906

Ilam Park by the River Manifold offers sweeping parkland nestled beneath limestone hills. You can walk from Ilam to Dovedale, home of the famous Stepping Stones, past spectacular rock formations and through ash woodlands. Alternatively, walk or cycle along the thickly wooded Manifold Valley. Rich in wildlife and wild flowers, the White Peak area offers superb walking all year. Winster Market House stands centrally in Winster village as testimony to the thriving fairs and markets of the past. Why not stay at our caravan site or bunkhouse in Ilam Park, or try the Wetton Mill holiday cottages in the Manifold Valley? **Note**: Ilam Hall is let to the Youth Hostel Association.

Eating and shopping: Manifold tea-room at Ilam Park with stunning views. Shops at Ilam Park and Dovedale Barn offering postcard-sized walk maps, gifts and information. Café at Wetton Mill (not National Trust) overlooking the River Manifold.

Making the most of your day: now you can discover Hinkley Hollow in Ilam Park, with natural play places by the river. Seasonal trails in the school holidays and free Friday walks across the wider estate. **Dogs**: under close control and on leads in areas with livestock.

Access for all: 🅿♿🚻🛗👁👂🌐
Ilam Park stableyard ♿♿ Winster Market House ♿
Ilam Park grounds ♿♿♿➡♿

Getting here: see website for details.
Parking: Ilam Park (pay and display).

Finding out more: 01335 350503 or peakdistrict@nationaltrust.org.uk

White Peak		M	T	W	T	F	S	S
Dovedale mobile barn								
29 Mar–28 Sep	11–5	M	T	W	T	F	S	S
Ilam Park shop and tea-room								
4 Jan–16 Feb	11–4	·	·	·	·	·	S	S
17 Feb–2 Nov	11–5*	M	T	W	T	F	S	S
3 Nov–23 Dec	11–4	M	T	W	T	F	S	S
26 Dec–31 Dec	11–4	M	T	W	·	F	S	S
Winster Market House								
29 Mar–2 Nov	11–5	M	T	W	T	F	S	S

*Tea-room open at 10:30. Tea-room and shop closed 24 and 25 December.

White Peak in Derbyshire, above and left, offers superb walking all year through wonderfully varied countryside, rich in wildlife and flowers

Attingham Park

Atcham, Shrewsbury, Shropshire SY4 4TP

Map (4) H4   🏠✿♿🍷 1947

Attingham was designed for 1st Lord Berwick by George Steuart in the 1780s and sits at the heart of a grand Repton landscape. You can discover how the Berwick fortunes rose and fell and how their legacy lives on today as the family's stories are brought to life. With acres of parkland and miles of walks, walled kitchen garden, large playfield and welcoming mansion, Attingham is the perfect all-day visit. Whether you are a family looking for activities both inside and out or someone in search of a traditional inspirational visit to a historic house and parkland stroll, you'll find it here. Attingham, Shropshire's leading year-round place to visit, has something to inspire and intrigue all our visitors. **Note**: 'Attingham Re-discovered Goes Through the Roof': conservation-in-action on John Nash's picture gallery and staircase.

The welcoming mansion at Attingham Park, Shropshire, sits within acres of parkland, with miles of paths, a walled kitchen garden and playfield

Eating and shopping: the four catering outlets and three shops offer a variety of experiences and styles, including Carriage House Café (open daily), Lady Berwick's waitress-service afternoon tea (bookings accepted), Mansion tea-room, Greedy Pig Catering, Butler's Pantry, Stables and Grooms' shops.

Making the most of your day: seasonal spectacles include displays of spring bluebells, summer blossom, autumn tree colour and winter snowdrops. Event highlights include Easter, Hallowe'en, Christmas in the mansion, themed tours and walks, food and craft fairs. Daily family trails and activities during all school holidays. Late park opening (until 7) in the summer. Visitors can witness the mansion's 'Attingham Re-discovered' project and the Walled Garden Project, which continue to transform, conserve and restore Attingham. All-costumed 'Mansion Regency Wednesdays'. Follow Attingham on Twitter, Facebook and You Tube. **Dogs**: welcome in grounds with identified on and off-lead areas. Dog walkers' guide available.

Access for all: 🅿️♿️🚻♿️💬🖼️👓•••📷

Mansion ♿️♿️⬆️♿️ **Carriage House Café** ♿️

Grounds ♿️➡️♿️♿️

Getting here: see website for details.
Parking: free, 25 to 100 yards from visitor reception.

Finding out more: 01743 708123 (Infoline).
01743 708162 or attingham@nationaltrust.org.uk

Attingham Park		M	T	W	T	F	S	S
Park, Walled Garden, Playfield and Stables Courtyard Café*								
1 Jan–30 Apr	9–6	M	T	W	T	F	S	S
1 May–30 Sep	8–7	M	T	W	T	F	S	S
1 Oct–31 Dec	9–6	M	T	W	T	F	S	S
Mansion**								
1 Mar–2 Nov	10:30–5:30	M	T	W	T	F	S	S
6 Dec–7 Dec	10:30–4	·	·	·	·	·	S	S
13 Dec–23 Dec	10:30–4	M	T	W	T	F	S	S
Mansion winter tours†								
3 Jan–28 Feb	11–3	·	·	·	·	F	S	S
7 Nov–23 Nov	11–3	·	·	·	·	F	S	S
Lady Berwick's Afternoon Tea††								
1 Mar–2 Nov	1–5	·	·	W	T	F	S	S
6 Dec–7 Dec	12:30–4	·	·	·	·	·	S	S
13 Dec–23 Dec	12:30–4	M	T	W	T	F	S	S

*Park, garden, playfield and café: January, February, November and December, 9 to 5 or dusk if earlier. Walled garden, playfield and café open 9 to 6:30 from May to October. **Mansion: March to November tours only 10:30 to 12:30, then free-flow from 12:30. Bank Holiday weekends free-flow from 11. December free-flow from 10:30. Last admission one hour before closing. †Winter tours: 12 bookable. ††Lady Berwick's: bookings not necessary. Mansion tea-room: from 11, daily 15 February to 2 November, 13 to 31 December and all other weekends. Greedy Pig Playfield Catering: from 11 weekends and daily during school holidays. Stables shops: daily from 10:30. Property closed 25 December.

Young visitors make friends and get baking at Attingham Park, above and below

Places may occasionally close for conservation, safety or events

Attingham Park Estate: Cronkhill

near Atcham, Shrewsbury, Shropshire SY5 6JP

Map (4) H5   1947

Significant and delightful Italianate hillside villa designed by Regency architect John Nash, with beautiful views across the Attingham Estate. **Note**: open six days a year. Ground floor of house, garden and stables open as part of visit. Property contents belong to tenants.

Finding out more: 01743 708162 or cronkhill@nationaltrust.org.uk

Baddesley Clinton, Warwickshire: wisteria flowers frame a view of the courtyard

Attingham Park Estate: Town Walls Tower

Shrewsbury, Shropshire SY1 1TN

Map (4) H4 1930

This last remaining 14th-century watchtower sits on what were once the medieval fortified, defensive walls of Shrewsbury. **Note**: open six days a year. Sorry no toilet or car parking and 40 extremely steep, narrow steps to top floor. Visit by guided tours.

Finding out more: 01743 708162 or townwallstower@nationaltrust.org.uk

Baddesley Clinton

Rising Lane, Baddesley Clinton, Warwickshire B93 0DQ

Map (4) K6  1980

The magic of Baddesley Clinton comes from its secluded, timeless setting deep in its own parkland. Yet its modest scale and homely feel can be deceptive – for a small manor house a surprising amount is known about its inhabitants and their often unexpected lives. This year the story of the Victorian Quartet continues; four writers and artists who restored the house they used as a retreat from the modern world. The gardens include medieval fish pools, lakeside walk, walled garden and wildflower meadow.

Eating and shopping: the Barn Restaurant serves hot meals, drinks and snacks and The Stables serves light refreshments. Shop sells seasonal gifts, local foods and plants. Second-hand bookshop.

Making the most of your day: events include supper lectures, open-air theatre and Murder Mystery evening. Family Fun every holiday, as well as Playful Journeys around the estate all year.

Welcome talks and garden tours, plus walking trails around the estate and surrounding countryside. Packwood House and Coughton Court are nearby. **Dogs**: welcome on leads in car park and public footpaths across estate. Assistance dogs only in gardens.

Access for all: [icons]
Building [icons] Grounds [icons]

Getting here: see website for details.
Parking: free, 100 yards.

Finding out more: 01564 783294 or baddesleyclinton@nationaltrust.org.uk

Baddesley Clinton		M	T	W	T	F	S	S
1 Jan–14 Feb	9–4*	M	T	W	T	F	S	S
15 Feb–2 Nov	9–5*	M	T	W	T	F	S	S
3 Nov–31 Dec	9–4*	M	T	W	T	F	S	S

*House open at 11. Admission to house by timed ticket, tickets available from reception (not bookable). Closed 24 and 25 December.

Flowers at Baddesley Clinton, Warwickshire, above, and the moated manor house, below

Parking charges for non-members may apply

A country house designed to impress, Belton House in Lincolnshire boasts fine furnishings and opulent decor

Belton House

Grantham, Lincolnshire NG32 2LS

Map ③ E4 🏠➕✿♔🔔🍴 1984

Belton was designed to impress; this perfect 17th-century English country house is set in delightful gardens with its own magnificent deer-park. Its honey-coloured symmetry, opulent decor and fine furnishings provided the perfect setting for lavish hospitality and entertainment on a grand scale. Home to the Brownlow family for 300 years, it reveals many fascinating layers of history. Each generation left its mark, employing top designers and craftsmen. Our theme this year 'Belton by Design' takes a closer look at the intricate details of the mansion interior as well as the grander vision of the Italian, Dutch and informal gardens and landscaped setting. Look out for special exhibitions, demonstrations, walks and talks. **Note**: trialling new ways of opening the house as part of the 'Changing Rooms' project.

Eating and shopping: Stables Restaurant and Ride Play Café. Garden and outdoor shop. Coach house gift shop. Second-hand bookshop in the Stables.

Making the most of your day: Belton by Design-themed events and demonstrations include a special exhibition by the Worshipful Company of Goldsmiths (during house opening times) and a contemporary silversmith working on a unique piece inspired by Belton (Saturdays, March to October). Daily Below-Stairs guided tours. Events and activities all year, including Food Fayre, Paint the Garden, open-air theatre, Hallowe'en Happenings, Christmas Food and Craft Market, Lantern Procession and Carol Evenings. Family trails, indoors and out, plus the Trust's largest outdoor adventure playground, with miniature railway rides. Indoor adventure play area. Woolsthorpe Manor, home of Sir Isaac Newton, is nearby. **Dogs**: welcome on leads in parkland and stableyard. Assistance dogs welcome all areas.

Figure from the fabulously detailed wallpaper frieze in the Chinese Bedroom at Belton House

Access for all: 🅿♿🚻♿🔊🖐📷📹♿👓📷

House 🔎♿♿ Grounds 🔎➡♿♿

Getting here: see website for details.
Parking: free. Please note: we ask all visitors (including members) to obtain an admission sticker from visitor reception on arrival.

Finding out more: 01476 566116 or belton@nationaltrust.org.uk

Belton House		M	T	W	T	F	S	S
House								
8 Mar–2 Nov	12:30–5	·	·	W	T	F	S	S
Park, gardens, shops, restaurant and Ride Play Café								
1 Jan–28 Feb	10:30–4	M	T	W	T	F	S	S
1 Mar–2 Nov	9:30–5:30	M	T	W	T	F	S	S
3 Nov–31 Dec	9:30–4	M	T	W	T	F	S	S
Adventure playground								
1 Mar–2 Nov	9:30–5:30	M	T	W	T	F	S	S

House: open Bank Holiday Mondays (March to October); guided tours replace free-flow on selected days; timed tickets in operation; daily below-stairs tours, tickets from reception. Bellmount Woods: open daily, access from separate car park. Bellmount Tower and Boathouse open occasionally. House closes in poor light. Closed 25 December.

Benthall Hall

Broseley, Shropshire TF12 5RX

Map ④ I5   🏛➕❀ 1958

Within this fine stone house, you can discover the history of the Benthall family from the Saxon period to the present day. Outside, the garden boasts a beautiful Restoration church, a restored plantsman's garden, with fabulous crocus displays in spring and autumn, and an old kitchen garden. **Note**: Benthall Hall is the home of Edward and Sally Benthall.

Eating and shopping: tea-room serving drinks, cakes and ice-creams only.

Making the most of your day: Elizabethan skittle alley open to visitors. Circular walks through the woodland. **Dogs**: in park and woodland only.

Access for all: 🅿♿🚻📷📷 Building 🔎

Benthall Hall		M	T	W	T	F	S	S
1 Feb–23 Feb*	1–4:30**						**S**	**S**
1 Mar–29 Oct	12:30–5:30**		**T**	**W**			**S**	**S**

*Only the ground floor is open in February. **House and
tea-room open at 1 and close 30 minutes earlier. Open Good
Friday and Bank Holiday Mondays. Closes dusk if earlier.

Berrington Hall

near Leominster, Herefordshire HR6 0DW

Map ④ H6   1957

Created as the perfect house in the perfect
setting, Berrington has many secrets to
uncover. Here in one of Henry Holland's
first houses, you can explore the family
rooms and walk in the servants' footsteps
down the back stairs, moving around the
house unseen by the family and guests.
You will find out what happened to William
Kemp, Lord Cawley's butler, and discover
the anguish of a grieving mother during the
First World War. Alternatively why not join
a below-stairs tour to see if you would have
liked being a servant at Berrington?

Eating and shopping: shop selling gifts,
local products and preserves made from
our fruit. Tea-room serving light lunches,
afternoon tea and cakes.

Benthall Hall in Shropshire, above, and children get to grips with churning at Berrington Hall, Herefordshire

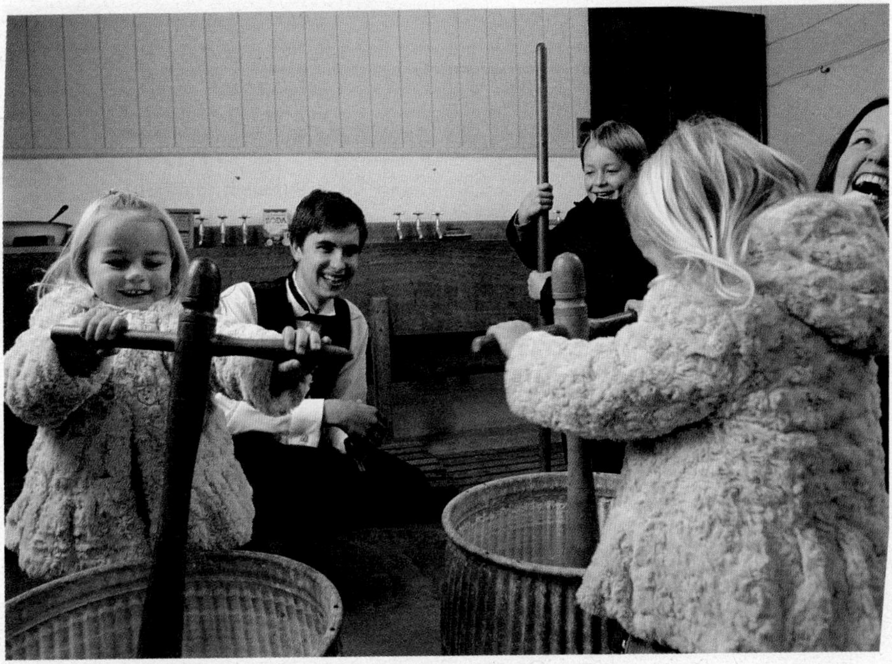

Making the most of your day: family events all year. Children's natural play and den-building area. Garden, parkland and architecture tours. House quizzes. Costume collection on view (by appointment). Waymarked estate walks.
Dogs: on leads on estate and in parts of garden.

Access for all: ⓟⒹ♿︎🚾♨️📷🖼️📺♿🅿️
Building 🏠🔕 **Grounds** ♿➡️♿

Getting here: see website for details.
Parking: free, 30 yards to visitor reception.

Finding out more: 01568 615721 or berrington@nationaltrust.org.uk

Berrington Hall		M	T	W	T	F	S	S
Below stairs, gardens, park, tea-room and shop								
1 Jan–6 Jan	10–4	M	·	W	T	F	S	S
27 Dec–31 Dec	10–4	M	T	W	·	·	S	S
Mansion, below stairs, garden, park, tea-room and shop								
11 Jan–9 Feb	10–4*	·	·	·	·	·	S	S
15 Feb–2 Nov	10–5*	M	T	W	T	F	S	S
8 Nov–14 Dec	10–4*	·	·	·	·	·	S	S
15 Dec–23 Dec	10–4*	M	T	W	T	F	S	S

*Mansion opens at 11. Last admission is one hour before closing.

Berrington Hall, Herefordshire, was created as the perfect house in the perfect setting

Biddulph Grange Garden

Grange Road, Biddulph, Staffordshire ST8 7SD

Map ④ J2 ❋ 1988

This amazing Victorian garden was created by Darwin contemporary, James Bateman, as an extension of his beliefs and scientific interests. His plant collection comes from all over the world – a visit takes you on a journey from an Italian terrace to an Egyptian pyramid, via a Himalayan glen and Chinese-inspired garden. We have a fabulous collection of rhododendrons, a dahlia walk and the oldest surviving golden larch in Britain, brought from China by the great plant hunter Robert Fortune. There is also a woodland nature path and tours of the unrestored Geological Gallery. A garden for all seasons. **Note**: there are 400 steps throughout the garden.

The temple in the Chinese-inspired garden at Biddulph Grange Garden in Staffordshire

Eating and shopping: self-service tea-room. Gift shop. Plant centre.

Making the most of your day: talks, guided tours, events and children's trails all year. Summer activities. **Dogs**: assistance dogs only in garden.

Access for all: 🅿️🎧📖⠿
Building 🦽 Grounds 🦽

Getting here: see website for details.
Parking: free, 50 yards.

Finding out more: 01782 517999 or biddulphgrange@nationaltrust.org.uk

Biddulph Grange Garden		M	T	W	T	F	S	S
1 Jan–16 Feb	11–3:30	M	T	W	T	F	S	S
17 Feb–26 Oct	11–5:30	M	T	W	T	F	S	S
27 Oct–2 Nov	11–4:30	M	T	W	T	F	S	S
3 Nov–31 Dec	11–3:30	M	T	W	T	F	S	S

Open Bank Holiday Mondays. Closes dusk if earlier.
Closed 25 December.

Birmingham Back to Backs

55-63 Hurst Street/50-54 Inge Street, Birmingham, West Midlands B5 4TE

Map ④ J5  🏠📷🍴 2004

An atmospheric glimpse into the lives of the ordinary people who crammed into Birmingham's last surviving court of back to backs: houses built, literally, back to back around a communal courtyard. Our guided tour will take you on a journey in time, from the 1840s through to the 1970s. With fires alight in the grates, and sounds and smells from the past, you will experience an evocative and intimate insight into life and work at the Back to Backs. **Note**: visits by guided tour only (advance booking essential).

Experience a long-forgotten world at the atmospheric Back to Backs, West Midlands

At the Back to Backs you can get a glimpse into the lives of the ordinary people who lived cheek by jowl in these humble dwellings

Eating and shopping: variety of mementoes available. Traditional 1930s sweetshop (not National Trust).

Making the most of your day: exciting year-round events. Ground-floor tour also available.

Access for all: [icons] Building [icons]

Getting here: see website for details. **Parking**: nearest at Arcadian Centre, Bromsgrove Street (not National Trust).

Finding out more: 0121 666 7671 (booking line). 0121 622 2442 or backtobacks@nationaltrust.org.uk

Birmingham Back to Backs		M	T	W	T	F	S	S
4 Feb–31 Aug	10–5	·	T	W	T	F	S	S
6 Sep–21 Dec	10–5	·	T	W	T	F	S	S

Admission by timed ticket and guided tour only, booking essential. Open Bank Holiday Mondays (but closed next day). During term time property closed 10 to 1 on Tuesdays, Wednesdays and Thursdays for schools. Last tour times vary in winter. Closed 1 September to 6 September.

Brockhampton Estate

Bringsty, near Bromyard, Herefordshire WR6 5TB

Map (4) I7   [icons] 1946

This ancient and unspoilt estate offers 687 hectares (1,700 acres) of traditional orchards and hedgerows, working farmland, woodland and a romantic 19th-century designed parkland. There are miles of walks, with breathtaking views across the surrounding countryside. Sitting at the heart of the estate is the picturesque medieval manor house at Lower Brockhampton. Surrounded by a moat and borders of seasonal flowers, the house is entered via a charming timber-framed gatehouse. A number of new rooms will be open from July. Enjoy the tranquillity as you sit in the damson orchard or stroll along the nature trail to discover a rich variety of wildlife.

Eating and shopping: seasonal menus offered at the Old Apple Store tea-room. Light lunches available in the Granary shop at Lower Brockhampton (new indoor seating area). Award-winning estate jams, honey and beer for sale. Second-hand bookshop. Picnics welcome.

We welcome dogs assisting visitors with disabilities

Making the most of your day: year-round events, including bushcraft days, damson picking, historical re-enactments and apple pressing. Family trails and games (school holidays). Natural play trail. Waymarked walks and orienteering routes. Guided tours most weekends. **Dogs**: welcome on leads in grounds, woods and parkland.

Access for all: ⬚⬚⬚⬚⬚⬚⬚⬚⬚
Building ⬚⬚⬚ **Grounds** ⬚➡⬚

Getting here: see website for details.
Parking: 100 yards and 1 mile.

Finding out more: 01885 482077 (Estate Office). 01885 488099 (house) or brockhampton@nationaltrust.org.uk

Brockhampton Estate		M	T	W	T	F	S	S
Estate								
Open all year	10–5	M	T	W	T	F	S	S
Tea-room								
1 Jan–5 Jan	10–4	·	·	W	·	·	S	S
11 Jan–9 Feb	10–4	·	·	·	·	·	S	S
15 Feb–2 Nov	10–5	M	T	W	T	F	S	S
8 Nov–21 Dec	10–4	·	·	·	·	·	S	S
27 Dec–31 Dec	10–4	M	T	W	·	·	S	S
House, grounds and shop								
15 Feb–2 Nov	11–5	M	T	W	T	F	S	S
8 Nov–21 Dec	11–4	·	·	·	·	·	S	S

Parkland at Brockhampton Estate, Herefordshire, above, and the gatehouse to Lower Brockhampton, below

Calke Abbey, Derbyshire, clockwise from above: the once-elegant Oak Bedroom now bears the scars of time, the grand façade and children gaze up at a skylight in the brew-house tunnels

Why not visit us on foot or by public transport? See page 4

Calke Abbey

Ticknall, Derby, Derbyshire DE73 7LE

Map ③ C4   🏠✝♿❀♿🐕🅿️🍽️
1985

With peeling paintwork and overgrown courtyards Calke Abbey tells the story of the dramatic decline of a grand country-house estate. The house and stables are little restored, with many abandoned areas vividly portraying a period in the 20th century when numerous country estates did not survive to tell their story. Outdoors there are beautiful, yet faded, walled gardens and the orangery, auricula theatre and kitchen gardens to explore. The more adventurous can discover the ancient and fragile habitats of Calke Park and its National Nature Reserve, a haven for wildlife. Enjoy a variety of walks in 243 hectares (600 acres), from newly restored limeyards and wetlands, to woodland and ponds. **Note**: everyone requires admission tickets for house and garden, including members (membership cards essential).

Eating and shopping: Threshing Barn Restaurant serving local produce, including estate-reared meat. Kiosk, coffee van and BBQ available at peak times. Large gift shop selling seasonal gifts, plants and local food.

Making the most of your day: events all year, whatever the weather, as well as activities such as guided park or garden walks. Family activities in Squirt's Stable at weekends and during school holidays, from March to October. We also offer Tracker Packs, discovery trails and geocaching. **Dogs**: welcome under control in park and on leads in stables.

Access for all: 🅿♿🚻♿♿🔊📖 VT 👓
Building ♿♿♿   **Grounds** ♿♿➡️

Getting here: see website for details.
Sat Nav: use DE73 7JF. **Parking**: free (membership cards essential for all passengers, otherwise charges apply). Charge for non-members.

Finding out more: 01332 863822 or calkeabbey@nationaltrust.org.uk

Calke Abbey		M	T	W	T	F	S	S
Calke Park National Nature Reserve								
Open all year*	7:30–7:30	M	T	W	T	F	S	S
House								
22 Feb–2 Nov**	12:30–5	M	T	W	.	.	S	S
House tours								
22 Feb–2 Nov†	11–12:30	M	T	W	.	.	S	S
27 Feb–31 Oct†	11–4	.	.	.	T	F	.	.
Garden and stables								
15 Feb–2 Nov	10–5	M	T	W	T	F	S	S
Restaurant and shop								
1 Jan–21 Feb	10–4	M	T	W	T	F	S	S
22 Feb–2 Nov	10–5	M	T	W	T	F	S	S
3 Nov–31 Dec††	10–4	M	T	W	T	F	S	S

*Closes dusk if earlier. **House admission by timed ticket. Last admission to house and garden 4:15. Guided tours may replace free-flow during adverse weather conditions. †Saturday to Wednesday last tour 11:45, Thursday and Friday last tour 3:30. ††Closed 25 December.

Canons Ashby in Northamptonshire: this tranquil Elizabethan house has remained virtually unaltered since 1710

Canons Ashby

near Daventry, Northamptonshire NN11 3SD

Map ③ D7　🏠 ✝ 🏛 ❊ 💺 1981

Tranquil Elizabethan manor house set in beautiful 18th-century gardens. Built by the Drydens using the remains of a medieval priory, the house and gardens have survived largely unaltered since 1710, and are presented as they were during the time of Sir Henry Dryden, a Victorian antiquary, passionate about the past. The warm and welcoming house features grand rooms, stunning tapestries and Jacobean plasterwork, contrasting with the domestic detail of the servants' quarters. Stroll in the historic parkland and catch glimpses of early medieval landscapes, while a wander through the priory church reveals the story of the canons of Canons Ashby.

Eating and shopping: Stables tea-room and tea-gardens. Coach House shop selling home and garden gifts. Second-hand bookshop (donations welcome).

Making the most of your day: events all year, including costumed weekends, live music in the gardens and priory church, guided walks, Hallowe'en and Christmas. Family fun activities and trails. **Dogs**: on leads in car park, paddock, tea-garden and parkland only.

Access for all: 🅿️♿🚐♿♿♿📷♿♿
Building ♿👫　Church ♿　Grounds ♿

Getting here: see website for details.
Parking: 218 yards.

Finding out more: 01327 861900 or canonsashby@nationaltrust.org.uk

Canons Ashby		M	T	W	T	F	S	S
Tea-room, gardens, shop, church and parkland								
1 Feb–14 Feb	10:30–3:30					F	S	S
House, tea-room, gardens, shop, church and parkland								
15 Feb–14 Mar*	10:30–3:30	M	T	W	T	F	S	S
15 Mar–2 Nov**	10:30–5	M	T	W	T	F	S	S
7 Nov–23 Nov	10:30–3:30					F	S	S
29 Nov–7 Dec*	10:30–3:30	M	T	W	T	F	S	S
13 Dec–14 Dec*	10:30–3:30						S	S

House closed on Thursdays, except 4 December. *Entry to house by tour only from 11:30. **Entry to house by taster tours between 11 and 1, free flow admission to house from 1.

Charlecote Park

Wellesbourne, Warwick,
Warwickshire CV35 9ER

Map ④ K7  1946

Charlecote has been home to the Lucy family
for 900 years. Their stories are told throughout
the house by their portraits and the objects
they collected from around the world.
Today you can see how Mary Elizabeth and
George Hammond Lucy lovingly extended and
furnished their home in Victorian times. Stroll
around the gardens to enjoy the formal
riverside parterre, colourful herbaceous
planting and shady woodland garden. The
'Capability' Brown parkland, rich in wildlife
and home to a herd of fallow deer since Tudor
times, offers level walks with views across the
River Avon. Explore how the family lived and
their servants worked in the outbuildings, which
include working Victorian kitchen and laundry,
brew-house, tack room and carriage collection.

The river at Charlecote Park, Warwickshire, top, and exploring the garden, above, with the turreted house beyond

Eating and shopping: Orangery restaurant serving hot meals and light snacks. Two retail outlets, Servants' Hall shop and Gatehouse shop, selling locally sourced produce. Picnics welcome.

Making the most of your day: events throughout the year. Wide range of guided walks and talks. Children's activities, including Easter Egg and treasure hunts during school holidays. Hands-on activities in the Victorian kitchen and laundry. The house is festively decorated during weekends in December. **Dogs**: assistance dogs only.

Access for all: 🅿️🅿️♿♿♿♿📷🔲📺♿
••🅰️ Building 👣👣♿ Grounds 👣➡️♿

Getting here: see website for details.
Parking: free, 300 yards.

Finding out more: 01789 470277 or charlecotepark@nationaltrust.org.uk

Charlecote Park		M	T	W	T	F	S	S
Park, gardens, restaurant shop and outbuildings								
1 Jan–28 Jan*	10:30–4	M	T	W	T	F	S	S
31 Jan–28 Feb*	10:30–4	M	T	W	T	F	S	S
1 Mar–2 Nov*	10:30–5:30	M	T	W	T	F	S	S
3 Nov–31 Dec*	10:30–4	M	T	W	T	F	S	S
House								
15 Feb–28 Mar	12–3:30	M	T	·	T	F	S	S
29 Mar–2 Nov	11–4:30	M	T	·	T	F	S	S
8 Nov–21 Dec	12–3:30	·	·	·	·	·	S	S

*Restaurant and shop close 30 minutes earlier. Closed: 29 and 30 January. 23, 24 and 25 December. May close at dusk if earlier. House: parts of ground floor open only in November and December. Some rooms closed in February.

Summer's evening at Charlecote Park

Clumber Park

Worksop, Nottinghamshire S80 3AZ

Map ③ D2   ✝️❀♿⛺️🍴 1946

With 1,537 hectares (3,800 acres) of picturesque parkland, gardens, woodland and a magnificent lake at its heart, Clumber Park still retains the grandeur of its past as the country estate of the Dukes of Newcastle. It's the perfect place to relax and enjoy the beautiful surroundings, year-round. We have the longest lime-tree avenue in Europe and a spectacular cedar avenue. This leads to the Walled Kitchen Garden, where there is a breathtaking glasshouse – the longest of any National Trust place. There's plenty to experience, from the history and beauty of the chapel to the peace and tranquillity of the ancient woodland and heathlands.

Tackling a ford at Clumber Park, Nottinghamshire, below, and fishing at the magnificent lake, opposite

Eating and shopping: café serving delicious home-cooked food, made using produce grown on site or sourced locally. Snacks, meals and cream teas. Children's menu. Additional catering options available at peak times. Gift shop. Plant sales. Bicycle hire and sales. BBQ site.

Making the most of your day: whether you're looking for peace and tranquillity or play and adventure, Clumber Park offers activities for all ages and interests to enjoy year-round. There are 20 miles of walking and cycle routes, tours, art and history exhibitions, as well as self-led or organised activities and workshops – on subjects as diverse as crafts and gardening. The under-threes will love The Burrow indoor play area, and there are also the Discovery Centre, outdoor play areas and bicycles for hire. Why not stay longer at our campsite? **Dogs**: welcome, some restrictions apply.

Access for all: 🅿️ 🚻 🚾 ⛽ 🎫 📷 🚶 👓 🎨
Buildings ♿ ⬇️ **Grounds** ♿ ➡️ ♿ ⬇️

Getting here: see website for details.
Parking: 250 yards.

Finding out more: 01909 544900 or clumberpark@nationaltrust.org.uk

Clumber Park		M	T	W	T	F	S	S
Visitor facilities								
1 Jan–29 Mar	10–4	M	T	W	T	F	S	S
30 Mar–25 Oct	10–5*	M	T	W	T	F	S	S
26 Oct–31 Dec	10–4	M	T	W	T	F	S	S
Walled Kitchen Garden								
11 Feb–23 Feb	10–4	M	T	W	T	F	S	S
30 Mar–1 Nov	10–5	M	T	W	T	F	S	S
2 Nov–28 Dec	11–3						S	S

*Closes at 6 on Saturday and Sunday. Visitor facilities include: café, tea-room, shop, plant sales, cycle hire, chapel, Discovery Centre and children's play areas. Open daily except 25 December.

Coughton Court

Alcester, Warwickshire B49 5JA

Map ④ K6 🏠✝♣🔔🍷 1946

Coughton has been home to the Throckmorton family for 600 years. Facing persecution for their Catholic faith, they were willing to risk everything. This year, you can discover their fascinating story through 'Coughton at War' – marking the centenary of the First World War with a look at the conflicts which have shaped Coughton over 600 years. Coughton is still very much a family home with an intimate feel; in fact the Throckmorton family still live here and created and manage the stunning gardens, which include a riverside walk, bog garden and beautiful display of roses in the walled garden.

Eating and shopping: the Coughton Kitchen serves lunch and teas. Drinks and ice-cream available from the Stables Coffee Bar. Coach House shop selling local food and seasonal gifts. Throckmorton family plant sales.

Coughton Court, Warwickshire: sideboard with bearskin and family photographs in Lady Lilian's room, below, and St Peter's Church as seen from the walled garden

Making the most of your day: events, including Family Fun every holiday, open-air theatre, concerts, Cheese and Pickle and Winter Festivals. Welcome talks. Children's playground and games. Walking trails. Baddesley Clinton and Packwood House nearby. **Dogs**: welcome on leads in car park and on public footpaths only. Assistance dogs only in gardens.

Access for all: 🅿️♿🚻♿♿📷📺♿👁️
House ♿♿♿ Grounds ♿➡️♿

Getting here: see website for details.
Parking: free, 150 yards.

Finding out more: 01789 400777 or coughtoncourt@nationaltrust.org.uk

Coughton Court		M	T	W	T	F	S	S
House, shop and restaurant*								
1 Mar–30 Mar	11–5	·	·	·	T	F	S	S
House, shop, restaurant and garden								
2 Apr–28 Sep	11–5	·	·	W	T	F	S	S
2 Oct–2 Nov	11–5	·	·	·	T	F	S	S
Taster tours**								
2 Apr–26 Sep	10:45–11:15	·	·	W	T	F	·	·
House, shop and restaurant†								
22 Nov–30 Nov	11–5	M	T	W	T	F	S	S

Open Bank Holidays. Closed Saturday 5 July and 6 September.
Admission by timed ticket on weekends and busy days.
*Parts of the house may be closed due to building work.
**One tour per day focusing on parts of the collection.
†Coughton Winter Festival.

Croft Castle and Parkland

Yarpole, near Leominster,
Herefordshire HR6 9PW

Map ④ H6

1957

Croft Castle is relaxed, peaceful and family friendly. Home of the Croft family for nearly 1,000 years, you can stroll along miles of woodland trails, picnic on the lawns, enjoy the beautiful scenery of the 607-hectare (1,500-acre) estate and then explore the Georgian interiors and discover the family portraits. You can learn about the family who have made Croft so special and go on a cellar tour, then relax in the walled garden or walk to the Iron Age hill fort at Croft Ambrey, past some of our 300 veteran trees, including the 1,000-year-old Quarry Oak. **Note**: trialling new ways of opening the house as part of the 'Changing Rooms' project. Parts of property may close in high winds or snow.

Eating and shopping: tea-room serving hot meals, homemade cakes, local beers, ciders, ice-cream and Sunday roasts. Dishes made using fruit and vegetables from the garden. Children's portions available. Shop selling local gifts, plant sales, home accessories and gardening gifts. Second-hand bookshop. Picnic area.

Making the most of your day: open-air theatre and historical re-enactments. Family activities, including Easter, Hallowe'en and Santa's workshop. Castle-inspired play area and family room. Servants and cellars tours. Waymarked walks and orienteering courses. **Dogs**: welcome, on leads in parkland only.

Access for all: 🅿️🚻♿🚾♿👁️🗄️📷⬆️
Castle ♿♿♿ Grounds ♿➡️♿

Getting here: see website for details.
Sat Nav: use HR6 0BL. **Parking**: 100 yards.

Finding out more: 01568 782120 or croftcastle@nationaltrust.org.uk

Croft Castle and Parkland		M	T	W	T	F	S	S
Tea-room, garden, play area and parkland								
1 Jan–3 Jan	10–4	·	·	W	T	F	·	·
4 Jan–9 Feb	10–4	·	·	·	·	·	S	S
27 Dec–31 Dec	10–4	M	T	W	·	·	S	S
Tea-room, garden, shop, play area and parkland								
15 Feb–23 Feb	10–4:30	M	T	W	T	F	S	S
1 Mar–2 Nov	10–5	M	T	W	T	F	S	S
8 Nov–21 Dec	10–4	·	·	·	·	·	S	S
Castle tours								
15 Feb–23 Feb	10:30–1	M	T	W	T	F	S	S
1 Mar–2 Nov	10:30–1	M	T	W	T	F	S	S
8 Nov–21 Dec	10:30–1	·	·	·	·	·	S	S
Castle								
15 Feb–23 Feb	1–4:30	M	T	W	T	F	S	S
1 Mar–2 Nov	1–5	M	T	W	T	F	S	S
8 Nov–21 Dec	1–4:30	·	·	·	·	·	S	S
Countryside								
Open all year	Dawn–dusk	M	T	W	T	F	S	S

Shop: opens 11. Tea-room open winter weekends 10 to 4.

A family enjoys a day out among the long autumnal shadows at Croft Castle and Parkland in Herefordshire

Members may have to pay on special events days

Croome

near High Green, Worcester,
Worcestershire WR8 9DW

Map ④ J7 🏠✝❀♨🔔🍽 1996

Expect the unexpected. Step into what remains of a secret wartime air base, now our visitor centre, where thousands of people lived and worked in the 1940s. Walk through a masterpiece in landscape design, which is 'Capability' Brown's first. Over the past 17 years we have restored what was once a lost and overgrown parkland and we're continuing this work today. Discover Croome Court, the home of the Earls of Coventry, at the heart of the park, which has been patiently waiting for its revival. Its time has come this year, as we pull this glorious, yet faded, house back from the brink. Explore unrestored spaces and view the intricate repair works which will see the house change for ever. **Note**: major repair project starts this year.

Eating and shopping: 1940s-style restaurant at the visitor centre. Shop selling gifts, local products and seasonal plants. Tea-room on the ground floor of the house. Second-hand bookshop in house basement (subject to house repair works) run by the Friends of Croome.

Croome, Worcestershire, clockwise from main picture: from sunny wildflower meadows to classical porticoes and fabulous statuary, there is far more to this unique place than meets the eye

Making the most of your day: events and activities throughout the year, including our regular guided tours of the park and house and outer eye-catcher open days. Experience something different at the house, where you can see the ongoing repair works up close, join a tour of the work and take part in hands-on activities. Daily family trails and explorer packs with special themed trails during the holidays. RAF-themed playground and natural play area next to the visitor centre. **Dogs**: welcome on leads. Assistance dogs only in house, restaurant and shop.

Access for all: 🅿♿🚻🏠🔦🎦🚶♿📷
House ♿🏠♿ Garden ▶♿♿

Getting here: see website for details.
Parking: free.

Finding out more: 01905 371006 or croome@nationaltrust.org.uk. Estate Office, The Builders' Yard, High Green, Severn Stoke, Worcestershire WR8 9JS

Croome		M	T	W	T	F	S	S
Park, restaurant and shop								
1 Jan–14 Feb	10–4	M	T	W	T	F	S	S
15 Feb–2 Nov	10–5:30	M	T	W	T	F	S	S
3 Nov–23 Dec	10–4	M	T	W	T	F	S	S
House								
1 Jan–14 Feb*	11–4	M	·	W	T	F	S	S
15 Feb–2 Nov	11–4:30	M	·	W	T	F	S	S
3 Nov–22 Dec*	11–4	M	·	W	T	F	S	S
House, park, restaurant and shop**								
26 Dec–31 Dec	11–4	M	T	W	·	F	S	S

*Winter weekdays house open for guided tours only before 1:30. **Winter weekdays house open for guided tours only. Parkland open until 6:30 in July and August.

Cwmmau Farmhouse

Brilley, Whitney-on-Wye,
Herefordshire HR3 6JP

Map ④ G7  1965

Impressive early 17th-century black-and-white
timbered farmhouse with many original
features, including stone-tiled roofs and
vernacular barns full of character.
Note: open four days in June and October –
available at other times as holiday cottage
(0844 800 2070).

Finding out more: 01568 782120 or
cwmmaufarmhouse@nationaltrust.org.uk

**Dudmaston Estate, Shropshire: as well as the Hall,
there are sweeping gardens and enchanting woodland
to delight visitors**

Dudmaston Estate

Quatt, near Bridgnorth, Shropshire WV15 6QN

Map ④ I5 1978

Enchanting wooded parkland, sweeping
gardens and a house with a surprise,
Dudmaston is something unexpected in the
Shropshire countryside. In the Hall, still a
thriving family home, you'll find atmospheric
family rooms and unexpected art galleries
created by the last owners, Sir George and
Rachel Labouchere, displaying their differing
art collections. The gardens provide amazing
vistas, while the orchard is the perfect place to
relax. A woodland playground and free trails
give plenty for younger visitors to enjoy.
For tranquillity and stunning views head to the
Big Pool and Dingle, while the wider estate
provides extensive walking for year-round
enjoyment. **Note**: the family home of
Mr and Mrs Mark Hamilton-Russell.

Eating and shopping: shop selling gifts, estate charcoal and woodland craft products. Tea-room offering lunch and afternoon tea. Ice-cream parlour. Second-hand bookshop.

Making the most of your day: traditional outdoor games and children's woodland playground. Introductory talks and garden tours. Varied events. **Dogs**: welcome on leads in parkland and orchard only.

Access for all: [P] [wc] [symbols] [symbols]
Building [symbols] **Grounds** [symbols]

Getting here: see website for details.
Parking: at The Holt, also at Hampton Loade, 1 mile.

Finding out more: 01746 780866 or dudmaston@nationaltrust.org.uk

Dudmaston Estate		M	T	W	T	F	S	S
Park, tea-room and shop								
15 Feb–23 Feb**	12–4	·	·	·	·	·	S	S
16 Mar–31 Mar	11:30–5	M	T	W	T	·	·	S
1 Apr–30 Sep	11–5:30	M	T	W	T	·	·	S
1 Oct–30 Oct	11:30–5	M	T	W	T	·	·	S
1 Nov–14 Dec**	11:30–4	·	·	·	·	·	S	S
Galleries and second-hand bookshop								
16 Mar–31 Mar	1–5	M	T	W	T	·	·	S
1 Oct–30 Oct	1–5	M	T	W	T	·	·	S
House, galleries and second-hand bookshop*								
1 Apr–30 Sep	1–5	M	T	W	T	·	·	S
Garden								
16 Mar–31 Mar	12–5	M	T	W	T	·	·	S
1 Apr–30 Sep	12–5:30	M	T	W	T	·	·	S
1 Oct–30 Oct	12–5	M	T	W	T	·	·	S

*House and galleries open at 2 on Sundays. No entry to the car park before 11. **Restricted park access – Dingle walks only.

Eyam Hall and Craft Centre

Main Street, Eyam, Derbyshire S32 5QW

Map ③ B2   [symbols] 2013

You can hear fascinating stories and learn about the legendary plague history of Eyam – situated in the beautiful Peak District. Eyam Hall, completed in 1672, is the historic home of the Wright family and a wonderfully unspoilt example of a gritstone Jacobean manor house, set within walled gardens. **Note**: may not open during winter if weather is bad.

Eating and shopping: shop and craft workshops. Buttery café (not National Trust) serving lunch and refreshments.

Making the most of your day: village and countryside walks, including our 'thought walks' on the stories of Eyam and its plague history. **Dogs**: welcome on 'thought walks' around village. Assistance dogs only in walled gardens.

Access for all: [P] [D] [wc] [symbols] [symbols]
Building [symbols]

Getting here: see website for details.
Parking: 43 yards.

Finding out more: 01433 639565 or eyam@nationaltrust.org.uk

Eyam Hall and Craft Centre		M	T	W	T	F	S	S
Craft centre								
Open all year*	10:30–4:30	M	T	W	T	F	S	S
Hall and garden								
15 Feb–2 Nov**	10:30–4:30	·	·	W	T	F	S	S
3 Dec–21 Dec†	10:30–4	·	·	W	T	F	S	S

*National Trust shop, information and walks open daily, independent craft units open as available. **Hall visits via tours, free-flow or timed tickets. †Christmas decorations: fewer rooms on display in December. Open Bank Holidays and closed 25 December.

Eyam Hall and Craft Centre, Derbyshire: the Riley graves contain seven plague victims – all members of one family

Farnborough Hall

Farnborough, near Banbury,
Oxfordshire OX17 1DU

Map (4) L7   🏠 ❄ 🚣 1960

Honey-coloured stone house with stunning
library and treasures collected during the
Grand Tour, surrounded by landscape garden
with country views. **Note:** occupied and
administered by the Holbech family.

Finding out more: 01295 690002
(Farnborough Hall). 01295 670266
(Upton House) or
farnboroughhall@nationaltrust.org.uk

The Fleece Inn

Bretforton, near Evesham,
Worcestershire WR11 7JE

Map (4) K7   🏠 🍴 🔔 🍷 1978

Originally a half-timbered medieval farmhouse,
now a traditional inn known for folk music,
morris dancing and asparagus.

Finding out more: 01386 831173 or
fleeceinn@nationaltrust.org.uk

Grantham House

Castlegate, Grantham, Lincolnshire NG31 6SS

Map (3) E4   🏠 ❄ 1944

Handsome town house, one of the oldest
buildings in Grantham, with riverside walled
garden. **Note:** leased by the National Trust and
the lessee is responsible for arrangements and
facilities. Appointments may be needed.

Finding out more: 01476 564705 or
granthamhouse@nationaltrust.org.uk

Greyfriars' House and Garden

Friar Street, Worcester,
Worcestershire WR1 2LZ

Map (4) J7   🏠 ❄ 🔔 1966

Set in the heart of historic Worcester,
Greyfriars is a stunning timber-framed
merchant's house – perfect for getting away
from the hustle and bustle. This unique house
and garden were rescued by two extraordinary
people with a vision to revive this medieval
gem and create a peaceful oasis.

Eating and shopping: refreshments served
in walled garden (in house during winter).
Plants grown at nearby Hanbury Hall for sale.
Second-hand books.

Making the most of your day: activities and
events throughout year, including garden
games for all ages and children's activity room.
Dogs: welcome in garden.

Access for all:  Building 🦽 ♿ 🚹

Greyfriars' House and Garden in Worcestershire

Getting here: see website for details.
Parking: no parking on site, nearest parking Corn Market, Kings Street and Cathedral Plaza (pay and display). Park and ride service from city outskirts.

Finding out more: 01905 23571 or greyfriars@nationaltrust.org.uk

Greyfriars		M	T	W	T	F	S	S
18 Feb–20 Dec	1–5	·	T	W	T	F	S	·

Open Bank Holiday Mondays.

Gunby Hall and Gardens

Gunby, Spilsby, Lincolnshire PE23 5SS

Map ③ G3  1944

Gunby Hall was the Massingberd family home from 1700 until 1967. The hall still feels homely and cherished, and many visitors remark 'I could live here'. It has a magnificent music room, dining-room and 3 hectares (8 acres) of gardens, which include immaculate lawns and a wonderful rose garden. **Note**: additional bedrooms, first-floor corridor and study now open.

Eating and shopping: courtyard tea-room offering homemade cakes, as well as hot and cold drinks.

Making the most of your day: events throughout year, from open-air theatre to apple days. First World War exhibition in basement to mark 2014 centenary. Public footpaths run across the wider historic park and estate. **Dogs**: welcome on lead in the gardens, courtyard tea-room terrace and grounds.

Access for all: ▢ ⬚ ⬚
Building ⬚ Grounds ⬚

Getting here: see website for details.
Parking: free.

Finding out more: 01754 890102 or gunbyhall@nationaltrust.org.uk

Gunby Hall and Gardens		M	T	W	T	F	S	S
Parkland and car park								
Open all year	11–5	M	T	W	T	F	S	S
Gardens, tea-room and basement**								
15 Feb–2 Nov	11–5*	M	T	W	T	F	S	S
House								
16 Feb–2 Nov	11–5	M	T	W	·	·	·	S

*Last admission to house and basement one hour before closing.
**Tea-room service ceases at 4. May close dusk or earlier.

Gunby Hall and Gardens, Lincolnshire, has a homely and cherished atmosphere, which makes visitors feel instantly at home

Gunby Hall Estate: Monksthorpe Chapel

Monksthorpe, near Spilsby,
Lincolnshire PE23 5PP

Map ③ G3 ✝ 2000

Remote late 17th-century Baptist chapel.

Finding out more: 01754 890102 or
monksthorpe@nationaltrust.org.uk

A family has fun exploring the formal
gardens at Hanbury Hall and Gardens
in Worcestershire

Hanbury Hall and Gardens

School Road, Hanbury, Droitwich Spa,
Worcestershire WR9 7EA

Map ④ J6  1953

This splendid early 18th-century house was built
by Thomas Vernon, lawyer and Whig MP for
Worcester. You can discover the story behind the
magnificent Sir James Thornhill wall- and
ceiling-paintings and the Hercules rooms, which
boast panoramic views of the formal gardens and
Malvern Hills. Outside, the restored George
London garden features include a parterre, grove,
bowling green and fruit garden. Why not see if
you can find the mushroom house and ice house?
For a longer walk, the 162-hectare (400-acre)
park offers paths up to the church, as well as
others leading to the Droitwich canal system.

Parking charges for non-members may apply

Eating and shopping: extended gardening range and plants grown in the walled garden for sale. Servants' hall tea-room serving meals made using home-grown produce (where possible) and home-baked cakes and sweet treats. Stableyard outdoor café (open busy days only).

Making the most of your day: regular garden tours and introductory talks. Varied events, including family activity days, concerts, open-air theatre, art exhibitions and themed weekends. Free park walks leaflet.
Dogs: on leads in the park and short leads in the stableyard only. Assistance dogs only in the gardens.

Access for all: ⓅⒹ♿🚾💺♿📷🅰
Building ♿♿♿ Grounds ♿♿➡♿

Getting here: see website for details.
Parking: free, 150 yards.

Finding out more: 01527 821214 or hanburyhall@nationaltrust.org.uk

Hanbury Hall and Gardens		M	T	W	T	F	S	S
House*, gardens, park, shop and tea-room								
1 Jan–29 Mar	11–4	M	T	W	T	F	S	S
26 Dec–31 Dec	11–4	M	T	W	.	F	S	S
House*, gardens, park, shop, tea-room and play area								
30 Mar–25 Oct	10:30–5	M	T	W	T	F	S	S
26 Oct–23 Dec	11–4	M	T	W	T	F	S	S

*January to 14 February, 3 November to 31 December, house admission by guided tour only. All tour tickets allocated on arrival (non-bookable). 6 to 21 December: limited free-flow access. 15 February to 2 November: house admission by guided tour until 1 (last tour at 12:20), 1 to 4 or 1 to 5 free-flow (depending on time of year as listed above). Whole property closed 24 and 25 December. Admission to house by timed ticket on busy days. Bank Holiday Mondays: free-flow access, 11 to 5.

Hardwick Estate: Stainsby Mill

Doe Lea, Chesterfield, Derbyshire S44 5RW

Map ③ D3 1976

Fully operational watermill giving a vivid evocation of the workplace of a 19th-century miller. Flour is ground regularly and is for sale throughout the season. **Note**: nearest toilets and refreshments at Hardwick Hall.

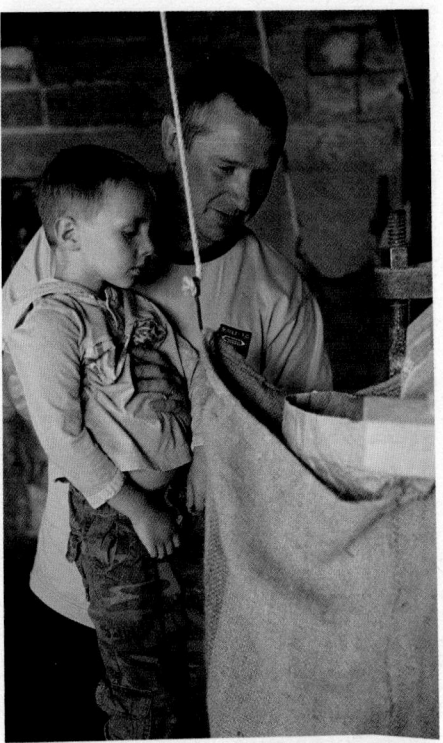
Learning all about flour at Stainsby Mill in Derbyshire

Eating and shopping: Stainsby freshly milled flour for sale. Restaurant and shop at nearby Hardwick Hall.

Making the most of your day: costumed millers bring the mill to life. Why not start your Hardwick adventure at Stainsby Mill, as it opens before the Hall? **Dogs**: welcome on leads in Hardwick Park.

Access for all: 📷💺♿📷🅰
Building ♿ Grounds ♿♿

Getting here: see website for details.
Parking: free limited on-road parking (not National Trust).

Finding out more: 01246 850430 or stainsbymill@nationaltrust.org.uk

Hardwick Estate: Stainsby Mill		M	T	W	T	F	S	S
15 Feb–2 Nov*	10–4	.	.	W	T	F	S	S

Open Bank Holiday Mondays. *National Mills weekend 10 and 11 May. 4 June to 7 September open until 5.

Always remember your current membership card

Hardwick Hall

Doe Lea, Chesterfield, Derbyshire S44 5QJ

Map ③ D3  1959

The Hardwick Estate is made up of stunning houses and beautiful landscapes that have been created by a cast of thousands. It was the formidable Bess of Hardwick who first built Hardwick Hall in the late 16th century. In the centuries since then gardeners, builders, decorators, embroiderers and craftsmen of all kinds have contributed and made Hardwick their creation. We want you to explore and enjoy Hardwick and in the process discover the lives, loves and adventures of the builders of Hardwick. As one of Derbyshire's leading year-round attractions, there is something to inspire at Hardwick every day, whatever the season. **Note**: Old Hall owned by the National Trust and administered by English Heritage (01246 850431).

Eating and shopping: Great Barn restaurant – inside and outside seating, Coach House kiosk for takeaway drinks, snacks and ice-cream. Picnic areas in the stableyard. Stable gift shop for locally sourced treats. Plant sales, propagated from the Hardwick nurseries and outdoor shop.

Making the most of your day: Tracker Packs available to help explore the park. 'Hands-on Hardwick' family activities in the house. Daily talks and tours of the house and gardens. Living History costume days each month. Circular walks through the picturesque parkland. Seasonal events, including Easter, Hallowe'en, Christmas, as well as behind-the-scenes tours, food fairs, themed walks, masterclasses. Family activities during school holidays. **Dogs**: welcome on leads in park and car park.

Access for all: 🅿️ 🚂 🚻 ♿ 🚪 🔁 🖥 📺 🚶 🅰️
Hall 🔁♿ Restaurant ♿ Garden ➡️♿

Getting here: see website for details.
Sat Nav: use S44 5RW. **Parking**: 600-space car park.

Finding out more: 01246 850430 or hardwickhall@nationaltrust.org.uk

Hardwick Hall		M	T	W	T	F	S	S
Garden, park, shop and restaurant								
Open all year	9–6**	M	T	W	T	F	S	S
Hall								
15 Feb–2 Nov	12–4:30	·	·	W	T	F	S	S
3 Dec–21 Dec*	11–3	·	·	W	T	F	S	S

Hall: during February and March we are trialling new combinations of tours or free-flow. Hall open Bank Holiday Mondays (April to August). *A reduced number of rooms are visible during the Christmas opening. **The restaurant and shop close dusk if earlier.

Hardwick Hall in Derbyshire, opposite and below, dates from the late 16th century and was built by the formidable Bess of Hardwick

Hawford Dovecote

Hawford, Worcestershire WR3 7SG

Map (4) J6   🏠 1973

Picturesque dovecote, which has survived virtually unaltered since the late 16th century, retaining many nesting boxes. **Note**: sorry no toilet or tea-room. Park carefully to one side of lane.

Finding out more: 01527 821214 or hawforddovecote@nationaltrust.org.uk

Kedleston Hall

near Quarndon, Derby, Derbyshire DE22 5JH

Map (3) C4   🏠✝️🍂🐄🛏️🔔🍷 1987

Kedleston is one of the grandest and most perfectly finished of all properties designed by architect Robert Adam as 'a temple of the arts' and location for grand entertainments.

The main house was never meant to be a family home; instead it was merely a canvas on which to showcase the finest collection of paintings, sculpture and furniture belonging to the Curzon family. Set in beautiful naturalistic parkland, which blends seamlessly into the surrounding countryside, the 332 hectares (820 acres) is perfect for walks, picnics and spotting wildlife, as well as being home to more than 100 ancient trees. **Note**: medieval All Saints church, containing many family monuments, run by the Churches Conservation Trust.

Eating and shopping: gift shop, plant sales and second-hand bookshop. The Great Kitchen Restaurant serving hot and cold lunches, cakes and teas made using fresh local produce. Refreshments available from coffee shop kiosk (peak times only).

Making the most of your day: events all year, whatever the weather, as well as activities such as children's trail, talks and guided tours. Five waymarked walks. Meet Mrs Garnett, our 18th-century housekeeper. **Dogs**: welcome on leads in park and pleasure grounds.

Access for all: 📶🐕♿🚻👐🦽🖐📷🖥️📺♿
⋮Ⓐ Ground floor ♿🦽   State floor ♿🦽
Grounds 🦽➡️

Kedleston Hall, Derbyshire, was designed by Robert Adam as a 'temple of the arts' rather than a family home

We welcome dogs assisting visitors with disabilities

Getting here: see website for details.
Sat Nav: do not use, follow brown signs.
Parking: 200 yards.

Finding out more: 01332 842191 or
kedlestonhall@nationaltrust.org.uk

Kedleston Hall		M	T	W	T	F	S	S
Park								
Open all year	10–4	M	T	W	T	F	S	S
Park and Pleasure Grounds								
15 Feb–2 Nov	10–6	M	T	W	T	F	S	S
House								
15 Feb–2 Mar	12–3	·	·	·	·	·	S	S
8 Mar–2 Nov	12–5	M	T	W	T	·	S	S
House tours								
17 Feb–6 Mar	11–3	M	T	W	T	·	·	·
Restaurant and shop								
15 Feb–2 Nov	10:30–5	M	T	W	T	·	S	S
8 Nov–21 Dec	10:30–4	·	·	·	·	·	S	S
26 Dec–31 Dec	10:30–3	M	T	W	·	F	S	S

Last entry to house 45 minutes before closing. House tours every 30 minutes from 11 to 3 (spaces limited, booking on day). Intro talk daily when house open, at 11. Open Good Friday. Park closes occasionally November to February. Closed 25 December.

Kinver Edge and the Rock Houses

Holy Austin Rock Houses, Compton Road, Kinver, near Stourbridge, Staffordshire DY7 6DL

Map ④ I5  1917

The Holy Austin Rock Houses, which were inhabited until the 1950s, are truly unique. Come and discover how a few extraordinary people carved a home for themselves in this famous sandstone ridge. There is an extra treat if you walk on to Kinver Edge – dramatic views stretching across three counties.

Eating and shopping: tea-room inside restored Rock House, serving drinks, cakes and snacks, including our famous rock cakes.

Making the most of your day: new Adder Adventure play trail and longer trails through miles of wood and heathland. Family events and activities every Thursday during school holidays. **Dogs**: on leads within grounds of Rock Houses.

Access for all: ⟨icons⟩
Building ⟨icon⟩ Grounds ⟨icon⟩

Getting here: see website for details.
Parking: by Warden's Lodge, Comber Road for the Edge and Compton Road or overflow car park on Kingsford Lane for the Rock Houses.

Finding out more: 01384 872553 or kinveredge@nationaltrust.org.uk

Kinver Edge and the Rock Houses		M	T	W	T	F	S	S
Countryside								
Open all year		M	T	W	T	F	S	S
Rock Houses and tea-room								
20 Feb–30 Nov	11–4	·	·	·	T	F	S	S

Guided tours on Thursdays 11 to 12 (booking essential).

Sandstone rock formations at Kinver Edge, Staffordshire

Kinwarton Dovecote

Kinwarton, near Alcester, Warwickshire B49 6HB

Map ④ K7 1958

Rare 14th-century circular dovecote with metre-thick walls, hundreds of nesting holes and original rotating ladder. **Note**: stock may be grazing. Sorry no toilet.

Finding out more: 01789 400777 or kinwartondovecote@nationaltrust.org.uk

Knowles Mill

Dowles Brook, Bewdley,
Worcestershire DY12 2LX

Map (4) I6    1938

Dating from the 18th century, the mill retains
much of its machinery, including the frames of
an overshot waterwheel. **Note**: mill open daily,
but Mill Cottage not open to visitors (please
respect the resident's privacy). Sorry no toilets
or tea-room. No parking at Mill Cottage.

Finding out more: 01527 821214 or
knowlesmill@nationaltrust.org.uk

Letocetum Roman Baths and Museum

Watling Street, Wall, near Lichfield,
Staffordshire WS14 0AW

Map (4) K5   1934

Remains of a once-important Roman staging
post and settlement, including *mansio* (Roman
inn) and bathhouse. **Note**: in the guardianship
of English Heritage.

Finding out more: 0870 333 1181 (English
Heritage) or letocetum@nationaltrust.org.uk

Lyveden New Bield

near Oundle, Northamptonshire PE8 5AT

Map (3) E6   1922

Set in the heart of rural Northamptonshire, the
mysterious Lyveden is a remarkable survival of
the Elizabethan age. Visitors can explore
Sir Thomas Tresham's garden, one of the oldest
in England which has remained incomplete
since work was abandoned in 1605, and see the
atmospheric garden lodge – destined never to

Atmospheric and mysterious Lyveden New Bield, Northamptonshire, is a remarkable survival of the Elizabethan age

be finished. Our audio guide will tell you all about Sir Thomas's dream and the troubled history of one of Northamptonshire's most famous families, and you can learn all about the hidden symbols of Catholicism and the family's involvement with the infamous Gunpowder Plot.

Eating and shopping: new cottage tea-room in a traditional Northamptonshire cottage serving delicious homemade, seasonal snacks. Locally produced ice-cream and drinks available from visitor reception. Picnics welcome.

Making the most of your day: free audio guide and volunteer-led tours (weekends, May to October). **Dogs**: welcome on leads only.

Access for all: ⬛⬛⬛⬛⬛⬛
Building ⬛ Grounds ⬛

Getting here: see website for details.
Parking: 100 yards.

Finding out more: 01832 205158 or lyveden@nationaltrust.org.uk

Lyveden New Bield		M	T	W	T	F	S	S
4 Jan–28 Dec	11–4	·	·	·	·	·	S	S
1 Mar–31 Oct	10:30–5	M	T	W	T	F	S	S

Open Bank Holidays. Open Good Friday, 10:30 to 5.

Middle Littleton Tithe Barn

Middle Littleton, Evesham, Worcestershire WR11 8LN

Map ④ K7   🏠 1975

The largest and finest restored 13th-century tithe barn in the country. **Note**: sorry no toilet.

Finding out more: 01905 371006 or middlelittleton@nationaltrust.org.uk

Morville Hall

Morville, near Bridgnorth,
Shropshire WV16 5NB

Map (4) I5    1965

Beautiful stone-built house set in attractive
gardens – of Elizabethan origin, enlarged and
expanded around 1750. **Note**: admission by
guided tour only arranged by written
appointment directly to tenants,
Dr and Mrs C. Douglas. Dower House
garden also open (not National Trust).

Finding out more: 01746 780838 or
morvillehall@nationaltrust.org.uk

Moseley Old Hall

Moseley Old Hall Lane, Fordhouses,
Wolverhampton, Staffordshire WV10 7HY

Map (4) J5   1962

Tread in the footsteps of a king at this
atmospheric Elizabethan farmhouse, which
holds many secrets. Charles II hid here while
fleeing for his life after the Battle of Worcester in
1651. You can see where he hid, the bed he slept
in and find out how he escaped from Cromwell's
army. Meanwhile daily life continued; discover
the domestic world of the 17th century and
warm yourself by the log fire. The garden is in
keeping with the period, with a knot garden and
an orchard. Beyond the garden is King's Walk
Wood, part of Monarch's Way Trail.

The knot garden at Moseley Old Hall in Staffordshire,
above, and admiring the lavender, below

Eating and shopping: tea-room serving light
lunches, homemade cakes and scones – freshly
baked throughout the day. Shop selling gifts
and plants. Second-hand bookshop.

Making the most of your day: guided tours,
family events, demonstrations, have-a-go
sessions and re-creations of 17th-century life
all year. Children's activities on family event
days and Mondays and Tuesdays in August.
Tracker Packs. **Dogs**: welcome on leads in
garden and grounds.

Access for all: ⓟ⅊ Dₑ 🚾 ♨ 🅹 ⌨ ♿ ∴ Ⓐ
House ♿⑂ Grounds ♿♿➡⑂

Getting here: see website for details.
Parking: free.

Finding out more: 01902 782808 or
moseleyoldhall@nationaltrust.org.uk

Moseley Old Hall		M	T	W	T	F	S	S
15 Feb–12 Mar	11–4	M	T	W	·	·	S	S
15 Mar–2 Nov	11–5	M	T	W	·	·	S	S
8 Nov–21 Dec	11–4				·	·	S	S
22 Dec–24 Dec	11–3	M	T	W	·	·		

House opens 30 minutes after property, except Bank Holidays.
In February, March, November, December, last entry is at 3
and, for safety reasons, access to top floor may be limited.
Rest of year at 4. Guided tours on Saturday, Sunday and
Wednesday with free-flow after 12:30. Timed entry other days.

The Old Manor

Norbury, Ashbourne, Derbyshire DE6 2ED

Map ③ B4 🏠❄🛏 1987

Medieval hall featuring a rare king post, Tudor door and 17th-century Flemish glass. **Note**: limited parking (cars only).

Finding out more: 01283 585337 or oldmanor@nationaltrust.org.uk

Packwood House

Packwood Lane, Lapworth, Warwickshire B94 6AT

Map ④ K6 🏠❄🛏🍴 1941

Surrounded by beautiful gardens and countryside, Packwood was described by a guest in the 1930s as 'a house to dream of, a garden to dream in'. Lovingly restored at the beginning of the 20th century by Graham Baron Ash, the house contains a wonderful collection of 16th-century furniture and textiles. The gardens include brightly coloured, 'mingled style' herbaceous borders, famous sculpted yews and an 18th-century gentleman's kitchen garden with herbs, flowers and vegetables. This year we have a new Garden Kitchen café and playful sculpture in the park.

Eating and shopping: new Garden Kitchen café serving hot food, soup, salads, sandwiches, cakes and snacks. Shop selling seasonal gifts, local foods and plants, many grown in our own nursery. Picnics welcome.

Making the most of your day: events, including Family Fun every holiday, open-air theatre and evening house and garden tours. Weekly garden talks, countryside walking trails and woodland Welly Walk. Baddesley Clinton and Coughton Court nearby. **Dogs**: welcome on leads in car park and on public footpaths in park. Assistance dogs only in gardens.

Access for all: 🅿♿ 🇩♿ 🦽 📷 ••
House 🚶♿🦽 **Grounds** 🚶♿🦽

Getting here: see website for details.
Parking: free, 150 yards.

Finding out more: 01564 782024 or packwood@nationaltrust.org.uk

Packwood House		M	T	W	T	F	S	S
House, garden, café and gift shop								
15 Feb–20 Jul	11–5	·	T	W	T	F	S	S
21 Jul–31 Aug	11–5	M	T	W	T	F	S	S
2 Sep–2 Nov	11–5	·	T	W	T	F	S	S
Café, shop and park								
1 Jan–14 Feb	9–4	·	T	W	T	F	S	S
15 Feb–20 Jul	9–5	·	T	W	T	F	S	S
21 Jul–31 Aug	9–5	M	T	W	T	F	S	S
2 Sep–2 Nov	9–5	·	T	W	T	F	S	S
4 Nov–31 Dec	9–4	·	T	W	T	F	S	S

Open Bank Holiday Mondays with admission to the house by timed ticket (not bookable). Tours of the house and garden 1 January to 14 February, 4 November to 31 December. Closed 24 and 25 December.

A quiet moment on the immaculate lawn at Packwood House, Warwickshire

Priest's House, Easton on the Hill

38 West Street, Easton on the Hill, near Stamford, Northamptonshire PE9 3LS

Map ③ E5  1966

A delightful small late 15th-century building, with interesting local architecture and museum exploring Easton on the Hill's industrial past. **Note**: open all year.

Finding out more: 01832 205158 or priestshouse2@nationaltrust.org.uk

Rosedene

Victoria Road, Dodford, near Bromsgrove, Worcestershire B61 9BU

Map ④ J6 1997

Restored 1840s cottage, organic garden and orchard illustrating the mid 19th-century Chartist Movement. **Note**: available to hire as a 'back to basics' holiday cottage. Visit by booked tours only (first Sunday of the month, March to December).

Finding out more: 01527 821214 or rosedene@nationaltrust.org.uk

Shugborough Estate in Staffordshire: this working, historic estate has a fine Georgian mansion at its heart

Shugborough Estate

Milford, near Stafford, Staffordshire ST17 0XB

Map ④ J4
1966

Shugborough is a working, historic estate, featuring a fine Georgian mansion, working servants' quarters, farm with costumed servants and redeveloped walled garden. Home to the Earls of Lichfield, Shugborough is set in 364 hectares (900 acres) of Grade I listed parkland, peppered with unusual monuments. **Note**: entirely operated by Staffordshire County Council. Charge for members for all areas, apart from the house and gardens.

Eating and shopping: licensed tea-room serving homemade cream teas and locally sourced dishes, including Shugborough's own-recipe sausage and mash and game casserole. Gift shop, ice-cream parlour, old-fashioned sweetshop and craft outlets making and selling handmade goods.

Making the most of your day: events all year, including craft fairs, theatre and family activities. Guided tours in mansion, 11 to 1 (£3 charge or included in all-sites ticket). Regular demonstrations of milling, baking and cheese-making. **Dogs**: on leads in parkland and gardens only.

Access for all:
Building **Grounds**

Longshaw and Eastern Moors

Longshaw, near Sheffield, Derbyshire

Map ③ C2 🏠🏛️🌸🦆🦅🐾 1931

There are traces of the past hidden among the ancient woods and heather moorland just waiting to be discovered. Renowned for their spectacular views, Longshaw and the Eastern Moors offer an excellent network of paths and bridleways and superb wildlife-spotting opportunities. This is a very special place for outdoor adventure and fun. **Note**: Eastern Moors managed in National Trust/RSPB partnership for the Peak District National Park Authority.

Eating and shopping: tea-room with terrace serving dishes made from fresh seasonal produce from the kitchen garden. Shop selling outdoor and wildlife-themed products.

Longshaw and Eastern Moors, Derbyshire: traces of the past lie waiting to be discovered in the ancient woodland and heather moorland

Making the most of your day: explore the magical world of Boggarts with Play Longshaw! Muck-in days, free walks (Wednesday and Sunday), Cycle to the Cinema and 'Longshaw Remembers the First World War'. Holiday cottage. **Dogs**: on leads at all times from early March to end of July.

Access for all: 🅿️♿️🚾♿️📷♿️
Building ♿️   Grounds ♿️♿️➡️

Getting here: see website for details.
Parking: for Longshaw at Woodcroft, Wooden Pole and Haywood; for the Eastern Moors at Curbar Gap, Birchen Edge and Shillito Wood. Additional car parks at Surprise View and Burbage, pay and display (not National Trust).

Finding out more: 01433 637904 (Longshaw). 01433 630316 (Eastern Moors) or peakdistrict@nationaltrust.org.uk

Longshaw and Eastern Moors		M	T	W	T	F	S	S
Tea-room and shop								
1 Jan–16 Feb	10:30–4	M	T	W	T	F	S	S
17 Feb–2 Nov	10:30–5	M	T	W	T	F	S	S
3 Nov–21 Dec	10:30–4	M	T	W	T	F	S	S
22 Dec–28 Dec	10:30–4	M	T	·	·	·	S	S
29 Dec–31 Dec	10:30–4	M	T	W	·	·	·	·

Closed 24 to 26 December. Longshaw Lodge not open to the public.

Getting here: see website for details. **Parking**: £3 (pay and display, including members). Refunded on purchase of all-sites ticket. Parking charges directly fund conservation on the estate.

Finding out more: 0845 459 8900 or shugborough@nationaltrust.org.uk

Shugborough Estate		M	T	W	T	F	S	S
House, servants' quarters, farm, walled garden								
21 Mar–24 Oct	11–5	M		W	T	F	S	S
Parkland, gardens, tea-room and shop								
21 Mar–24 Oct	11–6*	M	T	W	T	F	S	S
Shop								
25 Oct–23 Dec	11–4	M	T	W	T	F	S	S

Access to house by guided tour only 11 to 1. *Tea-room and shop close at 5.

Staunton Harold Church

Staunton Harold Estate, Ashby-de-la-Zouch, Leicestershire LE65 1RW

Map ③ C4 ✝ 1954

One of the few churches built between the outbreak of the English Civil War and the Restoration period. **Note**: toilets 500 yards (not National Trust). Parking not National Trust; Staunton Harold Estate, charges apply (including members).

Finding out more: 01332 863822 or stauntonharold@nationaltrust.org.uk

Mr Straw's House

5–7 Blyth Grove, Worksop, Nottinghamshire S81 0JG

Map ③ D2 🏠 ✽ 1990

Within this modest semi-detached home, the ordinary life of a grocer and his family has been preserved in an extraordinary way to provide a near-perfect time capsule from England in the 1920s. So you can enjoy your visit we operate timed tickets, which can be booked in advance.

The entrance of Mr Straw's House, Nottinghamshire

Eating and shopping: shop selling jam, biscuits, plants, souvenirs and gifts. Coffee area. Picnic benches. Tea and cakes available in the orchard on the first Saturday of each month (provided by the Friends of Mr Straw's House).

Making the most of your day: special tours, events and activity days throughout the year. Exhibition.

Access for all: ♿ 👓 🅰
Buildings ♿ 🚻 Garden ♿

Getting here: see website for details.
Parking: free.

Finding out more: 01909 482380 or mrstrawshouse@nationaltrust.org.uk

Mr Straw's House		M	T	W	T	F	S	S
11 Mar–1 Nov	11–4	·	T	W	T	F	S	·

Admission by timed ticket, booked in advance by telephone. Last tours start at 4. Closed Good Friday.

Sudbury Hall and the National Trust Museum of Childhood

Sudbury, Ashbourne, Derbyshire DE6 5HT

Map ③ B4 🏠 ♣ 🔔 ⊤ 1967

A visit here provides two days out in one. The quality and craftsmanship within the hall is world-class. Sudbury has one of the most surprising, light and beautiful long galleries in England and is the result of George Vernon's aspirations to create a perfect new home. You can get a glimpse of life 'below stairs' in the kitchen and basement, and picture yourself at home in some of the smaller family rooms. The Museum of Childhood is a place of fun and fascination for all ages. View childhood from the Victorian period to the present day; send your little one up a chimney, play with our hands-on toys and games and join a lesson in the Victorian Schoolroom.

Eating and shopping: gift shop, plant sales, sweets and toys. Tea-room serving light lunches and homemade cakes. Additional refreshments available at peak times.

Fun at the Museum of Childhood, Derbyshire

Making the most of your day: events throughout the year, whatever the weather. Take part in a range of family activities during school holidays. Why not pick up a trail sheet and test your skills in our woodland play area, discover the wildlife in the Boat House and find hands-on toys in the Museum? If you join one of our themed Hall tours, you can see behind the scenes and go to places not normally open to visitors.

Access for all: 🅿️ 🄳 🏨 ⚐ ⚐ ⚐ ⚐ ⚐ 🖥️ ⚐
⚐ 🄰 Hall ⚐ ⚐ Museum ⚐ ⚐ ⚐
Grounds ⚐ ⚐

Getting here: see website for details.
Parking: free, 500 yards.

Finding out more: 01283 585305 (Infoline). 01283 585337 or sudburyhall@nationaltrust.org.uk

Sudbury Hall		M	T	W	T	F	S	S
Hall								
15 Feb–2 Nov	1–5	·	·	W	T	F	S	S
Hall tours								
15 Feb–2 Nov	11:30–12	·	·	W	T	F	S	S
22 Apr–28 Oct	11:30–2:30	·	T	·	·	·	·	·
Museum, restaurant and shop								
15 Feb–20 Apr	10:30–5*	·	·	W	T	F	S	S
21 Apr–2 Nov	10:30–5*	M	T	W	T	F	S	S
6 Nov–21 Dec	10:30–4*	·	·	·	·	T	F	S	S
Grounds								
15 Feb–21 Dec	10–5	M	T	W	T	F	S	S

*Museum opens at 11 and closes at 4 November to December. Open Bank Holidays. Last admission 45 minutes before closing (Hall will close early if light level is poor). Hall tour Wednesdays to Sundays at 11:30 and Tuesdays between 11:30 and 2:30.

The south front of Sudbury Hall, Derbyshire, which boasts one of the most beautiful long galleries in the country

Midlands

Games on the lawn at Sunnycroft in Shropshire: a mini estate tucked away in the suburbs

Sunnycroft

200 Holyhead Road, Wellington, Telford, Shropshire TF1 2DR

Map ④ I4   🏠 ❄ 1999

This rare suburban villa and mini estate, tucked away in Wellington, is an Edwardian time capsule. Its original contents and features will transport you back to the pre-First World War 'country-house' lifestyle. Sunnycroft tells the story of a brewer, a widow and three generations of a local industrialist family. **Note**: no credit or debit card facilities.

Eating and shopping: Smoking Room tea-room serving light lunches, ice-cream and afternoon tea. Second-hand bookshop. Souvenirs available. Picnics welcome on the lawn.

Making the most of your day: free guided tours and children's trails in the house. Free garden tours and croquet on the lawn. Themed events, including summer fête, Edwardian Christmas and embroidery workshops.

Dogs: welcome on leads in grounds only.

Access for all: 🅿♿ 🐕♿ 🚻 📖 ♿
Building ♿ Grounds ♿ ➡

Getting here: see website for details.
Sat Nav: use address not postcode.
Parking: free, 150 yards. Additional free parking in Wrekin Road car park (not National Trust).

Finding out more: 01952 242884 or sunnycroft@nationaltrust.org.uk

Sunnycroft		M	T	W	T	F	S	S
4 Jan–23 Feb	10:30–3						**S**	**S**
28 Feb–3 Nov	10:30–5	**M**				**F**	**S**	**S**
8 Nov–7 Dec	10:30–3						**S**	**S**
13 Dec–21 Dec	10:30–4	**M**	**T**	**W**	**T**	**F**	**S**	**S**

Last admission to house one hour before closing. Entry by timed tickets with ten-minute introductory talk, then free-flow. Daily guided tours available in main season (not bookable). Free-flow throughout house on Bank Holiday weekends, 13 to 21 December and event days.

Tattershall Castle

Sleaford Road, Tattershall,
Lincolnshire LN4 4LR

Map ③ F3  1925

There are six floors to explore in this stunning red-brick medieval castle built by Ralph Cromwell, Lord Treasurer of England, in 1434. The castle has been a family home, a defensive tower and a cattle shed, before being saved from demolition by Lord Curzon of Kedleston in 1911. This iconic Lincolnshire landmark is a beautiful statement of 15th-century ambition and wealth, architecture and style. It is also a great place for watching the historic planes from the Battle of Britain Memorial Flight, based at nearby RAF Coningsby.

Eating and shopping: Guardhouse shop selling gifts and souvenirs, sandwiches, snacks, drinks and ice-cream. Picnics welcome.

Making the most of your day: events all year, including Living History Fortnight, Hallowe'en walks, Christmas market. Free audio guide. Children's activities. Battle of Britain Memorial Flight Centre tours (weekday) nearby.
Dogs: welcome in the grounds only.

Access for all: 🅿️ 🚻 ♿ 🎞️ 📷 ♿
Building ♿ ♿ ♿

Getting here: see website for details.
Parking: free, 150 yards.

Finding out more: 01526 342543 or tattershallcastle@nationaltrust.org.uk

Tattershall Castle		M	T	W	T	F	S	S
Castle, grounds and shop								
16 Feb–2 Nov	11–5	M	T	W	T	F	S	S
8 Nov–14 Dec	11–3	·	·	·	·	·	S	S
Countryside								
Open all year	Dawn–dusk	M	T	W	T	F	S	S

May close earlier than times stated or at dusk.

Tattershall Castle, Lincolnshire: at different times it has been a family home, defensive tower and even a cattle shed

Upton House and Gardens

near Banbury, Warwickshire OX15 6HT

Map ④ L7 🏠✳️🛏️🔔🎺 1948

Join the guests of Lord and Lady Bearsted and soak up the atmosphere of a 1930s millionaire's weekend house party. You can find out more about the family and their fortune, made from Shell Oil, then discover the red and silver Art Deco bathroom, the Sèvres and English 18th-century porcelain, and the internationally important art collection – which contains works by El Greco, Stubbs and Bosch. Outside, the garden has a sweeping lawn, which gives way to terraced and herbaceous borders leading to the mirror pool. There is also a kitchen garden, tranquil bog garden and spring bulb displays to explore.

Eating and shopping: restaurant serving hot lunches and teas. Afternoon teas in the 1930s kitchen on special days. Plant centre. Shop selling gifts, accessories, food and books.

Making the most of your day: Shell Oil advertising poster exhibition. House and garden tours. Art exhibitions, family activities, including woodland adventure, games, treasure boxes and dressing up. Home of National Collection of Asters. Holiday cottages.
Dogs: assistance dogs only in grounds.

Access for all: 🅿️♿🚼🚾🍽️📷📖📺♿🚫
House and gallery 👨‍🦽♿ Grounds 👨‍🦽♿

Getting here: see website for details.
Sat Nav: follow brown signs to car park entrance once you arrive at postcode location.
Parking: 300 yards.

Upton House and Gardens in Warwickshire: the billiard-room, above, and the *Adoration of the Magi*, attributed to Hieronymus Bosch, below – just one of the many masterpieces on display

Members may have to pay on special events days

Finding out more: 01295 670266 or uptonhouse@nationaltrust.org.uk

Upton House and Gardens		M	T	W	T	F	S	S
Gardens, restaurant, shop and tours*								
4 Jan–9 Feb	12–4						S	S
15 Feb–2 Nov	11–5	M	T	W		F	S	S
3 Nov–22 Dec	12–4	M				F	S	S
26 Dec–31 Dec	12–4	M	T	W		F	S	S
House and exhibition**								
4 Jan–9 Feb	12–4						S	S
15 Feb–2 Nov	1–5	M	T	W		F	S	S
3 Nov–22 Dec	12–4	M				F	S	S

Open every day in July and August. *November to February: gardens open as winter walk. 15 February to 2 November: taster tours 11 to 1 only. Timed tickets to all tours available on arrival (non-bookable). 26 to 31 December: no taster tours, exhibition open. **Bank holidays: house open 11 to 5 by timed tickets. 4 January to 9 February: house open for taster tours only. 3 November to 22 December: house open for taster tours on weekdays and free-flow at weekends (selected rooms only). Timed tickets to all tours available on arrival (non-bookable).

Eating and shopping: self-service tea and coffee available. Picnics welcome.

Making the most of your day: family trails daily during school holidays.
Dogs: assistance dogs only (other dogs allowed in car park).

Access for all: Grounds

Getting here: see website for details.
Parking: free.

Finding out more: 01981 590509 or theweir@nationaltrust.org.uk

The Weir		M	T	W	T	F	S	S
1 Feb–28 Feb	11–4	M	T	W	T	F	S	S
1 Mar–2 Nov	11–5	M	T	W	T	F	S	S

Last admission 45 minutes before closing.

The Weir

Swainshill, Hereford, Herefordshire HR4 7QF

Map ④ H7    1959

These stunning riverside gardens are perfect for exploring at any time of year. In spring there are carpets of spring bulbs, which give way to beautiful wild flowers in summer, while in autumn the colours change yet again. Don't miss the restored walled garden full of fruit and vegetables. **Note**: sturdy footwear advisable.

The Weir, Herefordshire: these stunning riverside gardens offer new delights every season, so one visit is never enough

Wichenford Dovecote

Wichenford, Worcestershire WR6 6XY

Map ④ I7   🏠 1965

Small but striking 17th-century half-timbered dovecote at Wichenford Court. **Note**: no access to Wichenford Court (privately owned). Sorry no toilet or tea-room. Please consider local residents when parking.

Finding out more: 01527 821214 or wichenforddovecote@nationaltrust.org.uk

![Perfect borders at Wightwick Manor and Gardens]

Perfect borders at Wightwick Manor and Gardens, West Midlands, above, and exploring the gardens, below

Wightwick Manor and Gardens

Wightwick Bank, Wolverhampton,
West Midlands WV6 8EE

Map ④ J5   🏛️ ❄️ 1937

Wightwick Manor was the haven of a romantic industrialist. With its timber beams and barley-twist chimneys, gardens of wide lawns, yew hedges and roses, rich William Morris furnishings and Pre-Raphaelite paintings, Wightwick is in every way an idyllic time capsule of Victorian nostalgia for medieval England. If you delve deeper, you will find stories of the remarkable politician, Geoffrey Mander, who fought social injustice and European fascism and felt the need to share this unique property with the nation. More than 75 years since that gift, the magic and warmth of the home is as enthralling and enchanting as ever. **Note**: all visitors need to go to reception in car park for tickets.

Eating and shopping: specialist shop with William Morris and Arts and Crafts-inspired ranges and plant centre (also available online). New tea-room in stable block serving hot food made with kitchen garden produce.

Making the most of your day: garden orienteering map and guided walks for all ages. Family activities in summer. Events, including specialist talks and tours. **Dogs**: welcome on leads in garden.

Access for all: 🅿️ 🐕 ♿ 🚻 👶 🔍 📷 🏛️ ♿
Manor ♿♿♿ Gardens ♿♿♿ ➡️

Getting here: see website for details.
Sat Nav: use WV6 8BN. **Parking**: free, entrance off A454.

Finding out more: 01902 761400 or wightwickmanor@nationaltrust.org.uk

Wightwick Manor and Gardens		M	T	W	T	F	S	S
House								
1 Jan–14 Feb	12–4	M	·	W	T	F	S	S
15 Feb–30 Jun	12–5	M	·	W	T	F	S	S
1 Jul–31 Aug	12–5	M	T	W	T	F	S	S
1 Sep–2 Nov	12–5	M	·	W	T	F	S	S
3 Nov–31 Dec	12–4	M	·	W	T	F	S	S
Garden, tea-room and shop								
1 Jan–14 Feb	11–4	M	T	W	T	F	S	S
15 Feb–2 Nov	11–5	M	T	W	T	F	S	S
3 Nov–31 Dec	11–4	M	T	W	T	F	S	S

Last entry to house one hour before closing. Closed 25 December. A reduced number of rooms will be open January to mid-February and after 26 December.

Wilderhope Manor

Longville, Much Wenlock, Shropshire TF13 6EG

Map (4) H5   1936

Beautiful Elizabethan manor house, restored by John Cadbury in 1936, surrounded by farmland managed for landscape and wildlife.
Note: popular youth hostel, so access to some rooms may be restricted. Open on Sundays throughout the year and Wednesdays during April to September.

Finding out more: 01694 771363 (Hostel Warden YHA) or wilderhope@nationaltrust.org.uk

Woolsthorpe Manor, Lincolnshire: Newton's birthplace

Woolsthorpe Manor

Water Lane, Woolsthorpe by Colsterworth, near Grantham, Lincolnshire NG33 5PD

Map (3) E4 🏛️ 🌿 ✤ 1943

A small manor house but the birthplace of a great mind – Sir Isaac Newton, world-famous scientist, mathematician, alchemist and Master of the Royal Mint. During the plague years of 1665–7, he returned to the family farm and produced some of his most important work on physics and mathematics here, including his crucial experiment to split white light into a spectrum of colours. Today you can still see the famous apple tree and explore some of Newton's ideas for yourself in the Science Discovery Centre.

Eating and shopping: small coffee shop and small shop in ticket office. Second-hand bookshop.

Making the most of your day: events, including regular 'Tales from Woolsthorpe' and science talks. Hands-on Science Discovery Centre. National Science Week (March), Apple Day (October). Summer holiday workshops. Belton House only 12 miles. **Dogs**: welcome in car park only.

Access for all:
House · **Discovery Centre**
Grounds

Getting here: see website for details.
Parking: free, 50 yards.

Finding out more: 01476 860338 or woolsthorpemanor@nationaltrust.org.uk. 23 Newton Way, Woolsthorpe by Colsterworth, near Grantham, Lincolnshire NG33 5NR

Woolsthorpe Manor		M	T	W	T	F	S	S
Manor house								
3 Jan–14 Mar	11–3	·	·	·	·	**F**	**S**	**S**
15 Mar–26 Oct	11–5	**M**	·	**W**	**T**	**F**	**S**	**S**
31 Oct–28 Dec	11–3	·	·	·	·	**F**	**S**	**S**
Science Discovery Centre, coffee shop and grounds								
1 Jan–14 Mar	11–3	**M**	**T**	**W**	**T**	**F**	**S**	**S**
15 Mar–26 Oct	11–5	**M**	**T**	**W**	**T**	**F**	**S**	**S**
27 Oct–31 Dec	11–3	**M**	**T**	**W**	**T**	**F**	**S**	**S**

From 3 January to 14 March and from 31 October to 31 December, access to the manor house is by timed tours only. At busy times during the year a system of timed tickets may be in operation. The manor house has limited lighting and on dark days may close early.

The Workhouse, Southwell

Upton Road, Southwell, Nottinghamshire NG25 0PT

Map ③ D3 2002

Follow in the footsteps of the Victorian poor as they sought refuge at The Workhouse. This austere building, the most complete workhouse in existence, was built in 1824 as a place of last resort for the poor and needy. Its architecture was influenced by prison design and its harsh regime became a blueprint for workhouses throughout the country. You can immerse yourself in the building's unique

The Workhouse, Southwell in Nottinghamshire was a place of last resort for the poor and needy

atmosphere and learn about the daily routine of those who lived and worked here in the 1840s, while reflecting on how society has tackled poverty through the centuries.

Eating and shopping: new refreshment room offering hot drinks and snacks. Shop selling gifts, seasonal produce from the vegetable garden. Picnics in the garden.

Making the most of your day: varied events programme, living history days, children's trails.

Access for all:
Building **Grounds**

Getting here: see website for details.
Parking: free, 200 yards.

Finding out more: 01636 817260 or theworkhouse@nationaltrust.org.uk

The Workhouse, Southwell		M	T	W	T	F	S	S
19 Feb–26 Oct	12–5	·	·	**W**	**T**	**F**	**S**	**S**
29 Oct–2 Nov	12–4	·	·	**W**	**T**	**F**	**S**	**S**

Guided tour of the outside and other buildings at 11 (places limited). Open Bank Holidays. Last admission one hour before closing.

North West

Majestic mountains, sweeping screes, riverside paths and utter peace characterise Wasdale in Cumbria

Outdoors in the North West

Join us in the North West and discover a stunning variety of places to explore, from deer-parks, moors and gardens, sweeping coastline at Formby or Whitehaven, to the hills and rare heathlands of Cheshire, then along the rivers and valleys into the awesome Lake District.

You'll find us out and about caring for landscapes, seascapes, wildlife havens, industrial heritage and many captivating out-of-the-way places. Walking is in our blood here, but there are also new outdoor trails offering cycling, running and orienteering at many places.

Above right: **the hare sculpture trail at Hare Hill, Cheshire**
Right: **Great Langdale, Cumbria**

The Lake District and Cumbria

Thanks to your help, we care for 20 per cent of the Lake District National Park, with England's highest mountain, Scafell Pike, and deepest lake, Wastwater, and many small fells and tiny tarns – special places in their own right. Your help enables us to look after these places, so come and soak up the spirit of each place. Some are busy and active, while others are tranquil and quiet – there is something for everyone. Find out more about our work at **www.nationaltrust.org.uk/lakedistrict**

Look out for our red-clad Ranger teams. They know our places inside out and we've captured their thoughts in our new *Ranger Guides*, available at our shops. Before you plan your next adventure, visit **www.ntlakesoutdoors.org.uk** and ask them a question or find their favourite secret places.

Holiday with us

Fancy camping, glamping or a cottage break at locations with a 'wow' factor?

We've four campsites – at Low Wray, Langdale, Wasdale and Hoathwaite – two stone bothies and 17 holiday cottages, so this is your opportunity to get back to nature and wake up to England's most dramatic views, all year round.

Why not stroll to a Lakeland inn, hike up a pike, take a bike ride or canoe paddle from your door? Check out adventure activities in the school holidays from Low Wray and Langdale campsites: moonlit canoeing, gorge scrambling, rock climbing and more. Every pound goes towards local conservation projects, so you're helping to look after the future, too. Book at **www.ntlakescottages.org.uk** and **www.ntlakescampsites.org.uk**

Cheshire, Merseyside and Lancashire

You'll find more great escapes close to Liverpool and Manchester – head to our gardens, parkland, woodland and great open spaces around Dunham, Lyme, Quarry Bank, Speke and Tatton, or the coastline at Formby, Arnside and Silverdale. All have walking trails and new activities for you to enjoy. For great escapes from the 'big smoke', visit Stubbins Estate and Holcombe Moor, north of Bury, the woods and heaths of the sandstone ridge in Cheshire and the magic of Alderley Edge and Hare Hill.

Bickerton Hill and Helsby Hill both have Bronze Age forts, and the folly of Mow Cop on the skyline always intrigues. Check out our websites for new outdoor events and activities, and a secluded holiday cottage tucked away at Lyme Park.

Above left: **dunes at Formby Beach, Lancashire**

Left: **family fun at Allan Bank, Cumbria**
Right: **playing football at the National Trust campsite at Wasdale Head, Cumbria**

Outdoors in the North West

From Cheshire's diverse countryside to the stunning Lancashire coast or the Lake District's inspiring landscape – the North West is one of the best places to enjoy the outdoors.

Alderley Edge

Nether Alderley, Macclesfield, Cheshire

Map (5) D8   🏛🖼 1946

The dramatic red sandstone escarpment of Alderley Edge has views over the Cheshire Plain and towards the Peak District. There are numerous paths winding through mature pine and beech woodland and walks to neighbouring Hare Hill. Alderley Edge is designated an SSSI for its geological interest and has a history of copper mining dating back to the Bronze Age. The site is also noted for its legend and the *Weirdstone of Brisingamen* novel. **Note**: toilets at Alderley Edge only.

Alderley Edge, Cheshire: the dramatic and far-reaching views over the Cheshire Plain to the Peak District

Eating and shopping: Wizard Tea-room (weekends and some Bank Holidays only) and Wizard Inn at Alderley Edge (neither National Trust). Picnic area and ice-cream vendor (when weather is fine).

Making the most of your day: summer guided walks; self-guided walks to Hare Hill. Orienteering trails. Derbyshire Caving Club opens mines twice yearly. Sites nearby – Bickerton, Bulkeley and Helsby Hills, Thurstaston Common, The Cloud, Mow Cop. **Dogs**: under close control. On leads where livestock present (particularly during bird-nesting season).

Access for all: Grounds 🏞➡

Getting here: see website for details.
Sat Nav: use SK10 4UB. **Parking**: at some properties (roadside elsewhere); non-members pay and display at Alderley Edge.

Finding out more: 01625 584412 or alderleyedge@nationaltrust.org.uk

Alderley Edge		M	T	W	T	F	S	S
Countryside								
Open all year	Dawn–dusk	M	T	W	T	F	S	S
Car park								
1 Jan–31 Mar	8–5	M	T	W	T	F	S	S
1 Apr–31 May	8–5:30	M	T	W	T	F	S	S
1 Jun–30 Sep	8–6	M	T	W	T	F	S	S
1 Oct–31 Dec	8–5	M	T	W	T	F	S	S

Formby

near Formby, Liverpool

Map (5) B7 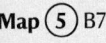  1967

This ever-changing sandy coastline set between the sea and Formby town offers miles of walks through the woods and dunes. You may glimpse a rare red squirrel or see a historic landscape levelled for asparagus. Prehistoric animal and human footprints can sometimes be found in silt beds on the shoreline. **Note**: toilets close at 5:30 in summer, 4 in winter.

Eating and shopping: ice-creams, soft drinks and coffee from mobile van.

Making the most of your day: guided walks and awareness days. Circular and longer walks linked to the Sefton Coastal Path. Formby Point audio guide trail. **Dogs**: under close control (vulnerable wildlife).

Access for all:  **Grounds**

Getting here: see website for details.
Sat Nav: use L37 1LJ.

Finding out more: 01704 878591 or formby@nationaltrust.org.uk

Formby		M	T	W	T	F	S	S
Countryside								
Open all year	Dawn–dusk	M	T	W	T	F	S	S
Car park								
1 Jan–26 Jan	9–4	M	T	W	T	F	S	S
27 Jan–30 Mar	9–4:30	M	T	W	T	F	S	S
31 Mar–26 Oct	9–5:30	M	T	W	T	F	S	S
27 Oct–31 Dec	9–4:30	M	T	W	T	F	S	S

Closed 25 December.

On the woodland trail near Aira Force in Cumbria

Lake District

Whether you want a great day out, a gentle stroll and splash in the lake, challenging hike to the mountaintops, or a picnic spot with a view, we've got it all.

Aira Force and Ullswater

near Watermillock, Penrith, Cumbria

Map (6) D7   1906

Ullswater is truly breathtaking. With its beautiful lake (above) nestled among towering fells, this valley begs to be explored. The tumbling waterfall of Aira Force drops an impressive 65 feet and can be reached by strolling through ancient woodland and landscaped glades. The perfect place for a family walk and picnic.

Eating and shopping: Aira Force tea-room (not National Trust) by car park. Side Farm tea-room (Trust farm) in Patterdale. Lakeshore picnics at Aira Green.

Making the most of your day: red squirrel trail at Aira Force. Willow birdwatching hide. Many walks in Ullswater. Canoe launching at Glencoyne car park. **Dogs**: under close control (stock grazing).

Access for all: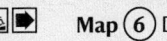

Getting here: see website for details.
Parking: at Aira Force, Aira Force High Cascades, Aira Force Park Brow and Glencoyne Bay (pay and display).

Finding out more: 017684 82067 or ullswater@nationaltrust.org.uk

Looking towards Windermere, Cumbria

Ambleside and Windermere

near Windermere, Cumbria

Map (6) D8  1927

The bustling Lakeland towns of Ambleside and Windermere are situated around England's longest lake. With fells, spring gardens, woodlands, lakeshore parks and a Roman fort on offer, this part of the Lake District is a great option for families looking for fun in the great outdoors.

Making the most of your day: seasonal displays of azaleas and rhododendrons at Stagshaw Gardens. Cumbria's tallest tree in Skelghyll woods. Galava roman fort. Bridge House, Ambleside's smallest building. Townend nearby. **Dogs**: welcome under close control (stock grazing).

Access for all: Bridge House 👤👤👤➡

Getting here: see website for details.
Parking: at Stagshaw Gardens.

Finding out more: 015394 63803 or windermere@nationaltrust.org.uk

Ambleside and Windermere		M	T	W	T	F	S	S
Stagshaw Gardens								
15 Mar–3 Aug	Dawn–dusk	M	T	W	T	F	S	S
Countryside								
Open all year		M	T	W	T	F	S	S

Bridge House, please see website for details.

Borrowdale

near Keswick, Cumbria

Map (6) D7  1902

You can enjoy 10,000 hectares (25,000 acres) of open fell in Borrowdale – taking a journey from lush lakeside woodland to the 'Jaws of Borrowdale', described by Wainwright as 'the loveliest square mile in Lakeland'. Our new shop and visitor centre is a great place to plan your visit. **Note**: charges apply to members on Force Crag Mine and Derwent Island House open days.

Eating and shopping: extended shop and visitor centre selling local souvenirs, ice-cream and refreshments. *Rangers' Guide* to intriguing places off the beaten track available. Tenant-run cafés at Rosthwaite, Watendlath and Stonethwaite serving local Herdwick lamb. Free-range eggs from Ashness or Stonethwaite farms.

Making the most of your day: events, including behind-the-scenes days at Force Crag Mine and Derwent Island House. Sights, tastes and smells of the 18th century at Wordsworth House and Garden in Cockermouth.
Dogs: under close control at lambing time.

Access for all: 🅿♿🚻 Island House 👤
Mine 👤🚶 Foreshore 👤

Borrowdale, Cumbria: there is so much to explore

Getting here: see website for details.
Sat Nav: for lakeside shop use CA12 5DJ; for Seatoller (at foot of Honister Pass) use CA12 5XN. **Parking**: at Great Wood, Ashness Bridge, Surprise View, Watendlath, Kettlewell, Bowder Stone, Rosthwaite, Seatoller and Honister.

Finding out more: 017687 74649 or borrowdale@nationaltrust.org.uk

Borrowdale
See website for Force Crag Mine and Derwent Island House opening arrangements.

Enchanting Buttermere in Cumbria

Buttermere, Ennerdale and Whitehaven Coast

near Cockermouth and Whitehaven, Cumbria

Map (6) C7   1935

There's plenty of choice here, in what we cheekily call the 'real' Lake District. Buttermere is paradise for fell walkers, Ennerdale's forest and lake walks are perfect to escape to on busy days, while Whitehaven and its coastline are full of hidden gems and stories about this proud industrial port. **Note**: sorry no toilets in Ennerdale. Landslips possible on Whitehaven coast path.

Eating and shopping: pubs and cafés in villages of Buttermere, Loweswater and Ennerdale and in Whitehaven town (none National Trust). Farm in Buttermere selling homemade ice-cream and café serving Butterbeer (neither National Trust).

Making the most of your day: coastal paths and four round-the-lake routes. Off-road cycling in Ennerdale and along Whitehaven coast. **Dogs**: under close control at lambing time.

Access for all: Grounds

Getting here: see website for details.
Sat Nav: use CA13 9UZ for Buttermere village; CA13 0RU for Loweswater village; CA23 3AU for Ennerdale Water; CA28 9AE for

Whitehaven Harbour. **Parking**: at Honister Pass, Buttermere village, Rannerdale, Cinderdale, Lanthwaite Green, Lanthwaite Wood near Crummock Water and Maggies Bridge at Loweswater. Also two car parks beside Ennerdale Water and on the Whitehaven Coast by harbour (none National Trust).

Finding out more: 017687 74649 or buttermere@nationaltrust.org.uk

Coniston and Little Langdale

near Coniston, Cumbria

Map (6) D8  1930

The countryside around Coniston and Little Langdale covers a large area of some of the Lake District's most scenic woodland, water and fells. There are numerous great routes to and from Coniston village and the accessible Blea Tarn in Little Langdale also has superb views and fine walking.

Eating and shopping: numerous places (not National Trust) to eat around the area, particularly in Coniston – some linked with Trust tenants. Refreshments usually available at Tarn Hows. Trust shop in nearby Hawkshead.

Making the most of your day: paths and bridleways around Coniston. Cruises on Steam Yacht Gondola, disembarking at Monk Coniston jetty for a walk through Monk Coniston grounds to Tarn Hows. **Dogs**: on leads (stock grazing).

Access for all: [P] Grounds [image] [image]

Getting here: see website for details.
Parking: at Glen Mary and Blea Tarn, also in Coniston (none National Trust).

Finding out more: 015394 41456 or coniston@nationaltrust.org.uk

---

Fell Foot Park

Newby Bridge, Windermere, Cumbria LA12 8NN

Map (6) D9 [image] 1948

The views of Lake Windermere from the park are truly breathtaking. A magical, and safe, environment for children and adults alike to enjoy the great outdoors, have a relaxed lunch around the boathouses, picnic or barbecue near the lakeshore, or take to the water in a rowing boat. **Note**: launch/slipway facilities available for a wide variety of craft (charges apply).

Eating and shopping: Boathouse Café serving drinks and snacks. Small selection of children's games, gifts and local food available.

Boathouse Café at Fell Foot Park, Cumbria

Making the most of your day: rowing boats for hire April to October (weather permitting). Events. Adventure playground. **Dogs**: welcome on leads.

Access for all: [P][D][image][WC][image] Grounds [image]

Getting here: see website for details.
Parking: two large car parks (charges for non-members).

Finding out more: 015395 31273 or fellfootpark@nationaltrust.org.uk

Fell Foot Park		M	T	W	T	F	S	S
Park								
1 Jan–3 Apr	Dawn–dusk	M	T	W	T	F	S	S
4 Apr–2 Nov	8–8	M	T	W	T	F	S	S
3 Nov–31 Dec	Dawn–dusk	M	T	W	T	F	S	S
Catering facilities								
15 Feb–3 Apr	11–4	M	T	W	T	F	S	S
4 Apr–14 Sep	10–5	M	T	W	T	F	S	S
15 Sep–2 Nov	11–4	M	T	W	T	F	S	S

Boat hire available daily 11 to 4 from 4 April to 2 November, weather permitting. Catering facility opening times may vary.

Hawkshead and Claife Viewing Station

near Hawkshead, Cumbria

Map (6) D8 [image] 1929

Hawkshead village, home to the Beatrix Potter Gallery, is surrounded by beautiful countryside, perfect for walks and exploration. Why not start your adventure at Claife Viewing Station on Windermere lakeshore, then follow the path up to Wray Castle? **Note**: toilets at Ferry House (near Claife Viewing Station) and in Hawkshead.

Eating and shopping: numerous catering options and shopping opportunities in and around Hawkshead village, including Hawkshead Trust gift shop and at Wray Castle (internet shop at www.shop.nationaltrust.org.uk/beatrixpotter)

Making the most of your day: Beatrix Potter Gallery in Hawkshead. National Trust campsite on lakeshore at Low Wray, next to Wray Castle. Numerous walks in the countryside which inspired Beatrix Potter. **Dogs**: allowed in countryside, under close control.

Claife Viewing Station on Windermere lakeshore, Cumbria

Access for all: Viewing Station 🔲 Courthouse 🔲

Getting here: see website for details.
Parking: Ash Landing and Harrowslack, near Windermere lakeshore for Claife Viewing Station.

Finding out more: 015394 41456 or hawkshead@nationaltrust.org.uk

Hawkshead and Claife

Hawkshead Courthouse: 29 March to 2 November by key from the National Trust shop in Hawkshead, no parking facilities.

Sticklebarn and Great Langdale

near Ambleside, Cumbria

Map (6) D8 ✚🔲🏛🔲🔲🔲⛺🍷 1925

Langdale is a natural playground of rugged fells, with walks and activities to suit all abilities. Nestling in the valley bottom you'll find Sticklebarn, the only National Trust-run pub. With crackling fires, real ales and great food, there is no better place to unwind after a day of adventure.

Eating and shopping: food and drink served all day. Outdoor eating. Wood-fired pizzas. Dishes made with fresh ingredients from National Trust farms and Lakeland producers. Hand-pulled real ales, wines by the glass and our own Sticklebarn Bedrock Gin.

Making the most of your day: fell walking, ghyll scrambling and rock-climbing. Live music and adventure film screenings at Sticklebarn. Campsite. **Dogs**: welcome under control.

Access for all: 🔲🔲🔲 Pub 🔲🔲 Grounds 🔲

Getting here: see website for details.
Parking: at Stickle Ghyll, Old Dungeon Ghyll and in Elterwater village.

Finding out more: 015394 63823 (Property Office). 015394 35665 (Grasmere Information Centre). 015394 37356 (Sticklebarn pub) or sticklebarn@nationaltrust.org.uk

Sticklebarn and Great Langdale

Sticklebarn open 12 to 11, food served all day until 9. Opening times vary from season to season. Closed 23 to 28 December.

Sticklebarn, Cumbria: Trust-run pub

Tarn Hows

near Coniston, Cumbria

Map (6) D8 🔲🔲 1943

Stunning Tarn Hows offers an accessible circular (1¾ miles) walk through beautiful countryside with majestic mountain views. A great place to walk and picnic, or to begin your wider Lake District countryside adventure. There are also rare Belted Galloway cattle and sturdy Herdwick sheep grazing by the tarn.

Eating and shopping: ice-cream and hot drinks van on site. Numerous catering options nearby, particularly in Coniston and Hawkshead. National Trust shop in nearby Hawkshead.

Making the most of your day: why not come to Tarn Hows via a Steam Yacht Gondola cruise on Coniston? Accessible circular walk around tarn. Wray Castle nearby is great for families. **Dogs**: on leads (stock grazing).

Access for all: 🅿️♿️🚾♿ Grounds ♿♿

Getting here: see website for details. **Parking**: free.

Finding out more: 015394 41456 or tarnhows@nationaltrust.org.uk

Wasdale, Eskdale and Duddon

near Seascale, Cumbria

Map (6) D8 ✝️🍽️🏛️♿🏊🚶🏕️ 1929

In Wasdale below Scafell Pike, England's highest mountain, lies Wastwater, its deepest lake, and the walled amphitheatre of Wasdale Head. Upper Eskdale is dominated by high mountains, yet has delightful riverside walks. Across the high mountain passes the ever-changing vistas of the Duddon Valley can be readily enjoyed.

Eating and shopping: shop at campsite.

Making the most of your day: walking in England's highest mountains. Paddling and wild swimming in Wastwater. Hardknott Roman Hill Fort. Wasdale Head Campsite. **Dogs**: under close control (stock grazing).

Access for all: Grounds ♿

Getting here: see website for details. **Parking**: at Wasdale Head.

Finding out more: 01946 726064 or wasdale@nationaltrust.org.uk

Morecambe Bay Coast

Sand dunes, cliffs, fascinating wildlife and amazing views make this coast a perfect backdrop for a day at the beach.

Arnside and Silverdale

near Arnside, Cumbria

Map (5) C4 🏛️🏊🚶 1929

With fine views over Morecambe Bay, and miles of footpaths, this coastal countryside is worth exploring. A wildlife-rich mosaic of limestone grassland, pavement, woodland and meadows. Arnside Knott (below) and Eaves Wood are renowned for butterflies and flowers; Jack Scout's cliffs for watching the setting sun or migrant birds passing through.

Eating and shopping: variety of small shops, galleries and cafés in and around Arnside and Silverdale villages (not National Trust).

Making the most of your day: toposcope viewpoint (short uphill from Arnside Knott car park). For easier walking follow the Silverdale Lots footpath to the cove. **Dogs**: welcome under control (stock grazing).

Getting here: see website for details. **Parking**: at Arnside Knott (signposted from Arnside Promenade) and Eaves Wood, Silverdale. Also parking in Silverdale village (not National Trust).

Finding out more: 01524 702815 or arnsidesilverdale@nationaltrust.org.uk

Scafell Pike, Wasdale in Cumbria

Twilight at Sandscale Haws National Nature Reserve, Cumbria: looking across the Duddon estuary

Heysham Coast

Heysham, near Morecambe, Lancashire

Map (6) D10   1996

Unique ruined Saxon St Patrick's Chapel and rock-cut graves. Clifftop walk with stunning views across Morecambe Bay to Lakeland Fells. **Note**: nearest facilities in village (not National Trust); park in the main village car park.

Finding out more: 01524 701178 or heysham@nationaltrust.org.uk

Sandscale Haws National Nature Reserve

Roanhead, Hawthwaite Lane, near Barrow in Furness, Cumbria LA14 4QJ

Map (6) D9   1984

Wild, grass-covered sand dunes and the windswept Roanhead Beach: home to some of Britain's rarest wildlife, including the natterjack toad. **Note**: toilets (not National Trust). Car park (open all year); ice-cream cabin (seasonal).

Finding out more: 01229 462855 or sandscalehaws@nationaltrust.org.uk

Car parks in the Lake District

Buttermere	
Lanthwaite Wood	NY 149 215
Buttermere	NY 172 173
Honister Pass	NY 225 135

Borrowdale	
Seatoller	NY 246 137
Rosthwaite	NY 257 148
Bowderstone	NY 254 167
Watendlath	NY 276 164
Kettlewell	NY 269 196
Great Wood	NY 272 213

Ullswater	
Aira Force	NY 401 201
Glencoyne Bay	NY 387 188
High Cascades	NY 397 211
Park Brow	NY 397 206

Wasdale	
Wasdale Head	NY 182 074

Langdale	
Blea Tarn	NY 295 043
Old Dungeon Ghyll	NY 285 062
Stickle Ghyll	NY 295 064
Elterwater	NY 329 047

Coniston	
Glen Mary	SD 321 998
Tarn Hows	SD 326 995

Windermere	
Red Nab	SD 385 995
Harrowslack	SD 388 960
Ash Landing	SD 388 955

West coast	
Sandscale Haws	SD 199 758

Acorn Bank

Temple Sowerby, near Penrith,
Cumbria CA10 1SP

Map (6) E7 🏛️🖼️🌸⚓🛏️ 1950

At the heart of the Eden Valley, with spectacular views across to the Lake District, Acorn Bank is a tranquil haven with an almost forgotten industrial past. There are walled gardens, sheltering a medicinal herb collection, and traditional orchards. Paths lead through woodland, along the Crowdundle Beck, to the watermill, now working again after more than 70 years. You can also explore the wider estate with its hidden gypsum-mining remains and abundance of wildlife. The unfurnished 17th-century sandstone house is partially open to the public while work to restore it progresses; the shop and charming tea-room are located within it. **Note**: access to fragile grass paths may be restricted after wet weather. Members pay on Apple Day, 12 October (opening arrangements differ on that day, see note in table for details).

Exploring the woodland at the tranquil haven of Acorn Bank in Cumbria

Eating and shopping: tea-room serving light lunches, cakes and scones made from local produce, herbs and fruit from the garden and flour from the mill. Shop selling plants and local and national products.

Making the most of your day: watermill machinery operates most weekend afternoons. Wild play area in the woods and secret places for children to discover. Apple Day is a great family day out. **Dogs**: welcome on leads on woodland walks/garden courtyard. Apple Day: assistance dogs only.

Access for all: 🅿️🚻♿🚾👶🦽📷🎧♿😊🐕
Watermill 🦽♿ House ♿🚻
Grounds 🦽♿🚻➡️🚻

Getting here: see website for details.
Parking: free.

Finding out more: 017683 61893 or acornbank@nationaltrust.org.uk

Acorn Bank		M	T	W	T	F	S	S
15 Feb–9 Mar	10–5*						S	S
15 Mar–2 Nov	10–5*	M		W	T	F	S	S

*Tea-room open 11 to 4:30. Apple Day: Sunday, 12 October, 11 to 4:30 (access for event only).

Parking charges for non-members may apply

Allan Bank and Grasmere

Allan Bank, Grasmere, Ambleside,
Cumbria LA22 9QB

Map ⑥ D8   🏯 🏛 🌸 ♨ 1920

A National Trust experience like no other,
Allan Bank is a place to relax in front of a warm
fire with a cup of tea while the children play.
Partially restored and undecorated, the house
offers you the opportunity to see and touch the
many layers of this home's fascinating history.
Make yourself at home, take time to explore the
intriguing woodland and soak up the stunning
views that once inspired William Wordsworth
and National Trust founder Canon Rawnsley.

Eating and shopping: National Trust shop in
Grasmere selling local gifts, snacks, books,
maps and our *Ranger's Guide to Grasmere*.
Light refreshments and free tea and coffee
available at Allan Bank. Picnics welcome.

**Allan Bank in Grasmere, Cumbria, below and right: so
many opportunities for families to relax and play**

Making the most of your day: family activities,
including painting or drawing in the art room
and board games. Woodland trail and walks
around Grasmere and Rydal Water.
Mountain Heritage Library. **Dogs**: welcome
under control.

Access for all: 🅿♿♿🚻♿♿♿
Allan Bank 🏠♿♿   Countryside ♿

Getting here: see website for details.
Parking: nearest in village, pay and display
(not National Trust).

Finding out more: 015394 35143 or
allanbank@nationaltrust.org.uk

Allan Bank and Grasmere		M	T	W	T	F	S	S
Allan Bank								
22 Mar–2 Nov	10–5	M	T	W	T	F	S	S
7 Nov–21 Dec	10:30–4	·	·	·	·	F	S	S
Grasmere gift shop								
22 Mar–2 Nov	10–5:30	M	T	W	T	F	S	S
3 Nov–31 Dec	10–4	M	T	W	T	F	S	S
Countryside								
Open all year		M	T	W	T	F	S	S

Grasmere gift shop: 1 January to 21 March – opening times
vary. Closed 25 to 26 December.

The Beatles' Childhood Homes

Woolton and Allerton, Liverpool

Map (5) C8   🏠 2002

A combined tour to Mendips and 20 Forthlin Road, the childhood homes of John Lennon and Paul McCartney, is your only opportunity to see inside the houses where the Beatles met, composed and rehearsed many of their earliest songs. You can walk through the back door into the kitchen and imagine John's Aunt Mimi cooking him his tea, or stand in the spot where Lennon and McCartney composed 'I Saw Her Standing There'. Join our custodians on a fascinating trip down memory lane in these two atmospheric period houses, so typical of Liverpool life in the 1950s. **Note**: access to these houses is by National Trust minibus tour only from Liverpool city centre or Speke Hall (charge including members).

Mendips, Liverpool: childhood home of John Lennon

Eating and shopping: guidebooks and postcards available at both houses and Speke Hall shop. Speke Hall's Home Farm restaurant serving local produce.

Making the most of your day: departures from convenient pick-up points (city centre and Speke Hall). Our comfortable minibus and easy online booking service allow you to relax, as we take the strain out of visiting.

Access for all: 🚻 ♿ 🖥 ♿ ⦂ 🅿   Building ♿

Getting here: see website for details.
Parking: for morning tours numerous public car parks in city centre (not National Trust). For afternoon tours, parking at Speke Hall.

Finding out more: 0844 800 4791 (Infoline). 0151 427 7231 (booking line) or thebeatleshomes@nationaltrust.org.uk

The Beatles' Childhood Homes	M	T	W	T	F	S	S
26 Feb–30 Nov	·	·	**W**	**T**	**F**	**S**	**S**

*Admission by guided tour only. Times and pick-up locations vary. Please visit website or call for details and to book tickets.

20 Forthlin Road, Liverpool: Paul McCartney's home

Beatrix Potter Gallery

Main Street, Hawkshead, Cumbria LA22 0NS

Map (6) D8   🏠 1944

This 17th-century building, once the office of Beatrix Potter's solicitor husband, is now a unique gallery housing the National Trust's internationally important collection of original Potter artwork. Each year, we show a different selection of rarely seen Potter paintings and items, and this year our exhibition takes you travelling with Beatrix. Through paintings, sketches, diary entries and photographs, you'll discover how Beatrix's travels inspired many of her stories. In addition, there's always a selection of the original artwork used to illustrate Beatrix's children's tales.
Note: nearest toilet 300 yards in main village car park (not National Trust).

Eating and shopping: shop in Hawkshead selling local products (online shop at www.shop.nationaltrust.org.uk/beatrixpotter). Meals and refreshments available in Hawkshead village (none National Trust).

Beatrix Potter Gallery in Cumbria, above and below, shows the author's rarely seen original artwork

Making the most of your day: exhibition of original artwork, with audio points and touchscreens. Hill Top and Wray Castle nearby.
Dogs: assistance dogs only.

Access for all: 🔖📷♿ ••🅿️   Gallery 🚶♿

Getting here: see website for details.
Parking: 300 yards, pay and display (not National Trust).

Finding out more: 015394 36355 (gallery). 015394 36471 (shop) or beatrixpottergallery@nationaltrust.org.uk

Beatrix Potter Gallery		M	T	W	T	F	S	S
Gallery								
15 Feb–27 Mar	10:30–3:30	M	T	W	T	·	S	S
29 Mar–22 May	10:30–5	M	T	W	T	·	S	S
24 May–28 Aug	10:30–5	M	T	W	T	F	S	S
30 Aug–2 Nov	10:30–5	M	T	W	T	·	S	S
Shop								
4 Jan–9 Feb	10–4	·	·	·	·	·	S	S
15 Feb–23 May	10–5	M	T	W	T	F	S	S
24 May–29 Aug	10–5:30	M	T	W	T	F	S	S
30 Aug–2 Nov	10–5	M	T	W	T	F	S	S
5 Nov–24 Dec	10–4	·	·	W	T	F	S	S

Open various Fridays throughout the year. At busy periods, timed entry system in operation.

Dalton Castle

Market Place, Dalton-in-Furness,
Cumbria LA15 8AX

Map (6) D9   🏠 1965

Eye-catching 14th-century tower built to assert
the authority of the Abbot of Furness Abbey.
Note: opened on behalf of the National Trust
by the Friends of Dalton Castle.

Finding out more: 015395 60951 or
daltoncastle@nationaltrust.org.uk

Dunham Massey is the Stamford Military Hospital

Altrincham, Cheshire WA14 4SJ

Map (5) D8   🏥✝🖼❄♿🍽 1976

During the First World War, this Georgian house,
set in a magnificent deer-park, was transformed
into a military hospital, becoming a sanctuary
from the trenches for almost 300 soldiers.

Dunham Massey is the Stamford Military Hospital, Cheshire: a much-needed sanctuary for almost 300 soldiers

We welcome dogs assisting visitors with disabilities

To mark the centenary we are turning the clock back, allowing you to discover what life was like for the patients and how the war changed everything for those who lived and worked at Dunham. As in the war years, family treasures will once again be stored in the Great Gallery, with a special exhibition showcasing some of the most fascinating objects in this significant collection. Dunham Massey has one of the north's great gardens, and has Britain's largest winter garden, as well as a stunning new rose garden. **Note**: all visitors require an entry ticket (free to members), available from visitor reception.

Eating and shopping: new café in visitor reception building with indoor and outdoor seating serving a range of food and drinks. Ice-cream kiosk. Stables Restaurant near clock tower serving hot lunches. Shop selling gifts, local products and wide range of plants.

Rosa '**Dunham Massey**' in the new rose garden

Making the most of your day: tour the Stamford Military Hospital: meet staff and patients. Experience the wartime 'fresh-air cure'. Free guided walks in the garden and deer-park. Children's trails in garden. The Mill: the oldest building on the estate. New visitor reception building. Events all year, including open-air theatre and garden parties. Family activities during school holidays. Cycling for under fives. **Dogs**: welcome under close control and on leads in deer-park.

Access for all: 🅿🄳♿🚾♿♿🤚📷♿♿
House ♿♿♿ Grounds ♿➡♿♿

Getting here: see website for details.
Parking: 200 yards.

Finding out more: 0161 942 3989 (Infoline). 0161 941 1025 or dunhammassey@nationaltrust.org.uk

Dunham Massey		M	T	W	T	F	S	S
House and mill*								
1 Mar–11 Nov	11–5	M	T	W	·	·	S	S
Garden								
1 Jan–28 Feb	11–4	M	T	W	T	F	S	S
1 Mar–11 Nov	11–5:30	M	T	W	T	F	S	S
12 Nov–31 Dec	11–4	M	T	W	T	F	S	S
Café and shop								
1 Jan–28 Feb	10–4	M	T	W	T	F	S	S
1 Mar–11 Nov	10–5	M	T	W	T	F	S	S
12 Nov–31 Dec	10–4	M	T	W	T	F	S	S
Park†								
Open all year	9–5	M	T	W	T	F	S	S

*Last entry to house at 4. House open Good Friday. Mill open 12 to 4. **Winter: closes at 4 or dusk if earlier. Wednesdays and Fridays throughout June: garden open from 11 to 8. †March to October: gates open until 7:30. Closed 26 November and 25 December. White Cottage open on last Sunday of each month from 30 March to 26 October, 2 to 5 (booking essential on 0161 928 0075).

Inside imposing Gawthorpe Hall in Lancashire

Getting here: see website for details.
Parking: 150 yards, narrow access road (passing places).

Finding out more: 01282 771004 or gawthorpehall@nationaltrust.org.uk

Gawthorpe Hall		M	T	W	T	F	S	S
House and tea-room								
29 Mar–2 Nov	11–5*	·	·	W	T	F	S	S
Grounds								
Open all year	8–7	M	T	W	T	F	S	S

*House opens at 12. Hall and tea-room also open Bank Holidays. Opening times may change.

The Hardmans' House

59 Rodney Street, Liverpool, Merseyside L1 9ER

Map (5) B8   2003

Step back in time and experience the 1950s. In this time capsule of post-war years, you will glimpse the life of an extraordinary couple. Renowned photographer E. Chambré Hardman and his talented wife Margaret lived and worked together in this remarkable Georgian house for 40 years, keeping everything, changing nothing. **Note**: admission by guided tour only – booking advised. Visitor entrance on Pilgrim Street.

The Hardmans' House, Liverpool, Merseyside

Gawthorpe Hall

Burnley Road, Padiham, near Burnley, Lancashire BB12 8UA

Map (5) D6    1972

This imposing house is set in the heart of urban Lancashire. In the 19th century, Sir Charles Barry created the opulent interiors we see today. The Hall displays textiles from the Gawthorpe Textile Collection, including needlework, lace and embroidery. The grounds are popular with dog walkers. **Note**: financed and run in partnership with Lancashire County Council.

Eating and shopping: tea-room serving light snacks.

Making the most of your day: events all year, including open-air theatre (July) and Victorian Christmas. **Dogs**: under close control in grounds.

Access for all: 🅿️♿🚻📶📷📷📷
Building 🏠 **Grounds** 🏠🏠🏠➡️

Eating and shopping: shop selling unique photographic prints, postcards and guidebooks.

Making the most of your day: tours (book your place to avoid disappointment). Virtual tour of house. Children's quiz trail.

Access for all: ⊞⊞⊞⊞⊞⊞⊞⊞⊞
Building ⊞⊞

Getting here: see website for details.
Parking: none on site. Car parks at Anglican Cathedral and Slater Street NCP (not National Trust).

Finding out more: 0151 709 6261 or thehardmanshouse@nationaltrust.org.uk

The Hardmans' House		M	T	W	T	F	S	S
19 Mar–1 Nov	11–3:30			**W**	**T**	**F**	**S**	

Admission by timed ticket only, booking advisable (places limited). Open Bank Holiday Mondays.

Spring at Hare Hill in Cheshire: glorious informality

Hare Hill

Over Alderley, Macclesfield, Cheshire SK10 4PY

Map ⑤ D8   ⊞⊞ 1978

This glorious, informal woodland garden, complete with bird hide, comes alive in spring with rhododendrons, azaleas and bulbs. At its heart is the delightful walled garden, a tranquil place to relax and admire the calming white border in the summer. There are lots of games for families to enjoy too.

Eating and shopping: hot drinks vending machine. Picnics welcome in walled garden.

Making the most of your day: carved wooden hares to spot. Bird hide. Circular walk through wider parkland. Events throughout the summer.
Dogs: under close control in estate only.

Access for all: ⊞⊞⊞ **Grounds** ⊞⊞

Getting here: see website for details.

Finding out more: 01625 584412 or harehill@nationaltrust.org.uk

Hare Hill		M	T	W	T	F	S	S
1 Mar–2 Nov	10–5		**T**	**W**	**T**	**F**	**S**	**S**

Open Bank Holiday Mondays. Last admission one hour before closing. Car park closes at 5.

Hill Top

Near Sawrey, Hawkshead, Ambleside, Cumbria LA22 0LF

Map (6) D8 🏠 ⛺ ❀ 1944

A time capsule of Beatrix Potter's life, this small house, with its fragile interiors, is full of her favourite things, while the garden is a haphazard mix of flowers, herbs, fruit and vegetables – just as it would have been in Beatrix's day. Visitors will be inspired by the sights and sounds loved by Beatrix. You can walk in her footsteps, warm yourself by her fire and even hear her clock strike the hour as you step back in time to Beatrix's 1914. Hill Top can be very busy and visitors may sometimes have to wait to enter the house. **Note**: timed-ticket entry system operating, early sell-outs possible (especially during holidays).

Above and below, inside and out at Hill Top in Cumbria: a time capsule of Beatrix Potter's life

Eating and shopping: Sawrey House Hotel and Tower Bank Arms (none National Trust) serve meals and refreshments. Hill Top shop sells a great range of Beatrix Potter books and collectables. Internet shop (www.shop. nationaltrust.org.uk/beatrixpotter) or mail-order (hilltop.shop@nationaltrust.org.uk).

Making the most of your day: children's garden trail. Combine with a visit to nearby Hawkshead and the Beatrix Potter Gallery. Why not visit by boat, bus, boot or bike? **Dogs**: assistance dogs only.

Access for all: 🅿️ 🖼️ 📖 ♿ ∴ 🗺️
House ♿ 👣 Shop ♿ Garden ♿ ➡️

Getting here: see website for details. **Parking**: limited.

Finding out more: 015394 36269. 015394 36801 (shop) or hilltop@nationaltrust.org.uk

Hill Top		M	T	W	T	F	S	S
House								
15 Feb–27 Mar	10:30–3:30	M	T	W	T	·	S	S
29 Mar–22 May	10:30–4:30	M	T	W	T	·	S	S
24 May–28 Aug	10–5:30	M	T	W	T	·	S	S
30 Aug–2 Nov	10:30–4:30	M	T	W	T	·	S	S
Shop and garden								
15 Feb–28 Mar	10:15–4	M	T	W	T	F	S	S
29 Mar–23 May	10–5	M	T	W	T	F	S	S
24 May–29 Aug	9:45–5:45	M	T	W	T	F	S	S
30 Aug–2 Nov	10–5	M	T	W	T	F	S	S
3 Nov–24 Dec	10–4	M	T	W	T	F	S	S

Entry by timed ticket (places limited). Small car park. Access to garden and shop free during opening hours. House open various Fridays throughout the year. Shop closes at 1 on 24 December.

Keld Chapel

Keld Lane, Shap, Cumbria CA10 3NW

Map ⑥ E7 ✝ | 1918 |

16th-century chapel, linked to Shap Abbey. **Note**: no facilities. Access daily (for key, see the notice on chapel door).

Finding out more: 017683 61893 or keldchapel@nationaltrust.org.uk

Little Moreton Hall

Congleton, Cheshire CW12 4SD

Map ⑤ D9 🏠 ✝ 🏛 ❀ | 1938 |

Lying close to the M6, Little Moreton Hall, one of the most famous buildings in Cheshire, still survives after 500 years. You can get a taste of Tudor life on a free guided tour and meet our Tudor gentlewomen. There are also family trails and games to enjoy, while the pretty knot garden and sweeping front lawn are the perfect setting for relaxing with friends. We are renowned for our homemade food, and our spacious shop stocks a wonderful selection of gifts and plants.

Eating and shopping: The Little Tea Room with outdoor seating and Mrs Dale's Pantry serve food produced in our bakery. Ice-cream kiosk open on sunny days. Large shop selling gifts, refreshments and local products.

Making the most of your day: guided tours, daily activities, costumes to try on and Tudor festivals all year. **Dogs**: on leads in car park and front lawn only.

Access for all: 🅿️ 🐕 ♿ 🚻 🔄 🖐 🅅🆃 🎞 ⦂ 🅰️
Hall ♿ 🏠♿ 🏠♿ ♿ Reception 🏠♿ ♿
Grounds 🏠♿ 🏠♿ 🏠♿ ➡️

Getting here: see website for details.
Parking: 100 yards.

Finding out more: 01260 272018 or littlemoretonhall@nationaltrust.org.uk

Little Moreton Hall		M	T	W	T	F	S	S
15 Feb–23 Feb	11–5	M	T	W	T	F	S	S
26 Feb–13 Apr	11–5	·	·	W	T	F	S	S
14 Apr–27 Apr	11–5	M	T	W	T	F	S	S
30 Apr–25 May	11–5	·	·	W	T	F	S	S
26 May–1 Jun	11–5	M	T	W	T	F	S	S
4 Jun–13 Jul	11–5	·	·	W	T	F	S	S
14 Jul–31 Aug	11–5	M	T	W	T	F	S	S
3 Sep–26 Oct	11–5	·	·	W	T	F	S	S
27 Oct–2 Nov	11–5	M	T	W	T	F	S	S
8 Nov–21 Dec	11–4	·	·	·	·	·	S	S

Open Bank Holiday Mondays. Upper floors may close early if light levels are poor.

Little Moreton Hall in Cheshire, offers a unique taste of life as it was lived in Tudor times

Please display current sticker for free parking (and show card when asked)

Lyme Park, House and Garden

Disley, Stockport, Cheshire SK12 2NR

Map (5) E8 ⬚✚✦✦✦ 1947

At Lyme there is a picture of a servants' ball painted at the height of the Edwardian age, when this great sporting estate was enjoying a golden era. This wonderfully atmospheric scene captures a moment when Lyme was at its best. Soon after, everything changed for ever with the tragedy of the First World War and life would never be the same again. Inside, you can explore lavish interiors filled with treasures and dip into experiences of a vanished age. What was life like before the ball ended? Outside, there is a beautiful garden set against sweeping moorland to discover. **Note**: owned and managed by the National Trust, but partly financed by Stockport Metropolitan Borough Council.

Eating and shopping: restaurant serving morning coffee, lunch and afternoon tea. Timber Yard Café serving light bites, drinks, cakes and snacks. Ice-cream kiosk. Gifts, books and plant shop.

Making the most of your day: why not get closer to the story and be a walk-on extra in the wardrobe department? You can also relax in the library, watch a cine film created by the Legh family, explore the butler's working rooms, then join in a play on the family stage and sit in the morning room to write a letter. Follow in the footsteps of Mr Darcy in the garden that featured as Pemberley in the BBC adaptation of *Pride and Prejudice*. Walking and running guides for the park. Crow Wood adventurous playscape for children between five and 12 years. Events and activities throughout the year. **Dogs**: under close control in park only (on leads in some areas).

Access for all: ⓟⒹⒹⓌⒸ♿♿♿ⓥⓣ••Ⓐ
House ♿♿ Grounds ♿♿♿

Getting here: see website for details.
Parking: 200 yards from house.

Lyme Park, House and Garden, Cheshire, opposite and above: experience the Edwardian golden era

Finding out more: 01663 762023 or lymepark@nationaltrust.org.uk

Lyme Park		M	T	W	T	F	S	S
House, restaurant and shop								
22 Feb–26 Oct	11–5	M	T		·	F	S	S
Garden								
22 Feb–26 Oct	11–5	M	T	W	T	F	S	S
Park								
Open all year	8–6	M	T	W	T	F	S	S
Timber Yard Café								
Open all year	11–4	M	T	W	T	F	S	S
Plant sales and Timber Yard shop								
4 Jan–16 Feb	11–4	·	·	·	·	·	S	S
22 Feb–26 Oct	10:30–5	M	T	W	T	F	S	S
2 Nov–28 Dec	11–4	·	·	·	·	·	S	S
Servants' Hall tea-room								
22 Feb–13 Apr	12–4	·	·	·	·	·	S	S
16 Apr–28 Sep	12–4	·	·	W	T	·	S	S
4 Oct–26 Oct	12–4	·	·	·	·	·	S	S
Winter exhibition, garden, shop and restaurant								
4 Jan–16 Feb	11–3	·	·	·	·	·	S	S
1 Nov–28 Dec	11–3	·	·	·	·	·	S	S

Closed 25 December. Last entry to house 4.

Nether Alderley Mill

Congleton Road, Nether Alderley, Macclesfield, Cheshire SK10 4TW

Map (5) D8 ⬚ 1950

This charming rustic mill is one of only four virtually complete corn mills in Cheshire.

Finding out more: 01625 527468 or netheralderleymill@nationaltrust.org.uk

Quarry Bank

Styal, Wilmslow, Cheshire SK9 4LA

Map (5) D8   🖼️❄️🏊🔔⊤ 1939

At Quarry Bank you can discover the compelling story of mill workers, entrepreneurs and the Industrial Revolution. There are hand-spinners working, the clatter of machinery and the hiss of steam engines – we also have Europe's most powerful working waterwheel. Guided tours take you to the Apprentice House, which housed the pauper children who worked in the mill. In the stunning garden, you can follow our progress with our Upper Garden Project. Nearby Styal village, built by the Gregs to house the mill workers, is still a thriving community. There are also woodland walks along the beautiful River Bollin.

Eating and shopping: shop selling gifts, mementoes and glass cloths produced in the mill. Plant sales. Mill Café serving lunch and afternoon tea. Coffee and ice-cream available from the Pantry (open during busy periods only). Picnic facilities.

Making the most of your day: events, including guided walks and open-air theatre. School holiday activities and trails for all the family. Family tours of the Apprentice House (summer) and children's play areas. Cycle route. **Dogs**: under close control on estate. On lead only in mill yard.

Access for all: 🅿️♿🚻♿♿📷📺:·🅰️
Building 🔼♿🔽   Grounds ♿➡️📶

Getting here: see website for details.
Parking: 200 yards down steep hill (61 steps, ramp available).

The Industrial Revolution comes to life at Quarry Bank in Cheshire, opposite and below

For all enquiries telephone 0844 800 1895 (seven days a week)

Finding out more: 01625 527468 or quarrybankmill@nationaltrust.org.uk

Quarry Bank		M	T	W	T	F	S	S
Mill and Apprentice House								
1 Jan–14 Feb	11–3:30	·	·	W	T	F	S	S
15 Feb–2 Nov	11–5	M	T	W	T	F	S	S
5 Nov–31 Dec	11–3:30	·	·	W	T	F	S	S
Garden								
15 Feb–2 Nov	10:30–5*	M	T	W	T	F	S	S
Shop, café and ticket/information office								
Open all year	10:30–5**	M	T	W	T	·F	S	S

Completely closed 6 to 10 January for essential maintenance. Closed 24 and 25 December, open daily 26 December to 5 January. Apprentice House: limited timed tickets only, available from ticket office (early arrival advised). Popular destination for schools. *Garden closes at dusk if earlier than advertised time. **Shop, café and ticket/information office: between 1 January to 14 February and 5 November to 31 December open Wednesday to Sunday 10:30 to 4.

Rufford Old Hall

200 Liverpool Road, Rufford, near Ormskirk, Lancashire L40 1SG

Map (5) C6 🏠 ❋ 🔔 🍴 1936

This romantic family home, with magnificent Tudor Great Hall, boasts nearly 500 years of Hesketh family history. If you stand in front of the carved screen, you can imagine a young Will Shakespeare entertaining Sir Thomas Hesketh in 1581. Listen to tales about Hesketh lives, loves and fortunes – here and in America. Downstairs, you can learn about the last children to live and be educated here in the 1920s, then step back in time to the 1840s as you climb the stairs to the drawing room, overlooking the beautiful formal gardens, where Lady Hesketh welcomed guests for afternoon tea. **Note**: additional charges may apply for some events (including members).

Eating and shopping: tea-room serving local food. Shop. Plant centre. Picnics welcome.

Making the most of your day: daily house talks and guided garden tours. Events, including open-air theatre. Seasonal children's trails inside and outside. Outdoor games, including giant jenga, swingball and croquet. Christmas experience with Santa's grotto. **Dogs**: on leads in courtyard and woodland only.

Access for all: 🅿️🄳♿🛗🅱️🔼🖼️♿🄰
Building 🔼♿♿♿ Grounds 🔼♿♿➡️♿

Getting here: see website for details.
Parking: free.

Finding out more: 01704 821254 or ruffordoldhall@nationaltrust.org.uk

Rufford Old Hall		M	T	W	T	F	S	S
15 Feb–19 Feb	11–4	M	T	W	·	·	S	S
22 Feb–2 Mar	11–4	·	·	·	·	·	S	S
8 Mar–30 Jul	11–5	M	T	W	·	·	S	S
2 Aug–31 Aug	11–5	M	T	W	T	·	S	S
1 Sep–29 Oct	11–5	M	T	W	·	·	S	S
1 Nov–14 Dec	11–4	·	·	·	·	·	S	S

Open Good Friday. Car park closes 30 minutes after times above. Tudor Great Hall occasionally closed until 1 on Saturdays for weddings.

The Tudor Great Hall at Rufford Old Hall, Lancashire, was once the stage for a young William Shakespeare before he was famous

Sizergh

Sizergh, near Kendal, Cumbria LA8 8AE

Map ⑥ E8 🏠 🍴 🏛 ❀ 🐾 🛏 1950

Sizergh – one family, one estate and more than 700 years of history. This much-loved family home stands proud in its natural setting. Still inhabited by the Strickland family, Sizergh has many tales to tell and certainly feels lived in, with centuries-old portraits sitting alongside modern family photographs. You can explore its gardens or venture into the 647 hectares (1,600 acres) of beautiful estate to spot the rich and diverse wildlife which also makes it their home. The atmosphere here is timeless, and it is an unexpected treasure on the edge of the Lake District. **Note**: Sizergh is a family home, consequently there are some opening restrictions.

Eating and shopping: licensed café. Shop selling local products and plants. Nearby Strickland Arms pub (tenant-run). Picnics available.

Sizergh, Cumbria, clockwise from main picture: the rock garden, dining-room and view across the former moat

Making the most of your day: activities, including estate walks and quizzes for children. Elizabethan carvings of international significance. Kitchen garden, with hens and bees. Bird hide and feeding area. National Trust's largest limestone rock garden. Footpaths through estate, guided walks and orienteering. **Dogs**: welcome on estate footpaths. Assistance dogs only in house and garden.

Access for all: 🅿️♿ 🇩♿ 🚾 ♿ 🔊 📷 📖 VT ♿
⦂🅰 Building ♿♿♿ Grounds ♿➡♿♿

Getting here: see website for details.
Sat Nav: use LA8 8DZ. **Parking**: 250 yards.

Finding out more: 015395 60951 or sizergh@nationaltrust.org.uk

Sizergh		M	T	W	T	F	S	S
House*								
9 Mar–2 Nov	1–5	M	T	W	T	·	·	S
Garden, café and shop**								
4 Jan–9 Feb	11–4	·	·	·	·	·	S	S
10 Feb–23 Feb	11–4	M	T	W	T	F	S	S
1 Mar–8 Mar	11–4	·	·	·	·	·	S	S
9 Mar–2 Nov	10–5	M	T	W	T	F	S	S
3 Nov–31 Dec	11–4	M	T	W	T	F	S	S
Estate**								
Open all year	9–7	M	T	W	T	F	S	S

*Two guided house tours available 12 to 1 (places limited). Entry by timed ticket on Sundays, Bank Holidays and school holidays. **Some parts of the garden are closed every Friday and Saturday and during the winter months of January, February, November and December. Closed 25 December. ***Estate: winter opening 10 to 4.

Speke Hall, Garden and Estate

Speke, Liverpool L24 1XD

Map ⑤ C8 🏛️❄️🏊🐾🔔 | 1944

A rare example of a Tudor manor house with Victorian interiors and original William Morris wallpaper. In this beautiful building, which has witnessed more than 400 years of turbulent history, you can uncover hidden Tudor secrets, take a guided tour or play billiards. Speke Hall is surrounded by gardens and woodland with seasonal displays of rhododendrons, daffodils and bluebells. There is a maze to explore or you can enjoy a bracing walk with stunning views of the Welsh hills. A perfect oasis from modern life. **Note**: administered and financed by the National Trust, assisted by a grant from National Museums Liverpool.

Eating and shopping: local gifts, products and plants available. Home Farm restaurant serving regional specialities, such as Scouse Pie and Wet Nelly. Stable tea-room, near the house, offering hot drinks and homemade cakes.

Making the most of your day: events all year, including Easter, Hallowe'en, Christmas, open-air theatre and themed Tudor and Victorian events, as well as period-costume guided tours. Gardens and woodland walks. Maze and restored kitchen garden. Children's playground and special activities. **Dogs**: on leads in woodland and on signed estate walks.

Access for all: 🅿️🚪♿🚻🍽️🪑📷🖥️♿ ⠿🅰️ Hall ♿♿♿ Grounds ♿➡️♿♿

Getting here: see website for details.
Parking: free.

Finding out more: 0844 800 4799 (Infoline). 0151 427 7231 or spekehall@nationaltrust.org.uk

Speke Hall, Garden and Estate		M	T	W	T	F	S	S
15 Feb–23 Feb	11–4	·	·	**W**	**T**	**F**	**S**	**S**
1 Mar–16 Mar	11–4	·	·	·	·	·	**S**	**S**
19 Mar–27 Jul	11–5	·	·	**W**	**T**	**F**	**S**	**S**
29 Jul–31 Aug	10:30–5	·	**T**	**W**	**T**	**F**	**S**	**S**
3 Sep–2 Nov	11–5	·	·	**W**	**T**	**F**	**S**	**S**
8 Nov–14 Dec	11–4	·	·	·	·	·	**S**	**S**

House: entry before 12:30 by guided tour only (places limited); free-flow access from 12:30. Hall open Bank Holiday Mondays. Some rooms under covers 15 February to 16 March for conservation reasons. Car park closes 30 minutes after times stated above.

Three views of Speke Hall, Garden and Estate in Liverpool: there are more than 400 years of turbulent history to uncover at this Tudor manor house

Steam Yacht Gondola

Coniston Pier, Lake Road, Coniston,
Cumbria LA21 8AN

Map (6) D8  1980

Steam Yacht Gondola, with her sumptuous,
upholstered saloons, is the perfect way to view
Coniston's spectacular scenery from the lake.
You can sail to Monk Coniston jetty at the
north of the lake, then walk through the Monk
Coniston garden to Tarn Hows. There is a
circular walk of four miles or you can disembark
at Brantwood to visit Ruskin's home.
Note: sails from Coniston Pier (sailings subject
to weather conditions). Sorry no toilet on
scheduled sailings. Full fare applies to all
passengers (including members).

**Sumptuous Steam Yacht Gondola, Cumbria:
a unique way to experience Coniston**

Eating and shopping: Bluebird Café (not
National Trust) at Coniston Pier serving local,
freshly prepared food. Disembark at
Brantwood jetty for Jumping Jenny's café
(licensed). Catering provided for private hire.
Gondola souvenirs available on board.

Making the most of your day: themed cruises
and guided walks. Special events.
Downloadable trails from Gondola's jetties.
Dogs: in outside areas only.

Access for all: 🅿♿🚾♿👁⊘ Gangway 👣♿

Getting here: see website for details.
Parking: 50 yards, pay and display, at
Coniston Pier (not National Trust).

Finding out more: 01539 432733 or
sygondola@nationaltrust.org.uk. Booking
Office, Low Wray Campsite, Low Wray,
Ambleside, Cumbria LA22 0JA

Steam Yacht Gondola

Daily sailing 1 April to 31 October. See website or call for
timetable. Piers at Coniston, Monk Coniston, Parkamoor
and Brantwood (not National Trust).

Townend

Troutbeck, Windermere, Cumbria LA23 1LB

Map (6) D8   🏠 ❄ 1948

The Brownes of Townend were a simple farming family, but their home and belongings bring to life more than 400 years of extraordinary stories. You will understand why Beatrix Potter described Troutbeck Valley as her favourite as you approach this traditional stone and slate farmhouse. Once inside, you are welcomed into the farmhouse kitchen, which has a real fire burning most afternoons and a quirky collection of domestic tools. Exploring further, you can marvel at the original intricately carved furniture and discover why the collection of books belonging to a farming family is of international importance.

Eating and shopping: small selection of souvenirs available. Second-hand books. Picnics welcome.

Making the most of your day: rag-rug making. Children's garden and house trail. Traditional games in the garden. Guided tours at 11 and 12. Downloadable circular walks.

Access for all: 🅿️ 🔼 🔼 🔼 🔼 🔼
Building 🔼   Grounds 🔼 🔼

Getting here: see website for details.
Parking: free, 300 yards.

Finding out more: 015394 32628 or townend@nationaltrust.org.uk

Townend		M	T	W	T	F	S	S
22 Mar–2 Nov	11–5*	·	·	**W**	**T**	**F**	**S**	**S**

*11 to 1 entry by guided tour only (places limited).
Open Bank Holiday Mondays. May close early due to poor light.

Townend, Cumbria: visitors can discover 400 years of extraordinary stories at this stone and slate farmhouse

Places may occasionally close for conservation, safety or events

Traditional toys and dressing up are all part of the fun at at Wordsworth House and Garden in Cumbria

Wordsworth House and Garden

Main Street, Cockermouth, Cumbria CA13 9RX

Map (6) C7   ⬛ ✦ 1938

You're guaranteed a warm welcome, whether you meet the maid, manservant or one of our knowledgeable 21st-century guides. They will give you a taste of history in the Georgian kitchen and you can marvel at stories brought to you by a ghostly hologram figure from the past. Outside, explore William's beloved garden. This inspired many of his poems and is full of 18th-century flowers, fruit and vegetables – all used in the house. Relax in the summerhouse and try the homemade cakes and scones in our café. Take in a talk, tasting or children's holiday activity. As featured on ITV.

Eating and shopping: shop selling Wordsworth and local souvenirs. Café serving light lunches and cakes.

Making the most of your day: house and garden tours, talks, harpsichord music, cooking demonstrations, Georgian recipe tastings, dressing up and traditional toys. Games and crafts. Family activities (during school holidays). **Dogs**: on leads in front garden only.

Access for all: 🐕‍🦺 🚻 🏍 🔎 🎧 📷 VT ⬆ ∴ Ⓐ
Building 🚽⬆♿   Grounds 🚽♿

Getting here: see website for details.
Parking: town centre car parks. Long-stay car park signposted as coach park (not National Trust), 300 yards, Wakefield Road.

Finding out more: 01900 820884 (Infoline). 01900 824805 or wordsworthhouse@nationaltrust.org.uk

Wordsworth House and Garden		M	T	W	T	F	S	S
House, garden and café*								
9 Mar–2 Nov	11–5*	M	T	W	T	.	S	S
Shop								
9 Mar–2 Nov	10–5	M	T	W	T	.	S	S
5 Nov–24 Dec	10:30–4	.	.	W	T	F	S	.

*Café: open 10:30 to 4:30. House: last entry 4.
Timed tickets may operate on busy days.

Wray Castle

Low Wray, Ambleside, Cumbria LA22 0JA

Map ⑥ D8   🏰🚲🛏️🏕️ 1929

Set in beautiful grounds on Windermere's western shore, with its own boathouse and jetty, you can explore this amazing mock-Gothic castle inside and outside, whatever the weather. Although empty of original furniture, it has something for all the family – feel free to run around and make noise! Come across on the boats, catch the bus or cycle along the lakeshore. This isn't your usual National Trust visit, so check out our website for more information about the changing activities at this exciting, newly opened National Trust property and to find out how it is developing.

Eating and shopping: we're still developing our offer but we will have a café in the castle serving locally produced snacks and a shop selling a range of items. Picnics welcome.

Making the most of your day: numerous family activities, including dressing-up, trails and castle building. Why not visit by boat, bus, boot or bike? **Dogs**: welcome in grounds on leads, assistance dogs only inside.

Access for all: 🅿️♿🚻♿🍴♿🔛♿
Castle ♿♿

Getting here: see website for details.
Parking: limited.

Finding out more: 015394 33250 or wraycastle@nationaltrust.org.uk

Wray Castle		M	T	W	T	F	S	S
Castle								
22 Mar–2 Nov	10–5	M	T	W	T	F	S	S
7 Nov–21 Dec	10:30–4	·	·	·	·	F	S	S
Grounds								
Open all year	Dawn–dusk	M	T	W	T	F	S	S

Young warriors do battle in front of mock-Gothic Wray Castle in Cumbria. Newly opened, the opportunities for adventure are immense – whatever the weather

Yorkshire and North East

A wonder of the Victorian age, Cragside in Northumberland is the house where modern living began

Outdoors in Yorkshire and the North East

Yorkshire and the North East are places of dramatic contrasts, each with a character and charm entirely its own.

There's so much to enjoy, from energetic adventures and family fun to the simple pleasures of a breathtaking view or watching wildlife; you'll find many ways to experience these great landscapes.

Walk alongside drystone walls through green valleys in the Yorkshire Dales or across wild moorland in the North York Moors. See unspoilt coastline and rugged countryside in Northumberland, or explore woodlands and beautiful beaches around Durham. Add to this a rock-climber's paradise and one of Europe's most exciting nature reserves and the scene is set for you to find your perfect place. Here's just a taster of what you can do.

Above: **walkers at Hadrian's Wall, Northumberland**

Walking

The Yorkshire Dales are a pleasure-ground for walkers. Waymarked trails, for all abilities, allow you to discover riverside beauty spots and limestone uplands. If you love tranquil walks, don't miss the woodlands at Allen Banks and Staward Gorge, Hardcastle Crags and Roseberry Topping. Or follow in the footsteps of Roman soldiers alongside Hadrian's Wall; we protect six miles of this World Heritage Site.

There's no better natural refreshment than a blast of sea air, and we care for 33 miles of coastline where you can find it. Escape to sandy beaches in Northumberland, find stunning clifftop views in Yorkshire or listen to crashing waves at Horden in County Durham.

You can download route maps from **www.nationaltrust.org.uk/walks**

Outdoor adventure

This July, the world's cycling elite will descend on Yorkshire as the Tour de France has its *Grand Depart* from the region. What better inspiration for discovering the freedom of cycling along routes through the Dales?

Hard-hat adventures also await in the Dales, where you can explore caves and mine tunnels. And from scrambling underground to soaring above it, Buckstones by Marsden Moor is a perfect base for paragliding and hang-gliding. Alternatively, take in the view from the colossal rocks at Brimham, with more than 470 climbs for all levels.

Rare and special nature

We care for one of Europe's finest seabird reserves on the Farne Islands. Most famous for the friendly-faced puffin, there's also England's largest colony of grey seals.

Marsden Moor is so rich in birdlife it's a designated International Special Protection Area. You may spot golden plover, curlew or snipe, and you'll find one of the few sanctuaries for our native red squirrel in Northumberland's vast woodlands – you may spot one around Allen Banks and Wallington.

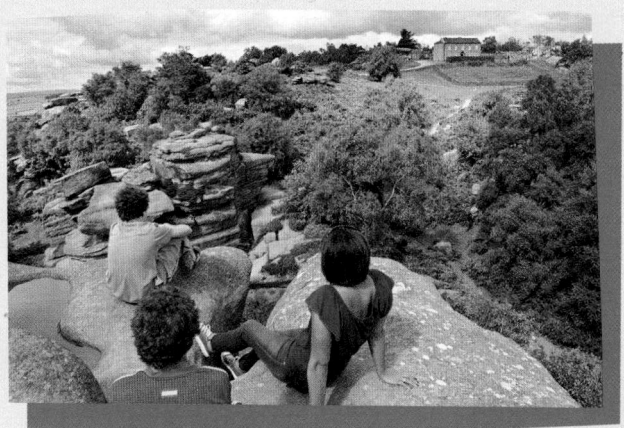

Above:
Brimham Rocks, Nidderdale, North Yorkshire
Above right:
puffins on the Farne Islands, Northumberland
Left: **mountain biking on the Malham Tarn Estate, Yorkshire Dales**

Stay on in a cottage

One day is never enough, so stay on in one of our characterful cottages among the dunes of the Northumberland coast or find the perfect walkers' cottage in the Dales. Visit **www.nationaltrustcottages.co.uk**

Try something new

Fancy getting active, but don't want to go it alone? We've hundreds of organised activities you can join, including mountain biking, climbing and family fun, like den building and rock-pooling. You can also follow our fantastic online Ranger blogs to keep up with the latest news and opportunities to get involved.

Visit our website for events and Ranger blogs, or connect with us on Facebook and Twitter – search for **NTYorkshire** and **NorthEastNT**.

Outdoors in Yorkshire and the North East

Between them, these two contrasting areas offer unspoilt coastline and beautiful beaches, as well as rugged countryside, moorland and green valleys.

Allen Banks and Staward Gorge

near Ridley Hall, Bardon Mill, Hexham, Northumberland

Map (6) F5   🏠🏛️⚡👤 1942

This spectacular gorge and river cuts through the largest area of ancient woodland in the county. There are miles of waymarked walks, interesting wildlife, the remains of a medieval pele-tower and a reconstructed Victorian summerhouse. Within the North Pennines Area of Outstanding Natural Beauty.

Allen Banks and Staward Gorge, Northumberland

Eating and shopping: numerous picnic spots, either at Allen Banks car park, in the woodland or by the river.

Making the most of your day: downloadable trails and events, including volunteering, bushcraft days and fungal forays.
Dogs: welcome under close control.

Access for all: ♿🚻🅿️ Grounds ♿

Getting here: see website for details.
Parking: pay and display at Allen Banks.

Finding out more: 01434 321888 or allenbanks@nationaltrust.org.uk

Bridestones, Crosscliff and Blakey Topping

Staindale, Dalby, Pickering, North Yorkshire YO18 7LR

Map (5) I3    1944

Spectacular all year, the Bridestones are a geological wonder – with moorland vistas, woodland walks and grassy valleys. **Note**: nearest toilets at Staindale Lake car park. Dalby Forest drive starting 2½ miles north of Thornton le Dale – toll charges (including members).

Finding out more: 01723 870423 or bridestones@nationaltrust.org.uk

Brimham Rocks

Summerbridge, Harrogate, North Yorkshire HG3 4DW

Map (5) F4   1970

Magnificent views and the clearest, freshest air can be enjoyed at these breathtakingly dramatic rock formations. A labyrinth of paths runs around the 320 million-year-old rocks and through glorious heather moorland and woodland. A natural playground for families and a premier climbing venue, within the Nidderdale Area of Outstanding Natural Beauty. **Note**: beware of cliff edges. Nearest toilets 600 yards from car park.

Eating and shopping: shop selling books and a range of gifts. Hot and cold refreshments and ice-cream available from kiosk. Picnic tables with views of the rocks and seating inside the visitor centre.

Brimham Rocks, North Yorkshire: fantastic walking

Making the most of your day: learn about the story of the rocks, local social history and conservation work in the visitor centre exhibition. Regular family activities, events and guided walks. **Dogs**: welcome on moors under control and on leads April to June (ground-nesting birds).

Access for all: ⬛⬛⬛⬛⬛⬛⬛⬛⬛⬛
Building ⬛⬛ Grounds ⬛⬛

Getting here: see website for details.
Parking: free (charge for non-members).

Finding out more: 01423 780688 or brimhamrocks@nationaltrust.org.uk

Brimham Rocks		M	T	W	T	F	S	S
Countryside								
Open all year	8–dusk	M	T	W	T	F	S	S
Visitor centre, shop and kiosk								
15 Feb–23 Feb	11–5	M	T	W	T	F	S	S
1 Mar–30 Mar	11–5	.	.	.	.	.	S	S
5 Apr–21 Apr	11–5	M	T	W	T	F	S	S
26 Apr–18 May*	11–5	.	.	.	.	.	S	S
24 May–28 Sep	11–5	M	T	W	T	F	S	S
4 Oct–19 Oct	11–5	.	.	.	.	.	S	S
25 Oct–2 Nov	11–5	M	T	W	T	F	S	S
8 Nov–28 Dec*	11–4	.	.	.	.	.	S	S

*Also open Bank Holiday 5 May, 26 December and 1 January.

Farne Islands

Northumberland

Map (6) H2 ✝ 🏛 ♿ 1925

Probably the most exciting seabird colony in England. A short boat ride off the Northumberland coast rewards you with unrivalled views of 23 nesting species, including 37,000 pairs of puffins, Arctic terns and guillemots. In autumn you can see a large grey seal colony, with over 1,000 pups. **Note**: basic toilet facilities on Inner Farne only. Access by boat from Seahouses (charge including members).

Eating and shopping: shop in Seahouses selling gifts and local produce.

Making the most of your day: Chapel of St Cuthbert with fine stained glass. Victorian lighthouse. Visitor centre. Easy access boardwalk. Seasonal tours. Views of Bamburgh Castle and the Cheviot Hills. Lindisfarne Castle and Northumberland coast nearby.
Dogs: no dogs allowed (including assistance dogs) due to the sensitive nature of the colony.

Seabirds galore at Farne Islands, Northumberland

Access for all: 🅿️ ♿ **Grounds** ♿

Getting here: see website for details.
Parking: in Seahouses opposite harbour, pay and display (not National Trust).

Finding out more: 01665 721099. 01289 389244 (Lindisfarne Castle) or farneislands@nationaltrust.org.uk

Farne Islands		M	T	W	T	F	S	S
Staple Island								
1 May–31 Jul	10:30–1:30	M	T	W	T	F	S	S
Inner Farne Island								
1 Apr–30 Apr	10–6	M	T	W	T	F	S	S
1 May–31 Jul	1:30–5	M	T	W	T	F	S	S

Landings only on Inner Farne and Staple Islands. Seahouses information centre and shop open all year, 10 to 5.

Hardcastle Crags

near Hebden Bridge, West Yorkshire

Map (5) E6  1950

This beautiful wooded valley, with its deep ravines, tumbling streams and glorious waterfalls, has miles of footpaths leading through woodlands rich in wildlife – listen out for the ever-changing birdsong. The seasonal colours are simply stunning, with carpets of bluebells in spring and golden leaves in autumn. Nestling alongside the river is Gibson Mill, a former cotton mill and entertainment emporium, now a visitor centre powered by sustainable energy. You can discover more about the valley's 200-year history here with exhibitions, tours and family fun.
Note: steep paths and rough terrain.

Eating and shopping: Weaving Shed Café serving sandwiches, soup, cakes and ice-cream. Shop selling books, gifts, cards and sweets.

Making the most of your day: seasonal family activities and events. Dress up in period costume at Gibson Mill. Regular workshops. Guided and themed walks. Circular walks, downloadable from the website. **Dogs:** under close control at all times.

Access for all: 🅿️ 🚗 ♿ 🚻 ♿ 💺
Building ♿ ⬆ 👤 **Grounds** ♿

Peaceful Hardcastle Crags in West Yorkshire

Getting here: see website for details.
Sat Nav: Midgehole car park: HX7 7AA. Clough Hole car park: HX7 7AZ. **Parking:** nearest 1 mile (pay and display), Clough Hole car park, Widdop Road (steep walk).

Finding out more: 01422 844518 (weekdays). 01422 846236 (weekends) or hardcastlecrags@nationaltrust.org.uk

Hardcastle Crags		M	T	W	T	F	S	S
Gibson Mill and Weaving Shed Café								
4 Jan–23 Feb	11–3						S	S
1 Mar–30 Oct	11–4		T	W	T		S	S
1 Nov–21 Dec	11–3						S	S
Weaving Shed Café								
3 May–28 Sep	10–5						S	S

Weaving Shed Café open 7 days and Gibson Mill open Saturday to Thursday during school holidays: 24 February to 2 March, 14 to 27 April, 26 May to 1 June, 22 July to 31 August, 26 October to 2 November (café open 11 to 3, from 1 November to 28 February). Open Bank Holidays.

Marsden Moor Estate

Marsden, Huddersfield, West Yorkshire

Map (5) E7  1955

Walk on the wild side at this ecological paradise, spanning the South Pennines and Peak District National Park. Start at Pule Hill or Buckstones for uninterrupted views across moorland – particularly magnificent at sunset. A Site of Special Scientific Interest, the landscape supports moorland birds and is important for carbon storage. **Note**: nearest refreshments and toilets in Marsden village.

Eating and shopping: tea-rooms, restaurants and shops in Marsden village (not National Trust).

Making the most of your day: seasonal events, family activities and guided walks. Exhibition room at estate office by Marsden railway station. Walking routes available (OS map required for walks). **Dogs**: welcome on leads.

Sunrise over Marsden Moor Estate, West Yorkshire

Access for all: Exhibition ♿ Grounds ♿

Getting here: see website for details.
Parking: free at Marsden village (not National Trust), Buckstones and Wessenden Head.

Finding out more: 01484 847016 or marsdenmoor@nationaltrust.org.uk

Northumberland Coast

Northumberland

Map (6) H2  1935

Northumberland Coast: mile upon mile of beautiful dunes

From Lindisfarne to Druridge Bay, enjoy wide open skies above white sands and blue seas. This unspoilt coastline boasts quaint fishing villages and deserted beaches, with excellent rock pools. You will also be able to spot wonderful wildlife, including seals, wading shorebirds and nesting terns at the Long Nanny. **Note**: coastal landscape of mixed terrain.

Eating and shopping: shops on Holy Island and Seahouses. Cafés, pubs and shops in coastal towns and villages (not National Trust).

Making the most of your day: little tern nesting colony at Long Nanny (June to August), access from High Newton. Events, including guided walks and wildlife spotting. Farne Islands, Dunstanburgh Castle and Lindisfarne Castle nearby. **Dogs**: welcome, some local restrictions may apply.

Getting here: see website for details.
Parking: limited at Druridge Bay. Local council parking at Holy Island, Seahouses, Beadnell, Newton by the Sea and Craster (not National Trust).

Finding out more: 01289 389244 or northumberlandcoast@nationaltrust.org.uk

Penshaw Monument

Chester Road, Penshaw, Tyne & Wear DH4 7NJ

Map (6) H5    1939

Enjoy walks and magnificent views from this 70-foot high tribute to the first Earl of Durham. An iconic Wearside landmark. **Note**: sorry no toilets. Access staircase to the top of the monument by guided tour only (advance booking advised).

Finding out more: 01723 870423 or penshaw.monument@nationaltrust.org.uk

Roseberry Topping

Newton-under-Roseberry,
North Yorkshire TS9 6QR

Map (5) G2   1985

Layers of human and geological history have shaped this iconic hill. Enjoy stunning views, woodland walks and wildlife.
Note: sorry no toilet.

Finding out more: 01723 870423 or roseberrytopping@nationaltrust.org.uk

Breathtaking views along the Yorkshire Coast

Yorkshire Coast

near Ravenscar, North Yorkshire

Map (5) I2    1976

Along the coastline from Saltburn to Filey you'll find breathtaking views, clifftop walks, cycling routes and sandy bays with excellent rock-pooling. Start your day with a warm welcome at Ravenscar Visitor Centre or see the coastal life exhibition at the Old Coastguard Station in Robin Hood's Bay.

Eating and shopping: Old Coastguard Station and Ravenscar Visitor Centre shops selling gifts, books, maps, children's toys etc. Hot and cold drinks, ice-cream, light refreshments available at Ravenscar. Indoor seating and outdoor picnic area.

Making the most of your day: regular art exhibitions at the Old Coastguard Station. Family events, geocaching, wildlife activities and guided walks from Ravenscar visitor centre and the Old Coastguard Station. Fossil hunting at Port Mulgrave. **Dogs**: welcome on lead at most events. Assistance dogs only in visitor centre and Old Coastguard Station.

Access for all: [icons]
Visitor centre [icon]   Grounds [icon]

Getting here: see website for details.
Parking: free on roadside at Ravenscar. Pay and display car parks at Saltburn, Runswick Bay and Robin Hood's Bay (not National Trust).

Finding out more: 01723 870423 or yorkshirecoast@nationaltrust.org.uk

Yorkshire Coast		M	T	W	T	F	S	S
Old Coastguard Station								
4 Jan–9 Feb	10–4	·	·	·	·	·	S	S
15 Feb–23 Feb	10–4	M	T	W	T	F	S	S
1 Mar–6 Apr	10–4	·	·	·	·	·	S	S
7 Apr–2 Nov	10–5	M	T	W	T	F	S	S
8 Nov–21 Dec	10–4	·	·	·	·	·	S	S
27 Dec–31 Dec	10–4	M	T	W	·	·	S	S
Ravenscar Visitor Centre								
4 Apr–2 Nov	10–4:30	M	T	W	T	F	S	S

Yorkshire Dales

Whatever your ability, you will find a walk that suits you here. There are riverside beauty spots, picturesque villages, limestone uplands and flower-rich meadows to discover.

Malham Tarn Estate

Waterhouses, Settle, North Yorkshire BD24 9PT

Map ⑤ D4 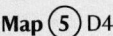  1946

Malham Tarn in the Dales, part of which is a National Nature Reserve, is the perfect place to enjoy the great outdoors. There are stunning views across limestone pavements and the tarn's rippling water. Popular with walkers and cyclists, it is wonderful for a stroll, picnic or family adventure. **Note**: nearest toilet Malham National Park car park, or Orchid House exhibition (weekends only).

Eating and shopping: tea-rooms, pubs and facilities in Malham village (not National Trust).

Making the most of your day: guided walks, events and outdoor activities. Accessible boardwalk through nature reserve. Cycle trail around the tarn. Family fun during school holidays. Orchid House exhibition room. Walking routes for all abilities. **Dogs**: welcome on leads due to roaming livestock.

Access for all: Town Head Barn Grounds 🚻▶

Getting here: see website for details. **Parking**: in Malham village, pay and display (not National Trust). Free at Watersinks car park, south side of Malham Tarn.

Finding out more: 01729 830416 or malhamtarn@nationaltrust.org.uk

Malham Tarn Estate		M	T	W	T	F	S	S
Town Head Barn								
15 Feb–31 Oct	10–4	**M**	**T**	**W**	**T**	**F**	**S**	**S**

Upper Wharfedale

near Buckden, North Yorkshire

Map ⑤ E4  1989

The spectacular landscapes in this part of the Dales are great for walking and cycling. The characteristic drystone walls and barns look striking in summer when surrounded by beautiful flowering hay meadows. Combined with river and valley-side woodland, this a wonderful place to relax and explore the great outdoors.

Eating and shopping: village tea-rooms, shops and pubs, farm shops (not National Trust).

Making the most of your day: guided walks, events, workshops and activities. Family fun during school holidays. Exhibition at Town Head Barn in Buckden. **Dogs**: welcome on leads due to livestock.

Access for all: 🅿♿🚾
Town Head Barn Grounds ▶

Getting here: see website for details. **Sat Nav**: use BD23 5JA. **Parking**: in Kettlewell and Buckden, pay and display (not National Trust).

Finding out more: 01729 830416 or upperwharfedale@nationaltrust.org.uk

Upper Wharfedale		M	T	W	T	F	S	S
Town Head Barn								
15 Feb–31 Oct	10–4	**M**	**T**	**W**	**T**	**F**	**S**	**S**

Cooling down in Upper Wharfedale, North Yorkshire, top

Beningbrough Hall, Gallery and Gardens

Beningbrough, York,
North Yorkshire YO30 1DD

Map ⑤ G4 🏠❄🦆🛏🔔🍷 1958

Set in the Vale of York, within easy reach of
Harrogate and Leeds, Beningbrough Hall is
the perfect location for works from the
National Portrait Gallery. Inside the
Italian-inspired house you'll find the
interactive galleries, Making Faces –
18th-Century Style, where you can discover
history and portraiture, and even sit for a
21st-century digital portrait. The grand rooms
are a perfect backdrop for the rich collection of
portraits, featuring people who have made, and
are making, British history and culture.
Outdoors, see what's in season in the working
Victorian walled garden and stroll among
luxurious Edwardian borders. The parkland is
perfect for longer walks, with plenty of space
and a play area for children to let off steam.

Eating and shopping: walled garden restaurant
serving hot lunches and snacks made using
local ingredients, including freshly picked
produce. Kiosk offering takeaway snacks and
sandwiches. Stable-block shop selling
souvenirs, gifts, lifestyle products, plus
extensive garden range, including plants
inspired by our borders.

Making the most of your day: Beningbrough's
series of interlocking gardens each offer their
own distinct seasonal interest – from wildlife
havens to colourful herbaceous borders – and
are inspirational all year. There are walks
through park and woodlands and beside the
river with stunning views of the hall, as well as
outdoor activities and natural play
opportunities for families. Art workshops,
dressing up, sculpture modelling and family
house trails are also on offer, plus a full
programme of events and regular tours. You
can get a taste of servant life in the Victorian
laundry and 'below stairs', then take an audio
tour of the house. **Dogs**: welcome on leads in
parkland. Assistance dogs only in gardens
and grounds.

The Victorian walled garden, opposite and above, at Beningbrough Hall, Gallery and Gardens, North Yorkshire

Access for all: [icons]
Mansion [icons]   Stable block [icons]
Grounds [icons]

Getting here: see website for details.
Parking: free.

Finding out more: 01904 472027 or beningbrough@nationaltrust.org.uk

Beningbrough Hall		M	T	W	T	F	S	S
Gardens, shop, restaurant, house and interactive galleries*								
1 Mar–6 Jul	11–5		T	W	T	F	S	S
7 Jul–31 Aug	11–5	M	T	W	T	F	S	S
2 Sep–2 Nov	11–5		T	W	T	F	S	S
Interactive galleries, gardens, shop and restaurant**								
4 Jan–16 Feb	11–3:30						S	S
18 Feb–23 Feb	11–3:30		T	W	T	F	S	S
8 Nov–28 Dec	11–3:30						S	S

*House and interactive galleries open at 12.
**Interactive galleries open at 11:30. Open Bank Holiday Mondays, 26 December and 1 January.

Braithwaite Hall

East Witton, Leyburn, North Yorkshire DL8 4SY

Map ⑤ E3   [icons] 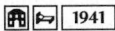 1941

Beautiful 17th-century tenanted farmhouse in Coverdale. **Note**: sorry no toilet. Open June, July and August (visits by arrangement in advance with the tenant).

Finding out more: 01969 640287 or braithwaitehall@nationaltrust.org.uk

Cherryburn

Station Bank, Mickley, Stocksfield,
Northumberland NE43 7DD

Map ⑥ G5   🏠 📷 ❄ ♣ 🍽   1991

Rare surviving Northumbrian farmstead and
Tyne Valley hidden gem, Cherryburn was the
birthplace and inspiration of Thomas Bewick,
the North East's most famous Georgian artist
and naturalist. After viewing Bewick's pioneering
wood engravings, relive his childhood outdoor
adventures, meet our unusual farm animals and
explore our tranquil gardens and orchard.

Eating and shopping: gift shop offering a wide
array of handmade Bewick prints and
souvenirs, plus local food, crafts and books.
Farmhouse café serving homemade cakes,
soups, sandwiches and ice-creams.
Farmyard picnic area.

Thomas Bewick's Cherryburn in Northumberland

Making the most of your day: family trail,
mini-adventure play area and school holiday
activities following in young Tom's footsteps.
Paddock walk. Regular folk music in the
farmyard. Printing demonstrations every
weekend. **Dogs**: welcome on short
leads in garden and grounds
(free-range hens in farmyard).

Access for all: 🅿 🔤 🚽 🏠 🗓 📷 🎢 ·· 🖼
Birthplace 🔣 🔣 🔣   **Café and museum** 🔣 🔣 🏛
Grounds 🔣 🔣 🔣 ➡

Getting here: see website for details.
Parking: free, 100 yards.

Finding out more: 01661 843276 or
cherryburn@nationaltrust.org.uk

Cherryburn		M	T	W	T	F	S	S
17 Feb–29 Jun	11–5	M	T	·	T	F	S	S
30 Jun–31 Aug	10–5	M	T	W	T	F	S	S
1 Sep–2 Nov	11–5	M	T	·	T	F	S	S

Cragside

Rothbury, Morpeth, Northumberland NE65 7PX

Map ⑥ G3   🏠 ❄ ♿ 🛏   1977

Trip the light fantastic to the home where
modern living began. Lord and Lady Armstrong
used their wealth, art and science in a most
ingenious way – Cragside house was the first in
the world to be lit by hydroelectricity, making it
a wonder of the Victorian age, while outside,
their shared passion for landscaping and
gardening was daring and demonstrated
engineering on a spectacular scale. There are
towering North American conifers and great
drifts of rhododendrons, as well as rocky crags
and tumbling water. The house is one of the
finest examples of Arts and Crafts workmanship
in the country. **Note**: challenging terrain and
distances (stout footwear essential).

Eating and shopping: tea-rooms serving hot
meals, hand-crafted sweet treats and local
ice-cream. Shop selling Northumbrian gifts,
books, cards, handmade items and plants.

Making the most of your day: you can see the
house lit by water power once again, now we
have installed the Archimedes Screw (new this
year). Lord Armstrong's hydroelectric
engineering collection and fantasy landscape.
Rhododendron labyrinth. Six-mile estate drive
through woodland. Lakeside trails and picnic
spots. Walks for all abilities, family strolls and
challenging hikes. Family activities, special
exhibitions and seasonal events throughout
the year. Courtesy bus between key features.
Visit nearby Wallington (15 miles) and
Lindisfarne Castle (37 miles).
Dogs: welcome on leads outdoors.

Exploring the grounds at Cragside, Northumberland, above and below: the home where modern living began

Access for all: [icons] House [icons] Visitor Centre [icons] Estate [icons]

Getting here: see website for details.
Parking: free. Nine car parks throughout estate.

Finding out more: 01669 620333 or cragside@nationaltrust.org.uk

Cragside		M	T	W	T	F	S	S
House								
4 Mar–4 Apr	1–5	·	T	W	T	F	·	·
1 Mar–30 Mar	11–5	·	·	·	·	·	S	S
5 Apr–21 Apr	11–5	M	T	W	T	F	S	S
22 Apr–23 May	1–5	·	T	W	T	F	·	·
26 Apr–18 May	11–5	·	·	·	·	·	S	S
24 May–1 Jun	11–5	M	T	W	T	F	S	S
3 Jun–18 Jul	1–5	·	T	W	T	F	·	·
7 Jun–13 Jul	11–5	·	·	·	·	·	S	S
19 Jul–1 Sep	11–5	M	T	W	T	F	S	S
2 Sep–24 Oct	1–5	·	T	W	T	F	·	·
6 Sep–19 Oct	11–5	·	·	·	·	·	S	S
25 Oct–2 Nov	11–5	M	T	W	T	F	S	S
Gardens and woodland								
1 Mar–2 Nov*	10–7	·	T	W	T	F	S	S
7 Nov–21 Dec	11–4	·	·	·	·	F	S	S

Open 15 to 23 February: house (ground floor only) 12 to 4, gardens and woodland 11 to 4. House open Bank Holiday Mondays 11 to 5. Entry is controlled (queueing at busy times). *Gardens and woodland open Mondays 10 to 7 when house is open. Last access to estate drive 5:30.

Dunstanburgh Castle

Craster, Alnwick, Northumberland NE66 3TT

Map ⑥ H3  1961

Iconic castle ruin occupying a dramatic position with spectacular views of the Northumberland coastline – a mere mile walk from Craster. **Note**: managed by English Heritage. National Trust members free. Sorry no toilets, see English Heritage website for further information.

Finding out more: 01665 576231 or dunstanburghcastle@nationaltrust.org.uk

East Riddlesden Hall

Bradford Road, Riddlesden, Keighley, West Yorkshire BD20 5EL

Map ⑤ E5  1934

Set in an estate which was once buzzing with farming activity, this intimate hall tells a story of survival. Originally the home of a 17th-century cloth merchant, today you can discover oak furniture and exquisite embroideries in the cosy rooms, all brought to life with fascinating stories shared by our room guides. The romantic, award-winning gardens

are the perfect place to relax and unwind, while active families can enjoy craft activities and dressing up or let off some steam in the natural play areas – where there is even a mud-pie kitchen for budding chefs.

Eating and shopping: tea-room with soups made using herbs from the garden. Plant sales and gift shop.

Making the most of your day: family trails and riverside walks. Seasonal events and exhibitions. Summer open-air theatre. Herb interpretation area and garden walks. Regular walking for health events. **Dogs**: assistance dogs only.

Access for all: 🅿️ 🄳 ♿ 🔔 🄸 📷 🖥️ 🎞️ ⠿ 🄰
Building ♿ ♿ ♿   Grounds ♿

Getting here: see website for details.
Parking: free, 100 yards.

Finding out more: 01535 607075 or eastriddlesden@nationaltrust.org.uk

East Riddlesden Hall		M	T	W	T	F	S	S
House, shop and tea-room								
15 Feb–2 Mar	10:30–4:30	M	T	W			S	S
8 Mar–16 Mar	10:30–4:30						S	S
22 Mar–2 Nov	10:30–4:30	M	T	W			S	S
Shop and tea-room								
8 Nov–21 Dec	11–4						S	S

Also open Good Friday. Entry to house may be by guided tour. Closed 6 July for private function. Last admission to tea-room 15 minutes before closing.

Intimate East Riddlesden Hall in West Yorkshire

Fountains Abbey and Studley Royal Water Garden

Fountains, Ripon, North Yorkshire HG4 3DY

Map (5) F4 🏠✝🏛✿🐾🛏🔔⚓🍴
1983

In this tranquil valley of the River Skell you'll find two masterpieces of creative genius. The first is the magnificent ruin of Fountains Abbey, established in the 12th century by Cistercian monks seeking a simpler life. The second is Studley Royal, a rare 18th-century water garden, created by the Aislabies to delight their friends and visitors. Today, you'll need a whole day to explore the dramatic ruins and Georgian pleasure gardens of this World Heritage Site. There are also 324 hectares (800 acres) of medieval deer-park, a Victorian high Gothic church, Jacobean manor house and the only surviving Cistercian corn mill. Visit all year round to enjoy the seasonal colour and charm of this beautiful landscape. **Note**: cared for in partnership with English Heritage.

Fountains Abbey and Studley Royal Water Garden, North Yorkshire, above and below

Eating and shopping: large restaurant serving locally sourced produce. Lakeside and abbey tea-rooms in spectacular settings. Large visitor centre shop selling souvenirs, gifts, garden and lifestyle products and plants. Smaller lakeside shop open weekends and school holidays.

Making the most of your day: abbey exhibition in Porter's Lodge. Events and talks all year. Daily guided tours and regular wildlife walks. Family activities, school holiday trails, geocaching and nature-spotter activity sheets. Playground and den-building area. Footpaths and trails through the woodland and lakeside. Discover the surprise view of the abbey, hidden follies and caves. Circular walk to the deer-park and St Mary's Church through estate. **Dogs**: welcome on short leads.

Access for all: ⬚⬚⬚⬚⬚⬚⬚⬚⬚
Building ⬚⬚⬚   Grounds ⬚⬚⬚⬚

Getting here: see website for details.
Parking: free. Main car park at visitor centre.

Finding out more: 01765 608888 or fountainsabbey@nationaltrust.org.uk

Fountains Abbey		M	T	W	T	F	S	S
Abbey and Water Garden								
1 Jan–1 Feb	10–5*	M	T	W	T	·	S	S
2 Feb–29 Mar	10–5*	M	T	W	T	F	S	S
30 Mar–25 Oct	10–6*	M	T	W	T	F	S	S
26 Oct–31 Dec	10–5*	M	T	W	T	·	S	S
Deer-park								
Open all year	7–9	M	T	W	T	F	S	S
St Mary's Church								
1 Apr–30 Sep	12–4	M	T	W	T	F	S	S

*Hall, mill, shop and restaurant close one hour earlier. Last admission one hour before closing. Studley Royal shop, Studley Royal tea-room and Abbey tea-room opening times vary. Completely closed 24 and 25 December.

George Stephenson's Birthplace

near Wylam, Northumberland NE41 8BP

Map ⑥ G5   ⬚⬚⬚  1949

The humble birthplace of railway pioneer George Stephenson, whose family lived in one tiny room. Our costumed guide shares the story of how challenging life was for mining families like George's, who once squeezed into this charming cottage, set in a pretty garden beside the Wylam Waggonway and River Tyne.

Eating and shopping: café and tea-garden serving light lunches, snacks and homemade cakes. Souvenirs and books for sale.

Making the most of your day: tiny room decorated as in 1781, the year of Stephenson's birth. Family-friendly walk and cycle path following the route of one of the world's first steam railways. **Dogs**: welcome on leads in garden.

Access for all: ⬚⬚⬚⬚⬚⬚
Birthplace ⬚   Café ⬚   Garden ⬚

Getting here: see website for details.
Sat Nav: use NE41 8HP. **Parking**: in village, pay and display (not National Trust), ½-mile walk along Wylam Waggonway.

Finding out more: 01207 541820 or georgestephensons@nationaltrust.org.uk

George Stephenson's Birthplace		M	T	W	T	F	S	S
Cottage, tea-room and tea-garden								
6 Mar–28 Sep	11–5	·	·	·	T	F	S	S
2 Oct–2 Nov	11–3	·	·	·	T	F	S	S
Tea-room and tea-garden								
4 Jan–2 Mar	11–3	·	·	·	·	·	S	S
8 Nov–28 Dec	11–3	·	·	·	·	·	S	S

Open Bank Holiday Mondays.

George Stephenson's Birthplace, Northumberland: in this humble cottage the railway pioneer's family lived in one tiny room

Tatton Park

Knutsford, Cheshire WA16 6QN

Map (5) D8
1960

One of the most complete historic estates open to visitors. The early 19th-century Wyatt house sits amid a 1,000-acre (400-hectare) deer-park and is opulently decorated, providing a fine setting for the Egerton family's collections of pictures, books, china, glass and specially commissioned Gillows furniture. The theme of Victorian grandeur extends into the garden, with its Fernery, Orangery, Rose Garden, Tower Garden, Pinetum, Walled Garden with glasshouses, plus Italian and Japanese gardens (viewed from the perimeter). Other features include a deer-park, 1930s working rare-breeds farm, children's play area, speciality shops, a restaurant and new garden tea-room. **Note**: managed/financed by Cheshire East Council. For tours, RHS show, Christmas and other events supplementary charges may apply (including members). Park car entry charge, £5 (including members).

Eating and shopping: Stableyard shopping and dining, including Stables self-service restaurant and new Gardener's Cottage table service tea-room. Speciality shops, including the stylish new-look gift shop, garden shop, Housekeepers' Store, local food and drink shop and tuck shop.

The Japanese Garden at Tatton Park, Cheshire

The imposing façade of Tatton Park, Cheshire

Making the most of your day: www.tattonpark.org.uk for more than 100 events. Members – free admission to house and gardens only; half-price to farm. Old Hall special openings. Large deer-park to explore on foot or bike. **Dogs**: on leads at farm and under close control in park only.

Access for all: [icons]
Building [icons] Grounds [icons]

Getting here: see website for details.
Sat Nav: use WA16 6SG. **Parking**: park car entry charge, £5 (including members).

Finding out more: 01625 374435 (Infoline). 01625 374400 or tatton@cheshireeast.gov.uk. www.tattonpark.org.uk

Tatton Park		M	T	W	T	F	S	S
Parkland, gardens, restaurant and tea-room								
1 Jan–28 Mar	10–5*	·	T	W	T	F	S	S
29 Mar–26 Oct	10–7*	M	T	W	T	F	S	S
28 Oct–31 Dec	10–5*	·	T	W	T	F	S	S
Mansion								
29 Mar–28 Sep	1–5	·	T	W	T	F	S	S
30 Sep–26 Oct	12–4	·	T	W	T	F	S	S
Farm								
4 Jan–23 Mar	11–4	·	·	·	·	·	S	S
29 Mar–26 Oct	12–5	·	T	W	T	F	S	S
1 Nov–28 Dec	11–4	·	·	·	·	·	S	S
Shops								
1 Jan–28 Mar	12–4	·	T	W	T	F	S	S
29 Mar–26 Oct	11–5	M	T	W	T	F	S	S
28 Oct–31 Dec	12–4	·	T	W	T	F	S	S

*Gardens, restaurant and tea-room close one hour earlier. Open Bank Holiday Mondays. Closed 25 December. Parkland, mansion, farm and garden last admission one hour before closing. Guided mansion tours Tuesday to Sunday 29 March to 28 September at 12 by timed ticket (places limited), small charge including members. Old Hall special opening arrangements. Check opening times before visiting.

Gibside

near Rowlands Gill, Gateshead,
Tyne & Wear NE16 6BG

Map 6 H5

1974

For a taste of the country on the edge of the city, escape to this stunning landscape park and nature reserve. Gibside was created by one of the richest men in Georgian England, and offers fantastic views, miles of walks, wide open spaces, fascinating historic buildings and ruins. After centuries of neglect we're bringing Gibside to life, restoring the gardens for people and wildlife, so there's always something new to discover. It's also the setting of Mary Eleanor Bowes' true story of torture and escape from her ruthless husband, inspiration for a Stanley Kubrick film and best-selling biography, *Wedlock*.

The portico of the chapel at Gibside, Tyne & Wear

Eating and shopping: Potting Shed café near entrance. New Carriage House coffee shop and second-hand books at Stables. Strawberry Castle family café at adventure play area. Gibside Larder selling local food, plants and gifts. Friday evening beer garden. Twice-monthly farmers' market.

Making the most of your day: see the walled garden come to life as we re-create historic features and much more. Events inspired by our stories, wildlife and food. Family-friendly trails and adventure play areas.
Dogs: welcome on leads.

Access for all: 🅿️ ♿ 🚻 ♿ 📷 🦻 ♿ ⬤ 🅰️
Chapel ♿ ♿ ♿   **Stables** ♿ ⬆️
Garden ♿ ♿ ♿ ➡️ ♿ ♿

Getting here: see website for details.
Parking: free. New car parks, 200 yards from café and shop.

Finding out more: 01207 541820 or gibside@nationaltrust.org.uk

Gibside		M	T	W	T	F	S	S
Landscape gardens, woodlands, café and shop								
1 Jan–2 Mar	10–4	M	T	W	T	F	S	S
3 Mar–2 Nov	10–6*	M	T	W	T	F	S	S
3 Nov–31 Dec	10–4	M	T	W	T	F	S	S
Chapel								
4 Jan–2 Mar	10–4	·	·	·	·	·	S	S
3 Mar–2 Nov	10–5	M	T	W	T	F	S	S
8 Nov–28 Dec	10–4	·	·	·	·	·	S	S
Beer garden and pub								
3 Jan–23 May	6–9	·	·	·	·	F	·	·
30 May–30 Aug	6–9	·	·	·	·	F	S	·
5 Sep–26 Dec	6–9	·	·	·	·	F	·	·

*Café, gift and food shop close at 5. Estate closed 24 and 25 December. Last entry: winter 3:30, summer 4:30.

Goddards

27 Tadcaster Road, York,
North Yorkshire YO24 1GG

Map (5) H5 🏠 ❄ 1984

The family home of Noel Terry, the famous York chocolatier, contains striking Arts and Crafts design. You can uncover family memories and find out about life at the Terry's factory, then relax in a shady spot in the garden beside flower-beds, ponds and a rockery.

Note: selected rooms open (also National Trust regional office).

Eating and shopping: 1930s-style tea-room in the dining-room serving lunches and cakes. Small gift shop. Picnic tables on the tennis lawn.

Making the most of your day: themed events and family activities. Chess to play in the sunny drawing-room. Exhibition about the Terry's chocolate factory – share your memories of factory life. **Dogs**: welcome on leads in garden.

Access for all: 🅿️♿🚻📖 House 🔗♿🚹
Grounds ♿➡️

Getting here: see website for details.
Sat Nav: enter 27 Tadcaster Road, York not the postcode. **Parking**: designated parking only. Nearest visitor parking in city centre car parks (1 to 2 miles), not National Trust (charge including members).

Finding out more: 01904 771930 or goddards@nationaltrust.org.uk

Goddards		M	T	W	T	F	S	S
1 Mar–2 Nov	11–5	·	·	W	T	F	S	S

Open Bank Holiday Mondays. On York race days, please call for opening arrangements. Closed for functions: 21 June, 3 to 5; 6 July, all day.

Goddards, York: striking Arts and Crafts design

Hadrian's Wall and Housesteads Fort, Northumberland: the wall snakes across the wild and rugged landscape

Hadrian's Wall and Housesteads Fort

Near Bardon Mill, Hexham, Northumberland NE47 6NN

Map (6) F5 1930

Running through wild landscapes with panoramic views, Hadrian's Wall was one of the Roman Empire's most northerly outposts. If you start your day at the new flagship visitor centre at Housesteads Fort, you can get a feel for military life and explore one of the best-preserved bases along the wall. **Note**: fort owned by National Trust, but maintained and managed by English Heritage.

Eating and shopping: new visitor centre at Housesteads Fort containing small shop, serving refreshments.

Making the most of your day: outdoor events, including family activities. Exhibition on military life at Housesteads Fort visitor centre, with CGI film reconstructing Housesteads. **Dogs**: welcome on leads.

Access for all:
Vistor centre **Museum**

Getting here: see website for details. **Parking**: National Park Authority parking covers Housesteads, Steel Rigg and Cawfields, pay and display (not National Trust), ½-mile walk to Houseteads Fort from visitor centre.

Finding out more: 01434 344525 or housesteads@nationaltrust.org.uk

Hadrian's Wall and Housesteads Fort

Closed 1 January and 24 to 26 December. Call or visit www.english-heritage.org.uk for opening arrangements.

Lindisfarne Castle

Holy Island, Berwick-upon-Tweed,
Northumberland TD15 2SH

Map ⑥ G1  1944

Location has always been the main attraction for the owners and occupiers of Lindisfarne Castle. From a former fort to the holiday home of a wealthy Edwardian bachelor seeking a quiet retreat, the idyllic location of the castle has intrigued and inspired for centuries. Enjoy shoreline walks to take in the unexpected grandeur of the lime kilns and the summer-flowering garden designed by Gertrude Jekyll.

Note: limited toilet facilities. Island accessed via tidal causeway (check safe crossing times at www.northumberland.gov.uk).

Eating and shopping: souvenirs, coffee machine, water, snacks and ice-cream available.

Making the most of your day: family trails and activities. Borrow a kite to fly or binoculars for wildlife spotting. Occasional seal spotting and rock-pooling activities. Regular events.
Dogs: welcome on leads. Assistance dogs only in castle.

Access for all: 🐕♿ Castle ♿👪 Grounds ♿

Getting here: see website for details.

Parking: use main island car park, 1 mile (signposted before village), pay and display (not National Trust). Private transfer available most days.

Finding out more: 01289 389244 or lindisfarne@nationaltrust.org.uk

Lindisfarne Castle		M	T	W	T	F	S	S
Castle								
8 Feb–3 Aug	Times vary	·	T	W	T	F	S	S
4 Aug–31 Aug	Times vary	M	T	W	T	F	S	S
2 Sep–2 Nov	Times vary	·	T	W	T	F	S	S

Opening times vary due to tides, either 10 to 3 or 12 to 5. Check times on our website or call before visiting. Open Bank Holiday Mondays. Some additional Monday openings throughout the season and some weekend openings in winter.

The idyllic location of Lindisfarne Castle in Northumberland has inspired and intrigued for centuries

Maister House

160 High Street, Hull, East Yorkshire HU1 1NL

Map ⑤ J6   1966

A merchant family's tale of fortune and tragedy is intertwined with the intriguing history of Maister House. **Note**: staircase and entrance hall only on show. Sorry no toilet.

Finding out more: 01723 870423 or maisterhouse@nationaltrust.org.uk

Middlethorpe Hall Hotel, Restaurant and Spa

Bishopthorpe Road, York, North Yorkshire YO23 2GB

Map ⑤ H5   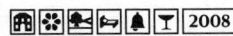 2008

William and Mary house, built in 1699, set in eight hectares (20 acres) of manicured gardens and parkland. **Note**: access is for paying guests of the hotel, including for luncheon, tea and dinner.

Finding out more: 01904 641241. 01904 620176 (fax) or info@middlethorpe.com. www.middlethorpe.com

Moulton Hall

Moulton, Richmond, North Yorkshire DL10 6QH

Map ⑤ F2   1966

Elegant 17th-century tenanted manor house with a beautiful carved staircase. **Note**: sorry no toilet. Visit by arrangement in advance with the tenant.

Finding out more: 01325 377227 or moultonhall@nationaltrust.org.uk

Mount Grace Priory

Staddle Bridge, Northallerton,
North Yorkshire DL6 3JG

Map ⑤ G3   ✝ | 1953 |

England's most important Carthusian ruin.
Entry is via 13th-century manor house and
garden, containing an exhibition and newly
refurbished rooms. **Note**: operated by English
Heritage; members free, except on event days.

Finding out more: 01609 883494 or
mountgracepriory@nationaltrust.org.uk

Nostell Priory and Parkland

Doncaster Road, Nostell, near Wakefield,
West Yorkshire WF4 1QE

Map ⑤ G6    | 1954 |

Home of the Winn family for more than 300
years, the Georgian mansion was built of the
finest materials on the site of a medieval priory.
Designed to show off the family's wealth, the
grand interiors were designed by Robert Adam
and contain a renowned collection of
Chippendale furniture – still in place in the
rooms they were made for 200 years ago.
There are impressive paintings by Brueghel,
Hogarth and Kauffman and we even have a
John Harrison longcase clock. Children will love
trying to find the mouse in our 18th-century
dolls'-house. Outside, the 121-hectare
(300-acre) parkland has secluded walks, lakes
and woodlands, while in the gardens you can
explore the maturing orchard, menagerie, rose
garden and kitchen garden.

Eating and shopping: Courtyard Café serving
hot food and refreshments. Kiosk offering
snacks and drinks. Shop selling gifts, souvenirs,
plants and ice-cream. Picnics welcome in the
park and gardens.

**Nostell Priory and Parkland, West Yorkshire,
opposite and right**

Making the most of your day: year-round
events, including craft fairs, open-air theatre
and live music. Guided parkland walks.
Regular tours of the house, specialist talks,
'Upstairs-Downstairs' tour of the servants'
quarters and library talks (bookable in
advance). Family activities and events during
school holidays. Geocaching trails. Children's
adventure playground. Special opening in
December, when the house is decorated for
Christmas. **Dogs**: on leads in park.
Exercise area in car park. Assistance
dogs only in gardens.

Access for all: 🅿️ 🅭 ♿ 🚻 🔔 🔍 📷 📱 ⊡ 🔲
House 🦽 ⬍ 🦵   **Grounds** 🦽 🦽 ➡ 🚗 🦵

Getting here: see website for details.
Sat Nav: use WF4 1QD. **Parking**: 500 yard
walk from car park to visitor facilities,
house and gardens.

Finding out more: 01924 863892 or
nostellpriory@nationaltrust.org.uk

Nostell Priory and Parkland		M	T	W	T	F	S	S
House								
1 Mar–2 Nov	1–5	·	·	W	T	F	S	S
29 Nov–14 Dec	1–4	·	·	·	·	·	S	S
Gardens, shop and tea-room								
1 Jan–23 Feb	11–4:30	M	T	W	T	F	S	S
24 Feb–2 Nov	10–5:30*	M	T	W	T	F	S	S
3 Nov–31 Dec	11–4:30	M	T	W	T	F	S	S
Parkland **								
Open all year	9–7	M	T	W	T	F	S	S

Last admission 45 minutes before closing. House open 11 to
12 for guided tours (places limited and allocated on arrival).
Open Bank Holiday Mondays. *Gardens open at 11. **Parkland
closes dusk if earlier. Property closed 25 December.

Nunnington Hall, North Yorkshire: spring-time blossom covers the trees in the orchard

Nunnington Hall

Nunnington, near York,
North Yorkshire YO62 5UY

Map ⑤ H4   🏠🍀 1953

Yorkshire manor house and gardens famed for their picturesque location, nestled on the banks of the River Rye. While exploring the hall, you will hear fascinating tales of the families which lived here – the rooms appear as though one of the family has just wandered off – and you can experience 1920s life, an era when the house was in its heyday. Outside, wander through the organic walled garden, taking in spring-flowering meadows and spotting the flamboyant resident peacocks. Our bird-spotter and bug hotel allow you to see wildlife at home, and you can even get messy in our mud-pie kitchen.

Eating and shopping: waitress-service tea-room (licensed), serving local produce and using ingredients from the Nunnington Hall garden. Picnic spots, kiosk, tea-garden. Shop selling local ranges.

Making the most of your day: regular events and high-profile exhibitions. Garden games, mud-pie kitchen, family activities and trails, dressing up. Carlisle Collection of miniature rooms. Visit nearby Rievaulx Terrace.
Dogs: welcome on leads in the garden.

Access for all: 🅿️♿🚾♿
Building 🅰️♿🔽 Grounds ♿🔽

Getting here: see website for details.
Parking: free.

Finding out more: 01439 748283 or nunningtonhall@nationaltrust.org.uk

Nunnington Hall		M	T	W	T	F	S	S
15 Feb–23 Feb	11–5	M	T	W	T	F	S	S
25 Feb–6 Apr	11–5	·	T	W	T	F	S	S
7 Apr–27 Apr	11–5	M	T	W	T	F	S	S
29 Apr–27 Jul	11–5	·	T	W	T	F	S	S
28 Jul–7 Sep	11–5	M	T	W	T	F	S	S
9 Sep–26 Oct	11–5	·	T	W	T	F	S	S
27 Oct–2 Nov	11–4	M	T	W	T	F	S	S
8 Nov–14 Dec	11–4	·	·	·	·	·	S	S

Open Bank Holiday Mondays.

Ormesby Hall

Ladgate Lane, Ormesby, near Middlesbrough, Redcar & Cleveland TS3 0SR

Map (5) G2  1962

Once home to the Pennyman family, the spirit of this Georgian mansion remains true to the kind couple who lived here last, Colonel Jim and his arts-loving wife Ruth. You can explore the garden and rambling house, with its Victorian kitchen, laundry and stylish legacy of 'Wicked' Sir James.

Eating and shopping: refreshments served in servants' hall or terrace.

Making the most of your day: activities and events, including lectures and tours. Model railway layouts (only ones owned by the National Trust). **Dogs**: welcome on leads in the park.

Access for all:
Building 🏛️♿ Grounds ➡️♿

Getting here: see website for details.
Parking: free, 100 yards.

Finding out more: 01642 324188 or ormesbyhall@nationaltrust.org.uk. Church Lane, Ormesby, Middlesbrough TS7 9AS

Ormesby Hall		M	T	W	T	F	S	S
8 Mar–3 Aug	1:30–5	·	·	·	·	·	**S**	**S**
7 Aug–28 Aug	1:30–5	·	·	·	**T**	·	**S**	**S**
6 Sep–2 Nov	1:30–5	·	·	·	·	·	**S**	**S**

Gardens open at 12:45. Open Bank Holiday Mondays and Good Friday. Open Thursdays in August for themed visits. Closures at short notice possible.

Georgian Ormesby Hall in Redcar & Cleveland

Rievaulx Terrace

Rievaulx, Helmsley, North Yorkshire YO62 5LJ

Map (5) H3  1972

Discover one of Ryedale's true gems; this 18th-century landscape offers one of Yorkshire's most spectacular views over Rievaulx Abbey. Stroll through the woodland to the beautiful unspoilt terrace – a mere half mile – with its unique views and temples at either end. In spring, a blanket of snowdrops covers the woodland floor, while in summer the terrace is the perfect place for a picnic. There's lots of fun to be had come rain or shine; borrow a brolly and take part in our wet weather trail. **Note**: no access to Rievaulx Abbey.

The Tuscan Temple at Rievaulx Terrace, North Yorkshire

Eating and shopping: ice-cream, cold drinks and sweet snacks available. Picnics welcome. Shop selling gifts and souvenirs.

Making the most of your day: seasonal events. Family trails and activities in school holidays; build a den, swing on a rope swing, natural play. Cloud spotting from the sky glade. Nunnington Hall nearby (8 miles). **Dogs**: welcome on leads.

Access for all: [P][D][WC][⌂][♿]
Visitor centre [♿] Temples [♿]
Grounds [♿][➡][♿][♿]

Getting here: see website for details. **Parking**: free, 100 yards.

Finding out more: 01439 798340 (summer). 01439 748283 (winter) or rievaulxterrace@nationaltrust.org.uk

Rievaulx Terrace		M	T	W	T	F	S	S
15 Feb–2 Nov	11–5	**M**	**T**	**W**	**T**	**F**	**S**	**S**

Last admission one hour before closing or dusk if earlier.

Seaton Delaval Hall

The Avenue, Seaton Sluice, Northumberland NE26 4QR

Map (6) H4 　[🏛][❀][♿][☂] [2009]

Designed by Sir John Vanbrugh, the architecture and stories at Seaton Delaval Hall tell a tale of the Georgian era at its most flamboyant. Welcome to the home of the Delavals, the most notorious Georgian family of party-goers, adulterers, actors and pranksters. They turned the estate into a stage for drama, revelry and romance, while the surrounding landscape fuelled the Industrial Revolution. The hall has survived fires, military occupation and potential ruin. Now a work in progress, you can see how we're bringing the hall and its colourful gardens back to life, and watch our conservation work in action. **Note**: ongoing building works, some areas may be inaccessible.

Eating and shopping: Stables café serving light lunch and snacks. Ice-cream, coffee and tea at the summerhouse in fine weather. Souvenir shop in ticket hut.

Making the most of your day: seasonal events, including arts and crafts, outdoor fun and children's activities. Family activity days and trails most school holidays. **Dogs**: welcome on leads in some areas (map available).

Access for all: [P][♿][WC][⌂][▭][♿] Hall [♿]
Stables [♿] Grounds [➡][♿]

Getting here: see website for details. **Parking**: free, 500 yards.

Finding out more: 0191 237 9100 or seatondelavalhall@nationaltrust.org.uk

Seaton Delaval Hall		M	T	W	T	F	S	S
Central hall, stables and gardens								
4 Jan–23 Feb	11–3	·	·	·	·	·	S	S
1 Mar–6 Apr	11–5	**M**	·	·	**T**	**F**	**S**	**S**
7 Apr–21 Apr	11–5	**M**	**T**	**W**	**T**	**F**	**S**	**S**
24 Apr–14 Jul	11–5	**M**	·	·	**T**	**F**	**S**	**S**
17 Jul–1 Sep	11–5	**M**	**T**	**W**	**T**	**F**	**S**	**S**
4 Sep–31 Oct	11–5	**M**	·	·	**T**	**F**	**S**	**S**
1 Nov–28 Dec	11–3	·	·	·	·	·	S	S
West wing								
1 Mar–2 Nov	11–5	**M**	·	·	**T**	**F**	**S**	**S**

Last admission 45 minutes before closing.
Access to West Wing may be limited on certain days and sometimes by tour only.

Members may have to pay on special events days

Souter Lighthouse in Tyne & Wear, above, has stood proud on the coastline since 1871

Seaton Delaval Hall, Northumberland, below, tells a tale of the Georgian era at its most flamboyant

Souter Lighthouse and The Leas

Coast Road, Whitburn, Sunderland, Tyne & Wear SR6 7NH

Map ⑥ I5   🏠 🏛 🚻 🛏 🍽 1990

Souter is an iconic beacon. Hooped in red and white it stands proud on the coastline between the Tyne and the Wear. Opened in 1871, it was the first purpose-built electric lighthouse in the world. Now, as then, Souter is a family affair, and visitors of all ages can learn the fascinating story of 'life in a lighthouse'. The Leas is a 2½-mile stretch of magnesian limestone cliffs with a wave-cut foreshore and coastal grassland, perfect for walking. The nearby cliffs and rock stacks of Marsden Bay are home to nesting kittiwakes, fulmars, cormorants, shags and guillemots.

Eating and shopping: coffee shop selling hot and cold drinks, lunches, cakes and lighter bites. Kiosk in Foghorn Field. Local dish Panacklety is a must-try.

Making the most of your day: events and family activities, including rock-pool rambles, bug hunting, birdwatching and geocaching. Annual pirate events and holiday crafts. Car boot sales. Outdoor play area, games and trails. Foghorn demonstrations. **Dogs**: welcome on leads outdoors.

Access for all: ⬛⬛⬛⬛⬛⬛⬛⬛⬛⬛
Building ⬛⬛ Grounds ⬛

Getting here: see website for details.
Parking: free.

Finding out more: 0191 529 3161 or souter@nationaltrust.org.uk

Souter Lighthouse and The Leas		M	T	W	T	F	S	S
15 Feb–23 Feb	11–5	M	T	W	T	F	S	S
24 Feb–6 Apr	11–5	M	T	W	T	·	S	S
7 Apr–20 Apr	11–5	M	T	W	T	F	S	S
21 Apr–25 May	11–5	M	T	W	T	·	S	S
26 May–1 Jun	11–5	M	T	W	T	F	S	S
2 Jun–30 Jun	11–5	M	T	W	T	·	S	S
1 Jul–31 Aug	11–5	M	T	W	T	F	S	S
1 Sep–26 Oct	11–5	M	T	W	T	·	S	S
27 Oct–2 Nov	11–5	M	T	W	T	F	S	S
8 Nov–21 Dec	11–4	·	·	·	·	·	S	S

Treasurer's House, York in North Yorkshire

Treasurer's House, York

Minster Yard, York, North Yorkshire YO1 7JL

Map ⑤ H5 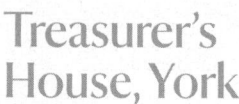 1930

This was the first house given to the Trust complete with its contents. Owned by Frank Green from 1897, you'll see his love for antiques in every room, and his collections of furniture, ceramics, paintings and textiles span a 300-year period. Famed for threatening to haunt us if we ever move the furniture – ask a guide about the studs on the floor – his ghost is one of many said to inhabit the house. Treasurer's has a 2,000-year history, from the Roman road in the cellar to Edwardian servants' quarters in the attics, both accessible on daily tours. **Note**: cellar tour charges (including members).

Eating and shopping: table service tea-room. Shop located in historic kitchen. Takeaway food and drinks available.

Making the most of your day: tours of the Roman ghost cellar and Edwardian servants' attics. Themed house tours in February and November. Regular events. Family trails and activities during school holidays.
Dogs: welcome on leads in garden.

Access for all: ⬛⬛⬛⬛⬛⬛⬛
Building ⬛⬛ Grounds ⬛⬛➡

Getting here: see website for details.
Parking: nearest in Lord Mayor's Walk. Park and ride service from city outskirts.

Finding out more: 01904 624247 or treasurershouse@nationaltrust.org.uk

Treasurer's House		M	T	W	T	F	S	S
House, garden, tea-room and shop								
15 Feb–27 Feb	11–3	M	T	W	T	·	S	S
1 Mar–2 Nov	11–4:30	M	T	W	T	·	S	S
3 Nov–30 Nov	11–3	M	T	W	T	·	S	S
Tea-room and shop								
1 Dec–22 Dec	11–3	M	T	W	T	·	S	S

February and November: house entry by guided tour only, some of the collection covered.

Wallington

Cambo, near Morpeth,
Northumberland NE61 4AR

Map (6) G4   ⊞ ❖ 🏄 🔔 │1941│

Gifted to you by Sir Charles Philips Trevelyan,
Socialist MP and 'illogical Englishman', this
5,260-hectare (13,000-acre) estate has
something for everyone. You can enjoy wild play
in the West Wood, visit our family-friendly
wildlife hide and look out for red squirrels,
just stroll by the river or refresh your mind
among the flowers in the Walled Garden.
Further afield, there are new walks across to
Broomhouse Farm and beyond, or you could
simply spend some time in the Trevelyan's
home. Wallington offers a relaxing day out,
whether you want to learn more about the
historic collections, enjoy the informal courtyard
with friends and family or just walk your dog.

Wallington, Northumberland, top, right and below: the impressive house and grounds offer something for everyone

Eating and shopping: Clocktower Café serving
brunch, lunch and afternoon tea. Refreshments
available from the Walled Garden kiosk
(seasonal). Take 'Tea the Trevelyan Way' in the
house. Gifts and new ranges for your home and
garden for sale in our shop.

Making the most of your day: like the
Trevelyan children, you can have your own
adventures in the West Wood, where there is
an adventure playground, play train and fort.
You may enjoy a stroll to Lady Trevelyan's
beloved Walled Garden, featuring the Mary
Pool and fragrant conservatory. The Trevelyans
entertained many people from the worlds of
theatre and politics, even welcoming 100
evacuees into their home, so be sure to spend
time in the house, soaking up the atmosphere
and discovering more about this well-travelled,
intellectual family. Events include talks, tours,
guided walks, hands-on activities, food and
craft festival, seasonal family fun and trails.
Dogs: welcome on leads throughout estate.

Access for all: 🅿️ 🐕 🚽 ♿ 🅱️ 🔎 📷 🖼️ 🎫
House ♿ ♿ ⬆️ ♿   Grounds ♿ ♿ ♿ ➡️ ♿ ♿

Getting here: see website for details.
Parking: free, 200 yards.

Finding out more: 01670 773600 or
wallington@nationaltrust.org.uk

Wallington		M	T	W	T	F	S	S
Woodland, garden and estate								
Open all year	10–dusk	M	T	W	T	F	S	S
Walled garden								
1 Jan–31 Mar	10–4*	M	T	W	T	F	S	S
1 Apr–30 Sep	10–7	M	T	W	T	F	S	S
1 Oct–31 Dec	10–4*	M	T	W	T	F	S	S
House**								
15 Feb–2 Nov	12–5	M	·	W	T	F	S	S
Shops and café								
1 Jan–14 Feb	10:30–4:30	M	T	W	T	F	S	S
15 Feb–2 Nov	10:30–5:30	M	T	W	T	F	S	S
3 Nov–23 Dec	10:30–4:30	M	T	W	T	F	S	S
27 Dec–30 Dec	10:30–4:30	M	T	·	·	·	S	S

*Walled garden closes at 6 in March and October, or dusk if earlier. **House open Tuesdays for special member events and tours. Last admission to house one hour before closing.

Washington Old Hall

The Avenue, Washington Village, Washington,
Tyne & Wear NE38 7LE

Map ⑥ H5  1956

This charming 17th-century hall was home to US President George Washington's ancestors. By 1860 the house had become a tenement and was saved from demolition in 1933. Today you can hear stories from Stanley Bone, who was born in the tenement, and see parts of the original 12th-century manor.

Eating and shopping: tea-room (run by Friends of Washington Old Hall). Souvenirs available from reception. Friends' bric-a-brac display. Picnics welcome in gardens.

Making the most of your day: seasonal garden trails, events and activities, including Fourth of July Independence Day ceremony.
Dogs: welcome on leads in garden only.

Access for all: ⬚⬚⬚⬚⬚⬚⬚⬚
Building ⬚⬚⬚   Grounds ⬚⬚➡⬚

Getting here: see website for details.
Parking: free. Additional parking on The Avenue.

Finding out more: 0191 416 6879 or washingtonoldhall@nationaltrust.org.uk

Washington Old Hall		M	T	W	T	F	S	S
30 Mar–29 Oct	11–5	M	T	W	·	·	·	S
Open 18 and 19 April.								

Charming 17th-century Washington Old Hall, Tyne & Wear

Wales

Grace and strength: Conwy
Suspension Bridge, Conwy –
the key to the town's prosperity

Outdoors in Wales

Croeso i Grymru! Wales is a small country with a huge variety of places to visit and things to do.

Some of the world's most unspoilt landscapes, glorious beaches, secluded islands, verdant woodlands and dramatic mountains are waiting for you to explore.

If you like your days out to be active, then you've come to the right place. Wherever you go in the Welsh countryside, you can find invigorating walks, peaceful cycle rides, energising water-sports and world-class wildlife watching. To unwind, you'll find that 'the land of song' is endlessly fascinating. With great locally produced food, an amazing wealth of history, age-old folklore and lively cultural activities, Wales has a pleasant surprise around every corner!

Above:
Pen y Fan in the Brecon Beacons National Park, South Wales

As a National Trust member you are helping care for 45,000 hectares (112,000 acres) of the finest countryside in Wales, including nearly 157 miles of coastline and ten of our highest mountains.

All of this and much more is waiting for you to discover and explore when you visit Wales.

Coastline gems and abundant wildlife
One of the glories of Wales is its amazingly diverse coastline, one mile in every ten of which is cared for by the National Trust. Our first property, Dinas Oleu – a hillside overlooking Cardigan Bay at Barmouth – was donated by a friend of our founders in 1895; and the first piece of coast saved by the Neptune Coastline Campaign, back in 1965, was Whiteford Burrows, just one of our places on the spectacular Gower Peninsula.

Opened in 2012, the 870-mile Welsh Coast Path links all 133 of the National Trust's coastal places. Among these are some of the best wildlife-watching sites in the UK. Mwnt in Ceredigion and Porth Ceiriad in Llŷn are excellent places to see dolphins and porpoises, while Braich-y-Pwll, Llŷn and St David's Head, Pembrokeshire, are both strongholds of the rare chough.

Pembrokeshire also boasts one of the top places to watch the elusive otter, at the astonishingly beautiful Bosherston lily ponds, near one of Wales' most perfect beaches, Barafundle Bay on the wonderful Stackpole Estate in Pembrokeshire.

Mysterious mountains and gentle countryside

In Snowdonia, more than 1,000 hectares (2,470 acres) of Snowdon, our highest mountain, forms part of the Trust's largest conservation farm, Hafod y Llan, its fragile habitats maintained by hardy native breeds of Welsh Mountain sheep and Welsh Black cattle. Nearby is the mysterious wooded crag of Dinas Emrys, said to be the birthplace of our national emblem, the red dragon, while just a mile away can be found the romantic legendary grave of Gelert, Prince Llywelyn's faithful hound.

In South Wales, in the heart of the Brecon Beacons, the footpath that climbs the highest peak in southern Britain, Pen y Fan, is regularly maintained by our skilled rangers, while nestling in gentler countryside further west in deepest Carmarthenshire is another of Wales' highlights, Dinefwr. This stronghold of the native Welsh princes in the Middle Ages combines an amazing wealth of history and wildlife, all easily accessible through a network of easy walks.

Above: **shepherds with their dogs at Hafod y Llan farm, Snowdonia**
Left: **Llŷn Peninsula, Gwynedd**
Right: **visitors on Pennard Cliffs, Gower**

Outdoors in Wales

From Snowdon's mystical lakes to Gower's golden beaches; from the temperate Celtic rainforest to the Trust's first property, the magical land of Wales awaits you.

Brecon Beacons

Powys

Map ④ F8  1936

Whether you are a serious mountain climber or prefer leisurely riverside rambles, the Brecon Beacons is the place to come. Dramatic peaks and waterfalls, glaciated valleys, rugged moorland and an 18th-century landscape park all provide outstanding walking. There are breathtaking views from the top of southern Britain's highest mountain, Pen y Fan, and you can explore the tallest waterfall at Henrhyd Falls. Take a day to trek across the vast wilderness of Abergwesyn Commons, or climb the iconic Sugarloaf or mythical Skirrid Fawr mountains to see the Usk Valley unfold before you, revealing the timeless Clytha Estate. **Note**: toilets at Pont ar Daf car park in the Brecon Beacons only.

Making the most of your day: guided walks throughout the year. Bunkhouse near Pen y Fan. Why not visit The Kymin nearby? **Dogs**: welcome on leads.

There are outstanding walks for every taste and ability at the Brecon Beacons in Powys

Getting here: see website for details.
Parking: several car parks throughout area (not all National Trust).

Finding out more: 01874 625515 or brecon@nationaltrust.org.uk

Carmarthenshire

Rugged, varied and full of undiscovered gems, often off the beaten track but worth discovering for yourself. Don't pass by – spend some time exploring.

Cwmdu

Llandeilo, Carmarthenshire SA19 7DY

Map ④ E8  1991

Georgian terrace, comprising holiday let, pub, post office, chapel and vestry, representing a rural Welsh village of the past. **Note**: pub and shop run by community (with National Trust support). Limited opening.

Finding out more: 01558 685088 or cwmdu@nationaltrust.org.uk

Dolaucothi Estate Woodland

Pumsaint, Llanwrda,
Carmarthenshire SA19 8US

Map ④ E7  1944

There are 1,012 hectares (2,500 acres) of woods, park and farmland with fascinating flora and fauna to discover.

Finding out more: 01558 650809 or dolaucothi@nationaltrust.org.uk

Paxton's Tower

Llanarthney, Carmarthen, Carmarthenshire

Map ④ D8  1965

Neo-Gothic folly erected in honour of Lord Nelson, situated on a hilltop near Llanarthney in the Towy Valley. **Note**: sorry no toilets or facilities. No access to the inside of the folly. Free of charge.

Finding out more: 01558 823902 or paxtonstower@nationaltrust.org.uk

Ragwen Point

Pendine, Carmarthenshire SA33 4NY

Map ④ C8  2000

Piece of land projecting onto a small beach with fine walks. The beach was used to practise the D-Day landings. **Note**: no facilities. Car park council operated – possible parking charge (including members).

Finding out more: 01558 823902 or ragwenpoint@nationaltrust.org.uk

Ceredigion

Wales' best-kept secret, with boundaries unchanged since the 5th century. Ceredigion's hidden, special, untouched qualities await discovery, exploration and pure enjoyment.

Mwnt

near Cardigan, Ceredigion SA43 1QF

Map ④ C7 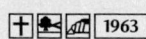 1963

Beautiful secluded bay with a sandy beach – perfect for relaxing, spotting dolphins, seals and other amazing wildlife. **Note**: steep steps down to beach. Small café and shop selling snacks and beach essentials.

Finding out more: 01545 570200 or mwnt@nationaltrust.org.uk

Penbryn

Sarnau, near Cardigan, Ceredigion SA44 6QL

Map ④ D7  1967

One of Ceredigion's best-kept secrets, this beautifully secluded sandy cove lies down leafy lanes, lined with flower-covered banks. **Note**: Cartws Café (open daily) serves a wide selection of snacks and drinks.

Finding out more: 01545 570200 or penbryn@nationaltrust.org.uk

Gower

The UK's first designated Area of Outstanding Natural Beauty, with sandy bays, secluded coves, ancient woodland and spectacular clifftop walks.

Gower: Rhossili Shop and Visitor Centre

Coastguard Cottages, Rhossili, Gower, Swansea SA3 1PR

Map (4) D9 1933

Perched on the clifftop, and overlooking the spectacular Rhossili Bay, the shop and visitor centre offers everything you need fully to enjoy this beautiful Area of Outstanding Natural Beauty. As well as local information and advice, there are gifts and tempting treats on offer. **Note**: car park charges (including members).

Eating and shopping: self-service refreshments and Swansea's famous Joe's ice-cream available all year. Shop also sells a wide range of books, souvenirs and quality gifts, reflecting its location.

Making the most of your day: free geocaching GPS units available (call to reserve at busy times). Exhibitions in Visitor Centre.
Dogs: welcome, on leads near livestock.

Access for all:
Visitor Centre **Grounds**

Getting here: see website for details.
Parking: 50 yards, not National Trust (charge including members).

Finding out more: 01792 390707 or rhossili.shop@nationaltrust.org.uk

Rhossili Visitor Centre		M	T	W	T	F	S	S
2 Jan–5 Jan	10:30–4	·	·	·	T	F	S	S
8 Jan–23 Feb	10:30–4	·	T	W	T	F	S	S
24 Feb–11 Apr	10:30–4	M	T	W	T	F	S	S
12 Apr–23 May	10:30–4:30	M	T	W	T	F	S	S
24 May–31 Aug*	10–5	M	T	W	T	F	S	S
1 Sep–3 Nov	10:30–4:30	M	T	W	T	F	S	S
4 Nov–23 Dec	10:30–4	M	T	W	T	F	S	S
27 Dec–31 Dec	10:30–4	M	T	W	·	·	S	S

The Visitor Centre closes 15 minutes before the shop.
*During August, the shop is open until 6 on Saturdays and Sundays only.

Glorious Rhossili Bay, Swansea, a perfect beach

Porth Meudwy

near Aberdaron, Gwynedd

Map ④ D4      1990

Nowhere expresses the essence of the area better than this sheltered cove on the wild and rocky coastline west of Aberdaron. It was from here that the Pilgrims set out to Ynys Enlli (Bardsey Island). Today fishermen still bring the daily catch in to the cove. **Note**: sorry no toilet.

Eating and shopping: in Aberdaron village (not National Trust).

Making the most of your day: the Llŷn Coastal Path – a birdwatchers' paradise – runs dramatically along the clifftop. **Dogs**: welcome.

Access for all: 🖐

Getting here: see website for details.
Sat Nav: use LL53 8DA. **Parking**: free.

Finding out more: 01758 760469 or porthmeudwy@nationaltrust.org.uk

The sheltered fishing hamlet of Porthdinllaen, Gwynedd

Fishing pots on the quay at Porth Meudwy, Gwynedd

Porthdinllaen

Morfa Nefyn, Gwynedd

Map ④ D3      1994

An old fishing village perched on the end of a thin ribbon of land stretching into the Irish Sea, with its clear sheltered waters lapping against stout stone houses, Porthdinllaen really is a jewel. You can watch fishermen bring in the daily catch while relaxing with a drink at the Tŷ Coch Inn. **Note**: nearest toilet in village (not National Trust).

Eating and shopping: refreshments available at Tŷ Coch Inn (not National Trust).

Making the most of your day: events during summer for all the family. Wonderful walking on the coastal path – maps and guides available at car park welcome cabin. Find out about village history at 'Caban Gruff'. **Dogs**: welcome.

Access for all: 🖐 🖐

Getting here: see website for details.
Sat Nav: use LL53 6DB. **Parking**: free.

Finding out more: 01758 760469 or porthdinllaen@nationaltrust.org.uk

Porthor

Aberdaron, Gwynedd

Map (4) C3   🖼 1981

This wonderful beach is famous for its 'whistling sands' and glistening waters. If the joys of sandcastles and sunbathing are not enough for you, then why not have a go at surfing. The sea here is perfect. In addition, the Wales Coast Path runs in both directions from the car park. **Note**: nearest toilet in car park.

Eating and shopping: beachside café and shop offering everything from lunch to sun cream.

Making the most of your day: famous beach and glorious clifftop coast path to explore. Children's adventure pack available from car park. **Dogs**: seasonal restrictions on beach apply from 1 April to 30 September.

Access for all: 🏷🚻

Getting here: see website for details. **Sat Nav**: use LL53 8LG. **Parking**: at Porthor.

Finding out more: 01758 760469 or porthor@nationaltrust.org.uk

The mysterious whistling sands of Porthor, Gwynedd

Pembrokeshire

Dramatically unspoilt, Pembrokeshire offers a world-class coastal landscape, where choughs, seals and otters are wildlife stars of the 60 miles the Trust cares for.

Marloes Sands, Pembrokeshire: perfect for sandcastles

Marloes Sands

Marloes, Pembrokeshire

Map (4) B8/9   🏛🖼✚ 1941

Laze on this long sandy beach or explore its interesting rock formations and rock pools. Take in the inland mere for its birdlife. **Note**: nearest toilets by Runwayskiln Youth Hostel.

Eating and shopping: shop, café and pub in Marloes village, plus information centre and shop at nearby Martin's Haven (none National Trust).

Making the most of your day: nature discovery Tracker Packs, available from car park, for rock-pooling, birdwatching and getting closer to nature. **Dogs**: welcome under close control on coast path to Martin's Haven.

Access for all: 🏷🚻➡

Getting here: see website for details. **Sat Nav**: use SA62 3BH. **Parking**: 1 mile west of Marloes village.

Finding out more: 01348 837860 or marloessands@nationaltrust.org.uk

Martin's Haven

near Marloes, Pembrokeshire

Map ④ B8  1981

The gateway to Skomer Island and a fabulously wild headland with fine panoramic views of St Bride's Bay. Combine spotting marine wildlife with traces of ancient settlements. **Note**: nearest toilets by the slipway.

Eating and shopping: information centre and shop at Martin's Haven, plus shop, café and pub in nearby Marloes village (none National Trust).

Making the most of your day: nature discovery Tracker Packs, available from car park, for rock-pooling, birdwatching and getting closer to nature. **Dogs**: welcome under close control when livestock grazing.

Access for all: 🦽➡

Getting here: see website for details.
Sat Nav: use SA62 3BJ. **Parking**: 2 miles west of Marloes village.

Finding out more: 01348 837860 or martinshaven@nationaltrust.org.uk

The coastal path at St David's Head, Pembrokeshire

St David's Visitor Centre and Shop

Captain's House, High Street, St David's, Pembrokeshire SA62 6SD

Map ④ A8  1974

Opposite The Cross in the centre of St David's, Wales' smallest historic city, the visitor centre and well-stocked shop is open all year. For a complete guide to the National Trust in Pembrokeshire, visitors can take a tour of our special places, beaches and walks using interactive technology. **Note**: sorry no toilet.

Eating and shopping: books, cards, maps, wide range of gifts and local produce. Walks leaflets available.

Making the most of your day: guided walks, evening talks and events. St David's Head and Abereiddi nearby.

Access for all: Building 🦽

Getting here: see website for details.
Parking: none on site.

Finding out more: 01437 720385 or stdavids@nationaltrust.org.uk

St David's Visitor Centre		M	T	W	T	F	S	S
2 Jan–22 Mar	10–4	M	T	W	T	F	S	
23 Mar–31 Dec	10–5	M	T	W	T	F	S	S

Closes 4 on Sundays. Closed 1 January, 25 and 26 December.

Stackpole

Stackpole, near Pembroke, Pembrokeshire

Map ④ B9

1976

A former grand estate stretching down to some of the most beautiful coastline in the world, including Broadhaven South, Barafundle and Stackpole Quay. Today Bosherston Lakes, famous for their superb display of lilies, and the dramatic cliffs of Stackpole Head are a National Nature Reserve. The former site of the grand Stackpole Court and nearby Lodge Park Woods give the historical background to this magnificent estate and reveal the story behind the designed landscape.

Eating and shopping: The Boathouse at Stackpole Quay serving fresh locally sourced food, including homemade cakes and scones, local seafood and Pembrokeshire heathland beef. Estate-grown produce for sale at Mencap walled gardens.

Making the most of your day: guided kayak and coasteering trips. Guided walks. Beach activity days. Coarse fishing. Theatre and music concerts. Wild camping with Rangers. Stay at holiday cottages or the Outdoor Learning Centre. **Dogs**: under control on estate.

Access for all: ♿ 🚻 ♿ ⬛
Building ♿ Grounds ♿ ➡

Getting here: see website for details.
Parking: at Stackpole Quay, Broadhaven South, Bosherston Lakes and Stackpole Court site (all pay and display).

Finding out more: 01646 661359 or stackpole@nationaltrust.org.uk

Stackpole		M	T	W	T	F	S	S
Estate								
Open all year	Dawn–dusk	M	T	W	T	F	S	S
Boathouse tea-room								
15 Feb–2 Mar	11–4	M	T	W	T	F	S	S
1 Mar–6 Apr	11–3:30	·	·	·	·	·	S	S
12 Apr–2 Nov	10–5	M	T	W	T	F	S	S
8 Nov–14 Dec	11–3:30	·	·	·	·	·	S	S
20 Dec–28 Dec	11–3:30	M	T	W	T	F	S	S

Boathouse tea-room closed 24 and 25 December.

The coastline at Stackpole in Pembrokeshire is among the most beautiful to be found anywhere in the world

Stackpole Outdoor Learning Centre

Old Home Farm Yard, Stackpole, near
Pembroke, Pembrokeshire SA71 5DQ

Map (4) B9      1976

Located in the heart of the Stackpole Estate,
our eco award-winning centre provides
residents with easy access to the Bosherston
Lakes, Stackpole Quay, award-winning
beaches – including Barafundle and
Broadhaven South – as well as the historic site
of Stackpole Court. The recently upgraded
residential centre can house up to 140 guests
and offers flexible accommodation with
modern facilities, including a theatre, meeting
and classroom space. It is ideal for educational
groups, corporate clients, private group hire,
family holidays and celebrations. We also offer
health and fitness retreats and special interest
breaks, covering subjects as wide-ranging as
photography and wildlife identification.
Note: contact the centre for activity
programmes, prices and availability.

Eating and shopping: self-catering or choose a
chef-catered option from our inhouse National
Trust catering team. All meals produced using
locally sourced seasonal produce, including
Pembrokeshire heathland beef. Full
entertainment licence for events with bar.
Residents' barbecue area. Shop and
information hub.

Making the most of your day: events,
including rock-pool rambles, wild camping,
guided walks, open-air theatre, music festivals
and concerts. Kayaking or coasteering, cycling
and otter-spotting! **Dogs**: assistance dogs only.

Access for all: ♿ 🚻 ♿ ♿ ♿ 🦽

Getting here: see website for details.
Sat Nav: follow brown signs. **Parking**: free
for residents.

Finding out more: 01646 661425 (reception).
01646 661359 (estate office) or
stackpoleoutdoorlearning@nationaltrust.org.uk

Stackpole Outdoor Centre

Please contact the centre for more information on residential
group bookings, courses and activities.

Stackpole Outdoor Learning Centre, Pembrokeshire

Snowdonia

From the mountainous terrain of the Carneddau massif to the delightful remote Tŷ Mawr Wybrnant, Snowdonia has beauty, excitement and tranquillity.

Accessible path to the grave of Gelert, Gwynedd

Craflwyn and Beddgelert

near Beddgelert, Gwynedd

Map (4) E3  1994

The 81-hectare (200-acre) Craflwyn Estate is set in the heart of beautiful Snowdonia. The area is steeped in legend: Dinas Emrys, where the famous Welsh dragon lies sleeping, is only a short walk away. Within a couple of miles of Craflwyn, there are great walks for all abilities, from a pretty village stroll at Beddgelert to longer woodland walks and more strenuous walking adventures. **Note**: Craflwyn Hall is run and managed by HF Holidays (the surrounding land is open to the public).

Eating and shopping: Beddgelert, near Craflwyn, has a selection of restaurants, cafés, taverns and hotels (none National Trust).

Making the most of your day: numerous footpaths to explore and waterfalls to discover. The village of Beddgelert has the grave of the legendary faithful hound which the village was named after. **Dogs**: welcome under control near livestock.

Access for all: 👤

Getting here: see website for details.
Sat Nav: use LL55 4NG. **Parking**: in Craflwyn.

Finding out more: 01766 510120 or craflwyn@nationaltrust.org.uk

Dolmelynllyn Estate

near Dolgellau, Gwynedd

Map (4) E4  1936

Dolmelynllyn Estate (below) covers 696 hectares (1,719 acres) and comprises two tenanted farms, with the remaining woodland managed by the Trust. Dolmelynllyn Hall is Grade II listed, with well-preserved formal gardens, walled kitchen garden, Britain's largest bee-bole wall, ornamental lake and parkland. **Note**: Dolmelynllyn Hall is a privately run hotel, not a pay-to-enter property.

Eating and shopping: two National Trust-owned but tenanted hotels on the estate offering refreshments and light meals. Picnic site.

Making the most of your day: estate walks leaflet guides visitors around the more interesting parts of the estate, such as Rhaeadr Ddu waterfall, Cefn Coch gold mines and the wildlife-rich oak woodlands. **Dogs**: welcome on leads.

Access for all: 👤

Getting here: see website for details.
Sat Nav: use LL40 2TF. **Parking**: free (donations welcome).

Finding out more: 01341 440238 or dolmelynllyn@nationaltrust.org.uk

Hafod y Llan

Nantgwynant, Beddgelert, Caernarfon,
Gwynedd LL55 4NQ

Map (4) E3   1998

Hafod y Llan, in the beautiful Nantgwynant
valley, is the largest farm run by the National
Trust. It extends from the valley floor to the
summit of both Snowdon and Cnicht, and
visitors are free to wander the many paths
which cross this unique landscape.
Note: as this is a working farm, access
to the farmyard is by foot only.

Eating and shopping: refreshments
available at nearby Gwynant Café
(not National Trust).

Making the most of your day: network of
paths cross Hafod y Llan, including the Watkin
Path leading to the summit of Snowdon.
For those preferring a more leisurely walk, a
path starts at the farm entrance which then
runs alongside the River Glaslyn.
Dogs: welcome on a lead.

Access for all:

Getting here: see website for details.
Parking: on farm for campsite only.
National Park car park near farm entrance
(not National Trust).

Finding out more: 01766 890473 or
hafodyllan@nationaltrust.org.uk

Idyllic Hafod y Llan, Gwynedd, below and above right

Car parks in Wales

Ceredigion	
Mwnt	SM 193 519
Penbryn	SM 296 520
Gower	
Pennard	SS 553 872
Llŷn Peninsula	
Aberdaron	SH 174 264
Llanbedrog	SH 331 335
Porthdinllaen	SH 284 408
Porthor	SH 166 296
Uwchmynydd	SH 155 264
Pembrokeshire	
Broadhaven	SR 977 938
Bosherston	SR 968 947
Marloes	SM 770 085
Martin's Haven	SM 758 091
Stackpole Quay	SR 992 958
Porthclais	SM 741 242
Stackpole Court	SR 976 962
Snowdonia	
Craflwyn	SH 599 489
Cregennan	SH 660 140
Nantmor	SH 597 463

Aberconwy House

Castle Street, Conwy LL32 8AY

Map ④ E2   1934

This is the only medieval merchant's house in Conwy to have survived the turbulent history of the walled town over seven centuries. Furnished rooms and helpful volunteers bring different periods in its history alive. **Note**: nearest toilets 50 yards. Steps to all parts of property.

Eating and shopping: gift shop.

Making the most of your day: ghost stories. Children's trail and guided tours. Easter and Hallowe'en activities. Living history events. Members' lounge. **Dogs**: assistance dogs only.

Access for all: ⬜🖼️🚻 Building ♿

Getting here: see website for details.
Parking: no parking on site.

Finding out more: 01492 592246 or aberconwyhouse@nationaltrust.org.uk

Aberconwy House		M	T	W	T	F	S	S
House								
1 Mar–29 Jun	11–5	M	T	W	T	F	S	S
30 Jun–31 Aug	10–5	M	T	W	T	F	S	S
1 Sep–2 Nov	11–5	M	T	W	T	F	S	S
8 Nov–28 Dec	12–3						S	S
Shop								
1 Jan–28 Feb	11–5		T	W	T	F	S	
1 Mar–1 Nov	10–5	M	T	W	T	F	S	
2 Mar–2 Nov	11–5							S
3 Nov–31 Dec	11–5	M	T	W	T	F	S	S

House and shop closed 25 December.

Aberdeunant

Taliaris, Llandeilo, Carmarthenshire SA19 6DL

Map ④ E8    1996

Traditional Carmarthenshire farmhouse in an unspoilt setting.

Note: administered by tenant. Sorry no toilet. Open once a month (booking essential).

Finding out more: 01558 650177 or aberdeunant@nationaltrust.org.uk

Once the home of a merchant, Aberconwy House in Conwy, left, somehow managed to survive the turbulent history of this walled town for more than 700 years

Aberdulais Tin Works and Waterfall, Neath Port Talbot

Aberdulais Tin Works and Waterfall

Aberdulais, Neath, Neath Port Talbot SA10 8EU

Map (4) E9   🖼️🏛️🎣🍷 1980

If you like archaeology, you'll love some of the secrets that have been uncovered here at Aberdulais – one of Britain's oldest tin works. As you wander through the site, you will find yourself at the very heart of the earliest industry in Britain. You will also discover how Aberdulais played its part in shaping the world as we know it today. If you think you've seen Aberdulais before, come again – we've made new discoveries and we're dying to share them with you. We aim to enthrall and fascinate all ages… Whoever thought history could be so much fun? **Note**: waterwheel and turbine subject to water levels and conservation work.

Eating and shopping: Old School House tea-room serving light lunches, soup, cakes and refreshments. Victorian-themed gift shop and second-hand bookshop.

Making the most of your day: activities, including Conservation in Action. Demonstrations and family Tin Detectives Packs. Painting, photography and archaeology days. 'Visit Wales' Tourist Information Centre on site. **Dogs**: welcome on leads.

Access for all: 🅿️ 🔽 ♿ 👶 🔽 🔽

Stable and Tin Exhibition ♿ ♿ ♿
Turbine House ♿ ♿ ♿ ♿ ♿
Grounds ♿ ♿ ♿ ➡️ ♿

Getting here: see website for details.
Sat Nav: follow brown signs. **Parking**: 50 yards.

Finding out more: 01639 636674 or aberdulais@nationaltrust.org.uk

Aberdulais		M	T	W	T	F	S	S
4 Jan–2 Mar	11–4						S	S
3 Mar–13 Apr	11–4	M	T	W	T	F	S	S
14 Apr–28 Sep	10:30–5	M	T	W	T	F	S	S
3 Oct–2 Nov	11–4	M	T	W	T	F	S	S
7 Nov–21 Dec	11–4					F	S	S

Tea-room opening varies, call for details.

Bodnant Garden

Tal-y-Cafn, near Colwyn Bay, Conwy LL28 5RE

Map ④ F2   [icons] 1949

A breathtaking garden; grand terraces overlooking Snowdonian mountains, a valley of giant conifers and cascading water, open grassy wildflower glades and shrub borders of dappled sunlight filled with plants from all over the world. Created by five generations of one family, this 32-hectare (80-acre) garden sits perfectly within its dramatic North Wales landscape. Rhododendrons, magnolias and camellias grown from seed and cuttings gathered by plant hunters more than a century ago light up the garden in spring, while summer herbaceous borders, fiery autumn-coloured shrubs, trees and a new winter garden provide interest throughout the year. **Note**: garden and tea-rooms managed on behalf of the National Trust by Michael McLaren.

Eating and shopping: two tea-rooms. Garden centre and craft shops (neither National Trust).

Making the most of your day: varied events programme, including tours, guided walks and family events. Adventure playground, family trails and Explorer backpacks. **Dogs**: welcome on short leads Thursday to Saturday (January/February, November/December); Wednesday evenings (May to August).

Access for all: [icons]
Grounds [icons]

Getting here: see website for details.
Parking: 150 yards from entrance.

Finding out more: 01492 650460 or bodnantgarden@nationaltrust.org.uk

Bodnant Garden		M	T	W	T	F	S	S
1 Jan–28 Feb	10–4	M	T	W	T	F	S	S
1 Mar–26 Oct	10–5	M	T	W	T	F	S	S
27 Oct–23 Dec	10–4	M	T	W	T	F	S	S
27 Dec–31 Dec	10–4	M	T	W	·	·	S	S

Garden open until 8 on Wednesdays from May to August.

Bodysgallen Hall Hotel, Restaurant and Spa

The Royal Welsh Way, Llandudno, Conwy LL30 1RS

Map ④ F2    2008

Grade I listed 17th-century house within 89 hectares (220 acres) of award-winning gardens – with follies, cascade, walled and rose gardens. **Note**: access is for paying guests of the hotel, including for luncheon, afternoon tea and dinner.

Finding out more: 01492 584466. 01492 582519 (fax) or info@bodysgallen.com www.bodysgallen.com

Breathtaking Bodnant Garden in Conwy, left, was created by five generations of one family

Chirk Castle

Chirk, Wrexham LL14 5AF

Map (4) G3 ▣ 🔊 ❀ 🛶 🛏 🔔 ⛋ 1981

Completed in 1310, Chirk is the last Welsh castle from the reign of Edward I still lived in today. Features from its 700 years include the medieval tower and dungeon, 17th-century Long Gallery, grand 18th-century state apartments, servants' hall and historic laundry. The newly refurbished east wing depicts the life of Lord Howard de Walden during the 1930s. The award-winning gardens contain clipped yews, herbaceous borders, shrub and rock gardens. A terrace with stunning views looks out over the Cheshire and Shropshire plains. The parkland provides a habitat for rare invertebrates and wild flowers and contains many mature trees.

Eating and shopping: tea-room and coffee shop serving home-grown produce. Farm and gift shops, plant sales and second-hand books.

Visitors come face to face with the past at Chirk Castle in Wrexham, below, and the magnificent exterior, above

Making the most of your day: our new leaflets tell you all about the many places to explore (including the fortress, gardens and woods), plus fascinating stories about servants' lives and the Myddelton family home.

Dogs: welcome on leads, assistance dogs only in formal gardens.

Access for all: 🅿️ 🄳 ♿ 🛗 🔲 🖼️ 🗓️ ♿ ⠿
State rooms ♿ 🖼️ 🛗   Adam Tower ♿
Gardens ♿ 🖼️ ➡️ 🛗

Getting here: see website for details.
Parking: at home farm, 200 yards (via steep hill).

Finding out more: 01691 777701 or chirkcastle@nationaltrust.org.uk

Chirk Castle		M	T	W	T	F	S	S
Estate								
Open all year	7–7	M	T	W	T	F	S	S
Garden, tower, shops and tea-rooms								
1 Feb–31 Mar	10–4	M	T	W	T	F	S	S
1 Apr–30 Sep	10–5*	M	T	W	T	F	S	S
1 Oct–2 Nov	10–4	M	T	W	T	F	S	S
8 Nov–7 Dec**	11–3						S	S
13 Dec–21 Dec	11–4	M	T	W	T	F	S	S
26 Dec–31 Dec†	11–3	M	T	W		F	S	S
State rooms								
1 Mar–31 Mar††	12–4	M	T	W	T	F	S	S
1 Apr–30 Sep††	12–5	M	T	W	T	F	S	S
1 Oct–2 Nov††	12–4	M	T	W	T	F	S	S
13 Dec–21 Dec	12–4	M	T	W	T	F	S	S

Estate closes dusk if earlier and open until 9, June to August.
*Garden open until 6. **Conservation guided tours of state rooms (places limited). †East Wing state rooms also open.
††State room highlights guided tours 11 to 12 (places limited).

Cilgerran Castle

near Cardigan, Pembrokeshire SA43 2SF

Map ④ C7   🏛 | 1938

Striking 13th-century castle in a stunning location, overlooking the Teifi Gorge. **Note**: in the guardianship of Cadw – Welsh Government's historic environment service. Dogs on leads allowed.

Finding out more: 01239 621339 or cilgerrancastle@nationaltrust.org.uk

Colby Woodland Garden

near Amroth, Pembrokeshire SA67 8PP

Map ④ C8   🌼🍽🏛🛏 | 1980

Running down to the coast, this hidden wooded valley, with its secret garden and industrial past, is a place made for play. There are fallen trees to climb, rope swings, stepping stones across the stream and quirky surprises everywhere. Spring brings bluebells, camellias, rhododendrons and azaleas, while the walled garden gives year-round colour, peace and seclusion. There are woodland walks, meandering streams and ponds in the wildflower meadow, and the whole valley teems with wildlife. Fun learning activities and exploration packs are available, and there are picnic and campfire spots in the meadow and free games to borrow. **Note**: house not open.

Eating and shopping: shop and plant sales. Bothy tea-room (Trust-approved concession). Gallery selling Pembrokeshire arts and crafts. Second-hand books. Summerhill farm shop (tenant-run).

Making the most of your day: rope swings, den building, pond-dipping, camp fires, duck racing, wildlife tracking, activity sheets, exploration packs, dam building and games equipment. Virtual tour and film. Easter trails,

Stepping stones at Colby Woodland Garden, Pembrokeshire

wildlife events and summer holiday activities. **Dogs**: under control in estate woodlands. On leads in garden and meadow.

Access for all: 🅿♿🚻♿♿🔊📷🔴♿
Grounds ♿➡♿

Getting here: see website for details.
Parking: free, 50 yards.

Finding out more: 01834 811885 or colby@nationaltrust.org.uk

Colby Woodland Garden		M	T	W	T	F	S	S
Woodland and walled gardens and bothy exhibition								
2 Jan–14 Feb	10–3		M	T	W	T	F	S	S
17 Nov–23 Dec	10–3	M	T	W	T	F	S	S
Woodland and walled gardens, shop and bothy exhibition								
15 Feb–16 Nov	10–5	M	T	W	T	F	S	S
Gallery and tea-room								
5 Apr–2 Nov	10–4:30	M	T	W	T	F	S	S

Car park open as woodland and walled gardens.
Closed 1 January, 24 to 31 December.

Elegant Conwy Suspension Bridge, Conwy

Conwy Suspension Bridge

Conwy LL32 8LD

Map (4) E2  1965

Designed in the 1820s by Thomas Telford, this graceful bridge with its beautifully restored tiny toll-keeper's house has stunning views over the Conwy Estuary. Kept open by a husband and wife at a time when trade and travel brought Conwy to life, it never closed, whatever the weather. **Note**: sorry no toilet.

Eating and shopping: bring your own picnic to enjoy on the grassed area.

Making the most of your day: superb views of the river and castle. **Dogs**: allowed.

Access for all: Building 👨‍🦽 Grounds 👨‍🦽

Getting here: see website for details.
Parking: none on site.

Finding out more: 01492 573282 or conwybridge@nationaltrust.org.uk

Conwy Suspension Bridge		M	T	W	T	F	S	S
Bridge								
1 Mar–2 Nov	10–4:30	M	T	W	T	F	S	S
Toll House								
1 Mar–29 Jun	11–4:30	M	T	W	T	F	S	S
30 Jun–31 Aug	10–4:30	M	T	W	T	F	S	S
1 Sep–2 Nov	11–4:30	M	T	W	T	F	S	S

Last entry into the Toll House and the Bridge is at 4:15.

Dinefwr

Llandeilo, Carmarthenshire SA19 6RT

Map (4) E8
1990

Dinefwr has held an iconic position in Welsh history since the Middle Ages, when it was the seat of Welsh royalty. The spirits of Welsh princes still inhabit this magical landscape, designed in the 18th century by the visionaries George and Cecil Rice. There are 323 hectares (800 acres) of parkland to explore – three-quarters of which is a National Nature Reserve – encompassing a ruined castle, bogland walk, deer-park, woodlands, hay meadows and streams. Newton House is not your traditional dressed period house; instead the rooms tell the story of Dinefwr across the centuries, giving visitors an atmospheric and hands-on experience. **Note**: castle owned by Wildlife Trust, in guardianship of Cadw, Welsh Government's historic environment service.

Eating and shopping: coffee cabin in summer offering light refreshments. Billiard Room Café (licensed) at Newton House serving meals and snacks with a Welsh flavour – Dinefwr venison, when available. Gluten-free menu.

Embarking on a family adventure at Dinefwr in Carmarthenshire, below, and a tour of Dolaucothi Gold Mines, Carmarthenshire, right

Making the most of your day: daily tours of Newton House. Seasonal tours of the National Nature Reserve and fallow deer herd. Trailer tours of estate. School holiday and family activities. Events. Holiday cottages.
Dogs: welcome on leads, in outer park only (cattle and sheep grazing).

Access for all: ⃞⃞⃞⃞⃞⃞⃞⃞⃞⃞
Newton House ⃞⃞⃞⃞⃞ Castle ⃞
Estate ⃞⃞⃞

Getting here: see website for details.
Sat Nav: do not use. **Parking**: 50 yards.
Charges for non-members.

Finding out more: 01558 824512 or dinefwr@nationaltrust.org.uk

Dinefwr		M	T	W	T	F	S	S
Parkland, boardwalk and deer-park								
1 Jan–30 Mar	10–4*	M	T	W	T	F	S	S
31 Mar–2 Nov	10–6*	M	T	W	T	F	S	S
3 Nov–31 Dec	10–4*	M	T	W	T	F	S	S
Newton House, gift shop and Billiard Room Café								
3 Jan–30 Mar	11–4					F	S	S
31 Mar–2 Nov	11–6	M	T	W	T	F	S	S
7 Nov–28 Dec	11–4					F	S	S
Play area								
31 Mar–2 Nov	10–5	M	T	W	T	F	S	S
Dinefwr Castle								
2 Jan–31 Dec	10–4	M	T	W	T	F	S	S

*Boardwalk and deer-park close one hour earlier. Property closed 24 and 25 December, open all other Bank Holidays. Newton House, café, shop and castle closed to non-festival goers 20 to 22 June for the Dinefwr Literature Festival. Cadw manage Dinefwr Castle and may alter opening times.

Dolaucothi Gold Mines

Pumsaint, Llanwrda,
Carmarthenshire SA19 8US

Map ④ E7   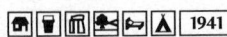 1941

These unique gold mines surrounded by wooded hillsides overlooking the Cothi Valley were abandoned 2,000 years ago by the Romans. Mining continued in the 19th and 20th centuries, finally ending in 1938 – the year the mine yard is presented as. There is still 1930s mine machinery on site, and guided tours allow you to glimpse the harsh conditions in the underground workings. Why not try gold panning and experience the frustrations of searching for gold, or take the self-led audio tour to see the Roman archaeology? It's the story of the search for gold in the Welsh hills. **Note**: steep slopes, stout footwear essential. Minimum height on underground tours; children may not be carried. Caravan park on site. Pitch charges (including members).

Eating and shopping: tea-room offering light refreshments. Small gift shop specialising in Welsh gold jewellery (also available from the National Trust online shop). Dolaucothi Arms offering food and accommodation. Picnic tables in the mine yard.

Making the most of your day: underground tours throughout day. Overground self-guided audio tour of Roman adits. 1930s machinery sheds. Walks around woodland estate.
Dogs: welcome on leads in mine yard only.

Access for all: ♿ 🅿 🚻 🔛 📷 🎧 👁
Office 📶 📶 📶 Machinery sheds 📶 Yard 📶 ➡

Getting here: see website for details.
Parking: free. Overflow car park opposite main entrance.

Finding out more: 01558 650809 or dolaucothi@nationaltrust.org.uk

Dolaucothi Gold Mines		M	T	W	T	F	S	S
Mines, shop and tea-room								
21 Mar–30 Jun	11–5	M	T	W	T	F	S	S
1 Jul–31 Aug	10–6	M	T	W	T	F	S	S
1 Sep–2 Nov	11–5	M	T	W	T	F	S	S
Estate and walks								
Open all year		M	T	W	T	F	S	S
Caravan site								
21 Mar–2 Nov		M	T	W	T	F	S	S
Dolaucothi Arms								
Open all year	12–11*	·	T	W	T	F	S	S

Last admission to the mine yard one hour before closing.
Peak season: Victorian tour 11, 12, 1, 1:30, 2:30, 3 and 4:30.
Roman Tour 12:30, 2 and 3.30. Off peak season: Victorian tour 11:30, 12:30, 2:30 and 3:30. Roman tour 12:30, 2 and 3:30.
*Open Tuesdays 6 to 11 and Sundays 12 to 10.

Dyffryn Gardens

St Nicholas, Vale of Glamorgan CF5 6SU

Map ④ G10   🏛 ❀ 🔔 🍽 2012

The gardens feature a stunning collection of intimate garden rooms, formal lawns, an extensive arboretum and a reinstated glasshouse, housing an impressive collection of cacti and orchids. Designed by the eminent landscape architect Thomas Mawson, the gardens are the early 20th-century vision of industrialist John Cory and son Reginald Cory. Recently restored Dyffryn House is on an ever-evolving journey, as it interprets the story of its most recent history and that of the Cory family. The spectacular symmetry of Mawson's lawn is best appreciated from the terrace of the Grade II* late-Victorian house – reminiscent of a French château.

The Vine Walk at Dyffryn Gardens in the Vale of Glamorgan

Eating and shopping: tea-room serving a selection of drinks, cakes and light lunches. Shop selling seasonal plants, gifts and books.

Access for all: ♿ 🚻 🔛 📷 House 📶 ⬍
Grounds 📶 📶 ➡ 📷 ♿

Getting here: see website for details.
Sat Nav: do not use. **Parking**: free.

Finding out more: 02920 593328 or dyffryn@nationaltrust.org.uk

Dyffryn Gardens		M	T	W	T	F	S	S
Gardens, tea-room and shop								
1 Jan–28 Feb	10–4	M	T	W	T	F	S	S
1 Mar–30 Mar	10–5	M	T	W	T	F	S	S
31 Mar–28 Sep	10–6	M	T	W	T	F	S	S
29 Sep–2 Nov	10–5	M	T	W	T	F	S	S
3 Nov–31 Dec*	10–4	M	T	W	T	F	S	S
House								
4 Jan–23 Feb	12–3	·	·	·	·	·	S	S
1 Mar–30 Mar	12–4	·	·	·	T	F	S	S
31 Mar–2 Nov	12–4	M	T	W	T	F	S	S
6 Nov–14 Dec	12–3	·	·	·	T	F	S	S

Last admission to the garden is one hour before closing.
*Closed on 25 and 26 December.

Erddig

Wrexham LL13 0YT

Map ④ H3   🏠✝🏛❖♿ 1973

At Erddig, you can immerse yourself in the life of a busy household during the early years of the last century. Your visit begins at the joiners' shop and smithy, followed by workyards with carriages and bicycles to discover. Entering the house via the laundry and kitchen, you get a sense of the once-bustling family home. Below stairs, portraits and verse record the lives of the servants, while upstairs, an array of original pieces evoke the lives of the Yorke family and their predecessors. Erddig's garden is one of the most important surviving 18th-century gardens in Britain.

Eating and shopping: gift shop and plant sales. Restaurant, tea-room and tea-garden.

Erddig, Wrexham: a young visitor enjoys the Yew Walk in the 18th-century gardens

Making the most of your day: events, including open-air theatre, festivals, craft fairs and Christmas weekends. Family activities all summer. Self-guided estate walks, children's explorer kits and natural play area – the Wolf's Den. **Dogs**: welcome on leads in country park only.

Access for all: 🅿️♿♿♿♿♿♿📷🏠 VT
♿••🅰️ Building ♿♿ Grounds ♿♿♿♿

Getting here: see website for details.
Parking: free, 200 yards.

Finding out more: 01978 355314 or erddig@nationaltrust.org.uk

Erddig		M	T	W	T	F	S	S
House								
1 Jan–7 Mar*	11:30–3:30	M	T	W	T	F	S	S
8 Mar–2 Nov	12:30–4:30	M	T	W	T	F	S	S
3 Nov–31 Dec*	11:30–3:30	M	T	W	T	F	S	S
Garden, restaurant and shop								
1 Jan–7 Mar	11–4	M	T	W	T	F	S	S
8 Mar–2 Nov	11–5	M	T	W	T	F	S	S
3 Nov–31 Dec	11–4	M	T	W	T	F	S	S

Last entry to house one hour before closing. *Ground-floor servants' quarters only, by guided tour. Closed 25 December.

Henfaes Centre: Porth y Swnt

Henfaes, Aberdaron, Pwllheli,
Gwynedd LL53 8BE

Map (4) C4 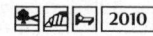 2010

This exciting new interpretation centre showcases the special qualities which make the Llŷn Peninsula so unique in terms of history, culture and environment. Come in and explore, learn, reflect and enjoy the natural environment, and get some great ideas for activities, walks, attractions and things to do on the peninsula. The centre is right at the heart of Aberdaron, so you can also immerse yourself in the joys of this beautiful fishing village. If you want to stay longer, our Henfaes holiday apartments are perfectly placed in the centre of the village, just a short walk from the beach.

Making the most of your day: walks and tranquil beaches at Porthor and Llanbedrog. Llŷn Coast Festival (throughout summer), events and activities, including beach fun days, seafood festival and guided walks.
Dogs: beach access restricted during summer.

Access for all: 🅿️♿🚾♿♿
Car park ♿♿

Getting here: see website for details.
Parking: free.

Finding out more: 01758 760469 or
henfaescentre@nationaltrust.org.uk

Henfaes Centre: Porth y Swnt		M	T	W	T	F	S	S
1 Mar–31 Mar	10–4	M	T	W	T	F	S	S
1 Apr–30 Jun	9–5	M	T	W	T	F	S	S
1 Jul–31 Aug	9–6	M	T	W	T	F	S	S
1 Sep–30 Sep	9–5	M	T	W	T	F	S	S
1 Oct–31 Dec	10–4	M	T	W	T	F	S	S

Closed 25, 26 and 31 December.

Henfaes Centre: Porth y Swnt, Gwynedd, sits right at the heart of the pretty village of Aberdaron

The Kymin, Monmouthshire: Georgian banqueting house

The Kymin

The Round House, The Kymin, Monmouth,
Monmouthshire NP25 3SF

Map (4) H8  1902

A Georgian banqueting house and unique
newly restored naval temple set atop a hill with
spectacular views and admired by Lord Nelson
and Lady Hamilton during their visit in 1802.
Set in woods and pleasure grounds, it's
ideal for picnics.

Making the most of your day: self-guided
walks, including bluebell walks in spring.
Garden games available to hire (when open).
Teddy bear hospital (April, July and October).
Dogs: allowed in grounds only.

Access for all: [symbols] Round House [symbols]
Naval Temple [symbols] Grounds [symbol]

Getting here: see website for details.
Parking: limited.

Finding out more: 01600 719241 or
kymin@nationaltrust.org.uk

The Kymin		M	T	W	T	F	S	S
Round House								
29 Mar–27 Oct	11–4	M	·	·	·	·	S	S
Grounds								
Open all year	7–9	M	T	W	T	F	S	S

Open Good Friday. Car park open during daylight hours only.

Llanerchaeron

Ciliau Aeron, near Aberaeron,
Ceredigion SA48 8DG

Map (4) D6  1989

Totally self-sufficient 18th-century Welsh minor
gentry estate. The villa, designed in the 1790s,
is the most complete example of the early work
of John Nash. It has its own service courtyard
with dairy, laundry, brewery and salting house,
giving a full 'upstairs downstairs' experience.
The walled kitchen gardens, pleasure grounds,
ornamental lake and parkland offer peaceful
walks, while the Home Farm complex has an
impressive range of traditional, atmospheric
outbuildings. A working farm, there are
Welsh Black cattle, Llanwenog sheep and
rare Welsh pigs.

Llanerchaeron, Ceredigion, was totally self-sufficient

Eating and shopping: café serving light meals
and cakes. Picnic site. Fresh garden produce
and plants, farm meat, local crafts, art, gifts
and books for sale. Second-hand bookshop.

Making the most of your day: activities during
local school holidays, including crafts,
gardening, nature activities and self-led
trails. Special events days. Cycle hire.
Dogs: welcome in the parkland only on leads.

Access for all: [symbols]
Visitor building [symbols] Villa [symbols]
Grounds [symbols]

Getting here: see website for details.
Parking: free, 50 yards.

Finding out more: 01545 570200 or
llanerchaeron@nationaltrust.org.uk

Llanerchaeron		M	T	W	T	F	S	S
Entire property								
24 Feb–28 Feb	11:30–3:30	M	T	W	T	F	·	·
24 Mar–31 Oct	10:30–5:30	M	T	W	T	F	S	S
Farm, garden, woodland walks and shop only								
1 Jan–5 Jan	11:30–3:30	·	·	W	T	F	S	S
11 Jan–23 Mar	11:30–3:30	·	·	·	·	·	S	S
1 Nov–5 Dec	11:30–3:30	M	T	W	T	F	S	S
8 Dec–31 Dec*	11:30–3:30	M	T	W	T	F	S	S
Christmas Fair								
6 Dec–7 Dec	11–3:30	·	·	·	·	·	S	S

Villa open 11:30, last entry 4, last entry to property one
hour before closing. Café open 24 February to 31 October.
*Closed 24 and 25 December. Geler Jones Collection open
Wednesday and Friday 12 to 4, 24 March to 31 October.
Farmland open daily.

Penrhyn Castle

Bangor, Gwynedd LL57 4HN

Map (4) E2  1951

Penrhyn was built to be remembered. Whether
it is its commanding position, the luxurious
decoration, or simply the vast principal rooms,
since 1830 visitors have come away with a
lasting impression. Presented at the time of the
visit of Edward, Prince of Wales, in 1894, you
can experience not only the parts of the castle
the family guests would have seen – the grand
dining-room, the finest art collection in North
Wales and the opulent bedrooms – but also the
'below stairs' areas, including the butler's
pantry and Victorian kitchens. An essential part
of any visit is a walk around the parkland,
where you can admire breathtaking views and
enjoy the tranquillity of the walled garden.

Eating and shopping: light meals and
homemade cakes available in our new
Stableyard Café; lunches in the tea-room.
Gift shop in the heart of the castle.

Making the most of your day: exhibitions and
events, including summer fun days. Tours to
hidden parts of the castle most days.

Climb aboard an engine or explore local
industrial history in the Railway Museum.
Art collection displayed in cathedral-like
interiors. Woodland walks and hidden parts of
garden to discover. **Dogs**: welcome on leads in
grounds. Assistance dogs only in castle and
walled garden.

Access for all: 〔symbols〕
Castle 〔symbols〕 Stableblock 〔symbols〕
Grounds 〔symbols〕

Getting here: see website for details.
Sat Nav: use LL57 4HT. **Parking**: free,
500 yards.

Finding out more: 01248 363219 (Infoline).
01248 353084 or
penrhyncastle@nationaltrust.org.uk

Penrhyn Castle		M	T	W	T	F	S	S
Castle, shop, tea-room and Victorian kitchens								
1 Mar–2 Nov*	11–5	M	T	W	T	F	S	S
8 Nov–28 Dec**	12–3	·	·	·	·	·	S	S
Railway Museum and grounds								
1 Jan–28 Feb	12–3	M	T	W	T	F	S	S
1 Mar–2 Nov	11–5	M	T	W	T	F	S	S
3 Nov–31 Dec	12–3	M	T	W	T	F	S	S
Coffee shop								
1 Jan–28 Feb	12–3	M	T	W	T	F	S	S
1 Mar–2 Nov	11:30–4:30	M	T	W	T	F	S	S
3 Nov–31 Dec	12–3	M	T	W	T	F	·	·

*Taster tours from 11 to 12. Free-flow from 12. Selected
showrooms in the Castle are open on Tuesdays, but by guided
tour only all day (no free-flow). **Parts of the Castle are open
for winter weekends (guided tour only).

Commanding Penrhyn Castle in Gwynedd, right, was
built to be remembered. Below, a view from the parkland
towards the Menai Strait

The dizzying heights of Pennard Cliffs, Swansea

Pennard, Pwll Du and Bishopston Valley

near Southgate, Swansea

Map (4) E9  1954

Spectacular cliffs, caves where mammoth remains have been found, rare birds, an underground river, bat roosts, silver lead mining, ancient woodland, smuggling and limestone quarrying are just a few of the wonders of this area. There are also numerous archaeological features and two important caves – Bacon Hole and Minchin Hole.

Eating and shopping: coffee shop, village stores, tea-rooms and a pub in Pennard (none National Trust). Picnics welcome.

Making the most of your day: Pennard provides a great starting point for a variety of walks, on which you can enjoy wild flowers and spot rare birds, such as choughs and Dartford warblers. **Dogs**: welcome on leads near livestock.

Access for all: [P♿]

Getting here: see website for details.
Sat Nav: use SA3 2DH. **Parking**: at Southgate car park.

Finding out more: 01792 390636 or pennard@nationaltrust.org.uk

Llŷn Peninsula

This is a hidden jewel of Wales. It's an ancient land, rich in culture and history, all set in a dramatic, beautiful coastal environment.

Llanbedrog Beach

Llanbedrog, Gwynedd

Map (4) D4 2000

Best known for its colourful beach huts, this wonderful stretch of sand has been enjoyed by generations. Its sheltered waters, fantastic views over Cardigan Bay and adjacent wooded and craggy landscape make this a real gem of Llŷn. **Note**: toilet (not National Trust).

Eating and shopping: shops and cafés at Llanbedrog and at nearby Pwllheli and Abersoch (not National Trust).

Making the most of your day: events during summer months. Maps and guides available at car park welcome cabin. Beach huts available to hire. **Dogs**: welcome.

Access for all: [♿]

Getting here: see website for details.
Sat Nav: use LL53 7TT. **Parking**: at beach.

Finding out more: 01758 760469 or llanbedrog@nationaltrust.org.uk

Colourful beach huts on Llanbedrog Beach, Gwynedd

Plas Newydd Country House and Gardens

Llanfairpwll, Anglesey LL61 6DQ

Map ④ D2
1976

This fine 18th-century mansion sits on the shores of the Menai Strait, with breathtaking views of Snowdonia. The surrounding gardens include an Australasian arboretum, formal Italianate terraces and an important rhododendron collection. After climbing up to our hand-crafted tree house, why not give croquet or Frisbee™ Golf a go? At the heart of the 1930s interior of the Marquess of Anglesey's ancestral family home, is Rex Whistler's 58-foot fantasy landscape mural (above).

Eating and shopping: Old Dairy tea-room. Coffee shop. Two gift shops. Second-hand bookshop.

Making the most of your day: events, including summer fair, Christmas craft and food fair. Specialist garden 'walks and talks'. New for 2014: discover our new viewing points of Snowdonia and the Menai Strait. **Dogs**: allowed in car park only.

Access for all: 🅿️♿ 🅳♿ 🔲 🔲 🔲 🔲 🔲 🔲
Building 🔲 🔲 🔲 Grounds 🔲

Getting here: see website for details.
Parking: free, 400 yards from main entrance.

Finding out more: 01248 714795 or plasnewydd@nationaltrust.org.uk

Plas Newydd		M	T	W	T	F	S	S
House								
1 Mar–9 Mar*	11–3	·	·	·	·	·	S	S
15 Mar–5 Nov**	12–4:30	M	T	W	·	·	S	S
Garden								
4 Jan–23 Feb	11–4	·	·	·	·	·	S	S
1 Mar–30 Jun	10:30–5:30	M	T	W	T	·	S	S
1 Jul–31 Aug	10:30–5:30	M	T	W	T	F	S	S
1 Sep–5 Nov	10:30–5:30	M	T	W	T	·	S	S
6 Nov–31 Dec	11–3	M	T	W	T	·	S	S
Shop, tea-room, playground and Frisbee™ Golf course								
4 Jan–23 Feb	11–4	·	·	·	·	·	S	S
1 Mar–5 Nov	10:30–5:30	M	T	W	T	F	S	S
6 Nov–31 Dec	11–3	M	T	W	T	F	S	S
Coffee shop and second-hand bookshop								
15 Mar–5 Nov	11:30–5	M	T	W	·	·	S	S

*Taster tours only, no free-flow. **Specialist tours 11 to 12.
Closed 25 to 27 December.

Plas yn Rhiw

Rhiw, Pwllheli, Gwynedd LL53 8AB

Map ④ C4  1952

The house was rescued from neglect and lovingly restored by the three Keating sisters, who bought it in 1938. The views from the grounds and gardens across Cardigan Bay are among the most spectacular in Britain. The house is 16th-century with Georgian additions, and the garden contains many beautiful flowering trees and shrubs, with beds framed by box hedges and grass paths. It is stunning whatever the season.

Eating and shopping: shop selling gifts, plants, guidebooks, photographs and prints of Honora Keating's landscapes. Hot or cold drinks, treats and ice-cream available. Tea-rooms opening in spring.

A homely corner at 16th-century Plas yn Rhiw, Gywnedd, which was rescued from neglect by three sisters in 1938

Making the most of your day: events. Grounds include beautiful woodland walks and a native apple orchard. Guided tours available by arrangement. Three stunning holiday cottages within walking distance of Plas yn Rhiw. **Dogs**: on woodland walk below car park only (on leads).

Access for all:
Building ⛪🦽 Grounds 🦽🏔

Getting here: see website for details.
Parking: 80 yards. Narrow lanes.

Finding out more: 01758 780219 or plasynrhiw@nationaltrust.org.uk

Plas yn Rhiw		M	T	W	T	F	S	S
27 Mar–26 May	12–5	M	·	·	T	F	S	S
28 May–21 Jul	12–5	M	·	W	T	F	S	S
22 Jul–1 Sep	12–5	M	T	W	T	F	S	S
4 Sep–29 Sep	12–5	M	·	·	T	F	S	S
2 Oct–2 Nov	12–4	·	·	·	T	F	S	S

Open Bank Holidays. Garden and snowdrop wood open occasionally at weekends in January and February.

Powis Castle and Garden

Welshpool, Powys SY21 8RF

Map ④ G5 🏰 ❀ 🛏 🔔 🍽 1952

The world-famous garden, overhung with clipped yews, shelters rare and tender plants. Laid out under the influence of Italian and French styles, it retains its original lead statues and an orangery on the terraces. The castle, originally built *circa* 1200, began life as a medieval fortress. Remodelled and embellished over more than 400 years, it reflects the changing needs and ambitions of the Herbert family – now the treasure house of Wales with a magnificent collection of paintings, sculpture, furniture and tapestries. A superb collection of treasures from India is displayed in the Clive Museum.

Eating and shopping: restaurant (licensed) and garden coffee shop. Gift shop and plant sales.

World-famous Powis Castle and Garden, Powys

Making the most of your day: daily introductory talks about the castle and garden, as well as themed castle tours. Castle and garden family fun trails. Children's activities during school holidays. **Dogs**: assistance dogs only.

Access for all: ♿🅿🚿♿🎫♿♿🖼️🚽👓
Building 🏢 **Grounds** 🏢♿➡️🚻

Getting here: see website for details.
Parking: free.

Finding out more: 01938 551944 (Infoline). 01938 551929 or powiscastle@nationaltrust.org.uk

Powis Castle and Garden		M	T	W	T	F	S	S
Castle								
4 Jan–23 Feb*	12–4	·	·	·	·	·	S	S
1 Mar–31 Mar**	11–4	M	T	W	T	F	S	S
1 Apr–30 Sep**	11–5	M	T	W	T	F	S	S
1 Oct–2 Nov**	11–4	M	T	W	T	F	S	S
3 Nov–23 Dec	12–4	M	T	W	T	F	S	S
Garden								
1 Jan–31 Mar	11–4	M	T	W	T	F	S	S
1 Apr–30 Sep	10–6	M	T	W	T	F	S	S
1 Oct–31 Dec	10–4	M	T	W	T	F	S	S
Clive Museum and restaurant								
1 Mar–31 Mar	10–4†	M	T	W	T	F	S	S
1 Apr–30 Sep	10–5†	M	T	W	T	F	S	S
1 Oct–23 Dec	11–4†	M	T	W	T	F	S	S
Shop								
1 Mar–23 Dec	11–4	M	T	W	T	F	S	S

*By guided tour. **Guided tours at 11, 11:30 and 12. Free-flow from 12:30. †Clive Museum opens at 12. Reduced number of state rooms open 4 January to 23 February and 3 November to 23 December. Coffee shop and small retail outlet open during January/February. Closed 25 December.

Segontium

Caernarfon, Gwynedd

Map ④ D2   🏛️ 1937

Fort built to defend the Roman Empire against rebellious tribes. **Note**: in the guardianship of Cadw – Welsh Government's historic environment service. Museum not National Trust.

Finding out more: 01443 336000 or segontium@nationaltrust.org.uk

Skenfrith Castle

Skenfrith, near Abergavenny, Monmouthshire NP7 8UH

Map ④ H8    1936

Remains of early 13th-century castle, built beside the River Monnow to command one of the main routes from England. **Note**: in the guardianship of Cadw – Welsh Government's historic environment service.

Finding out more: 01874 625515 or skenfrithcastle@nationaltrust.org.uk

Tredegar House

Newport, Newport NP10 8YW

Map ④ G9    2012

For centuries, this Grade I 17th-century house, one of the finest restoration houses in the British Isles, was home to the flamboyant Morgan family. Upstairs, you can immerse yourself in the stories of family life in the elegant state rooms, while 'below stairs', envisage work in the Victorian kitchens. The house is set within a 36-hectare (90-acre) park, with an impressive avenue of veteran oak trees, woodland walks, open parkland and a lake. Not to be missed are the impressive Grade I stables and the series of three walled formal gardens, including the distinctive parterre garden, which lie adjacent to the Orangery. **Note**: trialling new ways of opening the house as part of the 'Changing Rooms' project.

Eating and shopping: tea-room serving a selection of drinks, cakes and light lunches. Gift shop and independent craft workshops.

Making the most of your day: introductory talks about the house. Walks around the park and lake. Events, including Easter, Pirate Day, folk festival and vintage car rally. Summer family activities. **Dogs**: welcome on leads in garden and parkland only.

Tredegar House, Newport: the Orangery with the parterre in the foreground, above, and a well-polished *batterie de cuisine* has pride of place in the Great Kitchen, below

Access for all: ♿🚻🔣🔁📷

House 🔁   Grounds 🔁♿

Getting here: see website for details.
Parking: pay and display charge for non-members.

Finding out more: 01633 815880 or tredegar@nationaltrust.org.uk

Tredegar House		M	T	W	T	F	S	S
House and garden								
8 Feb–28 Feb*	11–4:30	M	T	W	T	F	S	S
1 Mar–2 Nov**	11–5	M	T	W	T	F	S	S
29 Nov–21 Dec	11–5	·	·	·	·	·	S	S
Tea-room and shop								
4 Jan–2 Feb	11–4	·	·	·	·	·	S	S
8 Feb–28 Feb	10:30–4:30	M	T	W	T	F	S	S
1 Mar–2 Nov	10:30–5:30	M	T	W	T	F	S	S
8 Nov–28 Dec	10:30–4:30	·	·	·	·	·	S	S
Park								
Open all year	Dawn–dusk	M	T	W	T	F	S	S

*Below stairs only. **Gardens open at 10:30 from 1 March to 2 November.

Tudor Merchant's House

Quay Hill, Tenby, Pembrokeshire SA70 7BX

Map (4) C9   1937

Imagine the life of a successful merchant and his family 500 years ago when Tenby was a busy trading port. This unaltered three-storey Tudor house and shop has been furnished with exquisitely carved replicas and brightly coloured wall-hangings to re-create the atmosphere of an earlier way of life.
Note: sorry no toilet.

Eating and shopping: shop range includes specially made Tudor-style pottery (design based on finds at the house), pewterware, horn cups, glass, beeswax candles and books about the Tudors.

Making the most of your day: Tudor Family Fortunes game, help lay the high table, costumes to try on and replica toys. Easter, Hallowe'en and Tudor-themed family events. Colby Woodland Garden and Stackpole nearby.
Dogs: assistance dogs only.

Access for all: ⬚ ⬚ ⬚ ⬚
Building ⬚

Getting here: see website for details.
Parking: very limited on-street parking within town walls. July to August: pay and display car parks or park and ride (charge including members).

Finding out more: 01834 842279 or tudormerchantshouse@nationaltrust.org.uk

Tudor Merchant's House		M	T	W	T	F	S	S
15 Feb–2 Mar	11–3	M	T	W	T	F	S	S
8 Mar–30 Mar	11–3						S	S
31 Mar–20 Jul	11–5	M		W	T	F	S	S
21 Jul–31 Aug	11–5*	M	T	W	T	F	S	S
1 Sep–2 Nov	11–5	M		W	T	F	S	S
8 Nov–28 Dec	11–3						S	S

Open Tuesdays of Bank Holiday weeks, 11 to 5. *Open until 7 on Tuesdays and Wednesdays 22 July to 27 August.

Tŷ Mawr Wybrnant

Penmachno, Betws-y-Coed, Conwy LL25 0HJ

Map (4) E3  1951

Hidden in the beautiful Conwy Valley, this traditional upland farmhouse was once home to Bishop William Morgan, who first translated the Bible into Welsh. This is one of the most important houses in the history of the Welsh language. An original rare copy of William Morgan's Bible is on display.

Eating and shopping: picnics welcome.

Making the most of your day: introductory talks, Tudor kitchen garden and woodland walks, exhibition room, family activity sheets and woodland animal puzzle trail.
Dogs: under close control.

Access for all: ⬚ ⬚ ⬚
Building ⬚ ⬚ **Grounds** ⬚

Getting here: see website for details.
Sat Nav: no access from the A470.
Parking: free, 500 yards.

Finding out more: 01690 760213 or tymawrwybrnant@nationaltrust.org.uk

Tŷ Mawr Wybrnant		M	T	W	T	F	S	S
3 Apr–2 Nov	12–5				T	F	S	S

Open Bank Holiday Mondays.

Tŷ Mawr Wybrnant, Conwy: traditional upland farmhouse

Northern Ireland

A rocky challenge, glistening golden sand and blue sea at Portstewart Strand, County Londonderry

Outdoors in Northern Ireland

Famed for its outstanding natural beauty, Northern Ireland's landscape is remarkably diverse. The haunting scenery ranges from the peaceful Fermanagh lakeland and drumlin landscape of Strangford Lough, to the bizarrely shaped basalt columns of the Giant's Causeway and the wild granite peaks of the Mourne Mountains. With many miles of beautiful coastline, huge stretches of countryside and panoramic views, we have a wealth of treasures for all to enjoy.

Above: **White Park Bay, County Antrim**
Below: **tranquil Crom, County Fermanagh**

Coastal adventures

Northern Ireland offers a spectacular range of walks for the serious rambler and for those who just want to take a short stroll. On the north coast, you can enjoy bracing walks and dramatic views at the Giant's Causeway. Nearby are the historic ruins of Dunseverick Castle and the majestic sweeping arc of White Park Bay. If you are feeling brave, you can cross Carrick-a-Rede rope bridge or marvel at the bustling seabird colonies at Larrybane and the views beyond to Rathlin Island and the west coast of Scotland. On Rathlin Island there are inspirational views from the path through Ballyconagan.

The tiny village of Glenoe near Larne, with its spectacular waterfall, is just waiting to be discovered, while the footpath along Skernaghan Point on the northern tip of Islandmagee leads to open headland, cliffs, coves and beautiful beaches.

The County Down coastline has much to offer, with rocky shore and heathland at Ballymacormick Point, and wildfowl, wading birds and gulls at Orlock Point. Strangford Lough, one of Europe's key wildlife habitats, offers bracing coastal walks, rock pools bursting with marine life and spectacular birdwatching. Further south, the fragile 6,000-year-old sand dunes of Murlough National Nature Reserve form an extraordinarily beautiful dune landscape which, with its network of paths and boardwalks, is perfect for walking.

Wild countryside

Visitors can escape to some of the best 'off-the-beaten track' experiences. Just a stone's throw from Belfast, the heathland-rich Divis and the Black Mountain provide the stunning backdrop to the city's skyline and a perfect haven for those in search of wild countryside. Other rural escapes in the Belfast area include the woodland paths of Collin Glen and the fine riverbank and meadows of Minnowburn, as well as the wonderful waterfalls at Lisnabreeny.

In mid-Ulster the woodland of Ballymoyer has the atmosphere and mystery of a fairy glen. While to the west of the region idyllic County Fermanagh is perfect walking country, boasting a kaleidoscope of tranquil landscapes to discover, including the woodland and wetlands of Crom on the serene shores of Lough Erne.

For a real walk on the wild side, the Trust's Mourne Mountain paths allow hikers to enjoy the dramatic scenery of Northern Ireland's highest mountain, majestic Slieve Donard, as well as neighbouring Slieve Commedagh. Visitors to Ballyquintin Farm, on the Ards Peninsula, can enjoy stunning views of Strangford Lough and learn how this critical site is managed for wildlife and conservation.

Above left: **Mourne Mountains, County Down**
Above right: **Rathlin Island, off the North Antrim coast**
Left: **the waterfall at Glenoe, County Antrim**

Further information

Euro notes are accepted by the Trust's Northern Ireland places.

Ulster Gardens Scheme facilitates opening of private gardens, providing income for Trust gardens in Northern Ireland.

For the 2014 events programme, telephone 028 9751 0721.

Outdoors in Northern Ireland

Famed throughout the world for our coastline, we also have wild mountains, peaceful lakes and huge stretches of idyllic countryside for you to enjoy.

Divis and the Black Mountain

Divis Road, Hannahstown, near Belfast, County Antrim BT17 0NG

Map ⑦ E6    2004

The mountains rest in the heart of the Belfast Hills, which provide the backdrop to the city's skyline, while the rich, varied archaeological landscape is home to a host of wildlife. There are walking trails along a variety of terrain – through heath, on stone tracks, along boardwalks and road surface.

Note: cattle roam freely during summer months.

Eating and shopping: tea and coffee available in the Long Barn.

Making the most of your day: guided walks – themes are biodiversity and archaeology. **Dogs**: welcome, but please note cattle roam freely during summer.

Access for all: 🅿️ 🚻 ♿ 👶

Visitor centre ♿   Mountain ♿

Getting here: see website for details. **Parking**: open all year.

Finding out more: 028 9082 5434 or divis@nationaltrust.org.uk

Divis and the Black Mountain

Car park open 9 to 8.

The rich and varied landscape of Divis and the Black Mountain in County Antrim, provides a home to a host of wildlife, as well as walking trails for every ability

Islandmagee

Larne Road, Larne, County Antrim BT40

Map (7) E5   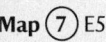  1996

Peninsula on the East Antrim coast steeped in history; with cottages, rolling fields, quiet villages and spectacular coastline teeming with bird life, it is a microcosm of the Northern Ireland countryside. The National Trust owns four stretches of the peninsula's coast with paths at Portmuck and Skernaghan Point. **Note**: paths are uneven and steep in places.

Eating and shopping: Chapter 1 café (not National Trust) serving food, tea and coffee in Mullaghboy village. The Rinkha (not National Trust) famous-ice cream in Ballystrudder village. Picnics welcome.

Making the most of your day: coastal walks and yearly guided walk at Portmuck.
Dogs: on leads only.

Access for all: Portmuck and Skernaghan 🦽

Getting here: see website for details.
Parking: free at Portmuck and Skernaghan Point (not National Trust).

Finding out more: 028 9064 7787 or islandmagee@nationaltrust.org.uk

Portmuck at the north-eastern point of Islandmagee, County Antrim

Lisnabreeny

Manse Road, Belfast, County Down BT8 6SA

Map (7) E6    1938

Nestling in the Castlereagh hills on the eastern edge of Belfast, Lisnabreeny consists of an intriguing range of landscapes and features. They include the woods and waterfall of Cregagh Glen and the grounds of Lisnabreeny House, as well as rolling farmland with spectacular views of the city and an ancient rath beyond. **Note**: sorry no toilets. Uneven paths and steep steps.

Intriguing Lisnabreeny, County Down, on the edge of Belfast

Making the most of your day: viewpoint and Second World War memorial commemorating US servicemen who died in Northern Ireland. Walks through glen, woodlands and ancient rath. Yearly guided walk.
Dogs: welcome on leads.

Access for all: Glen 🦽

Getting here: see website for details.
Parking: free on Lisnabreeny Road. No parking on Manse Road.

Finding out more: 028 9064 7787 or lisnabreeny@nationaltrust.org.uk

Minnowburn

Edenderry Road, Belfast,
County Down BT8 8LE

Map (7) E6  1952

Minnowburn is a paradox, set in beautiful
countryside and yet just a couple of miles from
Belfast city centre. Nestled in the heart of
Lagan Valley Regional Park, it offers
magnificent woodland walks, one of the finest
viewpoints in South Belfast and tranquil
riverbank trails leading to the Giant's Ring.
Note: sorry no toilets. Trails are uneven and
steep in places.

Eating and shopping: Piccolo Mondo catering
van (not National Trust) serves food, tea and
coffee in car park at weekends. Lock Keeper's
Inn (not National Trust) serving food, tea and
coffee, ¾ mile along riverside path. Picnic
tables in Terrace Hill garden.

Making the most of your day: guided walks,
including heritage, history and woodlands.
Waymarked walks, including the Giant's Ring
Trail. Sculpture trail. Riverside and pond walks.
Terrace Hill Garden, venue for 'Gig in the
Garden' music event. **Dogs**: on leads only.

Getting here: see website for details.
Parking: free.

Finding out more: 028 9064 7787 or
minnowburn@nationaltrust.org.uk

The tranquil river at Minnowburn, County Down

The Mournes

Newcastle, County Down

Map (7) E8  1992

Embraced by Shan Slieve, Chimney Rock and
Spences Mountains, the Mournes sweep down
to the sea while Slieve Donard, Northern
Ireland's loftiest mountain, dominates the
Down coastline. This is a place of ancient
smugglers' trails, Celtic ruins, bloody legends,
walls built as if by giants and views to die for.

The Mournes, County Down: a place of legends

Eating and shopping: picnics welcome.
Nearest shops, restaurants and cafés in
Newcastle (not National Trust).

Making the most of your day: outstanding
views from Bloody Bridge. Coastal path to
St Mary's Chapel ruins. Bird watching.
Dogs: welcome under control.

Getting here: see website for details.
Parking: for Slieve Donard park in Newcastle.
For Bloody Bridge park on A2, two miles
south of Newcastle.

Finding out more: 028 437 51467 or
mournes@nationaltrust.org.uk

Murlough National Nature Reserve

Keel Point, Dundrum, County Down BT33 0NQ

Map ⑦ E8   🏛🏖🚵🐕🛏 1967

Murlough is an extraordinarily beautiful dune landscape, fringing one of Northern Ireland's most popular beaches and overlooked by the rounded peaks of the Mourne Mountains. The fragile 6,000-year-old sand dunes, Northern Ireland's first nature reserve, are an excellent area for walking and spotting wildlife.
Note: limited toilet facilities.

Eating and shopping: beach café. Picnics welcome on beach or in car park.

Making the most of your day: self-guided nature walk, series of guided walks, volunteer events and family activities throughout year.
Dogs: welcome on leads, restrictions apply when ground-nesting birds breeding or cattle grazing.

Access for all: 🚾♿ Grounds ♿

Getting here: see website for details.
Parking: open all year.

Finding out more: 028 4375 1467 or murlough@nationaltrust.org.uk

Murlough		M	T	W	T	F	S	S
Facilities								
15 Mar–25 May	10–6	.	.	.	.	.	S	S
18 Apr–27 Apr	10–6	M	T	W	T	F	S	S
31 May–28 Sep	10–6	M	T	W	T	F	S	S
4 Oct–26 Oct	10–6	.	.	.	.	.	S	S

Open Bank Holiday Mondays and all other public holidays in Northern Ireland.

Murlough National Nature Reserve, County Down: the Mournes in the distance look down on this extraordinarily beautiful beach and dune landscape

Portstewart Strand

118 Strand Road, Portstewart,
County Londonderry BT55 7PG

Map ⑦ C3  1981

A rare and precious habitat, Portstewart Strand is a two-mile stretch of glistening golden sand and is one of Northern Ireland's finest and most popular beaches. The ancient sand-dune system is an area of special scientific interest and is a haven for wild flowers and butterflies.

Eating and shopping: beach toys and light refreshments available in newly improved visitor centre.

Making the most of your day: waymarked nature trail. Barmouth Estuary bird hide. Events during peak season. **Dogs**: on leads only.

Access for all: 🚻 ♿
Visitor centre 🏛 **Beach** ➡️

Getting here: see website for details.
Parking: on beach.

Both Portstewart Strand in County Londonderry, above, and Strangford Lough in County Down, right, are precious habitats

Finding out more: 028 7083 6396 or portstewart@nationaltrust.org.uk

Portstewart Strand		M	T	W	T	F	S	S
Beach								
Open all year	Dawn–dusk	M	T	W	T	F	S	S
Facilities								
11 Apr–2 May	10–5	M	T	W	T	F	S	S
3 May–29 May	10–6	M	T	W	T	F	S	S
30 May–31 Aug	10–7	M	T	W	T	F	S	S
1 Sep–28 Sep	10–6	M	T	W	T	F	S	S

Barrier to beach closes two hours after facilities close. Open Bank Holiday Mondays and all other public holidays in Northern Ireland. Closed 25 and 26 December. Facilities may open at other times.

Strangford Lough

County Down

Map ⑦ F7  1969

Strangford Lough is the largest sea lough in the British Isles. Covering 15,000 hectares (37,065 acres), it is one of only three marine nature reserves in the whole of the UK. More than 2,000 species of marine wildlife are found in or around the lough.

Eating and shopping: numerous restaurants serving dishes made from local produce, including meat produced on the surrounding land and seafood from the lough. Many arts and crafts shops.

Getting here: see website for details.
Parking: number of car parks on lough shores.

Finding out more: 028 4278 7769 or strangford@nationaltrust.org.uk

The traditional farmyard at Ardress House, County Armagh, complete with old agricultural implements and hens

Ardress House

64 Ardress Road, Annaghmore, Portadown, County Armagh BT62 1SQ

Map (7) D7   🏠 🎧 ✿ 🛏 1959

This charming 17th-century farmhouse, elegantly remodelled in Georgian times, offers fun and relaxation for all the family. Set in 40 hectares (100 acres) of countryside, there are apple orchards, beautiful woodlands and walks. The atmosphere of a working farmyard has been rekindled with the return of small animals.

Eating and shopping: drinks and ice-cream available. Picnics welcome in the garden or woodlands.

Making the most of your day: miniature Shetland ponies, pygmy goats, Soay sheep, ducks and chickens. Children's play area. Events, including 'Easter Egg Trail', 'Apple Fest' and 'Apple Press Day'. **Dogs**: on leads in garden only.

Access for all: 🚻 **Building** ♿ 🔆
Grounds ♿ ➡

Getting here: see website for details.
Parking: free, 10 yards.

Finding out more: 028 8778 4753 or ardress@nationaltrust.org.uk

Ardress House		M	T	W	T	F	S	S
Farmyard and house								
15 Feb–18 Feb	12–5	M	T	·	·	·	S	S
15 Mar–29 Jun	1–6	·	·	·	·	·	S	S
21 Apr–27 Apr	1–6	M	T	W	T	F	S	S
3 Jul–31 Aug	1–6	·	·	·	T	F	S	S
6 Sep–28 Sep	1–6	·	·	·	·	·	S	S
Lady's Mile Walk								
Open all year	Dawn–dusk	M	T	W	T	F	S	S

House: admission by guided tour, last admission one hour before closing. Open Bank Holiday Mondays and all other public holidays in Northern Ireland.

The Argory

144 Derrycaw Road, Moy, Dungannon,
County Armagh BT71 6NA

Map (7) C7 🏠✿♿🔔🍷 1979

Built in the 1820s, this handsome Irish gentry
house is surrounded by its 130-hectare
(320-acre) wooded riverside estate. The former
home of the MacGeough Bond family, a tour of
this Neo-classical masterpiece reveals it is
unchanged since 1900 – the eclectic interior
still evoking the family's tastes and interests.
Outside there are sweeping views, superb
spring bulbs, scenic walks, playground and
fascinating exhibitions.

Hide and seek in the grounds of The Argory in County
Armagh, above, and the West Hall, below

Eating and shopping: Courtyard Coffee Shop
serving light lunches and snacks. Gift shop and
second-hand bookshop, Blackwater Books.

Making the most of your day: events,
including children's, musical and general – such
as craft fairs. **Dogs**: on leads in grounds and
garden only.

Access for all: 🅿🚻♿👁 Grounds ♿➡

Getting here: see website for details.
Parking: 100 yards.

Finding out more: 028 8778 4753 or
argory@nationaltrust.org.uk

The Argory		M	T	W	T	F	S	S
Courtyard, café and shop								
1 Feb–23 Feb	12–5	·	·	·	·	·	S	S
17 Feb–18 Feb	12–5	M	T	·	·	·	·	·
House, courtyard, café and shop								
15 Mar–25 May	12–5	·	·	·	T	F	S	S
14 Apr–27 Apr	12–5	M	T	W	T	F	S	S
4 Jun–29 Jun	12–5	·	·	W	T	F	S	S
1 Jul–31 Aug	12–5	M	T	W	T	F	S	S
4 Sep–28 Sep	12–5	·	·	·	T	F	S	S
4 Oct–2 Nov	12–4	·	·	·	·	·	S	S
27 Oct–31 Oct	12–4	M	T	W	T	F	·	·
Grounds								
Open all year	10–5	M	T	W	T	F	S	S

House: admission by guided tour. Last tour one hour before
closing. Open Bank Holiday Mondays and all other public
holidays in Northern Ireland. Closed 25 and 26 December.

Carrick-a-Rede

119a Whitepark Road, Ballintoy,
County Antrim BT54 6LS

Map (7) D3    1967

Dare you cross the rope bridge to Carrick-a-Rede Island? This scary bridge crosses the Atlantic Ocean over a 30-metre deep drop and is 22-metres long. The bridge was traditionally erected by salmon fishermen and has been here for well over 250 years. Beyond the bridge you will discover unrivalled coastal scenery, beautiful sea views across the seas of Moyle to Rathlin Island and beyond, and spectacular bird watching opportunities. Carrick-a-Rede is a Site of Special Scientific Interest with unique geology, flora and fauna. There are two quarries on site, too – black and white. Come and find out more… **Note**: eight people maximum on bridge (open weather permitting).

Eating and shopping: new improved Weighbridge tea-room and gift shop offering hot food, snacks, sweets, gifts and souvenirs.

Making the most of your day: coastal path – part of the Causeway Coast Way from Portstewart to Ballycastle and the Ulster Way. Birdwatching and coastal scenery. Unique flora and fauna. Guided tours (by prior arrangement). **Dogs**: on leads (not permitted to cross bridge).

Access for all: [P] [♿] [WC] [♿] [♿] [⌖]
Grounds [♿] [♿] [▶]

Getting here: see website for details.
Parking: free.

Finding out more: 028 2076 9839 or carrickarede@nationaltrust.org.uk

Carrick-a-Rede		M	T	W	T	F	S	S
Bridge								
1 Jan–23 Feb	9:30–3:30	M	T	W	T	F	S	S
24 Feb–25 May	9:30–6	M	T	W	T	F	S	S
14 Apr–27 Apr	9:30–7:30	M	T	W	T	F	S	S
26 May–31 Aug	9:30–7:30	M	T	W	T	F	S	S
1 Sep–26 Oct	9:30–6	M	T	W	T	F	S	S
27 Oct–31 Dec	9:30–3:30	M	T	W	T	F	S	S

Last entry to rope bridge 45 minutes before closing.
Car park and North Antrim coastal path open all year.
Bridge open weather permitting. Closed 25 and 26 December.

Visitors need nerves of steel to venture across the rope bridge at Carrick-a-Rede, County Antrim

Castle Coole

Enniskillen, County Fermanagh BT74 6JY

Map (7) A7   🏛🏊🔔🍷 1951

Castle Coole is one of Ireland's finest Neo-classical houses and provides the perfect place for a great day out. The 18th-century mansion showcases what life was like in the home of the Earls of Belmore. With its opulent Regency interior, State Bedroom prepared for George IV and a fully intact basement revealing a wine cellar, plunge pool and working kitchen, a visit to this historic house is a real treat. For those with a passion for the outdoors, the parklands, lakeside walk and natural play area provide a further opportunity to explore this wonderful estate.

Eating and shopping: Tallow tea-room and shop selling souvenirs and gifts.

Making the most of your day: musical events throughout year. Guided tours of historic basement. Castle Coole was used as the setting for period drama *Miss Julie* (directed by Liv Ullmann), in cinemas this year.

Dogs: on leads in grounds only.

Access for all: 🅿️♿🚻♿📷📷
Building 🏛♿♿   Grounds ♿➡️

Castle Coole, County Fermanagh: the opulent Regency Saloon, above, and the stately Neo-classical façade, below

Getting here: see website for details.
Parking: 150 yards.

Finding out more: 028 6632 2690 or castlecoole@nationaltrust.org.uk

Castle Coole		M	T	W	T	F	S	S
Grounds								
1 Jan–28 Feb	10–4	M	T	W	T	F	S	S
1 Mar–31 Oct	10–7	M	T	W	T	F	S	S
1 Nov–31 Dec	10–4	M	T	W	T	F	S	S
House, tea-room and shop								
15 Mar–13 Apr	11–5	·	·	·	·	·	S	S
18 Apr–27 Apr	11–5	M	T	W	T	F	S	S
3 May–25 May	11–5	·	·	·	·	·	S	S
31 May–31 Aug	11–5	M	T	W	T	F	S	S
6 Sep–28 Sep	11–5	·	·	·	·	·	S	S

House: admission by guided tour (last tour one hour before closing). Open Bank Holiday Mondays and all other public holidays in Northern Ireland.

Castle Ward

Strangford, Downpatrick,
County Down BT30 7LS

Map ⑦ F7

Sitting boldly on a rolling hillside overlooking
Strangford Lough, the magnificent, eccentric
18th-century house oozes personality, boasting
two very different styles of façade – one
classical and the other Gothic. History meets
re-creation throughout the 332-hectare
(820-acre) walled demesne. A 16th-century
tower-house stands firmly in the farmyard,
while the working corn mill is a fine example of
Irish industrial heritage. The exotic garden and
21 miles of walking, cycling and equestrian
trails through woodlands and along the
shoreline are exceptional. An impressive
laundry, tack room, children's Victorian play
centre and adventure playground complete the
picture. **Note**: 1 March to 30 November
visitor access to livestock grazing areas may
be restricted.

Eating and shopping: Coach House tea-room.
Gift shop selling local produce and souvenirs.
Second-hand bookshop.

Making the most of your day: bicycles for
hire. Guided house tours. Farmyard with

Castle Ward, County Down: magnificent and eccentric

animals. Children's activities and Tracker Packs.
Events, including Pirates' Picnic, Pumpkinfest,
Book Fair and Santa's House. Caravan park and
pods. **Dogs**: on leads in grounds only (livestock
grazing areas out of bounds).

Access for all: ⊞ ⊞ ⊞ ⊞ ⊞ ⊞ ⊞ ⊞ ⊞
Building ⊞ ⊞ ⊞   Grounds ⊞ ⊞ ⊞ ➡

Getting here: see website for details.
Sat Nav: follow signs. **Parking**: free.

Finding out more: 028 4488 1204 or
castleward@nationaltrust.org.uk

Castle Ward		M	T	W	T	F	S	S
Parkland, woodland and garden								
1 Jan–30 Mar	10–4	M	T	W	T	F	S	S
31 Mar–28 Sep	10–8	M	T	W	T	F	S	S
29 Sep–31 Dec	10–4	M	T	W	T	F	S	S
House, laundry and pastimes centre								
15 Mar–29 Jun	12–5						S	S
12 Apr–5 May	12–5	M	T	W	T	F	S	S
30 Jun–31 Aug	12–5	M	T	W	T	F	S	S
6 Sep–26 Oct	12–5						S	S
Coach House tea-room, shop and second-hand bookshop								
11 Jan–16 Mar	12–5						S	S
19 Mar–11 Apr	12–5			W	T	F	S	S
12 Apr–5 May	12–5	M	T	W	T	F	S	S
7 May–29 Jun	12–5			W	T	F	S	S
30 Jun–31 Aug	11–5	M	T	W	T	F	S	S
3 Sep–21 Dec	12–5			W	T	F	S	S
Trailhead and refreshments								
30 Jun–29 Aug	12–5	M	T	W	T	F	S	S

Last admission to house is one hour before closing. Timed
tickets apply to guided house tours. Open Bank Holiday
Mondays and all other public holidays in Northern Ireland.
The Barn: open when primary schools are closed. The corn mill
operates on Sundays from Easter to September, 2 to 5.

One of Ireland's most important nature conservation areas, Crom in County Fermanagh is home to many rare species

Crom

Upper Lough Erne, Newtownbutler,
County Fermanagh BT92 8AP

Map (7) A8  1987

Breathtaking 810-hectare (2,000-acre) demesne, set amid the romantic and tranquil landscape of Upper Lough Erne. One of Ireland's most important nature conservation areas, Crom's ancient woodland and picturesque islands are home to many rare species. **Note**: castle not open to public.

Eating and shopping: afternoon tea, gifts and souvenirs available in visitor centre.

Making the most of your day: regular guided walks. Historic castle ruins. Cot trips (Bank Holiday Mondays). Stay for longer at one of our holiday cottages or campsite. **Dogs**: on leads only.

Access for all: ⓟ♿wc♿♿ ⠿
Building ♿♿ **Grounds** ♿➡♿

Getting here: see website for details.
Parking: 100 yards.

Finding out more: 028 6773 8118 or crom@nationaltrust.org.uk

Crom		M	T	W	T	F	S	S
Grounds								
15 Mar–31 May	10–6	M	T	W	T	F	S	S
1 Jun–31 Aug	10–7	M	T	W	T	F	S	S
1 Sep–31 Oct	10–6	M	T	W	T	F	S	S
Visitor centre								
15 Mar–30 Sep	11–5	M	T	W	T	F	S	S
4 Oct–26 Oct	11–5	·	·	·	·	·	S	S

Open Bank Holiday Mondays and all other public holidays in Northern Ireland. Last admission one hour before closing. Tea-room open as visitor centre (closed October).

The Crown Bar

46 Great Victoria Street, Belfast,
County Antrim BT2 7BA

Map (7) E6  1978

Wonderfully ornate interior of brightly coloured tiles, carvings and glass, with period gas lighting and cosy snugs. **Note**: run by Mitchells and Butlers.

Finding out more: 028 9024 3187 or info@crownbar.com

Derrymore House

Bessbrook, Newry, County Armagh BT35 7EF

Map (7) D8 🏠♿ 1953

Elegant 18th-century thatched cottage with a peculiar gentrified vernacular style.
Note: sorry no toilet.

Finding out more: 028 8778 4753 or derrymore@nationaltrust.org.uk

Downhill Demesne and Hezlett House

Mussenden Road, Castlerock,
County Londonderry BT51 4RP

Map (7) C3 🏠🏰♿⛲♣✕♿🔔☂
1949

From the dramatic clifftop views and colourful gardens to the quaint thatched cottage, Downhill Demesne and Hezlett House have everything an avid explorer needs for an inspiring day out. The striking 18th-century mansion of the eccentric Earl Bishop now lies in ruin, while Mussenden Temple sits perched on a cliff edge. To complete your day, visitors can learn about the reality of life in the rural 17th-century cottage of Hezlett House, one of Northern Ireland's oldest surviving buildings.

Downhill Demesne and Hezlett House, County Londonderry: Mussenden Temple, above right, and Hezlett House, below

Eating and shopping: tea and coffee facilities. Picnics welcome in gardens.

Making the most of your day: numerous events throughout year, including the Kite Festival, open-air theatre production, Hallowe'en and Christmas at Hezlett House. Guided tours on request (booking essential).
Dogs: on leads only.

Access for all: 🅿♿🚻 Building 🏠
Grounds 🏠

Getting here: see website for details.
Parking: at Lion's Gate.

Finding out more: 028 7084 8728 or downhilldemesne@nationaltrust.org.uk.
107 Sea Road, Castlerock,
County Londonderry BT51 4TW

Downhill and Hezlett		M	T	W	T	F	S	S
Hezlett House and facilities								
1 Mar–30 Mar	10–5	·	·	·	·	·	S	S
31 Mar–7 Sep	10–5	M	T	W	T	F	S	S
13 Sep–28 Sep	10–5	·	·	·	·	·	S	S
Downhill Demesne grounds								
Open all year	Dawn–dusk	M	T	W	T	F	S	S

Open Bank Holiday Mondays and all other public holidays in Northern Ireland. Closed 25 and 26 December.

Florence Court

Enniskillen, County Fermanagh BT92 1DB

Map (7) A7   🏠❄️🦐🛏️🔔🍷 | 1954 |

This great Irish estate provides a unique opportunity to step back in time, explore the home of the Earls of Enniskillen, experience the workings of a sustainable Irish estate and enjoy the unspoilt landscape that surrounds this magnificent home. Florence Court oozes with charm and appeal as visitors are invited to relax in the Colonel's room listening to 1920s music, discover fossils in the Rock Hound room, explore the estate on foot or by bike, soak up the views from the summerhouse and discover the parent of all Irish yew trees.

Eating and shopping: Stables restaurant. Coach House gift shop.

Florence Court in County Fermanagh, below and right, oozes charm and appeal, both inside and out

Making the most of your day: events throughout year. Children's Tracker Packs. **Dogs**: on leads in garden and grounds only.

Access for all: 🅿️♿🚻♿📷◻️◻️🅰️
Building 🔆♿ Grounds ♿➡️♿

Getting here: see website for details.
Parking: 200 yards.

Finding out more: 028 6634 8249 or florencecourt@nationaltrust.org.uk

Florence Court		M	T	W	T	F	S	S
Gardens and park								
1 Jan–28 Feb	10–4	M	T	W	T	F	S	S
1 Mar–31 Oct	10–7	M	T	W	T	F	S	S
1 Nov–31 Dec	10–4	M	T	W	T	F	S	S
House, tea-room and shop								
15 Mar–13 Apr	11–5	·	·	·	·	·	S	S
18 Apr–27 Apr	11–5	M	T	W	T	F	S	S
1 May–31 May	11–5	M	T	W	T	·	S	S
1 Jun–31 Aug	11–5	M	T	W	T	F	S	S
1 Sep–28 Sep	11–5	M	T	W	T	·	S	S
4 Oct–26 Oct	11–5	·	·	·	·	·	S	S

House: admission by guided tour (last admission one hour before closing). Open Bank Holiday Mondays and all other public holidays in Northern Ireland. Open Irish Bank Holiday 27 October.

Giant's Causeway

44 Causeway Road, Bushmills,
County Antrim BT57 8SU

Map ⑦ D3  1962

Northern Ireland's iconic World Heritage Site and Area of Outstanding Natural Beauty is home to a wealth of local history and legend. There are 40,000 basalt stone columns left by volcanic eruptions 60 million years ago to discover – visitors always enjoy searching for distinctive formations fancifully named the camel, the wishing chair, the granny and the organ. State-of-the-art interpretation within the visitor centre unlocks the mystery and stories of the landscape, offering a unique glimpse into this amazing place. Visitors can explore the upgraded walking trails and enjoy spectacular coastal scenery accompanied by an outdoor audio-guide or join an hourly guided tour. The site offers an innovative and enhanced visitor experience.

Giant's Causeway in County Antrim is a geological wonder, steeped in legend. The new visitor centre, below, unlocks many mysteries

Eating and shopping: light lunches and snacks available. Gift shop.

Making the most of your day: interactive exhibition brings the science and stories of the Causeway to life. Outdoor audio-guides (in a range of languages) reveal the many secrets of the landscape. Colour-coded walking trails, including the coastal path which extends 11 miles to Carrick-a-Rede Rope Bridge and a ½-mile all-accessible trail to the viewpoint and picnic area at Runkerry Head. Geology, flora and fauna of international importance. Guided tours available. Range of events and family activities throughout the year. **Dogs**: on leads only.

Access for all:
Visitor centre 🔲🔲 Grounds 🔲🔲➡

Getting here: see website for details.
Parking: on site and park and ride in
Bushmills village.

Finding out more: 028 2073 1855 or
giantscauseway@nationaltrust.org.uk

Giant's Causeway		M	T	W	T	F	S	S
Stones and coastal path								
Open all year	Dawn-dusk	M	T	W	T	F	S	S
Visitor centre								
1 Jan–31 Jan	9–5	M	T	W	T	F	S	S
1 Feb–31 Mar	9–6	M	T	W	T	F	S	S
1 Apr–30 Jun	9–7	M	T	W	T	F	S	S
1 Jul–31 Aug	9–9	M	T	W	T	F	S	S
1 Sep–30 Sep	9–7	M	T	W	T	F	S	S
1 Oct–31 Oct	9–6	M	T	W	T	F	S	S
1 Nov–31 Dec	9–5	M	T	W	T	F	S	S

Last admission to Visitor Centre is one hour before closing.
Closed 24, 25 and 26 December.

The stunning coastline at Giant's Causeway

Gray's Printing Press

49 Main Street, Strabane,
County Tyrone BT82 8AU

Map ⑦ B5   1966

A treasure trove of galleys, ink and presses
hidden behind an 18th-century shop front in
the heart of Strabane.

Finding out more: 028 8674 8210 or
grays@nationaltrust.org.uk

Mount Stewart House, Garden and Temple of the Winds

Portaferry Road, Newtownards,
County Down BT22 2AD

Map ⑦ F6   🏠✳🔔🍷 1976

Mount Stewart is famed around the world
for its grandeur and bold planting schemes,
using many rare and tender plants. While
the gardens thrive thanks, in part, to their
mild location, their mystery, magic and
artistry belong to their creator, Edith,
Lady Londonderry. The formal areas exude a
strong Mediterranean feel, resembling an
Italian villa landscape, while the wooded
areas support plants from all corners of
the world – ensuring there is something to
see whatever the season. An exciting
£7 million restoration project is underway
in the house, and visitors have the
opportunity to see conservation in
action – watching the experts at work
and learning about different conservation
techniques in the new conservation studio.
Note: restoration tour replaces the house
tour due to ongoing conservation project.

Eating and shopping: shop selling local craft
products. Plant shop. Award-winning Bay
Restaurant. Mount Stewart ice-cream.

The bold planting at Mount Stewart, County Down, above and left, is world famous

Making the most of your day: guided walks and garden tours. Lakeside walk and statuary to discover. Why not experience conservation in action on a guided restoration tour or enjoy one of our many events throughout the year, including jazz on Sundays and car boot sales during the summer? There is also an art and antiques fair, garden fête, Hallowe'en festival and Santa experience. Many events are aimed specifically at children. **Dogs**: on leads in all areas.

Access for all:
Building **Grounds**

Getting here: see website for details.
Parking: free, 200 yards.

Finding out more: 028 4278 8387 or mountstewart@nationaltrust.org.uk

Mount Stewart		M	T	W	T	F	S	S
Formal and lakeside gardens, restaurant and shop								
1 Jan–14 Mar	10–4*	**M**	**T**	**W**	**T**	**F**	**S**	**S**
15 Mar–2 Nov	10–5	**M**	**T**	**W**	**T**	**F**	**S**	**S**
3 Nov–31 Dec	10–4*	**M**	**T**	**W**	**T**	**F**	**S**	**S**
House								
15 Mar–2 Nov	12–5	**M**	**T**	**W**	**T**	**F**	**S**	**S**
Temple of the Winds								
16 Mar–2 Nov	2–5	·	·	·	·	·	·	**S**

*Restaurant and shop closes at 5 on Saturday and Sunday.
House: admission by guided tour (timed tickets only) and free-flow on busy days, Bank and public holidays.
Last admission to house and gardens one hour before closing.
Open Bank Holiday Mondays and all other public holidays in Northern Ireland. Formal and lakeside gardens, restaurant and shop closed 25 and 26 December.

The forge at Patterson's Spade Mill, County Antrim

Patterson's Spade Mill

751 Antrim Road, Templepatrick,
County Antrim BT39 0AP

Map ⑦ E6  1991

Visitors can hear the hammers, smell the forge and feel the heat of traditional spade-making in the last working water-driven spade mill in the British Isles. Guided tours vividly capture life during the Industrial Revolution and dig up the history and culture of the humble spade.

Eating and shopping: handcrafted spades on sale and made to specification. Tea and coffee available from drinks machine.

Making the most of your day: guided tours and demonstrations for all the family.
Dogs: on leads only.

Access for all: ♿🅿️🚻♿
Building ♿♿ Grounds ♿

Getting here: see website for details.
Parking: free, 50 yards.

Finding out more: 028 9443 3619 or
pattersons@nationaltrust.org.uk

Patterson's Spade Mill		M	T	W	T	F	S	S
18 Apr–27 Apr	12–4	M	T	W	T	F	S	S
3 May–1 Jun	12–4	·	·	·	·	·	S	S
2 Jun–31 Aug	12–4	M	T	W	·	·	S	S
6 Sep–28 Sep	12–4	·	·	·	·	·	S	S

Admission by guided tour (last admission one hour before closing). Open Bank Holiday Mondays and all other public holidays in Northern Ireland from 18 April to 30 September.

Rowallane Garden

Saintfield, County Down BT24 7LH

Map ⑦ E7   ❊ 🔔 1956

Rowallane contains a treasure trove of exotic plants from around the world, intriguingly mixed into County Down's drumlins. It was created by Reverend John Moore in the mid-1860s – he planted woodland and used interesting stone ornamentation to sculpt this informal landscape. His nephew, Hugh Armytage Moore, continued his work from 1903, mingling exotic species with native plants – giving the garden a dramatic atmosphere. All types of plants are represented. Trees, shrubs, herbaceous perennials and bulbs abound throughout the 21 hectares (52 acres), which includes a walled garden, rock garden, woodland and wildflower meadows. The new exhibition area provides an insight into the history of the garden, while new trails offer visitors the chance to discover and enjoy new views and vistas.

Rowallane Garden, County Down, below and right, includes woodland and wildflower meadows, a rock garden and walled garden

Northern Ireland

Rowallane Garden is a treasure trove of exotic plants from around the world, cleverly combined with native species to create drama

Eating and shopping: new garden café with stunning views across the gardens. Shop offering garden and outdoor products. Second-hand bookshop. Pottery providing unique Rowallane Garden items and garden pots.

Making the most of your day: events, including spring and autumn plant fair, Ghosts and Gourds and Yuletide market. Children's activity sheets. **Dogs**: on leads in garden only.

Access for all: [symbols] Grounds [symbols]

Getting here: see website for details.
Parking: free.

Finding out more: 028 9751 0131 or rowallane@nationaltrust.org.uk

Rowallane Garden		M	T	W	T	F	S	S
Garden								
1 Jan–28 Feb	10–4	M	T	W	T	F	S	S
1 Mar–30 Apr	10–6	M	T	W	T	F	S	S
1 May–31 Aug	10–8	M	T	W	T	F	S	S
1 Sep–31 Oct	10–6	M	T	W	T	F	S	S
1 Nov–31 Dec	10–4	M	T	W	T	F	S	S
Café and shop								
4 Jan–23 Feb	12–3:30	·	·	·	·	·	S	S
1 Mar–20 Apr	11–4	·	·	·	T	F	S	S
21 Apr–27 Apr	11–4	M	T	W	T	F	S	S
1 May–31 Aug	11–5	M	T	W	T	F	S	S
4 Sep–26 Oct	11–4	·	·	·	T	F	S	S
1 Nov–28 Dec	12–3:30	·	·	·	·	·	S	S

Café and shop open all Sundays from 12. Open Bank Holiday Mondays and all other public holidays in Northern Ireland. Closed 25 and 26 December.

Springhill

20 Springhill Road, Moneymore, Magherafelt,
County Londonderry BT45 7NQ

Map (7) C6 🏠 ✻ 👥 ⛺ 🔔 ⵌ 1957

Charming 17th-century 'Plantation' home, with
walled gardens and parkland, full of tempting
waymarked paths. Informative tours breathe
life into the fascinating past of this welcoming
family home. There are ten generations of
Lenox-Conyngham family tales to enthrall you,
an intriguing link with the *Titanic* through a
letter written on board, not forgetting the
stories of one of Ireland's most-documented
ghosts, Olivia. The old laundry houses the
celebrated Costume Collection, which features
some fine 18th- to 20th-century pieces that
highlight its great appeal and enthralling past.

Eating and shopping: tea-room serving cream
teas. Gift shop. Second-hand bookshop.
Picnics welcome in garden.

Making the most of your day: guided tours and
links with the world-famous ship, the *Titanic*.
Dogs: on leads in grounds only.

Access for all: 🅿️ 🚻 📷 🖥️ ♪ ⦂
Building ♿ ⟨b⟩

Springhill, County Londonderry, above and
below: 17th-century 'Plantation' home with
walled garden and parkland

Getting here: see website for details.
Parking: 50 yards.

Finding out more: 028 8674 8210 or springhill@nationaltrust.org.uk

Springhill		M	T	W	T	F	S	S
Visitor centre								
2 Feb–23 Feb	12–5	.	.	.	.	.	.	S
15 Feb–18 Feb	12–5	M	T	.	.	.	S	S
Visitor centre, house and costume collection								
15 Mar–27 Apr	12–5	.	.	.	.	.	S	S
14 Apr–27 Apr	12–5	M	T	W	T	F	S	S
2 May–31 May	12–5	.	.	.	.	F	S	S
1 Jun–29 Jun	12–5	.	.	.	T	F	S	S
1 Jul–31 Aug	12–5	M	T	W	T	F	S	S
6 Sep–28 Sep	12–5	.	.	.	.	.	S	S
Grounds								
Open all year	10–5	M	T	W	T	F	S	S

House admission by guided tour (last admission one hour before closing). Open Bank Holiday Mondays and all other public holidays in Northern Ireland. Closed 25 and 26 December. Visitor centre has refreshment area and shop. Servants' Hall tea-room also open at weekends when visitor centre is open.

Wellbrook Beetling Mill

20 Wellbrook Road, Corkhill, Cookstown, County Tyrone BT80 9RY

Map ⑦ C6 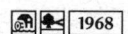 1968

Set in an idyllic wooded glen with lovely walks and picnic spots, this, the last working water-powered linen beetling mill, offers a unique experience for all the family. You can try scutching, hackling and weaving as part of the hands-on demonstrations, set against the thundering cacophony of beetling engines.

Eating and shopping: tea and coffee available · on request. Small cottage shop. Picnic tables near river.

Making the most of your day: mill tours cover history and linen-making processes. Walks up to the head-race. **Dogs**: on leads in grounds only.

Access for all: 🅳♿🚻📷♿
Building ♿♿ **Grounds** ♿♿

Getting here: see website for details.
Parking: free, 10 yards.

Finding out more: 028 8675 1735 or wellbrook@nationaltrust.org.uk

Wellbrook Beetling Mill		M	T	W	T	F	S	S
15 Mar–29 Jun	2–5	.	.	.	.	.	S	S
21 Apr–27 Apr	2–5	M	T	W	T	F	S	S
3 Jul–31 Aug	2–5	.	.	.	T	F	S	S
6 Sep–28 Sep	2–5	.	.	.	.	.	S	S

Admission by guided tour (last admission one hour before closing). Open Bank Holiday Mondays and all other public holidays in Northern Ireland.

Wellbrook Beetling Mill, County Tyrone, is the only remaining working water-powered linen beetling mill in Northern Ireland

Your visit

Welcoming families

Most places have baby-changing and baby-feeding areas – some also have parent and baby rooms. Restaurants and cafés have highchairs, children's menus and colouring sheets. Unfortunately it is usually difficult to accommodate prams and pushchairs inside historic houses, as they can impede other visitors and cause accidental damage, so you may be asked to leave them at the entrance.

Front-carrying slings for smaller babies and hip-seat carriers or reins for toddlers are often available to borrow. We welcome baby back-carriers wherever we can, although where space is limited (and at very busy times) it may not be possible to admit them.

Many places have guides, trails or quizzes for children and families, and some have special activity kits, such as Tracker Packs (bags packed with activities to do as you explore). These are free to borrow, although a deposit may be required. Many sites have discovery rooms and play areas. Obviously everyone is welcome to play in our gardens and parkland, although there may be restrictions due to conservation reasons or the time of year, such as the nesting season. Staff are happy to advise on the best areas to go to. Throughout the year there are things to get involved with, from spring lambing to autumn harvests. Visit www.nationaltrust.org.uk/visit/families/family-activities

Eating and shopping

Every time you buy something in our shops, restaurants, tea-rooms and coffee shops, your purchase helps our work.

Shops: our many property-based shops offer a wide range of merchandise, much of which is exclusive to the National Trust. You can buy many Trust gifts online at www.shop.nationaltrust.org.uk

Restaurants and tea-rooms: we open about 150 tea-rooms and cafés – often in very special buildings, such as stable blocks or hothouses. Many offer special winter and Christmas food events.

Parking

Parking in Trust car parks is free for members displaying current stickers, although a valid membership card should always be shown to a member of staff on request.

Dogs

We always try to provide facilities such as water, areas where dogs can be exercised and shady spaces in car parks (though dogs should not be left in cars). Dogs are welcome at most countryside places, where they should be kept under close control at all times.

Please observe local notices on the need to keep dogs on leads, particularly at sensitive times of year. Dogs should be kept on a short lead on access land between 1 March and 31 July, and always when near livestock.

In some areas, particularly on beaches, there may be restrictions, usually seasonal.

Please clear up dog mess and dispose of it responsibly. Where dog-waste bins are not provided, please take the waste away with you.

A family enjoys a day out at Arlington Court in Devon

Your questions answered

Where can I take photographs? We welcome amateur photography out of doors at our places and indoors – without flash (for visitor comfort, not conservation reasons) or tripods – when houses are open, at the discretion of the Property/General Manager and where owners of loan items have granted permission.

The use of mobile phones with built-in cameras is similarly permitted indoors (again, no flash please). At most places special arrangements can be made for interested amateurs (as well as voluntary National Trust speakers, research students and academics) to take interior photographs by appointment outside normal opening hours. Requests to arrange a mutually convenient appointment must be made in writing to the place concerned, giving your address. This facility isn't offered everywhere and we may make an admission charge (including National Trust members).

All requests for commercial, non-editorial filming and photography need to go through the Broadcast and Media Manager (020 7824 7128).

May I use my mobile? We'd be really grateful if you could turn off your mobile or put it on silent before going into one of our houses. Just as in a theatre, mobiles can really disrupt the atmosphere and detract from other people's experience.

Is there somewhere to leave large or bulky bags? You will be asked to leave large items of hand luggage at the house entrance. This is standard practice at museums and galleries worldwide to prevent accidental damage and to improve security.

The restriction includes rucksacks, large handbags, carrier (including open-topped) bags, bulky shoulder bags and camera/camcorder bags.

What types of footwear are restricted? Any heel which covers an area smaller than a postage stamp can cause irreparable damage to floors, carpets and rush matting. So sharp-heeled shoes aren't allowed. Overshoes may be provided and boot-scrapers and brushes are available for ridged-sole shoes, as well as plastic slippers for visitors with unsuitable, wet or muddy footwear.

What may I touch? We'd love you to be able to touch as much as possible, but many objects and surfaces are simply too fragile to be handled.

Volunteer room guides and staff will guide you on what can be touched. At some places you are welcome to play a piano or even try your hand at snooker.

Where may I sit down? We want you to be able to rest and relax, so we are increasing the seating in our houses and gardens. Room guides will be happy to show you where it is safe to sit.

Kingston Lacy in Dorset

Why is it dark inside some historic rooms? This is to slow down the deterioration of light-sensitive contents, especially textiles and watercolour paintings. We recommend that you allow time for your eyes to adapt to these darker conditions.

What happens during winter? Many historic houses offer special tours during the winter months, when house staff share the secrets of their traditional housekeeping practices and explain why we have to close many of our houses during at least part of the winter.

Why is it so cold inside some houses in winter? The heating systems in National Trust houses were not designed for the levels of domestic heating that we have become used to in our own homes.

We suggest that you dress warmly – just like our hardy staff and volunteers! – when you visit during the winter.

Joining in with the Trust

Volunteering

As a charity we rely greatly upon additional support to protect and manage the coastline, countryside, historic buildings and gardens in our care. You can help us by volunteering. Contact your local place or visit website for details.

Supporter groups

You can also help us by joining a supporter group, where you can get together with people who feel passionate about the same things as you do. You might be constructing a footpath, building a fence or helping to restore natural coastal habitats. Visit website for details.

Events

We offer a variety of events throughout the year, from wildflower walks to family fun at Easter and Hallowe'en. There are live summer concerts, living history events, countryside open days and open-air theatre productions. Our lecture lunches and 'behind-the-scenes' tours explain the work of our gardeners and house staff, while our 'Conservation in Action' events provide opportunities for you to see conservation specialists at work and talk to them about their techniques. The year ends with Christmas craft fairs, carol concerts and winter walks.

Weddings and private functions

The bell and glass symbols at the top of entries indicate that the place is licensed for civil weddings (bell symbol) and/or available for private functions (glass symbol), such as wedding receptions and family celebrations. Contact your local place or visit website for details.

Supporting us

Heritage Lottery Fund

Using money raised through the National Lottery, the Heritage Lottery Fund (HLF) sustains and transforms a wide range of heritage for present and future generations to take part in, learn from and enjoy. From museums, parks and historic places to archaeology, natural environment and cultural traditions, we invest in every part of our diverse heritage. The HLF has supported over 35,000 projects, allocating more than £5.4 billion across the UK. Recent National Trust projects supported by the HLF include:

Castle Drogo, Devon
Chedworth Roman Villa, Gloucestershire
Clumber Park, Nottinghamshire
Croome, Worcestershire

Giant's Causeway, County Antrim
Hardwick Hall, Derbyshire
Ickworth, Suffolk
Morden Hall Park, London
Stowe, Buckinghamshire
Tyntesfield, North Somerset

If you would like to find out more please visit **www.hlf.org.uk**

Art Fund

The National Trust is grateful to the Art Fund (**www.artfund.org**) for its continuing generous support in the acquisition of historic contents (a Brueghel painting for Nostell Priory and Seaton Delaval Hall are recent examples). We warmly welcome Art Fund members, who may visit places which have benefited directly, free of charge.

National Gardens Scheme

The National Trust acknowledges with gratitude the generous and continuing support of the National Gardens Scheme Charitable Trust.

The Royal Oak Foundation

Through the generous support of its members and donors across the US, Royal Oak makes grants to the Trust. Royal Oak members receive free entry and parking at all properties.

Have your say

Governance

A guide to the Trust's governance arrangements is available on our website **www.nationaltrust.org.uk/ about-us** and on request from The Secretary.

Our Annual Report and Accounts are available online at **www.nationaltrust.org.uk/ annualreport** or by email.

Please send the request to **annualreport@nationaltrust. org.uk**

Annual General Meeting

Every autumn we hold our Annual General Meeting (AGM). This event is for our members and gives you the opportunity to meet our Trustees and staff, and to help steer the organisation through contributing to debates and voting on resolutions.

The AGM is also a great opportunity for us to talk to you about the ways we work, to show you what's been happening over the past year and update you on our recent campaigns and appeals.

We send the formal papers for our AGM – including voting papers – with the autumn magazine. We hope you will consider attending this year's AGM. However, you don't need to come to the meeting to join in. You can follow the event and share your views with us by watching the live webcast (see **www.nationaltrust.org. uk/agm**). You can also let us know your views by returning your voting papers – or voting online – ahead of the meeting.

In addition, you have the opportunity to elect members of our Council. The Council is made up of 52 members, 26 elected by you and 26 appointed by organisations whose interests coincide in some way with those of the National Trust.

This mix of elected and appointed members appoints our Trustees and ensures that the Trust takes full account of the wider interests of the nation, for whose benefit it exists. The breadth of experience and perspective which this brings also enables the Council to act as the Trust's conscience in delivering its statutory purposes.

Privacy Policy

The National Trust's Privacy Policy sets out the ways in which we process personal data. The full Privacy Policy is available on our website **www.nationaltrust.org.uk** The National Trust makes every effort to comply with the principles of the Data Protection Act 1998.

Use made of personal information

Personal information provided to the National Trust via our website, membership forms, fundraising responses, emails and telephone calls will be used for the purposes outlined at the time of collection or registration in accordance with the preferences you express.

By providing personal data to the National Trust you consent to the processing of such data by the National Trust as described in the full Privacy Policy. You can alter your preferences as explained in the following paragraph.

Verifying, updating and amending your personal information

If, at any time, you want to verify, update or amend your personal data or preferences please write to:

National Trust,
Supporter Services Centre,
PO Box 574,
Manvers,
Rotherham,
S63 3FH.

Verification, updating or amendment of personal data will take place within 28 days of receipt of your request.

If subsequently you make a data protection instruction to the National Trust which contradicts a previous instruction (or instructions), then the Trust will follow your most recent instruction.

Subject access requests

You have the right to ask the National Trust, in writing, for a copy of all the personal data held about you (a 'subject access request') upon payment of a fee of £10.

To access your personal data held by the National Trust, please apply in writing to:

The Data Protection Officer,
National Trust,
Heelis, Kemble Drive,
Swindon,
Wiltshire,
SN2 2NA.

Your membership

Through your membership of the National Trust you not only have free access to visit more than 400 places listed in this *Handbook*, as many times as you like all year, and the right to park free of charge in Trust car parks on coast and countryside sites, but reassurance that your subscription forms a significant part of the financial bedrock of the Trust. As an independent registered charity this support is absolutely vital to us – thank you very much indeed.

- Membership of the National Trust allows you free parking in Trust car parks and free entry to most Trust places open to the public during normal opening times and under normal opening arrangements, provided you can present a current valid membership card.
- **Remember to display your current car-parking sticker.**
- **Please check that you have your card with you before you set out on your journey. Without it, we regret that you may not be admitted free of charge, nor will we subsequently be able to refund any admission charges.**
- Membership cards are **not transferable**.
- If your card is lost or stolen, please contact the Supporter Services Centre or telephone 0844 800 1895.
- A temporary card can be sent quickly to a holiday address or emailed to you.
- Members wishing to change from one category of life membership to another, or requiring information on pensioner membership, should contact the Supporter Services Centre for the scale of charges.
- In some instances an entry fee may apply. Additional charges may be made:

  - when a special event is in progress;

  - when we open specially for a National Gardens Scheme open day;

  - where the management of a place is not under the National Trust's direct control, for example Tatton Park, Cheshire;

  - where special attractions are additional and/ or separate elements of the property, for example Steam Yacht Gondola in Cumbria, Dunster Watermill in Somerset, and the model farm and museum at Shugborough in Staffordshire;

  - where special access conditions apply, for example The Beatles' Childhood Homes in Liverpool, where access is only by minibus from Speke Hall and Liverpool city centre, and all visitors (including Trust members) pay a fare for the minibus journey.

Educational Group Membership
Visitors from the educational sector and special interest groups are welcome. We recommend that teachers make a preliminary visit, which can be arranged free of charge. Frequent visitors should consider Educational Group Membership. Visit www.nationaltrust.org.uk/membership/educational-group-memberships

Reciprocal visiting
National Trust members enjoy reciprocal visiting arrangements with certain overseas National Trusts, including Australia, New Zealand, Barbados, Bermuda, Canada, Italy and – closer to home – Jersey and Guernsey. A similar arrangement is in place with the Manx Museum and National Trust on the Isle of Man (your current membership card is always needed). A full list is on our website and may be obtained from the Supporter Services Centre.

Entry to places owned by the Trust but maintained and administered by English Heritage or Cadw (Welsh Government's historic environment service) is free to members of the Trust, English Heritage and Cadw.

National Trust for Scotland (NTS)
Members of the National Trust are also admitted free of charge to properties of the NTS, a separate charity with similar responsibilities. NTS places include the famous Inverewe Garden, Bannockburn, Culloden and Robert Adam's masterpiece, Culzean Castle. Full details are contained in *The National Trust for Scotland Guide to Properties* (£5, including post and packaging), obtained by contacting the NTS Customer Service Centre (0844 493 2100). Information is also available at **www.nts.org.uk**

Area maps

For clarity, the nine regions covered in this *Handbook* have been broken down into 12 areas on the maps (please see the key on the right). The seven maps show those places which have individual entries, as well as many additional coast and countryside sites in the care of the National Trust.

In order to help with general orientation, the maps show main roads and population centres. However, the plotting of each site serves only as a guide to its location. Please note that some countryside places, for example those in the Lake District, cover many thousands of hectares. In such cases the symbol is placed centrally as an indication of general location.

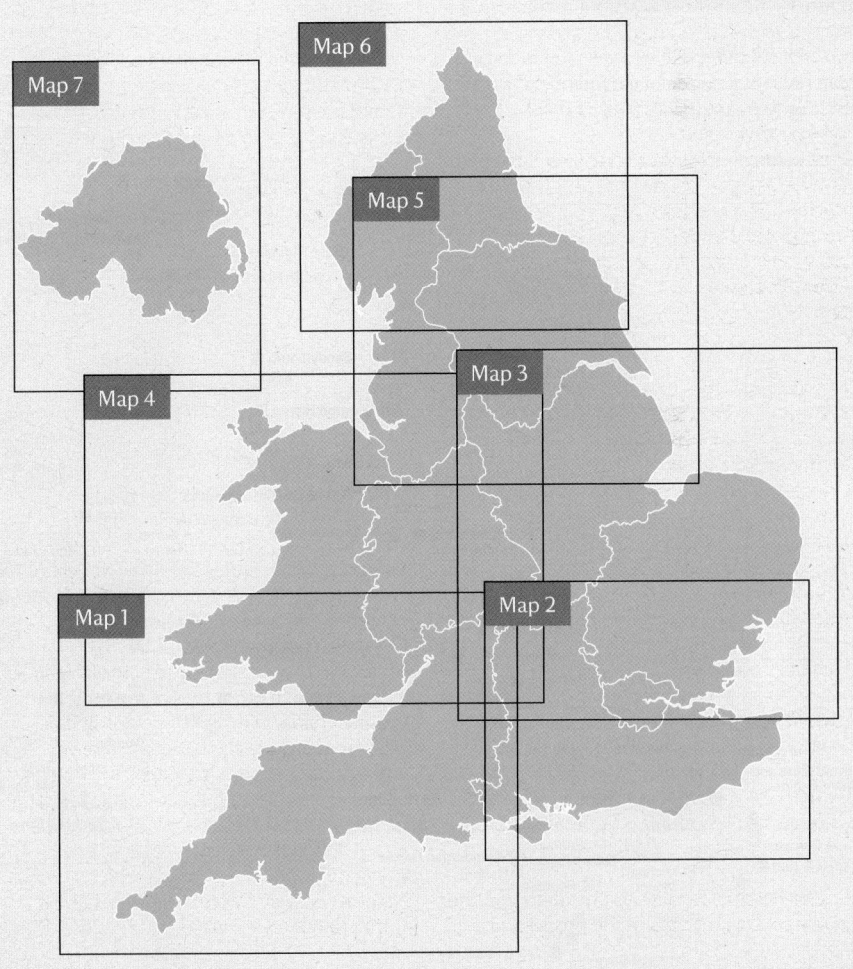

London Partners ⦿

- Freud Museum London
- Museum of Brands
- Leighton House Museum
- Strawberry Hill House ⦿
- Keats House
- Foundling Museum
- Dr Johnson's House
- Bevis Marks Synagogue
- ⦿ The Fan Museum
- Danson House ⦿
- Handel House Museum
- The Old Operating Theatre Museum
- Benjamin Franklin House
- Hall Place and Gardens

Map 2

South East page 89
London page 159

- ▲ Buildings and gardens
- ■ Coast and countryside
- ⛴ Historic House Hotel
- ⦿ London Partners

0   10   20 miles
0 10 20 30 kilometres

Mildenhall
Theatre Royal
Eye
Dunwich Heath ■ and Beach

G — res
Waterbeach ○ Burwell
Histon ○
CAMBRIDGE
Anglesey Gardens and Lode Mill
Wimpole Estate
Royston
Saffron Walden
Hav
Bishop's Stortford
Hatfield Forest
Ware
Hertford
Harlow
Hoddesdon
Danb and E
enton House and Garden
Willow Road
Bre

National Reserve
A1120
M25
M11
M1
M4
M25
A1307
A505
A507
M11
A602
A10
A414
M25
M11
A12

National reserve

Sutton House
Eastbury Manor House
Rainham Hall
Southend-on-Sea
Canvey Island
yle's House
George Inn
75 Wandsworth oad
Morden Hall Park
Red House
St John's Jerusalem
Rochester
Cobham Wood and Mausoleum
Owletts
Coldrum Long Barrow
Sheerness
Whitstable
Herne Bay
Margate
Selsdon Wood
rmeads
Quebec House
Knole
Old Soar Manor
Ightham Mote
Maidstone
Faversham
Canterbury
Ramsgate
Chartwell
ate Hill
Gatton
Emmetts Garden
Toys Hill
Stoneacre
Deal
South Foreland Lighthouse
Standen
Wakehurst Place
Nymans
Sheffield Park and Garden
ddlescombe Farm d Newtimber Hill
Ditchling Beacon
vil's Dyke
Monk's House
Alfriston Clergy House
Frog Firle Farm
Chyngton Farm
Birling Gap and the Seven Sisters
Crowlink
Sissinghurst Castle
Scotney Castle
Tunbridge Wells
Smallhythe Place
Royal Military Canal
Bodiam Castle
Bateman's
Battle
Hailsham
Hastings
Bexhill-on-Sea
Lewes
Brighton
Newhaven
Eastbourne
Haywards Heath
Tenterden
Ashford
Dover
The White Cliffs of Dover
Folkestone
Hythe
New Romney
Rye
Lamb House
Sheerness
Sheffield
M25
M20
M26
M23
A2
A21
A26
A22
A23
A24
A25
A229
A20
A2070
A259
A265
A267
A271
A26
A27
A28
A257
A256
A2
A299
A428
M2
M20

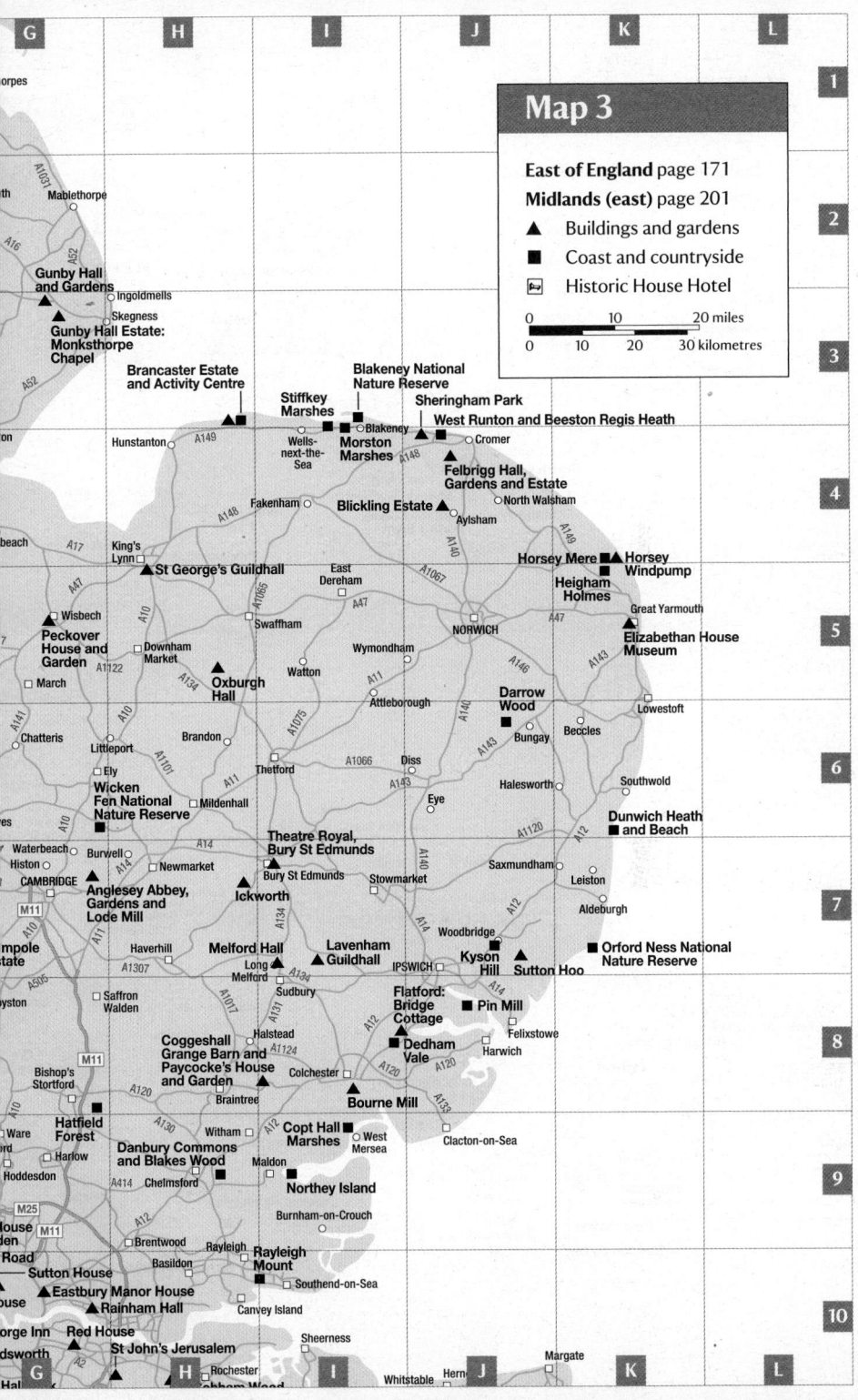

Map 3

East of England page 171
Midlands (east) page 201

▲ Buildings and gardens
■ Coast and countryside
⌂ Historic House Hotel

0 .... 10 .... 20 miles
0 .. 10 .. 20 .. 30 kilometres

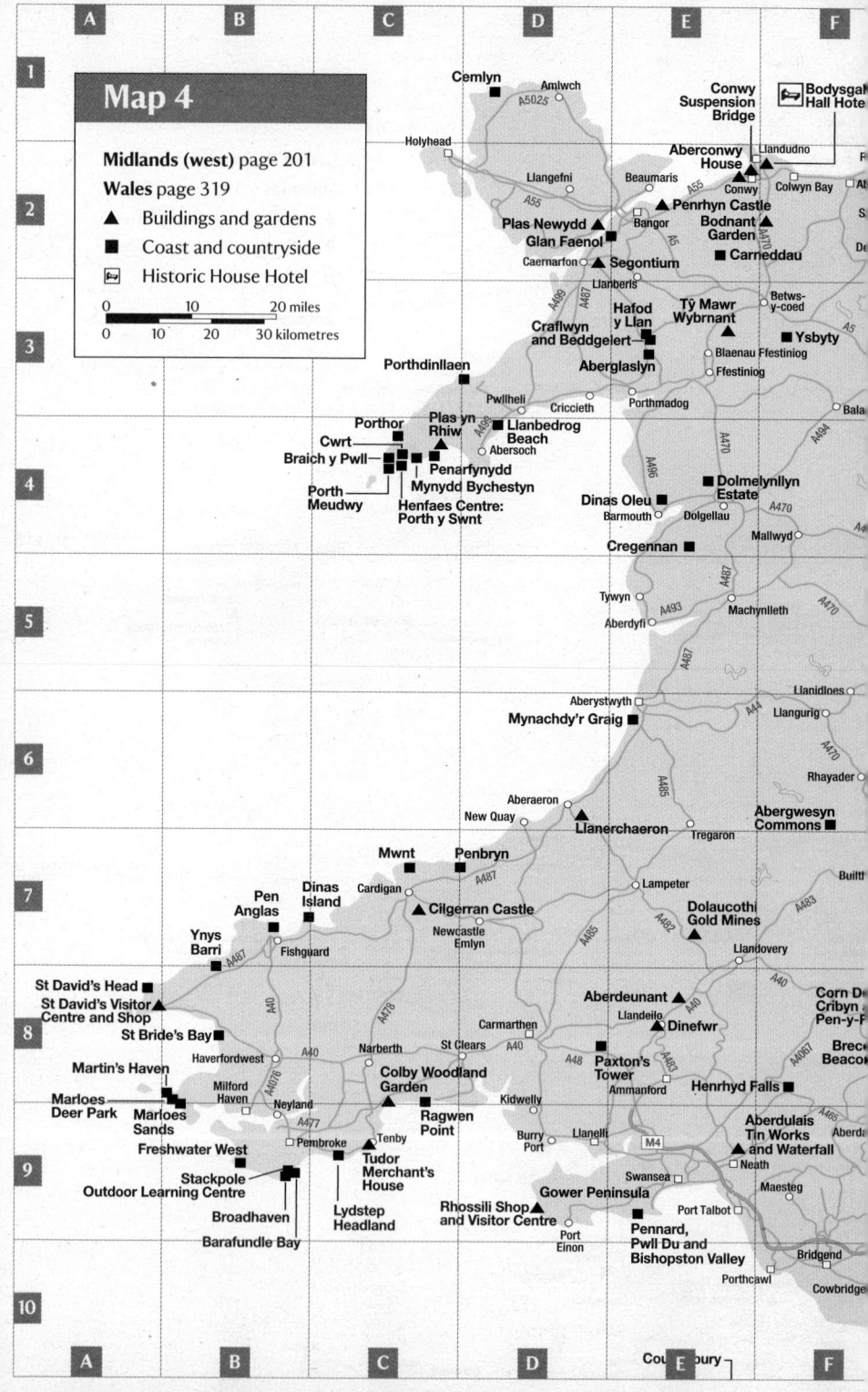

Map 4

Midlands (west) page 201

Wales page 319

▲ Buildings and gardens

■ Coast and countryside

⌂ Historic House Hotel

0	10	20 miles
0	10	20	30 kilometres

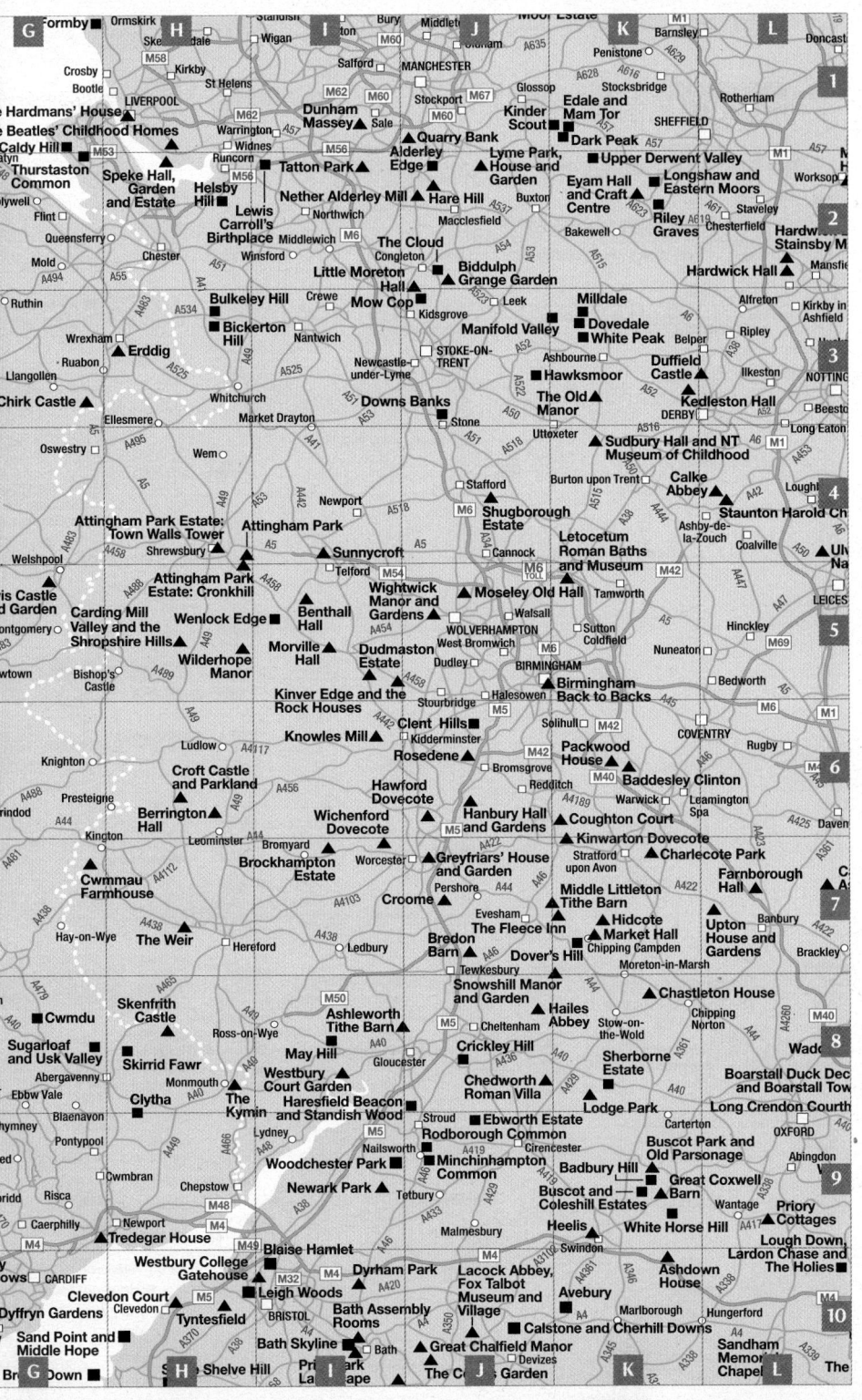

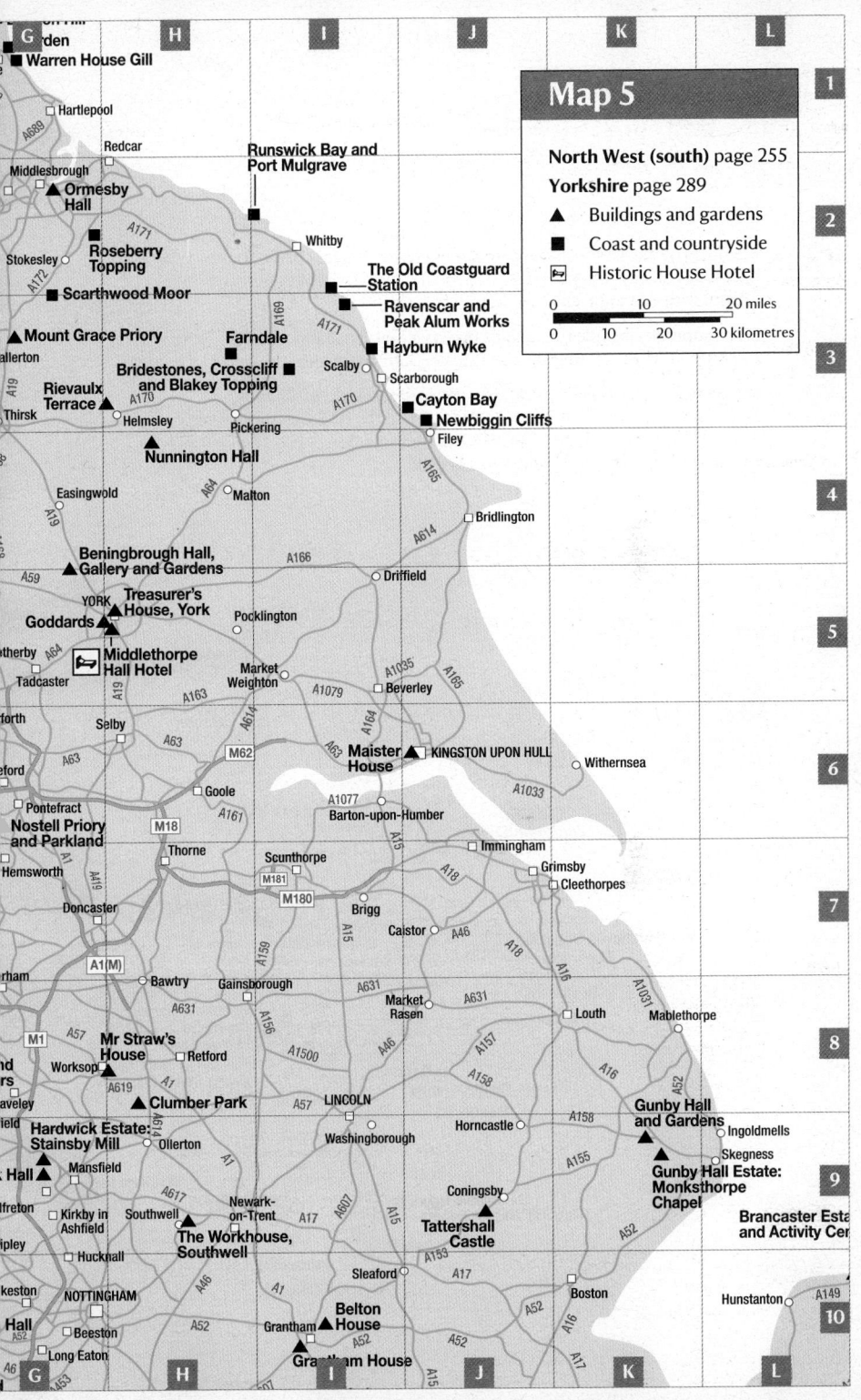

Map 5

North West (south) page 255

Yorkshire page 289

▲ Buildings and gardens

■ Coast and countryside

🏠 Historic House Hotel

0 — 10 — 20 miles
0 — 10 — 20 — 30 kilometres

Warren House Gill

Hartlepool

Redcar

Middlesbrough

Ormesby Hall

Stokesley

Roseberry Topping

Scarthwood Moor

Mount Grace Priory

allerton

Rievaulx Terrace

Thirsk

Helmsley

Runswick Bay and Port Mulgrave

Whitby

The Old Coastguard Station

Ravenscar and Peak Alum Works

Farndale

Bridestones, Crosscliff and Blakey Topping

Hayburn Wyke

Scalby

Scarborough

Pickering

Nunnington Hall

Cayton Bay

Newbiggin Cliffs

Filey

Easingwold

Malton

Bridlington

Beningbrough Hall, Gallery and Gardens

A166

Driffield

YORK

Treasurer's House, York

Goddards

Pocklington

Middlethorpe Hall Hotel

wetherby

Tadcaster

Market Weighton

Beverley

forth

Selby

Maister House

KINGSTON UPON HULL

Withernsea

eford

Goole

Pontefract

Barton-upon-Humber

Nostell Priory and Parkland

Hemsworth

Thorne

Immingham

Scunthorpe

Grimsby

Cleethorpes

Doncaster

Brigg

Caistor

rham

Bawtry

Gainsborough

Market Rasen

Louth

Mablethorpe

Mr Straw's House

Worksop

Retford

LINCOLN

Horncastle

Gunby Hall and Gardens

Ingoldmells

Clumber Park

Washingborough

Skegness

Hardwick Estate: Stainsby Mill

Ollerton

Gunby Hall Estate: Monksthorpe Chapel

Hall

Mansfield

Coningsby

Brancaster Estate and Activity Cen

lfreton

Kirkby in Ashfield

Southwell

Newark-on-Trent

The Workhouse, Southwell

Tattershall Castle

ipley

Hucknall

Sleaford

Boston

keston

NOTTINGHAM

Hunstanton

Hall

Beeston

Grantham

Belton House

Long Eaton

Grantham House

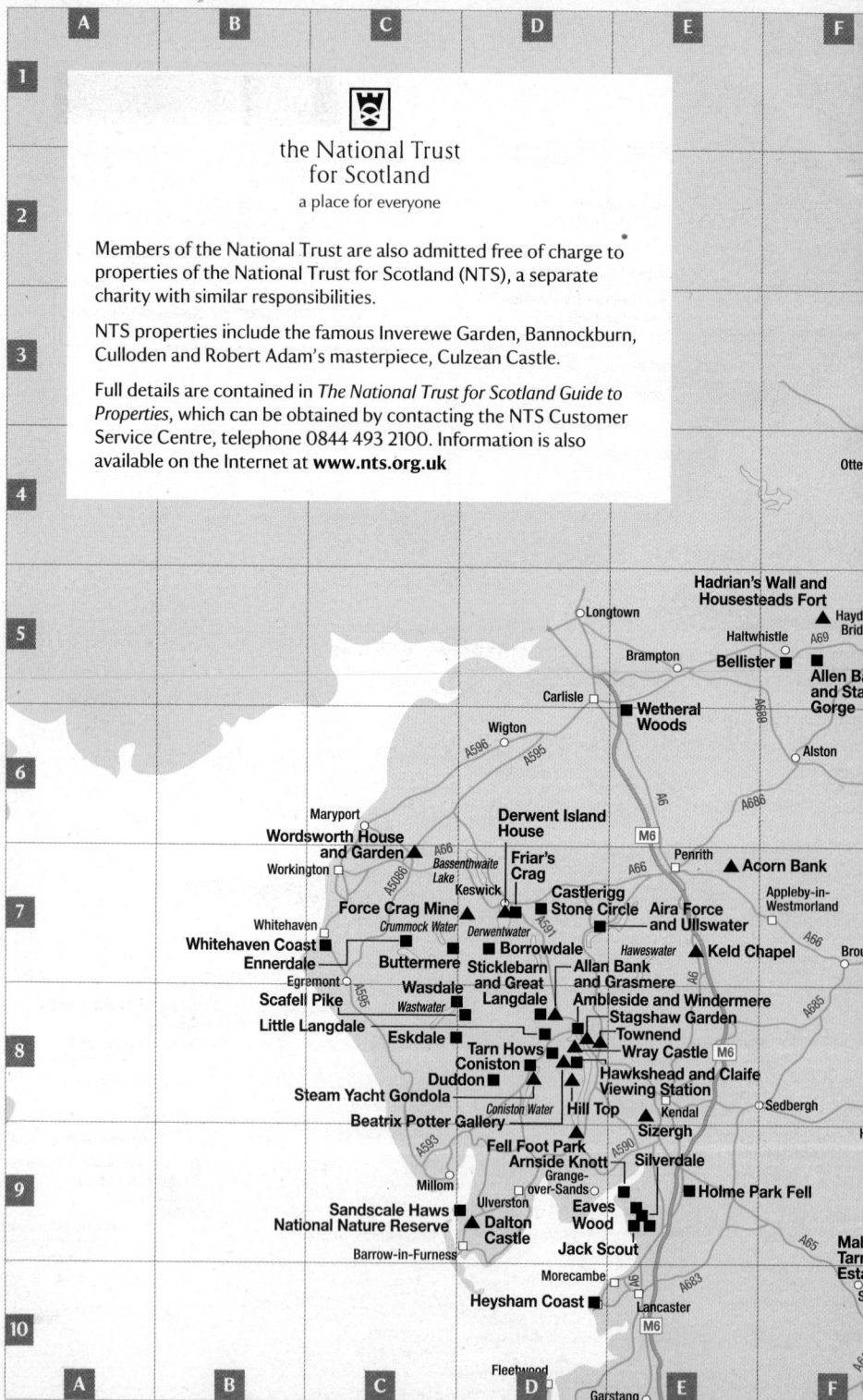

the National Trust
for Scotland
a place for everyone

Members of the National Trust are also admitted free of charge to properties of the National Trust for Scotland (NTS), a separate charity with similar responsibilities.

NTS properties include the famous Inverewe Garden, Bannockburn, Culloden and Robert Adam's masterpiece, Culzean Castle.

Full details are contained in *The National Trust for Scotland Guide to Properties*, which can be obtained by contacting the NTS Customer Service Centre, telephone 0844 493 2100. Information is also available on the Internet at **www.nts.org.uk**

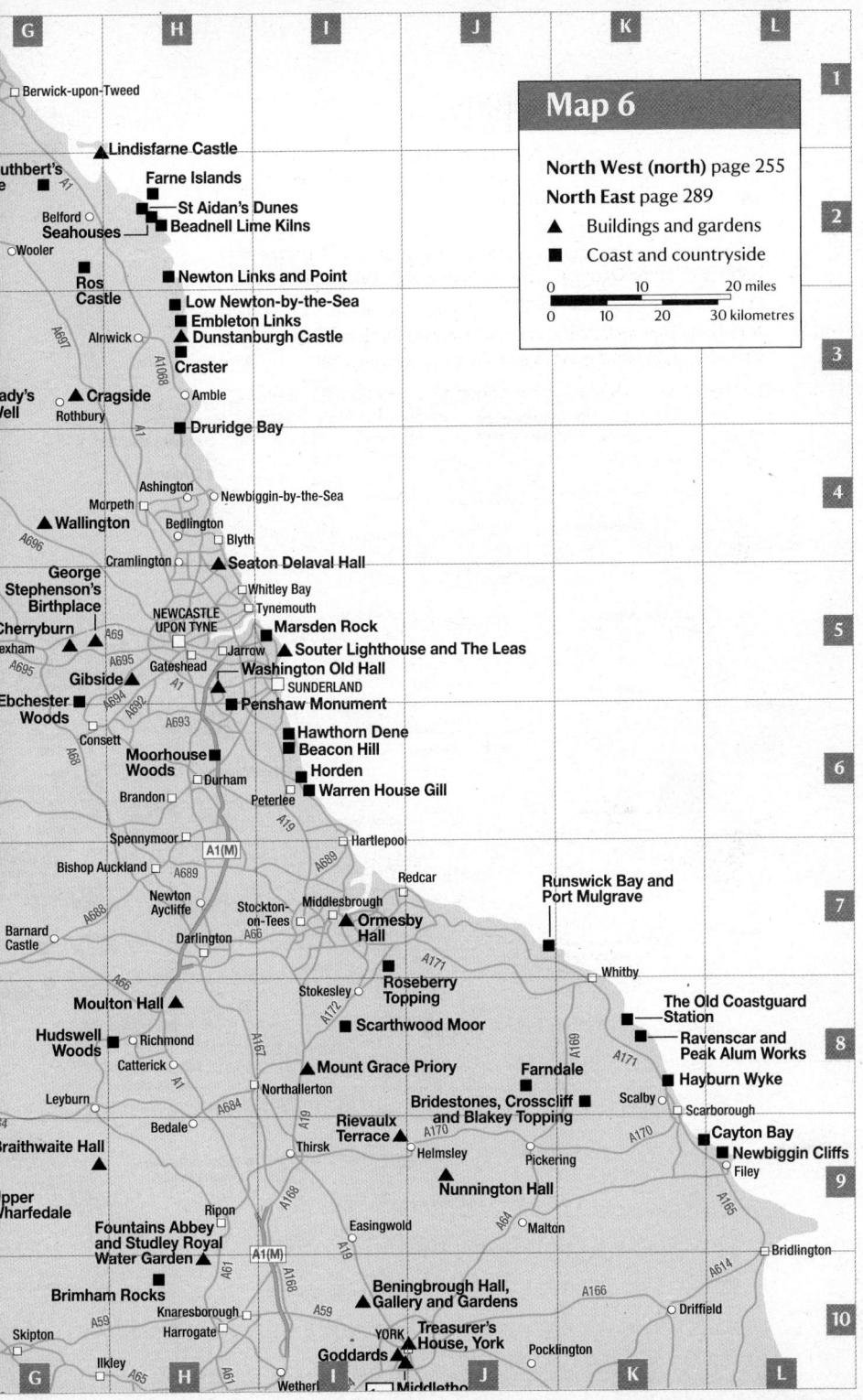

Map 6

North West (north) page 255

North East page 289

▲ Buildings and gardens

■ Coast and countryside

0   10   20 miles

0   10   20   30 kilometres

□ Berwick-upon-Tweed

▲ Lindisfarne Castle

uthbert's e ■

■ Farne Islands

Belford ○
Seahouses ○

○ Wooler

■ St Aidan's Dunes
■ Beadnell Lime Kilns

■ Ros
Castle

■ Newton Links and Point

■ Low Newton-by-the-Sea
■ Embleton Links
▲ Dunstanburgh Castle

Alnwick ○

▲ Craster

ady's
ell ○

Rothbury ○

▲ Cragside

○ Amble

■ Druridge Bay

Ashington ○

○ Newbiggin-by-the-Sea

Morpeth □

▲ Wallington

Bedlington ○

□ Blyth

Cramlington ○

▲ Seaton Delaval Hall

George
Stephenson's
Birthplace

□ Whitley Bay
□ Tynemouth

NEWCASTLE
UPON TYNE

Cherryburn

exham

▲ Marsden Rock

Gibside ▲

Gateshead

Jarrow ▲ Souter Lighthouse and The Leas

Washington Old Hall

□ SUNDERLAND

Ebchester
Woods ■

▲ Penshaw Monument

Consett ○

Moorhouse
Woods ■

□ Durham

■ Hawthorn Dene
■ Beacon Hill
■ Horden
■ Warren House Gill

Brandon □

Peterlee ○

Spennymoor □

□ Hartlepool

A1(M)

Bishop Auckland □

A689

Newton
Aycliffe ○

□ Redcar

Barnard
Castle ○

Stockton-
on-Tees □

Middlesbrough

Darlington ○

▲ Ormesby
Hall

Runswick Bay and
Port Mulgrave

■

Moulton Hall ▲

Stokesley ○

Roseberry
Topping

○ Whitby

Hudswell
Woods ■

○ Richmond

Catterick ○

▲ Scarthwood Moor

The Old Coastguard
Station

■ Ravenscar and
Peak Alum Works

Leyburn ○

Northallerton ○

▲ Mount Grace Priory

■ Farndale

Scalby ○

■ Hayburn Wyke

□ Scarborough

Braithwaite Hall
▲

Bedale ○

Rievaulx
Terrace ▲

Bridestones, Crosscliff ■
and Blakey Topping

□ Cayton Bay
■ Newbiggin Cliffs
Filey ○

pper
harfedale

Thirsk ○

Helmsley ○

Pickering ○

Fountains Abbey
and Studley Royal
Water Garden ▲

Ripon □

▲ Nunnington Hall

Easingwold ○

○ Malton

□ Bridlington

Brimham Rocks

A1(M)

Skipton □

Knaresborough □

Harrogate □

Beningbrough Hall,
▲ Gallery and Gardens

○ Driffield

Ilkley ○

Wetherl

YORK ▲ Treasurer's
House, York

Goddards ▲

Pocklington ○

Middletho

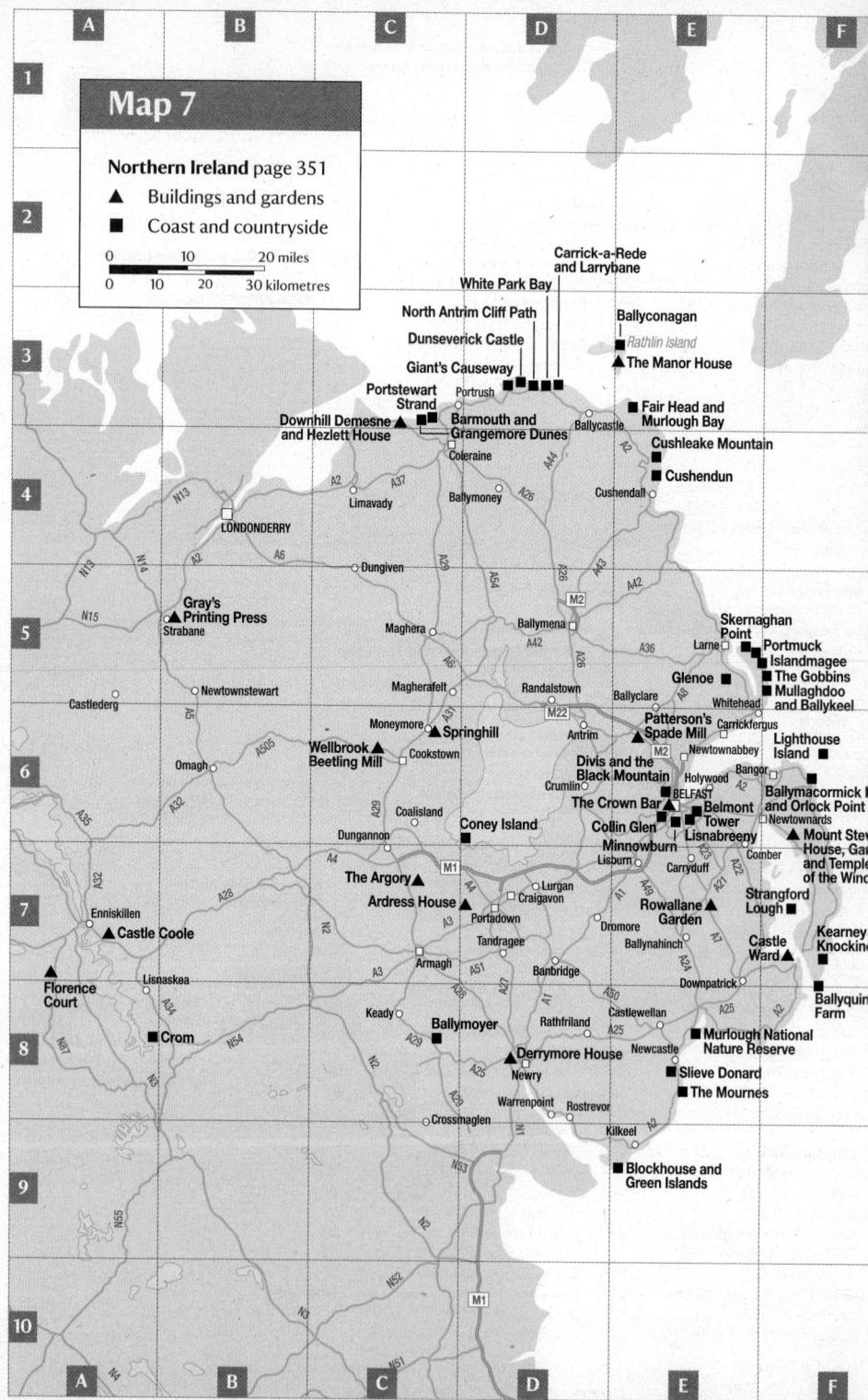

Map 7

Northern Ireland page 351

▲ Buildings and gardens

■ Coast and countryside

0   10   20 miles
0 10 20 30 kilometres

Carrick-a-Rede and Larrybane

White Park Bay

North Antrim Cliff Path

Dunseverick Castle

Giant's Causeway

Ballyconagan
Rathlin Island
▲ The Manor House

Portstewart Strand

Portrush

Downhill Demesne and Hezlett House ▲

Barmouth and Grangemore Dunes

Ballycastle

■ Fair Head and Murlough Bay

Coleraine

Cushleake Mountain

■ Cushendun

Limavady

Ballymoney

Cushendall

LONDONDERRY

Dungiven

Gray's Printing Press ▲
Strabane

Maghera

Ballymena

Skernaghan Point

Portmuck

Larne

Islandmagee

■ The Gobbins

Newtownstewart

Magherafelt

Randalstown

Glenoe ■

Mullaghdoo and Ballykeel

Castlederg

Whitehead

Ballyclare

Patterson's Spade Mill ▲

Carrickfergus

Lighthouse Island ■

Omagh

Moneymore

Springhill ▲

Antrim

Newtownabbey

Bangor

Wellbrook Beetling Mill ▲
Cookstown

Divis and the Black Mountain

Crumlin

Holywood

BELFAST

Ballymacormick and Orlock Point

The Crown Bar ▲

Belmont Tower

Newtownards

Coalisland

Coney Island ■

Collin Glen

Lisnabreeny

Dungannon

Minnowburn

Lisburn

Carryduff

Comber

▲ Mount Stewart House, Garden and Temple of the Winds

The Argory ▲

Lurgan

Craigavon

Ardress House ▲

Portadown

Rowallane Garden ▲

Strangford Lough ■

Enniskillen

Tandragee

Dromore

▲ Castle Coole

Armagh

Banbridge

Ballynahinch

Castle Ward ▲

Kearney Knockin

▲ Florence Court

Lisnaskea

Keady

Ballymoyer ▲

Rathfriland

Downpatrick

Ballyquin Farm

■ Crom

Derrymore House ▲

Castlewellan

Newry

Newcastle

■ Murlough National Nature Reserve

Crossmaglen

Warrenpoint

Rostrevor

■ Slieve Donard

■ The Mournes

Kilkeel

■ Blockhouse and Green Islands

Index

Places not in italics have an individual entry.
* Denotes properties shown only on maps.

© 2014 National Trust

Editor
Lucy Peel

Editorial assistance
Anthony Lambert
Penny Shapland
Wendy Smith
Dee Maple

Production
Graham Prichard

Art direction
Craig Robson
Wolff Olins

Content management
Roger Shapland
Dave Buchanan

Design
LEVEL Partnership

Maps © **Blacker Design**,
Maps in Minutes™/Collins
Bartholomew 2013

Origination
Zebra

Printed
Wyndeham,
Peterborough

NT LDS stock no:
73801/14

ISBN 978-0-7078-0427-9

Sponsor
Louise McRae

Publisher
John Stachiewicz

Acknowledgements
National Trust Images'
photographers and
copyright holders:
Matthew Antrobus
Steve Atkins
Cristian Barnett
Bill Batten
Mark Bolton
Daniel Bosworth
Michael Boys
Jonathan Buckley
Andrew Butler
Michael Caldwell
Neil Campbell-Sharp
Brian and Nina Chapple
Peter Cook
Val Corbett
Joe Cornish
Stuart Cox
Nick Daly
James Dobson
Graham Eaton
Britainonview/Rod
    Edwards
Rod Edwards
Andreas von Einsiedel
Geoffrey Frosh
Dennis Gilbert

Nick Guttridge
John Hammond
Jerry Harpur
Paul Harris
Ross Hoddinott
Sue Jones
Chris King
David Kirkham
Chris Lacey
Britainonview/David
    Levenson
David Levenson
Nadia Mackenzie
Leo Mason
Nick Meers
John Millar
Paul Mogford
Andrew Montgomery
Robert Morris
Nina Elliot-Newman
Clive Nichols
David Noton
Alasdair Ogilvie
Anthony Parkinson
Patrick Prendergast
Magnus Rew
Kevin Richardson
Phil Ripley
Derry Robinson
Stephen Robson
David Sellman
Ben Selway
Arnhel de Serra
Ian Shaw
Mark Sunderland
Megan Taylor
Layton Thompson

Martin Trelawny
Rupert Truman
Penny Tweedie
Angus Wainwright
Ian West
Mike Williams

Additional images
supplied by:
Bob Anderson
J. Anderson
Phil Barnes
Wyn Barnes
Janet Baxter
Heather Bradshaw
Bernie Brown
Paul Canning
David Clarke
Melanie Clarke
Chris Clennett
DACS
Joshua Day
David Dixon
James Dobson
Lucy Evershed
Ian Fairweather
John Faulkner
Jonathan Gardner
Greenway Ferry
    Company
David Griffen
Marie-Louise Halpenny
Paul Harris
Will Hawkins
Steven Haywood
Rob Hewer
Chris Hill

Eddie Hyde
David Kirkham
    (Fisheye Images)
Jason Ingram
JRUL
George Kavanagh
Roger Kinkead
Robert Ledbury
George Littler
Graham Lubbock
Sarah Mason
Kippa Matthews
Sarah McCarthy
John Miller
Mischief/Sam Lewis
Peter Muhly
Philip Mynott
Hugh Palmer
Josie Phillips
Christine Shaw
Kate Sheard
George Littler and Peter
    Spooner
Wolfgang Stuppy
Jenny Sutton
Mark Sykes
Claire Takacs
John Bigelow Taylor
Robert Thompson
Robert Thrift
A. Tryner
Art Ward
David Watson
Linda Whiting
David Williams
Emma Williams
Rob Wright

Getting in touch

The National Trust supports the National Code of Practice for Visitor Attractions. We are very willing to answer questions and keen to receive comments. Many National Trust places provide their own comment cards and boxes. All your comments will be read, considered and action taken where necessary, but it is not possible to answer every comment or suggestion individually.

Enquiries by telephone, email or in writing should be made to the Trust's Supporter Services Centre (see opposite), open seven days a week (9 to 5:30 weekdays, 9 to 4 weekends and Bank Holidays). (Our 0844 numbers are charged at 5p per minute from BT landlines, charges from mobiles and other operators may vary.) You can also obtain information from our website **www.nationaltrust.org.uk**

National Trust Supporter Services Centre
PO Box 574, Manvers, Rotherham S63 3FH.
0844 800 1895, 0844 800 4410 (minicom)

Email **enquiries@nationaltrust.org.uk** for all general enquiries, including membership.

Central Office
The National Trust and National Trust (Enterprises) Ltd, Heelis, Kemble Drive, Swindon, Wiltshire SN2 2NA.
01793 817400, 01793 817401 (fax)

National Trust Holiday Cottages
0844 800 2072 (brochures)
0844 800 2070 (reservations)

To contact the Editor email
lucy.peel@nationaltrust.org.uk